I0788514

Center for Basque Studies
Conference Papers Series, No. 1

Empire & Terror:

Nationalism/Postnationalism in the New Millennium

EDITED BY

Begoña Aretxaga, Dennis Dworkin,
Joseba Gabilondo, & Joseba Zulaika

Center for Basque Studies
University of Nevada, Reno
Reno, Nevada

This book was published with generous financial support from the Basque Government.

Center for Basque Studies
Conference Papers Series, No. 1
Series Editors: Joseba Zulaika and Cameron J. Watson

Center for Basque Studies
University of Nevada, Reno
Reno, Nevada 89557
http://basque.unr.edu

Library of Congress Cataloging-in-Publication Data

Empire and terror : nationalism/postnationalism in the new millennium / edited by
Begona Aretxaga ... [et al.].
       p. cm. -- (Center for Basque Studies conference papers series ; no. 1)
   Papers presented at the academic conference on "Nationalism, Globalization, and
Terror: A Debate on Stateless Nations, Particularism/Universalism, and Radical
Democracy," sponsored by the Center for Basque Studies of the University of Nevada,
Reno in April 2002.
   Includes bibliographical references and index.
   ISBN 1-877802-48-4 (pbk.) -- ISBN 1-877802-49-2 (hardcover)
   1. Nationalism--Congresses. 2. Self-determination, National--Congresses. 3. Group
identity--Political aspects--Congresses. 4. Democracy--Congresses. 5. País Vasco
(Spain)--Politics and government--21st century--Congresses. I. Aretxaga, Begoña. II.
University of Nevada, Reno. Center for Basque Studies. III. Title. IV. Series.

JC311.E495 2005
320.54--dc22

                                                                              2004031055

*For Ernest Lluch, murdered by ETA:
a friend whose vision helped shape the conference
on which this book is based.*

CONTENTS

Introduction 9

Part I
NATIONALISMS, POSTNATIONALISMS

Democracy and National Self-Determination: Yesterday, Today, and Tomorrow 15
    WALKER CONNOR

Postnationalist Identities: A New Configuration 29
    RICHARD KEARNEY

Intellectual Adventures in the Isles 41
    DENNIS DWORKIN

The Persistence of the Palestinian Question 57
    JOSEPH MASSAD

The Art of Forgetting 71
    XAVIER RUBERT DE VENTÓS

Part II
POPULISM AND RADICAL DEMOCRACY

Queering the Nation: Some Thoughts on Empire, Nationalism,
    and Multiculturalism Today 79
    JOHN BEVERLEY

From the Spains Defeated to the Spains Restored: Around a Map 93
    ERNEST LLUCH

Populism: What's in a Name? 103
    ERNESTO LACLAU

Nourishment by the Negative: National Subalternity, Antagonism,
    and Radical Democracy 115
    JOSEBA ZULAIKA

A Basque Referendum: Resolution of Political Conflict or the Promised Land of Error? ... 137
WILLIAM A. DOUGLASS and PEDRO IBARRA GÜELL

Out of Their Minds?: On Political Madness in the Basque Country ... 163
BEGOÑA ARETXAGA

Self-Fulfilling Prophecy and Unresolved Mourning:
Basque Political Violence in the Twenty-First Century ... 177
ALFONSO PÉREZ-AGOTE

Part III
POST 9/11

How to Live with Catastrophes? ... 201
SLAVOJ ŽIŽEK

The Second Cold War and Postmodern Terror ... 217
CHRIS HABLES GRAY

Performing Populism: A Queer Theory of Globalization, Terror, and Spectacle
(on *Lord of the Rings* and 9/11/2001) ... 237
JOSEBA GABILONDO

Index of Concepts ... 265

Index of People ... 281

Index of Places ... 287

List of Contributors ... 289

Introduction

Stateless Nations and Their Terrors

The demise of the Eastern European socialist bloc and the upsurge of neoliberal globalization promised a peace dividend. Rather we see a proliferation of virulent and intractable forms of ethnic movements demanding their own independent nation-states. This expansion has taken place at a time when right-wing movements within established nation-states in Europe and elsewhere are on the rise. In the Balkans, nationalist aspirations have been harnessed to authoritarian political traditions, continual reminders of a traumatic past. In Spain the advent of democracy after decades of dictatorship has represented a decisive break. The success of the Spanish democratic transition is undeniable, evinced by economic success and a growing international presence. Still the ongoing ethnic violence in the Basque Country (now being led by a whole new generation of youth born and raised in a democratic regime) constitutes a threatening and haunting reminder of both the former authoritarian regime and the fragility of democracy. In Northern Ireland, one of the few places where eventual reconciliation of two warring nationalist contingents seems possible, the Good Friday agreement is continually under threat of being undermined. Even at this juncture, more than five years following the signing of the peace treaty there, the devolved democratic machinery is on hold.

The ongoing crisis in the Basque Country, however, is the point of departure for this book. In spring 2002, the Center for Basque Studies at the University of Nevada, Reno, held a conference entitled "Nationalism, Globalization, and Terror: A Debate on Stateless Nations, Particularism/Universalism, and Radical Democracy." The impetus of the conference was a growing recognition by scholars in Basque studies that the Basque situation needs to be thought about in broader terms. On the one hand, its dynamic unfolding calls for a comparative analysis with other nationalist crises—from Canada to Kashmir. On the other hand, and most important, the Basque situation can no longer be geographically isolated. At a time when globalization is rapidly making and remaking the world and when nation-states no longer operate as coherent entities—if they ever did—that which is internal *and* external to the Basque crisis is unclear. The global ramifications of

September 11th for terrorist discourse underscore this, but also need to be better understood.

What began as an effort to expand the notion of Basque studies in that conference ended up as a wide-ranging discussion of the relationship between nationalism, globalization, terrorism, democracy, and culture. The conference brought together scholars from several disciplines—anthropology, history, cultural studies, and political science, among others—working in numerous geographical areas, including the British Isles, Scandinavia, Spain, and Latin America. They presented scholarly papers that were intensively discussed by the participants. And a number of public lectures were attended by the broader university community. The talks were so well received that they gave rise to an additional public lecture series held in fall 2002. Among those who delivered public talks were the political theorist Ernesto Laclau, the philosopher Richard Kearney, the historian Joseph Massad, the sociologist and feminist theorist Minoo Moallem, and the critical theorist and psychoanalyst Slavoj Žižek. This collection of essays draws from both the conference papers and the public talks.

Stateless nationalisms in Europe and elsewhere provide dramatic instances of democracies constituted through exclusions of people that return to haunt them. In addition to the Basque Country, regions such as Northern Ireland, Catalonia, Chechnya, Kashmir, Quebec, and Palestine come to mind. Whether described as terrorism-prone or ethnicity-tainted, or both, they confront contradictions that arise from striving for political sovereignty as well as democracy. Is it possible, some of our authors ask, to create a state based on national identity that is firmly participatory and that does not tramp on minority rights? Such seemingly intractable conflicts demand new kinds of theory and politics.

The cases of nationalist violence examined in this volume explore crucial issues regarding the articulation of politics at the beginning of the new millennium, in terms of both the mimesis of authoritarian forms and new democracies' efforts to throw off the weight of a dictatorial past. Contributors raise questions about contemporary political configurations. What does sovereignty in the state mean in the contemporary world of neoliberal capitalism? What is the status of democracy at a time when it has become a hegemonic discourse on capitalist belonging and fetishism? How is it possible to reconcile political claims that are universalistic yet are founded on specific identities? How do we come to grips with the specter of new authoritarian politics of the left, right, and center?

We do not see the concrete and specific cases discussed here in merely particularistic and exceptional terms. Rather we think of them as providing specific political contexts in which are dramatized crucial questions about contemporary relations of power, sovereignty, statehood, ideology, and fantasy. We see them as sites of psychic investments in the particular that nonetheless have implications for the universal dimension. Particularistic claims, such as self-determination, ultimately appeal to universal principles. Moreover, specific interests, if they are not to be merely relational or differential, invariably end up in conflict with other such interests, mediated by a field of power relations that is structured by forms of dominance, subordination, and exclusion.

As globalization becomes the new hegemonic discourse of late capitalism and as new suprastate realities emerge, some analysts have referred to the new nationalist formations as "postnationalist." They remain rooted in "imagined communities" of national identities and citizenship but are not exhausted by them. Their political form, the nation-state, is no longer a clearly delineated repository and expression of sovereignty. Postnationalism is an emerging political current or kernel that is simultaneously undermining the state and extending its boundaries. It seems as if neither the traditional Left nor the pundits and analysts of global capitalism are able to conceptualize, harness, and symbolize it. Has its spectral existence become the site of political universality?

In such a world—where the very existence of a "proper state" is being seriously undermined by financial markets, global threats, and transnational institutions and cultures—unavoidable questions emerge relating both to the hegemonic strategies used by nation-states to perpetuate their power and to new forms of antagonism produced by stateless nations seeking to regain lost ground. How can stateless nations claim theoretical and political rights to "sovereignty" in this new scenario, and how can this concept be (re)framed in the era of globalization? What are the implications of the theoretical paradox whereby the universal is nothing more than a dominant particular and the purely particular without any appeal to the universal is self-defeating? How does it affect our thinking about the articulations between suprastate formations, nation-states, quasi-states, regions, transnational corporations, and particular groups? Given that sovereignty appears necessary but impossible—an object presupposed and articulated by hegemonic logics but ultimately unachievable through them—is it helpful here? And are such paradoxes the very precondition for democracy?

A genuinely democratic society permanently shows the contingency of its foundations, the gap between the ethical moment and the normative order. Critical in this context are antagonisms, which have no objective meaning and which produce empty signifiers with no necessary attachment to any precise content. While authority attempts to establish an objective order of social relationships, it is subverted by antagonisms that lack a definitive ground. At the level of political subjectivity, historical analysis shows that oppositional identities are simultaneously antagonistic to and dependent on the status quo from which their opposition and hence identity is derived. Issues pertaining to antagonism and oppositional identities repose at the center of our reflections.

Such considerations call to mind the role that ideology plays in masking the impossible task that a society grounded in antagonisms faces in representing its fullness. Here, ideological constructs acquire a positive existence in the guise of some "big other" who ultimately controls social order. The societal vision of stateless nations fighting for sovereignty tends to become identified with a clear demand: attaining independent statehood. The negativity that prevents such nations from achieving their fullness exists in the form of historically and politically suppressed marginal nations. Ideological fantasy seeks to grind up the panoply of social and cultural paradoxes and contradictions. It mystifies the epistemological confusions that are continually generated by the impossibility of giving expression either to the fullness of society or to overcoming historical obstacles. The big "other" of the domineering nation-states becomes the locus of ideological antagonism and political fantasy.

Thus the contributors to this volume consider questions about the psychic investments and dynamics that animate both capitalist democratic practices and nationalist movements. What kinds of ideological fantasies, they ask, dominate the drive for an ethnic nation state? What kinds of fantasies, they wonder, sustain the hegemonic democratic form? What kinds of relations are established between the law of the state and the state of "terrorist" law? What kinds of fantasmic investments configure the state as an object of desire, identification, or threat? What are the psychic organizations of political trauma? And what are the consequences of silence regarding historical violence?

The events of 9/11 in New York City, Washington, D.C., and Pennsylvania and the subsequent ideological hegemony of terrorism in the global political discourse have added dramatic urgency to these issues. Some of the contributors to this volume discuss these and associated questions in the new post-9/11 international context. But ultimately the volume's goal is to stimulate productive ways of thinking simultaneously about the dynamics articulating the concrete situation of identity politics or violence (such as the Saami, Irish, Palestinians, Catalans, or Basques) and the global rhetoric of international terrorism that has come to dominate all political discourse.

As scholars, we are concerned with issues of particularism/universalism and democracy. The spiraling circle of violence and the narrowing scope of the discussion about it likewise preoccupy us. We see this volume as a contribution to expanding that debate beyond the idea that terrorism is intrinsically evil and therefore can only be condemned, or the notion that it is part of an inevitable clash of civilizations. Situating terrorism within different historical contexts and analyzing how it functions as a stimulus for discourse are the preconditions for opening up that discussion beyond today's stultifying polarities.

Part I

NATIONALISMS, POSTNATIONALISMS

Democracy and National Self-Determination: Yesterday, Today, and Tomorrow

WALKER CONNOR

Abstract

What follows is a discussion of the relationship between democracy and the multinational state. It addresses the question of whether democratic multinational states are necessarily destined to fragment along ethnonational lines. The conclusion, based on an array of comparative data, is that democracy and ethnonational heterogeneity are not intrinsically incompatible, but that the leadership of a democratic multinational state must be prepared to countenance significant decentralization of political power as the price of containing separatist sentiment.

A Thumbnail History of National Self-Determination Movements

The dismemberment of the former Soviet Union, the Federal Republic of Yugoslavia, and the recognition of East Timor are only the most recent manifestations of the challenge that ethnonationalism poses to the survival of the multihomeland state. In the 130-year period that separated the Napoleonic Era and the end of World War II, all but three of Europe's states either lost significant territory and population to ethnonational aspirations or were themselves newly created in the name of national self-determination. (One of the exceptions, Portugal, was ethnically homogeneous; the other two, Spain and Switzerland, while remaining intact, have not been free of ethnically inspired discord.) Ethnonational aspirations continued to challenge multihomeland political structures in the post–World War II period, and, by 1965, more than half of all states had experienced significant levels of ethnonational unrest.

At the bottom of all this unrest is a concept of political legitimacy that makes ethnicity the ultimate standard for judging legitimacy. It holds that a national group—just because it considers itself to be a separate nation—has the right, if it so desires, to its own state. At first untitled, later referred to as "the principle of nationalities," and more recently as "national self-determination," this concept of political legitimacy now manifests itself universally in antistate movements.

Significantly, no particular classification of country has proven immune. Afflicted countries are to be found in Africa (for example, Nigeria), Asia (Sri Lanka), Eastern Europe (Romania), Western Europe (France), North America (Guatemala), South America (Guyana), and Oceania (New Zealand). The list includes countries that are old (the United Kingdom) as well as new (Bangladesh), large (Indonesia) as well as small (Fiji), rich (Canada) as well as poor (Pakistan), authoritarian (Sudan) as well as democratic (Belgium), Marxist-Leninist (China) as well as militantly anti-Marxist (Turkey). The list also includes countries that are Buddhist (Burma), Christian (Spain), Moslem (Iran), Hindu (India), and Judaic (Israel).

A Note on Terminology and on Homelands and Homeland Psychology

Terminology

Improper and inconsistent use of the key terms has bedeviled the study of nationalism. In this essay, the following terms are used as follows:

Ethnic—derived from *ethnos,* the ancient Greek word for a nation *(qv)* in the latter's pristine sense of a group characterized by common descent; the prefix *ethno* therefore means *national.*

Ethnocracy—an ethnically homogeneous political unit; it can vary in size from a small village to a modern state.

Ethnonationalism—a redundancy, coined in response to the general tendency to *misuse* the word *nationalism (qv)* to convey loyalty to the state rather than to one's national group; it is designed to leave no doubt in the reader's mind that the author is discussing loyalty to the nation.

Gemeinschaft—an association resting on a sense of kinship, real or imagined; gemeinschaft groupings include the family, band, tribe, and nation.

Gesellschaft—an association of individuals resting on the conviction that their personal self-interest can be best promoted through membership in the group; the gesellschaft society is largely a product of rational self-interest (in political philosophy, the case for the political legitimacy of the gesellschaft state has been closely tied to the notion of the social contract).

Nation—a group of people sharing a myth of common ancestry; it is the largest grouping that can be mobilized by appeals to common blood (nation is often *improperly* employed as a synonym for *state,* as in the League of Nations, or the United Nations, or as a synonym for the citizenry of a state regardless of its ethnic complexity, as in references to "the American nation").

Nationalism—identity with and loyalty to one's nation in the pristine sense of that word; nationalism is often *incorrectly* used to refer to loyalty to the state.

Nation-state—that relatively rare situation in which the borders of a state and a nation closely coincide; a state with an ethnically homogeneous population.

Patriotism—devotion to one's state and its institutions.

State—the major political unit in world politics; country.

The principal confusion caused by improper terminology has been the tendency to substitute *nationalism* for *patriotism* when referring to loyalty to the state. The most current vogue, a slight refinement on the nationalism-equals-loyalty-to-the-state malapropism, is to refer to loyalty to the state as civic nationalism and loyalty to the nation as ethnic nationalism. But this only tends to propagate the misconception that we are dealing with two variants of the same phenomenon. If writers prefer to use civic identity or civic loyalty in preference to patriotism, fine. But the fundamental dissimilarities between state loyalty and nationalism should not be glossed over by employing the noun nationalism to refer to two quite different phenomena. The two loyalties represent two very different order of things. Loyalty to state is sociopolitical in nature and is based in large part on rational self-interest. Loyalty to nation is intuitive rather than rational and is predicated on a sense of consanguinity. When the two are viewed as being in irreconcilable conflict, loyalty to the nation customarily proves the more powerful.

Homelands and Homeland Psychology

Although it is now commonplace to note that the overwhelming number of states are multinational, it is much more rare for authors to note that most states are multihomeland as well. Yet the fact that states tend to be multihomeland is of the greatest significance when assessing the probable political instability of tomorrow's world, for the demands of ethnonational movements tend to be coterminous with their homeland. In terms of geography, it is for their homeland that ethnonational groups demand greater autonomy or full independence. For example, in the last stages of the Soviet Union, it was precisely over the homeland—over mother Armenia, Estonia, Georgia, Latvia, Lithuania, and so forth—that the non-Russian peoples demanded of Gorbachev greater control. It is over Euskadi, Corsica, Kashmir, Nagaland, and Tibet that the Basques, the Corsicans, the Kashmiri, the Nagas, and the Tibetans demand greater control. The principal slogan of the Québecois, "Maîtres Chez Nous," captures this attitude nicely. The Québecois must be masters in their home—meaning the homeland of Quebec.

It is possible, of course, that an autonomy or independence movement may be based on regionalism rather than an ethnic homeland. This is true of the movement that separated Eritrea from Ethiopia and is also true of a much weaker and nonviolent movement to separate British Columbia and other western provinces from Canada. But the great number of autonomy and secessionist movements that pockmark the globe are being waged by homeland peoples. It is the multihomeland state that is the target of ethnonational demands for autonomy or independence.

The Self-Determination Impulse

National self-determination is treated by intellectuals with cavalier superficiality. Usually the phrase is prefaced by "the principal of" or the "the doctrine of" and its creation attributed to one or another individual or school. During 1999, I attended a conference sponsored by the Carnegie Corporation of New York. More than fifty ostensible specialists on national self-determination were in attendance. During the conference the origin of the phrase was uncritically—albeit erroneously—attributed to Woodrow Wilson, and there was an evident consensus among participants that Wilson was to be criticized for unleashing a pernicious doctrine; had he not, the implication was, this would be a more ordered and peaceful world. So far as I can determine, the phrase *national self-determination* first appeared publicly in the First International's *Proclamation on the Polish Question* (1865) and became thereafter a staple in the writings of Marx, Engels, and Lenin, as well as in various proclamations and documents associated with their movement.[1] In any event, well before the coining of this particular phrase, the same phenomenon was being described within French circles as *le principe des nationalités.*

But this history of phraseology is beside the point. Neither Wilson, nor Marx, nor the French coiner of *le principe des nationalités* created the phenomenon to which they attached a name. The phrase did not give rise to the phenomenon; the phenomenon gave rise to the phrase. Self-determination is much more than a principle or a doctrine. It is a popular impulse to resent and resist control by those deemed aliens. As such, the urge for group self-determination is a fixture throughout history, antedating the age of nationalism. The history of empires, both ancient and modern, is riddled by incidents, riots, and uprisings through which indigenous peoples expressed their unhappiness with rule by an alien *them.* The commonness of such manifestations is the more telling because large numbers of people dwelling within an empire were not ruled directly by the center. Leaders of major portions of the ancient empires often had only a tributory relationship to the emperor, and a very similar system of vassal states existed in more recent empires through the device of the protectorate. Moreover, even within regions of an empire that were ruled directly from the center as colonies, "indirect rule" was often practiced through local headmen. Moreover, it is relatively safe to assume that prior to the twentieth century ostensible control over an extensive land area was more fictional than real. On this point the classic study is that of Eugen Weber's *Peasants into Frenchmen.*[2] Although France had long been viewed as an integrated society, Weber established that most people living within France in the late 19th and early 20th centuries dwelt in rural villages that were cultural

---

1. For details, see W. Connor, *The National Question in Marxist-Leninist Theory and Strategy* (Princeton: Princeton University Press, 1984), Chapters 1 and 2.

2. Eugen Weber, *Peasants into Frenchmen: The Modernization of Rural France, 1870–1940* (Stanford: Stanford University Press, 1976).

isolates. People were fractured into tiny units, each speaking a local patois and seldom aware of an identity shared with those beyond the locale. Further research establishes that this highly decentralized pattern was not unique to France. Prior to the twentieth century the ethnic identity of rural people seldom corresponded with that of the national group to which the outside world assigned them (e.g., to a French or German or Chinese or similar category).[3]

In sum, then, what were represented on maps as empires or states were in fact arrays of local ethnocracies, within which the inclination to resent domination by the ethnic "other" did not come into play. However, wherever it could come into play—where subordination to an intruding people was actually experienced—resistance to alien rule was common. Thus, within Britain, Anglo-Saxons long chafed under "the Norman Yoke";[4] Ireland was the scene of periodic local uprisings against English overseers long before Irish nationalism was a reality;[5] Welsh anti-English insurrections and rebellions date to the late thirteenth century;[6] and the many Scottish anti-English uprisings and wars with England date to this same period.[7]

National self-determination describes this deeply rooted aversion to domination by others when the group is the nation. But again, the impulse permeating national self-determination has been manifest in behavior patterns throughout history.

Despite all this, it has been and remains a common conceit of policy-makers and academicians that they can dictate the limits of self-determination. With regard to policy-makers, I wrote three decades ago:

> But as the host of ethnopolitical struggles to which we alluded at the outset makes clear, the dynamic of self-determination operates quite independently of the wishes and perceptions of such leaders. Following World War I, the peacemakers believed that they could establish limits to self-determination, restricting it essentially to Eastern Europe and limiting it further therein so as to prevent the "balkanization" of the area. But Croatian, Slovene, Slovak, Macedonian, and other unsatisfied nationalisms plague Eastern Europe a half-century later, and the self-determination concept has been instrumental in demolishing the empires of Belgium, Britain, France, Spain, and the Netherlands throughout Africa and Asia. And, as Biafra, Bangladesh, and a series of other separatist movements attest, the leaders of the new states are not apt to prove any more successful in their attempt to legislate the limits of the self-determination impulse. Governmental resistance accounts for the poor record of self-determination to date, but the prospect is for proliferating and escalating challenges to this posture.[8]

---

3. For details, see Walker Connor, "From Tribe to Nation?" *History of European Ideas* 13, nos. 1\2 (1991), 5–18, and "When Is a Nation?" *Ethnic and Racial Studies* 13 (Jan. 1990), 92–103.

4. The most well-known account can be found in Christopher Hill, *Puritanism and Revolution* (London: Secker and Warburg, 1958), 50–122.

5. For a table chronologically itemizing a number of such insurrections, see Bertrand Roehner, *Separatism and Integration* (New York: Rowman and Littlefield, 2002), 200–201.

6. See the table in Roehner, ibid., 267–68.

7. Centuries of clan and subclan warfare attest to the fact that highland Scotland and Ireland were aggregates of localized ethnocracies throughout most of their histories.

8. "The Politics of Ethnonationalism" *Journal of International Affairs* 27, no. 1 (1973), 14.

As to academicians, the Carnegie conference that was alluded to earlier was suffused with implicit and explicit examples. The conference began with papers and lengthy discussion addressing normative standards by which the legitimacy of national self-determination movements should be judged and subsequently endorsed or rejected. At a later session one participant, the head of a think tank, recalled with pride that he had told a representative of one of the nations of Yugoslavia that he didn't see why he should feel constrained to recognize ethnicity rather than some other element as a basis for self-determination claims. Others expressed the opinion that we should create larger rather than smaller states. (I found this particularly whimsical, not only in light of the above quotation, but also since it was uttered only a decade after the dismemberment of the Soviet Union.) A similar mind-set is evident in the many articles and books questioning whether national self-determination has or has not become an accepted "principle" of international law, the assumption being that, if not, self-determination is not a reality. But again, the self-determination impulse has not proven noticeably responsive to the will of political leaders, the ruminations of academicians, or its status in international law.

National Self-Determination and Democracy

National self-determination, though destined to become a universal force, arrived without benefit of intellectual heralds. It was unanticipated by the sages of political philosophy and gained their attention only after it had become an undeniable force in the real world, as opposed to the world of ideas. The explanation for this seeming enigma appears to lie in the intricate and complex relationship between national self-determination and popular sovereignty. Prior to the eighteenth century, political rule was legitimized as a gift from the gods (divine right), a prerogative of royal blood, the rightful reward of conquest, an inheritance, the result of royal marriage, a fidelity owed because of protection or other services rendered (feudalism), a right inherent in the title to the land on which people lived, or some combination of the foregoing. All these rationales shared the common premise that the right to rule emanated from above; it did not emanate from below, that is to say, from those who were ruled. The masses were viewed solely as the object, not the font, of political authority. And if the masses were not germane to the issue of political legitimacy, it follows that their ethnicity was not. And so, the borders of empires, princely states, and even the post-1648 so-called modern states were usually drawn with little regard for the geographic distribution of ethnic groups. But a single theory of legitimacy—popular sovereignty, which holds that ultimate political authority resides in the people and that the consent of the governed is therefore the *sole valid basis,* the sine qua non, of political legitimacy—undermined all of these theories simultaneously and set the scene for ethnic identity to become *the* standard of political legitimacy.

Popular sovereignty had its devotees among political philosophers dating back to ancient times. It grew progressively more popular among theorists, and the renowned German scholar Otto Gierke has informed us that well before the close of the Middle Ages it had become almost *the theory* of legitimacy among philosophers: "From the end of the thirteenth century it was the axiom of political theory that the justification of all government lay in the voluntary submission of the community ruled."[9] But if philosophers were infatuated with popular sovereignty by the thirteenth century, why the lapse of five hundred years before this concept ignited the imagination of activists? As it emerged from the writings of philosophers, the notion of *the people* in whom the right to rule was said to be vested was too abstractly intellectual, too remote from human experiences and feeling, too bloodless to serve as a centerpiece for a crusade.

The time lag between the period when popular sovereignty had captured the imagination of theorists and its much later popularization in the world of action is therefore a reflection of humankind's tendency to abhor universal views of self. What breathed life into the overly sterile concept of *the people* was the inclination to substitute *my* for *the*. It was not in the name of *the* people but in the name of *my people*—that is, a *Greek, Irish,* or *Norse* people—that movements, insisting on an incontrovertible right of a human collective to determine its own political destiny, would most commonly be waged.[10]

What all this adds up to is that national self-determination is a conception—the most frequent and emotional objectification—of popular sovereignty. Consonant with this propensity to equate one's own people with *the people,* it was through political demands for the Albanian, Basque, Bulgarian, Catalan, Croat, Czech, Estonian, Finnish, Galician, Icelandic, Lett, Lithuanian, Magyar, Polish, Romanian, Serbian, Ukrainian, or other specific national group that the notion that holds that the consent of the governed is the paramount determinant of political legitimacy customarily manifested itself in Europe between the Napoleonic Wars and World War II. Events both within and without Europe since World War II clearly reinforce this trend.

As the most frequent objectification of popular sovereignty, national self-determination could accurately be described as "*popular* popular sovereignty." The conclusion that national self-determination is itself popular sovereignty as most commonly conceived goes well beyond simply noting—as many scholars have done—that popular sovereignty was a necessary precondition for the germination of the idea of national self-determination. Indeed, recognizing national self-determination as popular sovereignty in its most commonly conceived form contradicts the conclusion of many authorities who, having noted that national self-determination is a very recently emerged concept in terms of the overall history of political ideas, infer therefrom that the concept is apt to prove short-lived.

Contrary to this view of its short history, we have noted, first, that national self-determination rests on an impulse to resent rule by those perceived as aliens, an impulse that has resonated throughout history. Second, national self-determination appeared in the world of action before and independent of its recognition and captioning by wordsmiths. Third, the rationale for national self-determination is inseparable from the rationale for

---

9. Cited in C. E. Merriam, *History of the Theory of Sovereignty Since Rousseau* (New York: The Columbia University Press, 1900), 12.

10. The psychological predisposition or predilection to perceive *my nation* in references to *the people* is perhaps suggested by the fact that the word used by many peoples to *self*-describe their nation literally translates as "the people." The Eskimo word *Innuit*, the Navajo word *Diné*, and the Welsh word *Cymru* are examples.

popular sovereignty and there is no reason to believe that it will ebb as a political force in a world in which popular sovereignty shows no sign of receding.

The case for popular sovereignty as the foundation of political legitimacy cannot be developed logically. Just as with the claims to political legitimacy that preceded popular sovereignty (divine right of kings, rightful reward of conquest, an accompaniment to title to the land, and the like), popular sovereignty is ultimately an assertion or credo. As did Jefferson, one can aver it to be a "self-evident truth," despite the fact that it was not at all "self-evident" until quite recent times, that is, history does not support a claim to self-evidency for popular sovereignty. By contrast, what we have termed "*popular* popular sovereignty" or national self-determination would appear to be a better candidate for classification as "a self-evident truth," since it grows out of a human aversion to domination by "the other" that can be detected throughout history.

Democracy and National Self-Determination: Myth and Reality

Democracy presumes popular sovereignty, but the reverse is not true. So long as those in power pay lip service to the notion of the people as the source of their power and enjoy a significant measure of popularity, the system's legitimacy is said to be based on popular sovereignty. Democratic elections and the like are not necessary.

The national self-determination variant of popular sovereignty also does not presume the existence of a democracy. Some ethnocracies in history may have been democratically run, as were purportedly the Germanic tribes of the early Middle Ages, and as are a number of essentially ethnically homogeneous states in contemporary Western Europe. But ethnocracies prior to the twentieth century were certainly far more apt to be authoritarian than democratic in orientation, and the perpetuation of ethnocratic authoritarianism into the twentieth century could be seen in, among other countries, pre-1945 Japan, Nazi Germany, Salazar's Portugal, and Hoxha's Albania. It was Adolf Hitler who wrote:

> We, as Aryans, are therefore able to imagine a State only to be the living organism of a nationality which not only safeguards the preservation of that nationality, but which, by a further training of its spiritual and ideal abilities, leads it to the highest freedom.[11]

It should not be surprising that ethnocracies cover the spectrum from democratic to despotic. Despite its *ism* suffix, nationalism is not an ideology. Beyond positing the idea that one's nation is the most important unit of humankind and deserving of unwavering loyalty, it is remarkably contentless. Over generations it has accommodated monarchists, republicans, fascists, Leninists, Maoists, and what have you, often simultaneously. It is this contentless quality that accounts for the nearly universal tendency of nationalist movements to factionalize. The current fragmentation of nationalists between followers of the moderate Basque National Party and more militant Basques is hardly unique. The (Northern Ireland) Irish, Walloon, Corsican, and Breton movements are among the many

---

11. Adolf Hitler, *Mein Kampf* (New York: Reynal & Hitchcock, 1940), 595.

that manifest profound ideological cleavages. Some nationalists are far less committed to democratic procedures than are others.

National self-determination is therefore democratic only in that it assumes a collective right inherent in every national group to choose its political attachments, but it contains no assumptions concerning the governmental system that the national group must adopt. It assumes ethnocracy but not democracy.

There is, nevertheless, an important relationship between national self-determination and the modern, democratic, multinational political system, in that such a system is the most intrinsically vulnerable to self-determination demands. The authoritarian government can, with logical consistency, deny any legitimacy to such demands, since the case the regime makes for its own legitimacy does not rest on democratic foundations. It is far more embarrassing and manifestly hypocritical for a self-styled democracy to deny the self-determination principle. It is not pure chronological chance that Basque and Catalan national aspirations, effectively squelched under Franco, should be extended concessions in post-1975, democratic Spain. If Madrid desired a country-wide democracy, it had little choice. Moreover, the likely results of a contrary policy—such as long-term occupation forces maintaining order over an unwilling population throughout large sectors of the country—would be totally alien to democracy.

One Nation, One State?

Does this mean, then, that the British scholar Ernest Barker was correct in his assertion that a democratic state would tend to dissolve into as many states as there were nations within it?[12] Seemingly not. The essence of self-determination is choice, not result. As noted, it holds that any nation has the right to secede, *if it so desires*. But opinion surveys and election data drawn from a number of democracies indicate that the typical member of a national minority in a modern democratic state is prepared to settle for something less than secession. The following are some of the more pertinent attitudes that have been documented:[13]

1. Members of ethnonational minorities manifest substantially less affection toward the state than do members of the dominant group.
2. Different minorities of the same state can differ significantly in this regard.
3. For most persons, however, the matter is not perceived in either/or terms. Affective ties to the state coexist with ethnonational consciousness.
4. In most cases in which a separatist movement is active, large numbers, usually a majority of the involved group, do not favor secession.
5. In some cases, the percentage represented by prosecessionists has remained relatively constant; in other cases it has evidenced profound trends.

---

12. Ernest Barker, *National Character and the Factors in Its Formation* (London: Methuen, 1927), 125–26.

13. For details, see W. Connor, "A Primer for Analyzing Ethnonational Conflict," in *Ethnic Conflict: Religion, Identity, and Politics*, ed. S.A. Giannakos (Athens, Ohio: Ohio University Press, 2002), particularly 31–35.

6. Regardless of their attitude toward secession, a preponderant number do favor major alterations in the political system that would result in greater autonomy.

7. Where separatist parties are allowed to contest elections, their vote is not an adequate index to separatist sentiment.

8. In all cases for which there are attitudinal data, members of ethnonational groups overwhelmingly reject the use of violence carried out in the name of the national group.

9. However, a large percentage, including many who do not favor separation, empathize with those engaged in violence and place the blame for the violence on others.

10. Separatists draw their support from all social strata and age groups.

11. Disproportionate support, however, comes from those under thirty-five years of age, with above-average education and income.

12. Lack of support is particularly pronounced among those over fifty-five years of age.

13. Professional people are disproportionately represented among separatists.

All these findings are consonant with our earlier discussion. Members of a politically nondominant nation manifest less loyalty to the state than do those of the dominant nation (finding #1) because they do not perceive the state as the political extension or expression of the nation. The primary focus of an ethnonational minority is the nation and the homeland. It follows that if a national minority popularly perceives its loyalty to the state and to the nation as being in irreconcilable conflict, loyalty to the nation will win the competition. It should, however, elicit little surprise that the state should enjoy a significant measure of loyalty in the absence of such a perception (finding #3). The state has powerful means for politically socializing (programming) its citizens to respect both itself and its institutions, not the least of which is control of education (and especially control of the manner in which history is taught). Particularly in the modern welfare state, the fear of losing state-conferred benefits, such as old-age assistance, can dampen the ardor for separation, most markedly among the elderly (finding #12). In the case of the Basques, the complexity of self-identity to which state socialization of this sort can give rise is suggested in a poll in which some 10 percent of respondents chose the identity category "More Basque than Spanish" in preference to simpler category of "Basque." At least to this 10 percent, "Basque,"[14] while being considered the more important identity, was not perceived as excluding a significant measure of affinity for the Spanish state. In like manner, in a 1992 poll only 19 percent of Scots elected to describe themselves as "Scottish not

---

14. Richard Gunther, "A Comparative Study of Regionalism in Spain" (paper presented to the Society for Spanish and Portuguese Historical Studies, Toronto, Canada, April 24–25, 1981). See also the table in Goldie Shabad and Richard Gunther, "Language, Nationalism, and Political Conflict in Spain," *Comparative Politics* 14 (July 1982), 449. A more recent newspaper article cites surveys suggesting that 60 percent identify themselves as both Spanish and Basque, while only 30 percent say they are Basque. *New York Times*, Aug. 11, 2000.

British," while 40 percent selected "more Scottish than British" and 33 percent elected "equally Scottish and British."[15]

Even if the state is viewed with only marginal sympathy, it is not incongruous that most members of the national minority are prepared to settle for autonomy (findings #4 and #6). Autonomy has the potential for satisfying the principal aspirations of the group. Ethnonational aspirations, by their very nature, are more obsessed by the dream of *freedom from* domination by outsiders than by *freedom to* conduct relations with states. Ethnocracy need not presume independence, though it must presume *meaningful* autonomy at the minimum. As earlier noted, the conviction that the nation must exert control over its own destiny is captured in the chief slogan of the Québècois, *Maîtres Chez Nous*. The Québècois must be masters in their own home, meaning the homeland of Québèc. They are convinced that within the homeland they must have the ultimate power of decision-making over those matters most affecting ethnonational sensibilities and nation-maintenance.

Unfortunately, central authorities have tended to perceive any demand for a significant increase in autonomy as tantamount to secession, or an important step toward it. Governments have been inclined to guard their prerogatives zealously and to resist any move toward decentralization. In doing so, they often further the very result that they ostensibly wish to avoid, for there is an inverse relationship between a government's willingness to grant meaningful autonomy and the level of separatist sentiment. For example, when the Spanish government first granted an autonomy statute to the Basques in 1979, the proportion of Basques desiring independence dropped from 36 percent to 12 percent.[16] Recent events in Canada illustrate this same phenomenon in reverse. Denied a request that the constitution be altered to recognize the French-speaking people of Québèc as "a distinct society," those Québècois in favor of separation rose dramatically, from less than 20 percent to well over 50 percent.[17]

The message therefore is clear: Governments of multinational states refuse to countenance demands for decentralization at the peril of increasing separatist sentiment. Decentralization of important powers is the price of maintaining democratic institutions in a multinational setting.

Switzerland, while certainly not immune to ethnically inspired dissension, demonstrates that a multinational democracy can survive if the political system is sufficiently decentralized. The confederal, cantonal structure of the country, combined with its ethnic map, minimizes the possibility of domination or even the perception of domination by the

---

15. Lynne Bennie, Jack Brand, and James Mitchell, *How Scotland Votes: Scottish Parties and Elections* (Manchester: Manchester University Press, 1997), 155.

16. A *New York Times* article (Aug. 11, 2000) suggests that separatist sentiment subsequently increased to perhaps 30 percent.

17. Separatist sentiment subsequently dropped and in 2003 the separatist Parti Québècois (PQ) lost its majority in the Québec Assembly. However, the Québècois vote was divided into two parties, one of which (the PQ) promised a vote on separatism within 1,000 days, while the other, without denying the desirability of separation, stood for its indefinite postponement in order to tackle serious social problems. Analyzing the vote is precarious because the population of the province is more than 20 percent non-Québècois. However, it would appear that only an approximate one-fourth of the Québècois voters voted for the party which opposed separatism both now and in the future.

numerically predominant Germanic element. In the case of the one canton within which a sizable French-speaking minority was dominated by the Germanic element, a successful secessionist movement was waged by the Francophones during the 1970s. But, most instructively, the secessionists aspired to secede only from the German-dominated canton of Bern, not from Switzerland. Given their own ethnocracy (a canton), they considered their right to national self-determination fulfilled. Following, if somewhat haltingly, this same path, a number of western democracies—most notably Belgium, Canada, Italy, and Spain—have at least partially assuaged ethnonational aspirations through the recent granting of substantial autonomy.

The Shifting Meaning of Autonomy

Why assuaged rather than satisfied? It was earlier noted that most members of a national minority are prepared to settle for *meaningful* autonomy. Autonomy is an amorphous concept meaning quite different things to different people. It may refer to very limited home rule or to regional control over everything other than foreign policy. That is to say, it can depict any situation on the continuum between total subordination to the center and total independence.

Even when discussion is limited to the three modern democracies of Belgium, Canada, and Spain, it is difficult to generalize concerning the specifics of autonomy. For example the power to conduct foreign policy, being a defining characteristic of state sovereignty, is usually considered to be beyond the confines of the most extreme definition of autonomy. Yet, the government of Québec has entered directly into a number of bilateral arrangements with foreign countries. Perhaps the broadest generality that can be made concerning the specifics of autonomy is that governments have been far more inclined to grant demands for autonomy in the cultural than in the political realm. In Belgium, for example, the Flemish-, French-, and German-speaking communities are constitutionally authorized to legislate in the areas of education, cultural affairs, and health and social assistance, and, more broadly, to formulate "socioeconomic policies." As to the use of minority languages, contemporary democracies have shown a willingness to permit the local language to be used in the courts and other public forums, including its use as the language of instruction in the schools. In Belgium and Canada, although not in Spain, the coequal status of a homeland language has been extended throughout the country as a whole by declaring it an official state language.

An issue of seemingly unavoidable conflict between the center and homeland peoples involves the migration of peoples. Central governments control not only the movement of people across the state's borders (immigration/emigration) but also the movement of people within the country. Democratic governments customarily insist that all legal residents have the right to live wherever they choose. Typical is the wording of the Canada Act of 1982, guaranteeing to every citizen and permanent resident of Canada, "the right (a) to move to and take up residence in any province; and (b) to pursue the gaining of a livelihood in any province." On the other hand, few if any matters will be deemed more of an exclusive prerogative by a homeland people than the issue of who is to be permitted to live within the nation's home. An influx of significant numbers of nonmembers of the nation is apt to trigger resentment and a rise in separatist sentiments. This linkage between separatism and the movement of nonindigenes into the homeland holds true even if the nonindigenes are fellow citizens. But the linkage has taken on a new intensity within the democratic states of Western Europe and Canada as they have become the targets of unprecedented numbers of foreign migrants. Thus, in the recent general elections in Belgium, the party that has gained the largest percentage increase in parliamentary seats is the Vlams Block; a hitherto marginal party advocating separate statehood for Flanders, it has substantially increased its representation in the Parliament by adding to its platform a demand for the repatriation of immigrants. Even immigration policy, a former preserve of the central government, is therefore also becoming a matter increasingly viewed by homeland peoples as falling within their notion of autonomy.

Notions of what constitutes an acceptable level of autonomy therefore differ (1) between the view from the palace and the view from the homeland, (2) among individuals, and (3) over time. The multifaceted meanings of autonomy account for the dismal record of attempts to implement it. Typically, there will be those associated with the center who will tend to view even minimal devolution as tantamount to secession and will pressure the government to concede in practice as little as possible. On the other side, those who hold a maximalist view of autonomy will perceive any manifestation of the center's presence in the homeland as violating the spirit of autonomy. More moderate homeland leaders will be under pressure from the maximalists, to say nothing of the separatists, to squeeze more concessions from the center if they desire to maintain their following. In this atmosphere, mutual recriminations and charges of bad faith abound.

Simply agreeing to introduce autonomy is therefore no guarantee of peaceful accommodation. The search for adjustments in the system sufficiently acceptable to both sides may fail. But a democratic milieu is the most conducive to finding an acceptable balance.

A paradox of democracy, then, is that while it is the most vulnerable to demands for national self-determination, it is the most likely to sufficiently sate those demands and thus avoid secession. As noted, the level of separatist sentiment correlates with the level of frustration of nationalist aspirations. Working, enduring autonomy requires continuous adjustments in the relationship of the center to the minority in response to changing circumstances and perceptions. And this presupposes an atmosphere and institutions conducive to give-and-take conciliation, a situation most apt to prevail in those political systems closest to the democratic pole on the authoritarian–democratic continuum.

Conclusion

1. The Rationale for Ethnocracy Was Furnished by Democratic Doctrine

Prior to the American Declaration of Independence and the French Declaration of the Rights of Man and Citizen, ethnocracy was without a rationale. It was restricted to the local scene, devoid of an articulated principle for creating a sovereign polity. Its rationale proved to be embodied in popular sovereignty. The right of nations to self-determination was a sequacious application of the notion that sovereignty resides in the people. What the philosophers had advanced as the rationale for a *Gessellschaft* society unexpectedly furnished the rationale for the *Gemeinschaft* society in the form of the principle of nationalities and national self-determination.

Significance: As the most infectious interpretation of popular sovereignty, national self-determination is not apt to lose its *popular* status as a categorical imperative so long as popular sovereignty remains the nearly universally accepted justification for the exercise of political power.

2. The Democratic Multinational State Is the Most Vulnerable to National Self-Determination Demands

Both logically and institutionally, the democratic state, primarily because of its genuine commitment to popular sovereignty, offers the most favorable milieu for successfully pursuing the goal of national self-determination.

Significance: The modern democratic multinational state cannot deny the aspirations of its national minorities without undermining its claim to be a democracy.

3. Although the Most Vulnerable to National Self-Determination Demands, Democracy Is Best Equipped to Satisfy Those Demands Without Recourse to Secession

National minorities tend to view their loyalty to nation and loyalty to state as compatible, if the center is prepared to grant substantial autonomy. A formula for power-sharing will be difficult to achieve and, if achieved, will be subject to periodic demands for alterations. However, attitudinal polls, the history of Switzerland, and developments in such democracies as Belgium, Canada, Spain, and the United Kingdom indicate that successful accommodation need not be illusion.

Significance: As contrasted with other forms of government, democracy exerts pressure to find a peaceful solution to the problems posed by ethnonational heterogeneity. The price of remaining a democratic state, while retaining present borders, is likely to be greater decentralization. An autonomy agreement will not create a stable, fixed-for-all-time division of authority between the government and nondominant ethnic elements. As in Switzerland, the balancing of authority will be a dynamic process, subject to continuous redefinition in the face of new problems and new demands. But again, this imperfect prospect would appear more consonant with the self-interest of governing elites than would the most stable hegemony coercively maintained over hostile, noncooperative peoples.

Postnationalist Identities: A New Configuration

Richard Kearney

As we move into the third millennium, people are becoming increasingly aware that nationality is a necessary but by no means sufficient source of identity. In addition to the national identity afforded by one's belonging to a nation-state (or a nation in search of a state, viz. the Kurds, Palestinians, and Basques), it is now commonplace for people to lay claim to a model of *multiple identity,* extending from subnational categories of region, province, or county to transnational categories such as the EU or UN. In the case of Ireland and Britain, which I concentrate on in this paper, this third category would also include the British-Irish Council. If the first step in this set of expanding concentric circles is epitomized by Patrick Kavanagh's statement that "the parish is my world," the ultimate step is captured by Socrates's famous assertion that he is "neither Athenian, nor Greek, but a citizen of the world." Between the *ego sum* and the *mundanus sum* there are many worlds to be traversed, and each has its proper place in the postnational jigsaw of identities.

1

While this is new in some respects, it is a very old idea in others. To concentrate on the example of Ireland, it is important to recall that the literature of this land is replete with references to multiple identities. The first book recording its history and genealogy is entitled, tellingly, *The Book of Invasions;* and this serves to remind us that Ireland is not, and never has been, an ethnically homogenous, continuous nation but is composed of layers of migrations and transmigrations making up a palimpsest of differing identities ranging from the Tuatha De Danann and Milesians to the Celts, Vikings, Danes, Normans, and Anglo-Saxons, among others. That is why it is no accident that one of the first lines recorded by an Irishman in English—that of Captain McMorris in Shakespeare's *Henry V*—assumes the form of a question: "What is my nation?" To be Irish is to be someone who asks the question what it means to be Irish. Ireland is a country that exists in the interrogative mode.

This question of multiple identity reflects itself in turn in the complex question of *sovereignty*. There are four provinces in Ireland—Leinster, Munster, Ulster, and Connaught—but the Gaelic word for a province is *coicead* or "fifth." So where is the fifth province? The fact is that nobody knows and never has known. Some claimed it was in Tara, others in Uisneach, others in Meath (*Meatha* meaning the "middle" of Ireland); but the general view was that it did not actually exist in any territorial location. The Fifth Province was an extraterritorial or place-less place (*u-topos*) that provided the unifying symbolic space for the other four provinces to come together and interact. Without it, the land fell back into division and conflict. Indeed, as most Celtic scholars like Proinsias McCana and Myles Dillon agree, there never was a concept of political sovereignty in Ireland prior to the creation of a High Kingship (*Ard Ri*) in response to the Viking and Anglo-Norman invasions. The creation of a centralized, homogenous nation was therefore a historical strategy in reaction to violence inflicted from without rather than anything inherited or God-given. And this strategic construction was further consolidated when King Donald O'Neill wrote to the Pope in Rome in 1371 declaring himself sovereign leader of the whole nation of Ireland (*totus hiberniae*), which, he argued, laid claim to the unbroken lineage of a single nation (*nacio* or *gens*) going back to time immemorial. This was of course a mimetic response to the claim of the invading English (*Sasanach*) that *they* were the true and pure *gens* who, as divinely appointed gentlemen of the gentry, had a natural right to the land. This latter claim was copperfastened in the Statutes of Kilkenny (1366), which drove a legal wedge between those colonial planters residing "inside the pale" (*gens*) and those dislodged natives now residing "outside the pale" (*de-gens*): For the former to intermingle or intermarry with the latter was to become "degenerate." The two "opposed" peoples were in fact ethnically and genetically identical (indeed, to this day the peoples of the islands of Ireland and Britain enjoy the same gene pool), but for political reasons it was felt necessary to keep them apart by artificial categories and conventions of law, residence, property, apparel, language, and manner.

This colonial campaign of segregation began earlier than the States of Kilkenny, however. Already in 1185, Gerald of Cambrensis visited Ireland in the entourage of the English Prince John and composed an influential *History and Topography of Ireland* in which he cast the native Irish as a "wild and inhospitable people who lived like beasts"—and were, consequently, in dire need of colonial conquest. These unruly natives included, in Gerald's account, such odd folk as the bearded lady from Limerick with a mane running down her spine and the Cowman of Wicklow (both progeny of human–animal congress), not to mention the infamous King of Tirconnell who mated with a white mare and then bathed in the broth of her flesh of which he and his people partook. Gerald's portrait of the Hibernian landscape was no less flattering: "Ireland is a country of uneven surface and rather mountainous. The soil is soft and watery, and there are many woods and marshes. Even at the tops of high and steep mountains you will find pools and swamps…" This representation of the rural Irish landscape as "degenerate" and "uncultivated" was to enjoy a long lineage of portraiture evidenced in the "sublime" paintings of subsequent generations that inspired terror and awe in the public (see Edmund Burke's *Essay on the Beautiful and the Sublime*). Such portraits were contrasted with the "beautiful" urban gardens of the colonial Pale and other garrison towns (e.g., the Pleasure Grounds painted by Joseph O'Connor). The Celts could stay sublime and stay put—while the Planters moved about at leisure.

Cambrensis was, needless to say, on a mission of conquest and therefore graphically underscored Ireland's need for enlightened Anglo-Angevin rule. As Michelle Brown aptly remarks: "Gerald depicts Ireland as a source of savage bestiality, as a land filled with grotesque and uncivilized figures… That the Papal Bull eventually approving Henry II's annexation of Ireland did so on grounds of the land's alleged immorality—including bestiality—suggests that Gerald may have helped to legitimize that political enterprise and encourage public support of it."[1] It is also worth noting that the famous Land War of 1879, when the natives sought to reclaim the land, occasioned a series of portraits of the Irish Frankenstein—and other monstrous personifications—in the pages of *Punch Magazine* (see the illustrations in Perry Curtis, *Apes and Angels,* 1997).

But while Ireland was annexed by England, it was never a happy marriage. Irish literature kept appealing to idealized figures of sovereignty—from the ethereal motherland to the dream woman (*speirbhean*) or inaccessible goddess (Kathleen ni Houlihan, Dark Rosaleen, Roisin Dubh, and others)—who might one day return to restore unity to the land. And there are many instances in English literature too of the destabilizing effect that Ireland had on England, as when Shakespeare's Richard II returns from a visit there to the mainland only to find himself at a loss to know who he is *qua* sovereign: "I had forgot myself, am I not King?… Is not the King's name twenty thousand names?" (act 3, scene 2). At worst, then, the Irish were considered subversive inferiors who threatened to undo the sovereign unity of the English (and later British) Crown. At best, they were portrayed as exotic creatures capable of composing great fantasies, music, and poetry but incapable of governing themselves. Indeed one of the most impassioned celebrants of the cultural genius of the Celts, Mathew Arnold, was an equally impassioned opponent of the Home Rule for Ireland Bill of 1886.

This is all by way of saying that the equation of sovereignty-territory-nation-state in Ireland was never an easy one. In fact, even when the Irish Free State emerged after the War of Independence in the 1920s it was in the form of a partitioned state, with the Northern Six Counties remaining part of Great Britain. This led in turn to a clash of sovereignty claims by both nationalists and unionists—the former for a United Ireland, the latter for a United Kingdom. Indeed the official constitutions of both the Irish Republic and Britain claimed exclusive unitary sovereignty over the same territory of Northern Ireland. But since sovereignty is by definition "one and indivisible" and since two into one

---

1. Michelle Brown, "Shaping and Mis-shaping: Visual Impressions of Ireland in Illuminated Manuscripts," in *Éire/Land,* ed. Vera Kreilkamp (Boston: McMullen Museum of Art; Boston College, 2003), 44.

won't go, the inevitable consequence of this clash of mutually incompatible sovereignty claims was conflict and war. It was not until the Fifth Province returned in the guise of paragraph 6 of the Good Friday Agreement of 1998—declaring that the citizens of Northern Ireland could be "British or Irish or *both*"—that the fatal equation of unitary sovereignty and national territory was dissolved and transcended. Ireland and Britain thus entered a new "postnational" configuration as envisaged in (a) the British-Irish Council and European Union on the one hand, and (b) the simultaneous devolution and decentralization of power to subnational regions on the other.

2

My argument is that postnationalism involves a radical rethinking of the whole notion of sovereignty.

Territorial sovereignty cannot be exercised by two separate nation-states over the same people at the same time. And this is especially the case, as in the Irish–British conflict, where we are talking "absolutist" sovereignty and take this to mean something like "one and indivisible"—as defined by Hobbes, Bodin, and Rousseau.

The Belfast Agreement of spring 1998 means that the British and Irish nations are compelled to redefine themselves. The "hyphen" has been reinserted into their relations, epitomized in the new British-Irish Council of Isles (BIC), which had its first meeting on December 18, 1999, and whose aim, as the Agreement tells us, is "to promote the harmonious and mutually beneficial development of the totality of relationships among the peoples of the British and Irish islands." Membership of the Council is drawn from the British and Irish governments, the devolved assemblies of Scotland, Wales, Northern Ireland, the Isle of Man, and the Channel Isles. It acknowledges the fact that the citizens of both islands are inextricably intermingled thanks to centuries of internal migration, cultural mixing, and political exchange. And it purports to deal with a whole range of common interests running from the environment and transport to the knowledge economy (see in particular the meeting held in Jersey Island on June 15, 2002). Speaking at the launch of the BIC in Lancaster House in 1999, Prime Minister Tony Blair described its inaugural session as "an extraordinary and historical event that we have all the people of these islands finally coming together and saying we share certain things in common, that we can resolve our differences. The British and Irish people feel closer together now than at any time in their lifetime."[2] And the vintage Scottish political theorist Tom Nairn hailed it as "an imagined community disconcertingly different from anything in the political arsenal of the old British State."[3] The fact that the BIC was able to secure the enthusiastic support not only of both sovereign governments but also of the two leaders of the traditionally opposed republican and unionists communities of Ulster—John Hume and David Trimble—was decisive.

---

2. Quoted by Dennis Dworkin, "Intellectual Adventures in the Isles" in this volume.

3. Tom Nairn, "Farewell Britannia," *New Left Review* 7 (2001), 60; see also his *After Britain: New Labour and the Return of Scotland* (London: Granta, 2000).

The sea-change signaled by the establishment of the BIC was reflected in a radical paradigm shift in the constitutional relations between the two islands. The Irish government endorsed the removal of articles 2 and 3 from the Constitution of the Republic (a move ratified by the vast majority of the electorate), while the British government redrafted the 1922 Government of Ireland Act and held referenda to establish regional assemblies in Scotland, Wales, and Northern Ireland. The zero-sum game of mutually exclusive "national identities" seemed over at last.

The emerging postnationalist scenario permits, according to the model I sketched at the outset, that citizens of Northern Ireland profess differing degrees of allegiance to an expanding range of identifications: from regional townland, parish, or province to national constitution (British or Irish or both) and, larger still, to the transnational union of Europe. As John Hewitt prophetically wrote to his fellow Ulster poet John Montague: "I always maintained that our loyalties had an order: to Ulster, to Ireland, to the British archipelago, to Europe, and that anyone who skipped a step or missed a link falsified the total."

If, in the Irish context, the issue of unitary national sovereignty was always, as suggested above, in question—a matter of aspiration rather than acquisition, of imagination rather than possession—this was not always the case for Britain. Indeed it could be said that the British crisis of sovereignty only reached its peak in recent times. This was brought on by a variety of different factors: (1) the final fracturing of the long-enduring empire (with the Falklands, Gibraltar, and Hong Kong controversies); (2) the end of the Protestant hegemony (with the mass immigration of non-Protestants from the ex-colonies—including India, Pakistan, the Caribbean, and of course Ireland); (3) the entry of the UK, however hesitantly, into the Single European Union, which ended Britain's isolationist stance vis-à-vis its traditional "alien-nations" in Europe, namely Ireland and France; (4) the ineluctable impact of global technology, finance, and communications; (5) the devolution of power from overcentralized government in Westminster to the various regional assemblies of Edinburgh, Cardiff, and Belfast—and most probably, in due course, to different English regions also (a 1999 MORI poll, conducted by the *Economist,* showed 50 percent versus 27 percent of the English in favor of more devolved power to English regions); and finally, (6) the ultimate acknowledgment, with the mourning of Princess Diana and the election of Blair's New Labour, that Britain is now a multiethnic, multicultural, multiconfessional community that can no longer sustain the illusion of an eternally perduring sovereignty. The old Tory vision of Great Britain as a timeless Anglo-Saxon Empire presided over by indomitable "little Englanders" is well and truly spent. Influential recent publications like the Parekh Report, *The Future of Multi-Ethnic Britain* (2000), Yasmin Alibhai Brown's *Who Do We Think We Are Now? Imagining the New Britain* (2000), and Andrew Marr's *The Day Britain Died* (2000) all cogently demonstrate that new modes of postnational politics are now as ineluctable as they are desirable.

To be sure, Thatcherism represented one last desperate exercise in "denial" fantasy, finding its perfect foil in the IRA. Terrorist bombings of London and Birmingham momentarily served to rally the British people against the alien Irish in their midst: people who looked and spoke like them but were secretly dedicated to their destruction. But even the IRA at its most menacing—and however associated with similar anti-British "monsters" like Galtieri, Gadafy, and Sadam Hussein—could not save Britain from itself. Thatcher's last stand to revive one-nation Toryism was just that, a *last* stand. It could not prevent the dissolution of absolute unitary power, ultimately leading to the formation of regional parliaments in Edinburgh, Cardiff, and Belfast. (The British and Scottish Election Studies of 1997, for example, already showed that less than 4 percent of the inhabitants of Scotland considered themselves British not Scottish.) The breakup of Britain was as inevitable as it was overdue. So much so that the enormous outpouring of grief at Princess Diana's demise was mourning not just for a particular person but for an entire imperial nation.

If Ireland was present at the origin of the British *nacio,* as I suggested in my account of the Statutes of Kilkenny, then it is equally present today—in the guise of the Ulster crisis and resolution—precipitating its end. Ireland is the deconstructive seed at the heart of the British body politic. A cracked mirror reflecting Royal Britannia's primal image of its split-self. John Bull's other island sending shock waves back to the mainland. An island behind the island returning to haunt its inventor.

3

The British-Irish "Council of Isles" is now a reality. This third spoke of the 1998 Agreement's wheel—alongside the internal Northern Ireland Assembly and the North–South cross-border bodies—harbors, I suggest, particular promise. What the transnational model effectively recognizes is that citizens of Britain and Ireland are inextricably bound up with each other: mongrel islanders from east to west sharing an increasingly common civic and economic space. In addition to the obvious contemporary overlapping of our sports and popular cultures, we are becoming more mindful of how much of our respective histories is shared: from the Celtic, Viking, and Norman settlements to our more recent entry into the European community. For millennia the Irish Sea served as a waterway connecting our two islands, only rarely as a *cordon sanitaire* keeping us apart. And this is becoming true again in our own time with almost 30,000 trips being made daily across the Irish Sea, in both directions. It is not entirely surprising then that over eight million citizens of the United Kingdom today claim Irish origin, with over four million of these having an Irish parent. Indeed a recent survey shows that only 6 percent of British people consider Irish people living in Britain to be foreigners. And we don't need reminding that almost a quarter of the inhabitants of the island of Ireland claim to be at least part British. Finally, at a symbolic level, few can fail to have been moved by the recent unprecedented image of the president of the Irish Republic, Mary MacAleese, standing beside the Queen of England on the battlefield of Flanders commemorating their respective dead—Irish and British. Poppies and shamrocks are no longer considered irreconcilable symbols of identity.

In light of this reawakening to our common memories and experiences, it was not surprising to find Tony Blair receiving a standing ovation from both houses of the Parliament of the Irish Republic on November 26, 1998, in the wake of the Good Friday Agreement. Such a visitation had not occurred for over a century, and the ghost of Gladstone was not entirely absent from the proceedings. Blair acknowledged openly on this occasion that Britain was at last leaving its "post-colonial malaise" behind it and promised that a newly confident Republic and a more decentralized UK would have more common tasks in the scenario of European convergence than any other two member states. East–West reciprocity was back on track for the first time since the divisive Statutes of Kilkenny.

Although no one is shouting about it, a *practical* form of joint sovereignty has been endorsed by the Irish and British peoples. The pluralization of national identity, epitomized by the provision of the BIC, entails a radical redefinition of the hallowed notion of sovereignty. In essence, it signals the *deterritorialization* of national sovereignty—namely, the attribution of sovereignty to peoples rather than land. (A fact that finds symbolic correlation in the Agreement's extension of national "belonging" to embrace the Irish diaspora, now numbering over seventy million worldwide).

The term *sovereignty* (from the Latin *superanus*) originally referred to the supreme power of a divine ruler, before being delegated to divinely elected "representatives" in this world—kings, pontiffs, emperors, monarchs—and, finally, to the "people" in most modern states. A problem arose, however, in that many modern democracies recognize the existence of several *different* peoples within a single state. And many peoples mean many centers of sovereignty. Yet the traditional concept of sovereignty, as already noted, was always *unitary,* that is, "one and indivisible." Whence the dilemma: How divide the indivisible? This is why, today, sovereignty has become one of the most controversial concepts in political theory and international law, intimately related to issues of state government, national independence, and minority rights.

Inherited notions of absolutist sovereignty are being challenged both from within nation-states *and* by developments in international legislation. With the Hague Conferences of 1899 and 1907, followed by the Covenant of the League of Nations and the Charter of the UN, significant restrictions on the actions of nation-states were laid down. A system of international checks and balances was introduced limiting the right of sovereign states to act as they pleased in all matters. Moreover, the increasing *interdependence* of states—accompanied by a sharing of sovereignties in the interests of greater peace, social justice, economic exchange, and information technology—qualified the very principle of absolute sovereignty. "The people of the world have recognized that there can be no peace without law, and that there can be no law without some limitations on sovereignty. They have started, therefore, to pool sovereignties to the extent needed to maintain peace; and sovereignty is being increasingly exercised on behalf of the peoples of the world not only by national governments but also by organisations of the world community."[4]

---

4. "Sovereignty" in *Encyclopedia Britannica* 11, 57.

If this pertains to the "peoples of the world" generally, how much more does it pertain to the peoples of the islands of Britain and Ireland? This is why I argued in *Postnationalist Ireland* (1997) for a surpassing of the existing nation-states in the direction of both an Irish-British Council and a federal Europe of regions. The nation-state has become *both* too large *and* too small as a model of government. Too large for the growing needs of regional participatory democracy; too small for the increasing drift toward transnational exchange and power-sharing. Hence my invocation of the Nordic Council as a model for resolving our sovereignty disputes—in particular the way in which these five nation-states and three autonomous regions succeeded in sorting out territorial conflicts, declaring the Aland and Spitsbergen islands to be Europe's two first demilitarized zones. Could we not do likewise under the aegis of a new transnational British-Irish Council, declaring Northern Ireland a third demilitarized zone?

To date, such sovereignty sharing had been largely opposed by British nationalism, which went by the name of Unionism. It was, ironically, the Irish republican tradition (comprising all democratic parties in the Irish Republic as well as the SDLP and Sinn Fein in the North) that was usually labeled "nationalist," even though the most uncompromising nationalists in the vexed history of Northern Ireland have been the Unionists. It was the latter, after all, who clung to an anachronistic notion of undiluted British sovereignty, refusing any compromise with their Irish neighbors, until Tony Blair blew the whistle and moderate unionism realized the tribal march was over. The final showdown probably came when the Unionists faced off against Her Majesty's Army in Drumcree, prepared to do combat with the very Crown to which they swore unconditional loyalty. At that fateful moment it must have dawned on even the most fervid loyalist that the United Kingdom was no longer united. By contrast, John Hume's "new republicanism"—a vision of shared sovereignty between the different peoples of this island—had little difficulty with the new "postnationalist" scenario. Indeed Hume had called himself a "postnationalist" for many years without many taking heed. And, curiously, one might even argue that Michael Collins was himself something of a postnationalist when he wrote that as a "free and equal country" Ireland would be willing to "cooperate in a free association on all matters which would be naturally the common concern of two nations, living so closely together" as part of a "real league of nations of the World";[5] a sentiment echoed by Linda Colley in her Downing Street address on the status of Britishness in the wake of the Belfast Agreement, where she concluded that "these islands may actually move closer together in the next century."[6]

That the Blair government was prepared to grasp the sovereignty nettle and acknowledge the inevitable long-term dissemination of Britain, *qua* absolute centralized state, was to its credit. But it is not a decision taken in a vacuum. There were, of course, precedents for sovereignty-sharing in Britain's recent experience, including Westminster's consent to a limitation and dilution of sovereign national power in its subscription to the European Convention on Human Rights, the Single European Act, the European Com-

---

5. *Manchester Guardian*, Dec. 1921.

6. Linda Colley, "Britishness in the 21st Century," *10 Downing Street Magazine* (1999). At <http://www.number-10.gov.uk/output/page3049.asp>.

mon Defence Policy, and the European Court of Justice. If Britain had been able to pool sovereignty in these ways with the other nation-states of the EU, surely it was only logical to do so with its closest neighbor, the Irish Republic. Moreover, the EU principles of subsidiarity and local democracy, promoted in the European Charter of Self-Government, already signaled a real alternative to the clash of British–Irish nationalisms that had paralyzed Ulster for decades.

Nor should one forget that the forging of Britain into a multinational state constitution was predicated, at its best, on a *civic* rather than *ethnic* notion of citizenship. We need only recall how dramatically the borders of the British nation had shifted and altered in history (e.g., in 1536, 1707, 1800, and 1921) to envisage how they might shift and alter yet again—perhaps this time so radically as to remove *all* borders from these islands. The fact that British nationalism was often little more than English nationalism in drag does not detract from its salutary constitutional principle of civic (rather than ethnic) belonging.

The implications of the Good Friday Agreement are especially relevant here: The conflict of sovereignty claims exercised over the same territory by two independent governments—issuing in decades of violence—is now, as we have been suggesting, superseded by a postnational paradigm of intergovernmental power. The dual identities of British–Irish relations have long belied the feasibility of "unitary" forms of government and shown the necessity of separating the notion of *nation* (identity) from that of *state* (sovereignty) and even, to some extent, from that of *land* (territory). Such a separation is, I submit, a precondition for allowing the coexistence of different communities in the same society and, by extension, amplifying the models of identity to include more pluralist forms of association—a British-Irish Council, a European network of Regions, and the Irish and British diasporas. In sum, it is becoming abundantly clear that Bossuet's famous seventeenth-century definition of the nation as a perfect match of people and place—where citizens "lived and died in the land of their birth"—is no longer tenable.

The fact is there are no pristine nations around which definitive state boundaries —demarcating exclusivist sovereignty status—can be fixed. (Germany's attempts to do this from Bismarck to Hitler led to successive and disastrous wars.) The Belfast Agreement recognized the historic futility of both British and Irish constitutional claims on Northern Ireland as a natural and necessary part of their respective "national territories." Instead, the Council of Isles (BIC) promises a network of interconnecting regional assemblies guaranteeing parity of esteem for cultural and political diversity and an effective comanagement of such practical common concerns as transport, environment, social equity, and e-commerce (the main items on the agenda for the second meeting of the BIC in June 2000). We are being challenged to abandon our mutually reinforcing myths of mastery (largely British) and martyrdom (largely Irish) and to face our more mundane postimperial, postnationalist reality. Might the BIC not, as Simon Partridge suggests, even serve as an inspiration to other parts of Europe and the globe still embroiled in the devastations of ethnic nationalism?

Conclusion

What the new Agreement allows, in short, is that the irrepressible need for identity and allegiance be gradually channeled away from the fetish of the nation-state, where history has shown its tenure to be insecure and belligerent, to more appropriate levels of regional and federal expression. In the Irish–British context, this means that citizens of these islands may come to express their identity less in terms of rival sovereign nation-states and more in terms of (a) locally empowered provinces (Ulster, Scotland, Wales, North and South England, the Republic, etc.); and (b) larger international associations (the BIC, EU, World Court, etc.). The new dispensation, I repeat, fosters variable layers of compatible identification—regional, national, and transnational—allowing anyone in Northern Ireland who wishes to declare allegiance to the Ulster region, the Irish and/or British nation, the European community, and, in the widest sense, the cosmopolitan order of world citizenry.

Citizens of the British-Irish islands might, I suggest, do better to think of themselves as mobile mongrel islanders than as eternal dwellers of two pure, God-given nation-states. There is no such thing as primordial nationality. If the nation is indeed a hybrid construct, an "imagined community" as Benedict Anderson says, then it can be reimagined again in alternative versions. The task is to embrace this process of hybridization from which we derive and to which we are committed. In the face of resurgent nationalisms in these islands and elsewhere, fired by rhetorics of purity and purification, we do well to recall that we are all mongrelized, interdependent, marvelously mixed up. So doing, we might be emboldened to replace the nationalist template of homogeneous identity with a postnationalist palimpsest of multiple identities.

What is true for the Irish-British situation is equally true for sovereignty crises in other parts of the world. One thinks of Bosnia, the Basque country, Chechnya, Cyprus, and, of course, Israel and Palestine. Several thinkers have been gesturing toward a postnationalist vision of politics from Kant and Voltaire in the eighteenth century to more recent theorists like Hannah Arendt and Habermas in Germany, Derrida and Ricoeur in France, and Vattimo and Agamben in Italy.

Arendt and Habermas point in such a postnationalist direction when they call for a move beyond the equation of sovereignty and national independence toward a more cosmopolitan model of coexistence between citizens and peoples. Arendt first outlines her critique of sovereignty in an essay entitled "The Decline of the Nation-State"[7] where she argues that human rights cannot depend upon national law if these rights truly derive from the fundamental status of human beings as humans—that is, as cosmopolitan citizens bearing universal moral rights over and above those granted by the legislatures of sovereign nation-states. But her critique of nationalist sovereignty becomes even more explicit in her later book *Crises of the Republic* (HBJ, New York, 1972), where she claims that so long as "national independence and the sovereignty of the state are identified" no solution to the problem of war is conceivable and "a guaranteed peace on earth is as utopian as the squaring of the circle."[8]

---

7. In *The Origins of Totalitarianism* (San Diego: Harcour, 1948).
8. Hannah Arendt, *Crises of the Republic* (New York: HBJ, 1972), 229.

Jurgen Habermas is moving in a similar direction with his notion of a "constitutional patriotism" for the European community that would place constitutional ideals and laws above questions of ethnic allegiance or national origin. He speaks accordingly of a new cosmopolitanism based on a "postnational constellation." Noting the erosion of the territorial sovereignty of nation-states, Habermas expresses the hope that this may open up a new space for: (1) cultural hybridization, (2) transnational mobility and emigration, (3) cosmopolitan solidarity, predicated on a neorepublican balance between private and civic liberties opposed to the neoliberal disregard for social justice, and (4) constitutional patriotism on a federal European scale inspired by principles of coordinated redistribution and egalitarian universalism.[9] But Habermas is not naïve. He knows that such a postnational project has many obstacles to confront. One of the most challenging questions is, he insists, "whether the European Union can even begin to compensate for the lost competencies of the nation-state."[10] And the related question of the EU's ability to act effectively, motivating citizens toward social solidarity, will depend in turn on "whether political communities form a collective identity beyond national borders, and thus whether they can meet the legitimate conditions for a postnational democracy."[11] If these questions cannot be answered in the affirmative then no meaningful "Federal States of Europe" is possible. Or in Habermas's own words: "If Europe is to be able to act on the basis of an integrated, multilevel policy, then European citizens, who are initially characterized as such only by their common passports, will have to learn to mutually recognize one another as members of a common political existence beyond national borders."[12] This calls for a radical rethinking of both identity politics (the question of recognition and belonging) and constitutional politics (the question of rights and justice). And I fully agree with Habermas that the most promising context for such rethinking is that of a new postnational paradigm. But while I hope to have indicated certain signs of a paradigm shift in the British–Irish context, we are, I believe, still at the beginning. A postnational Europe is not a *fait accompli* but a task.

The Italian thinker Georgio Agamben seems to be pursuing a similarly postnationalist vision when he calls for a postsovereignty solution to the Israeli–Palestinian crisis. It is necessary, he says, that the nation-states find the courage to question the "trinity of state-nation-territory" and to entertain the possibility that Jerusalem become—"simultaneously and without territorial partition—the capital of two different states." This paradoxical condition of what he calls "reciprocal extra territoriality" (or aterritoriality) could, he suggests, in turn be generalized as a model of new international relations (*Means without End: Notes on Politics,* 2000). Here Agamben seems to endorse Derrida's argument in *On Cosmopolitanism and Forgiveness* (2002) that a future postnationalist configuration would be based on the model of open cities rather than sovereign bordered states. This means viewing citizens less as homogenous natives than as nomadic residents whose identity remains

---

9. Jurgen Habermas, *The Postnational Constellation* (Cambridge: Polity Press, 2001), 68f., 73–76, 103f.
10. Ibid., 90.
11. Ibid.
12. Ibid., 99.

flexible and plural. Similarly he recommends reconsidering Europe in terms of an "aterritorial or extraterritorial space in which all the residents of he European states would be in a position of exodus." The status of European would then become the "being-in-exodus of the citizen" rather than the being indigenous of the native. European space would thus mark an "irreducible difference between birth (*nascita*) and nation in which the old concept of people (which, as is well known, is always a minority) could again find a political meaning, thus decidedly opposing itself to the concept of nation (which has so far unduly usurped it)." Agamben concludes on a note of utopian urgency: "This space would coincide neither with any of the homogeneous national territories nor with their topographical sum... European cities would rediscover their ancient vocation as cities of the world by entering into a relation of reciprocal extraterritoriality." For he claims that only in a world "in which the spaces of states have been thus perforated is the political survival of humankind today thinkable."

I cite these contemporary political thinkers in conclusion to indicate that the postnationalist scenario I have been outlining above with respect to British–Irish relations is not an isolated or idiosyncratic dream but a significant part of a jigsaw that is at last taking shape. There are, to be sure, several missing pieces to fill in before the puzzle of sovereignty is solved. But each piece counts.

Intellectual Adventures in the Isles

DENNIS DWORKIN

In spring 2002, I saw an episode of the BBC soap opera *Eastenders* in which Frank Butcher—confidence man, used car salesman, and publican—made a guest appearance after a year's absence from the show. He had left Walford after his wife Peggy had discovered his affair with his long-time passion and ex-wife Pat, who was supposed to run off with him but at the last minute had a change of heart. As it happened, Frank reappears in a Spanish seaside resort, where he had faked his own death and was now operating under the name of Nigel, a lame attempt at producing an aura of English respectability. Frank's Spanish sojourn is not all that unusual for *Eastenders*. Characters are seldom allowed to break free of the claustrophobic and oppressive world of London's East End. When they do, they frequently escape to Spain for fantasy holidays that usually come back to haunt them. Here, Spain represents England's other: good weather, open space, relaxed sexuality, and casual hedonism. It is a place where working-class English people can go and momentarily forget that they are, well, working-class English people.

If *Eastenders* is granted, which I think it deserves, a key role in producing English identity, then what this says about Spain is worth noting. For though Spain is no longer portrayed as a reactionary, antidemocratic, and Catholic power as in former days, "other" it undoubtedly still is. And such comparisons do not stop at *Eastenders*. In political and economic discussions the English, and the British more generally, despite a well-deserved reputation for insularity, compare themselves to many others: Americans, the French, the Germans, the Japanese, Arabs, and South Asians. Seldom do they compare themselves to the Spanish.

Upon closer inspection, Britain and Spain have more in common than the world of *Eastenders* suggests. The Iberian Peninsula and the British Isles are both distinct geographical regions, and Britain and Spain are former imperial powers with overseas empires. They have been shaped by being part of an Atlantic world and are now being reshaped by membership in the European Union. They even both still have monarchies. Like Spain, Britain is a multinational state, which is undergoing conflict between its center and its constituent parts. Both central states have already ceded autonomy to the regions. Catalonia—with its heritage of industrial development, its pride in its cultural distinctiveness, and its achievement of regional autonomy—has much in common with the stateless nation of Scotland but also with Wales. The same can be said of the Basque country, but the political struggle within it is more analogous to that found in Northern Ireland. In short, there are good reasons why the politics of contemporary Spain is relevant to Britain. In the present context—a discussion of nationalism and postnationalism, whose point of departure is the Basque case—what is taking place in Britain (and Ireland) is conceivably relevant to Spanish (and Basque) politics as well.

My contribution concerns the transformed intellectual landscape that has placed national identity and nationalism—as well as possibly postnationalism—at the center of political and intellectual discussions in the "British" Isles. I say the "British" Isles here, rather than simply Britain, because the rethinking of the component parts of Britain—or more precisely the United Kingdom—entails just that: a reconfiguring of the relationships in the entire archipelago. Indeed, many feel that the "British Isles" is no longer a viable term, given the imperialist associations with "British." Atlantic Isles and North Atlantic Isles are among those terms that have been put forward as substitutes. I have settled on "the Isles," certainly the most general term possible and one given currency by Norman Davies in his best-selling history *The Isles* (1999). Given the historical antagonism between Britain and Ireland, and the very different intellectual cultures that they have produced, intellectual discussions across the Irish Sea have not been in abundance. They are, however, beginning to take place, and, even when they are faint it is possible to detect a theoretical space that is being carved out from contributions on both sides of the Irish/British divide. I am trying to sketch out some of the elements of what a postnationalist and contemporary intellectual history of "the Isles" looks like.

I look at this intellectual milieu in two ways. First, I discuss (what I take to be) some of the most important discursive shifts relevant to nationalism and cultural identity. Here, I am not interested in particular thinkers as much as in mapping the new terrain. Second, I analyze the thought of two of the most important thinkers on nationalism in the Isles: Tom Nairn from Scotland and Richard Kearney from Ireland. Taken together, their work not only deconstructs Britishness and the pieties espoused in the Irish–British conflict, but also is concerned, though in different ways, with a reordering of the relationships in the Isles as a whole, a reordering that involves production of a postnational space.

I

Nationalism as discourse did not figure prominently in Britain until the 1960s and 1970s. Indeed, with the exception of sporadic murmurings from the "Celtic fringe" (a name that says it all), it was not supposed to be a place where nationalism flourished. What happened? A shorthand answer is British decline. The combined effect of the loss of empire, frustrations at defining a world role, and relative—if not absolute—economic decline in an expanding globalized world have produced a sense of precariousness and insecurity, a belief in the vulnerability of the British state, and a breeding ground for challenges to received cultural identities. In a popular vein, Jeremy Paxman draws together decline, Englishness, and the end of empire in a passage from his best-selling book *The English: A Portrait of a People*. "The belief that something has rotted in England is widely held: a people cannot spend decades being told their civilization is in decline and not be affected by it… The English put their faith in institutions, and of these, the British Empire has evaporated, the Church of England has withered away and Parliament is increasingly irrelevant" (1998: 17). Not only does Paxman draw our attention to an identity crisis grounded in cultural, imperial, and political decline, but he also recognizes that discourses of decline have themselves played a constitutive role in the making of postwar English identity and implicitly the fragmentation of Britishness. This is the site on which Scottish and Welsh nationalists, black and South Asian Britons, supporters of intensified European integration, and advocates of constitutional reform have challenged the legitimacy of the British state and the very meaning of Britishness itself.

The challenge to Britishness has been articulated in multiple ways. In music, the singer Billy Bragg has expressed it in "Millennium Song":

> Take down the Union Jack, it clashes with the sunset
> And put it in the attic with the emperor's old clothes.
> Britain isn't cool you know, it's really not that great,
> It's not a proper country, it doesn't even have a patron saint,
> It's just an economic union that's past its sell-by date (Bragg 2002).

It is evident in such texts as Yasmin Alibhai-Brown's *Who Do We Think We Are Now?: Imagining the New Britain* (2000), which envisions British identity in multicultural terms, signified by the computer-generated photograph of a black Queen Elizabeth II on its cover. It is manifested in Andrew Marr's *The Day Britain Died* (2000). Marr's travels in England and Scotland reveal that Britishness meant nothing in Scotland and a mass of confusion south of the border. That Marr's book accompanied a BBC television series and that he himself would subsequently become the BBC's political editor suggest a transformation in cultural identification at the heart of the establishment.

What Marr discovered in his travels is borne out by a mid-nineties survey. Respondents throughout Britain were asked about their perception of their national identity (McCrone 2001). Of those interviewed in Scotland, more than 60 percent saw themselves as being "more Scottish than British"; in Wales about 40 percent claimed "Welshness over Britishness" (probably an underestimate given the number of people who are English or are from English backgrounds living there); and in England, about 25 percent of the respondents saw themselves as being "more English than British." The fact that almost half of those surveyed in England viewed themselves as being equally English and British, while only about a quarter of the respondents in Scotland and Wales claimed being Scottish or Welsh as being as important as being British, confirms what many commentators have suggested. In Scotland and Wales, people tend to have a fairly clear perception of the distinction. In England, the difference between Englishness and Britishness tends to blur. Indeed, in England there is a tendency to see being English and being British as the same, which, of course, from the Scottish and Welsh viewpoint is the root of the problem.

Percentage in column	Scotland	Wales	England
X not British	23	13	8
More x than British	38	29	16
Equally x and British	27	26	46
More British than x	4	10	15
British not x	4	15	9
None of these	4	7	9
Sample sizes	882	182	2,551

The idea of Britishness is traceable to the monarchy of James I, which unified the crowns of England and Scotland in 1603 and had aspirations of uniting the parliaments as well. It was clearly given a boost by the 1707 Act of Union between England and Scotland, which created Great Britain. In what by now is the standard historical account, Linda Colley's *Britons: Forging the Nation, 1707–1837* (1992), Britishness is seen as being produced by the building of a Protestant nation, notably through the more than century-long struggle with Catholic France, culminating in the Napoleonic Wars. It is also the product of a worldwide empire, where the ethnic differences between the English, the Welsh, and the Scots—sometimes even the Irish—are displaced by a common British identity, reflected, for instance, in the critical role that the old ethnic minorities played in imperial expansion. Colley's work is part of a broader movement among British historians, for whom the English can no longer be treated as if they constitute the whole of British history: They are connected to the other ethnic and national groups in the Isles. Historians such as Hugh Kearney (1989) and Norman Davies (1999) have been in the forefront of writing four-nation history and the history of the Isles.

Despite the indispensable role that a British identity played in the expansion of the centralized state and the Empire, it was always at its foundation a political identity: A Briton could likewise be a citizen of Edinburgh, a Lowlander, *and* a Scot. As its underpinnings have been eroded, challenges have proliferated to the identity that it produced. Indeed, only two groups remain in the UK that still embrace a British identity with any enthusiasm: (1) unionists in Northern Ireland whose allegiance to the Protestant tradition of William of Orange—or King Billy—is based on an image of Britishness that is unique by any definition, and (2) significant numbers of the black and Asian population living in England, that is, those who have a stake in the British political system but feel themselves to be outsiders to the dominant English culture.

Black and Asian Britons might embrace a British identity with greater ease than, say, the Welsh or the Scots, but their self-identification is by no means unproblematic. In this context, we might consider the recently published *The Future of Multi-Ethnic Britain* (Britain 2000) or the Parekh report. Commissioned by the Runnymede Trust, an independent think tank, the report was produced by a committee of twenty-three prominent academics, journalists, writers, and professionals. Its chair, Bhikhu Parekh, is a political philosopher of Indian birth who has lived in Britain for most of the last forty years and in 2000 was awarded a life peerage. New Labour publicly blessed the commission. Indeed, at its public launch, Jack Straw, the home secretary, said it was setting off with "a very strong wind. We are going to take it very seriously" (Johnston 2000).

When the Parekh report was published, "seriously" is precisely what the government ended up not taking it. For despite hundreds of pages of analysis and recommendations on numerous subjects, the media and the political right focused on the report's few pages analyzing the meaning of British identity, claiming that the report equated Britishness with racism. In fact, what the report argued was that British identity had been historically racialized and that for black and Asian Britons it was inscribed with collective memories of imperial domination. It called for widening the scope of Britishness rather than rejecting it, and it advocated, among other things, a recasting of British history so that it was germane to a multicultural society. Defending the Parekh report in the *Guardian*, Stuart Hall, a Runnymede report commissioner, wrote: "We did say that, historically, the idea of Britishness carried 'largely unspoken racial connotations'—meaning that, in common understandings, the nation is usually imagined as white... We nowhere suggested that this was destined to remain so until the end of time" (2000).

The report was denounced from several quarters. That the *Telegraph*'s home affairs editor, Phillip Johnson, should portray it as "a predictable and unjustified denunciation of race relations in Britain, underpinned by assumptions about what it meant to be British that eclipsed worthwhile recommendations" should come as no surprise (2000). Jack Straw's condemnation was another matter altogether. Acknowledging the merit of many of the Report's recommendations, Straw distanced himself from its attack on British identity. "Unlike the Runnymede Trust, I firmly believe there is a future for Britain and a future for Britishness" (Travis 2000). He went on to broaden his attack, suggesting that the report's sentiments were symptomatic of the Left's lack of patriotic feeling. "Given the tendency of some of the left to wash their hands of the whole notion of nationhood, it is perhaps not surprising that some people's perception of Englishness and Britishness became a narrow, exclusionary, conservative one. That's a view of Britishness that I don't recognize" (Travis 2000). In part, Straw's response can be seen as part of New Labour's eternal quest to produce a political line that is palatable to middle England, and at the time Straw was designated as the man for the job. However, his comments should also be seen in relationship to New Labour's fears that, having set the devolution train in motion, it might not be able to control it—neither the pulling away of the newly devolved parliaments nor the surfacing of an ethnically based and reactionary English nationalism that plays into a Tory vision of "little England." It is Straw after all who proclaimed on a Radio 4 program that the English have a "propensity for violence." He subsequently remarked: "We want to celebrate our achievements in England as well as in the United Kingdom, but in order to do that we have to have an understanding about why the English people's sense of nationalism is a somewhat distorted one from that of the Scots, Welsh and Irish" (Tran 2000). In short, Straw's attitude toward Englishness and Britishness underscores a crisis in identity that is being played out not only in the mass media and the serious press but also at Westminster itself.

No writer has done more for articulating the crisis in Britishness than the Scottish writer Tom Nairn. Arguably the most famous Scottish intellectual writing today, Nairn has since the early 1970s produced a powerful analysis of the fragmentation of the British state and the rise of ethnic nationalisms in the UK, particularly as found in Scotland, that has constituted a discursive force in that very fragmentation. The classical statement of Nairn's position is found in the path-breaking *The Break-up of Britain* (1977). It was written from within the emerging Scottish nationalist movement of the 1970s at a time when Britain was reeling from the combined effects of high inflation and unemployment, the International Monetary Fund loan, and the two miners' strikes.

For Nairn, Britain's major failing has been its inability to create a modern state—popular sovereignty, a written constitution, and the rest. Ironically, Britain had pioneered the initial stage in nation-state building in 1688 yet had never actually become a nation-state itself. It is closer in spirit to the defunct Hapsburg Empire than to a genuine modern nation such as France or the United States. In Nairn's view, while the English were slow to grasp the dilemma, the UK's peripheral nationalities understood its implications all too well. "The larger story," he writes, "is that of the fall of one of history's great states, and of the tenacious, conservative resistance of its English heartland to this fate. Within the more general process, the disruptive trends of the periphery emerge as both effect and cause: products of an incipient ship-wreck, they also function—often unwittingly—as contributors to the disaster itself, hastening a now foreseeable end" (1977: 73).

What did this mean for Scotland? For Nairn, it has many of the qualities that inspired nineteenth-century nationalist movements—a state religion, its own educational system, the collective memory of nationhood. However, while other small nations were defining themselves in opposition to the imperialist center, Scotland was flourishing within it. "It has given up statehood for a hugely profitable junior partnership in the New Rome" (1977: 129). Thus, nineteenth-century Scotland had all the trappings of cultural nationalism but none of its political aspirations. It experienced a separation between head and heart, emotional attachment to the past accompanied by political prostration. "It could only be 'sub-nationalist', in the sense of venting its national content in various crooked ways—neurotically, so to speak, rather than directly" (1977: 156).

For Nairn, then, British decline and a revived Scottish nationalist movement are part of a general historical process. Britain is the victim of precocious modernization; Scottish national aspiration, sacrificed to this unprecedented leap forward, reemerged in the late

1960s and early 1970s as civic or neonationalism, the result of "over" rather than "under" development. Under Thatcherism, Scottish national aspiration was held in check, but, following New Labour's sweeping victory and the Tories' loss of its parliamentary seats in Scotland and Wales in 1997, it found a government with a sympathetic ear. The referendums that produced a devolved Scottish parliament and a Welsh Assembly followed later the same year.

Nairn's efforts at understanding life after devolution have been collected in the essays comprising *After Britain* (2000). The book argues that, as a consequence of the devolved parliaments and the Good Friday agreement, Britain is on an inevitable course of disintegration. As in the *Break-up of Britain,* Nairn's analysis follows two tracks. On the one hand, he analyzes the politics and structure of the British state; on the other hand, he looks at the Scottish political situation. Nairn's treatment of Britain inevitably leads to an analysis of New Labour. Nairn commends Blair and company for recognizing the urgency of reform on various fronts, but he argues that the government sees these steps as concessions that bolster rather than weaken the centralized state. In the end, Nairn sees New Labour as "another long-lived 'regime' of decline-management—a generational reign, as it were, comparable to that of Mrs. Thatcher in 1979–97. Once more, 'radicalism' would boil down to staying afloat" (2000: 55).

If Nairn views New Labour as plugging the holes of a sinking ship, holes they remain. "Blairism has reformed just enough to destabilize everything, and make a reconsolidation of the once-sacred earth of British sovereignty impossible" (2000: 272). In the case of Scotland, 1997 was a historical divide: not just a vote for devolution but a reestablishment of Scottish identity, a symbolic overthrow of the union. While Nairn can imagine that such a momentous moment is capable of producing a wave of anti-English feeling, he believes that it is more likely to produce a constitutional crisis, whereby the devolved Scottish parliament confronts the limits imposed on it by the centralized state. Arguing that both nation and state in Scotland have not disappeared but "have collapsed into a miserable and parlous condition, through dependency, mediocrity, routine and habitual patience," he advocates national deconstruction over nation building" (2000: 252). This means producing a community of citizenship founded on a constitution. Such an act would be an expression of popular identity; and it would define Scotland as a European nation. Nairn sees the writing of a constitution as a challenge to the foundations of the British union.

Nairn's vision of Scottish civic nationalism is based on a view of history where constitutions, popular sovereignty, and democratic machinery are the normal course of modernity. Having concluded that Marx underestimated the potential of the nation-state, he cannot imagine any progressive development that does not entail its centrality. Taking his cue from the French and the American revolutions, Nairn equates progress with constitution making, and his long-term antagonism toward Britain derives from, among other things, his feeling that its political culture in such regard does not measure up. But a constitution does not a democracy make, even though it might be indispensable. As Francis

Mulhern rightly points out in a review of *After Britain,* the United States is "the most pure-ly civic of nations historically; its constitution is held sacred as an act of creation; democ-racy and equality are watchwords of the official culture." Yet such civic nationalist authen-ticity does not stop it from "assuming an international role without comparison in its destructive egoism" (Mulhern 2000: 65). At a time when the state itself is being under-mined by globalization, and is deemed by many as being simultaneously too large and too small, it might just turn out that a reformed UK political structure has something to rec-ommend it. Assuming that closer ties to Europe are just a matter of time, a state with multiple forms of sovereignty might find real appeal. Having missed out on the modern, perhaps Britain will find the postmodern more to its liking.

II

The political discourse of national identity and nationalism might have been a relatively recent development in Britain, but in Ireland this of course is far from the case. Indeed, the problem has been quite the reverse, as two forms of essentialized and fixed national-ist formations—Irish and British, republican and loyalist—have fought a life and death struggle, which has tended, as is clear from its latest incarnation in Northern Ireland, to overwhelm alternative forms of political definition. The Good Friday Agreement is undoubtedly a major step forward, and the IRA's hitherto largely symbolic act of putting weapons beyond use has been a major step. Certainly there is a widespread feeling that no alternative exists. Yet Northern Ireland remains dominated by two segregated and hos-tile communities. Efforts at opening up a space for cross-community relations and alter-native forms of identity have struggled to take root.

Once subscribing to Eamon de Valera's insular and protectionist vision of "a people who valued material wealth only as the basis of right living," the Republic has reinvented itself as the Celtic Tiger. A service-based economy that has thrown itself open to the EU and the globalized economy, it has established itself as the software, computer, and net-work center of Europe. It is the fastest-growing economy in the EU, if not the Western World, although the cost of throwing itself open to the multinationals has been growing income disparities. Northern Ireland, by contrast, is mired in a postindustrial malaise, intensified by civil war. It has suffered from a shrinking manufacturing sector, the high-est unemployment in the UK, and an intensified dependency on public-sector employment. Still, like the Republic, the North is increasingly enmeshed in the world economy and dependent on outside investment. According to Peter Shirlow, the middle classes in the North and South increasingly possess transnational identities "in which relationships with London, Brussels, Washington and Tokyo predominate over a previously strong associ-ation with their respective parts of Ireland" (1997: 105). For Neville Douglas, the North can no longer be adequately described in purely binary terms. He views it as "a society in transition," which has seen a "decline in the blind acceptance of derogatory stereotypes" and where identity "evokes answers of greater diversity, complexity and subtle caveats" (1997: 168).

A writer who brilliantly evokes the intractable nature of the Northern Irish conflict as well as the opening up of new identity spaces is Robert McLiam Wilson, whose 1996 novel *Eureka Street* (1999) actually lives up to the subtitle of its American edition: *A Novel of Ireland Like No Other.* Wilson's representation of Belfast evokes the traumatic and numbing effects of the Northern Irish troubles as well as the efforts of a handful of individuals to rise above them. He achieves this largely by creating characters who refuse to succumb to the fixed political, religious, and cultural positions that have been assigned to them. They produce contradictory, multiple, and transnational identities that continually resist being dwarfed by the violence and sectarian madness surrounding them. Consider, for example, Chuckie Lurgen, an illegitimate and unemployed, thirty-year-old, working-class Protestant whose friends are exclusively Catholic and whose most treasured possession is a photograph that was taken of him and the Pope (along with throngs of other people). "Sure the guy was a Tag, a Fenian, the logical extension of all that was Catholic in the world. But no one could deny that he was famous" (1999: 29). On the one hand, Chuckie resists Protestant stereotypes. A committed hedonist, he wants wealth and fame, but without embracing the self-sacrifice, discipline, and frugality that is associated with the Protestant ethos. Yet it turns out that Chuckie's greatest talent is a Catholic-associated gift of the gab that takes him from unemployment checks and bus riding to government boards, global capitalist ventures, a beautiful American wife, and a Mercedes that he has not the faintest notion of how to drive. In what amounts to a subversion of the rags-to-riches story, Chuckie cannot help but make money. He comes to embody what can happen in Northern Ireland when the old rules are thrown out the window.

In Irish intellectual circles, the deconstruction of stereotypes is traceable to the *Irish Historical Studies* project of the 1930s. It began as a modest effort at producing a history of Ireland based on the expansion and critical reading of sources. It developed the broader aims (brought about in part by the return of the Troubles) of deconstructing nationalist pieties of English tyranny and Irish victimhood: those interpretations of Irish history that P. S. O'Hegarty once called "the story of a people coming out of captivity." By no means an iconoclast, F. S. Lyon in his 1972 Oxford Ford lecture, *Culture and Anarchy in Ireland* (1979), characterized Ireland's history as a clash of civilizations—English, Gaelic, Anglo-Irish, and Scottish-Presbyterian—thus giving a powerful rebuttal to the idea that Ireland's history could be read along unitary lines. Arguably Roy Foster, the first historian of Ireland to hold a chair at Oxford—the Carrell Professor of Irish history—has emerged as the leading revisionist historian today. In "The Varieties of Irishness" (a revisiting of Lyon's lectures) he argues that Lyon's account gives too much weight to inevitable conflict. And he suggests that alternative readings of the history justify the "hope that the discovery of an outward-looking and inclusive cultural nationalism, not predicated upon political and religious differences, will be the salient business of young and not so young intellectuals and educators at this current crisis in both Irish states" (Foster 1993: 38). In his 1994 inaugural address at Oxford, Foster deconstructs the historical process that produced "the story of Ireland," recapturing in the process uncertainties and contingencies while recovering the voices of historical actors.

If the achievement of revisionist historiography is indisputable, it has been subject to trenchant criticisms. In deconstructing nationalist mythology, revisionists have at times skirted dangerously close to letting England off the hook, a charge that is bolstered by the fact that they have spent a disproportionate amount of their time dismembering the republican and nationalist, rather than the loyalist and unionist, ideologies. A complementary but contrasting development that has likewise played a significant role in problematizing Irish identity is the Field Day project. Originally founded in Derry in the early 1980s as a theater company, it has subsequently published pamphlets and books and produced an ambitious three-volume revision of the Irish canon, *The Field Day Anthology of Irish Writing* (Deane, Carpenter, and Williams 1991). In the preface to its first pamphlets, published in book form as *Ireland's Field Day,* the directors see Field Day as contributing "to the solution of the present crisis by producing analyses of the established opinions, myths and stereotypes which had become both a symptom and a cause of the current situation" (Deane 1985: vii). Where historical revisionists tend to view the Anglo–Irish conflict as being historically contingent, writers associated with Field Day are more likely to view it as a colonial relationship whereby Irish nationalism is overdetermined by its British other. The idea of Ireland, Declan Kiberd suggests, is "largely a fiction created by the rulers of England in response to specific needs at a precise moment in British history." The Irish notion of England, on the other hand, is "a fiction created and inhabited by the Irish for their own pragmatic purposes" (Deane 1985: 83). Field Day's original inspiration was a united Ireland, but it does not stand for a monolithic nationalism. "Our desire," as Seamus Deane states it, "would be to create through Field Day, and through certain kinds of writing and theatre, a vision of…the cultural, social, political unification that is possible in Ireland between all the different groupings and sects" (Regan 1992: 26). Critical to the Field Day project is the contention that Ireland's crisis is bound up with language and discourse, and critics such as Kiberd have openly espoused ideas derived from postcolonial theory. Field Day writers have engaged in a deconstruction of the dominant discourses. Like the revisionists, they regard the mystique of Irishness as an impediment to realizing a pluralist and united island.

Among those associated with the Field Day project, Richard Kearney has emerged as perhaps its most imaginative thinker. A philosopher by training, Kearney has for nearly two decades sought to deconstruct the language of the Anglo–Irish conflict while at the same time imagining how it might be alternatively construed. His most ambitious attempt in this vein is found in his *Postnationalist Ireland: Politics, Culture, Philosophy* (Kearney 1997). Kearney's analysis, like others connected to Field Day, is founded on the belief that Irish and British nationalism are "Siamese twins" and thus must be deconstructed together, a position that is plausible now that Britishness is in crisis. "Far too often," Kearney writes, "the sins of nationalism have been laid exclusively on the Irish side, with the result that Britain's implication in the nationalist quarrel is conveniently occluded. This, I would argue, has been one of the most ingenious ploys of British (or more particularly English) nationalism: to pretend that it *doesn't exist,* that the irrational and unreasonable claimants to sovereignty, territory, power and nationhood are always *others...*" (1997: 9). Here, Kearney occupies a theoretical space that is akin to that filled by the Scottish journalist Neal Ascherson, but more importantly he relies on Tom Nairn's historical analysis of the British state and the current crisis of Britishness. Kearney regards the "spectre of Irish nationalism" as "Britain's return of the repressed," which "compels it to look in the mirror and see its own cracked image" (1997: 11). From this point of view, the survival of British nationalism beyond the peace process in Ulster is an open question.

For Kearney, an essential component of unraveling the binary opposition of Britishness and Irishness is to grapple with what makes the opposition lethal in the first place. This involves looking anew at the concept of sovereignty. Kearney argues that at the heart of the Northern Irish conflict is an untenable notion of absolute sovereignty—a unity, of people, nation, and territory—that by definition sees the province as being part of either the UK or the Republic, the property of either British or Irish nationalism; and thus it assumes that either London or Dublin is best placed to represent the community of Ulster as a whole. Such a nation is incompatible with the pluralist nature of Ulster, and it inevitably reproduces opposition. Alternatively, Kearney advocates separating the notion of the nation from the notion of the state in order to think about sovereignty in a pluralist way. He believes that such thinking points beyond traditional nationalism, toward a postnationalism that preserves what is valuable in cultural memories of nationality while superseding them.

Kearney's vision of postnationalism involves establishing forms of state that make possible the free expression of multiple forms of identity. His ultimate goal is to supplant the nation-states of Europe with a European union of regions that would allow people to "be Irish and British in (Ulster), Spanish and British (in Gibraltar), Spanish and Catalan (in Catalonia), Basque and French (in *Le Pays Basque*), Arab and French (in Marseilles), Flemish and Belgian (in Northern Belgium), Swiss and Italian (in Tyrol)—while being *European* in all" (1997: 59–60). In the case of the British–Irish conflict, Kearney advocates a joint sovereignty solution in Northern Ireland. In the end, he advocates a complete political reordering of the Isles: "a Council of the Islands of Britain and Ireland, eventually evolving towards a federal British-Irish archipelago in the larger context of a Europe of regions" (1997: 11). Kearney draws his image of the Council of the Islands from the Nordic Council. Founded in 1952, comprising five nations and three autonomous regions, it is a parliamentary and ministerial body that has successfully resolved territorial disputes on the Scandinavian peninsula, transforming it into a "highly successive network of transnational communities" (1997: 92).

III

Published a year before the Good Friday Agreement, *Postnationalist Ireland* has something of a prophetic air, especially in connection to the Agreement's third strand, the proposal for a British-Irish Council of Isles whose aim is "to produce the harmonious and mutually beneficial development of the totality of relationships among the peoples of the British and Irish islands." The British-Irish Council—otherwise known as the Council of the Isles–was established as a consultative body whose members include the British and the Irish governments; the devolved parliaments of Northern Ireland, Scotland, and Wales; and the governments of the Isle of Man and the Channel Islands. That the birth of the Council began as a concession to the Unionists for accepting the cross-border North-South Ministerial Council should not serve to minimize the accomplishment. David Trimble is often credited with the idea, although the *Irish Times* suggested that it came from the Progressive Unionists. In fact, the idea has a complex intellectual history. Yet it is certainly shares the spirit of Kearney's proposal in *Postnationalist Ireland.* Writing in the *Irish Times,* after the proposal for a council became part of the peace talks, Kearney and Simon Partridge portray it as a means of "finding an imaginative and structured institutional form of expressing the reality that the peoples of these islands are—through internal migration and cultural borrowing—'intermingled'" (1998). By "the peoples," they mean the old ethnicities of the Isles, together with black and Asian Britons, the growing Chinese community in Northern Ireland, and emigrants to a "more self-confident" Republic. In response to James Anderson's and Douglas Hamilton's contention that the existing British–Irish interparliamentary body provided the East–West link desired by Unionists and that the analogy of the Nordic Council was both inappropriate and a distraction, Kearney and Partridge give a twofold response (Anderson 1998). First, they argue that the Nordic Council model was never to be taken literally: Since it had been rooted in older civil institutions "we drew parallels between this association and the extraordinary density of civic links between these islands." Second, they point out that the existing East–West link, the British–Irish interparliamentary body, was hated by the Unionists because of its association with the 1985 Anglo-Irish Agreement (Kearney 1998).

Of the various commentators on the Council of the Isles, the Scottish nationalist Tom Nairn is undoubtedly among the most important. At first, he endorsed the idea, seeing it as "an imagined community disconcertingly different from anything in the political arsenal of the old British State" (2001: 60). He admits that the Council's aspiration to develop the totality of relationships in the Isles can mean "everything or nothing," but he argues that a multiplicity of vested interests are likely to keep it afloat, including the Channel Islands, the New Labour government, the two devolved parliaments, and the Irish Republic. More recently, in *Pariah: Misfortunes of the British Kingdom* (2002), Nairn has had a change of heart, revealing a raging cynicism regarding anything touched by New Labour, and states that he has lost all hope in the Council's potential. "The 'British-Irish Council,'" he has written, "was in truth the Un-British-and-Irish Council of the Isles, intended to foster an aureole of hope and credulous aspiration among those taking it seriously. It was another part of the Redemption variety show—an audience-befuddler, prompting reveries of life after Unionism. But the point of the dream was to keep Unionism alive, not to transcend it" (Nairn 2002: 112). Nairn further argues that since England and the English regions have no representation, except via Westminster, and that since the devolved governments simultaneously represent themselves and are represented by Westminster, contradictions are bound to arise. He concludes that "on any politically important matter, the British-Irish Council would therefore have amounted to a classical form of idiocy: Ukania communing with Herself, via the assorted parts of Herself, occasionally punctuated by bits of negotiation with Dublin (which could quite well have been carried out anywhere else)" (Nairn 2002: 112–13). If Nairn points to genuine challenges that the Council of the Isles faces, he appears to object to New Labour's last-ditch Unionism rather than the principle on which the Council is founded. Given that he waited thirty years for the reality of the devolved parliaments, Nairn should know that unforeseen political contingencies could just as easily produce a more viable Council of the Isles as a neutered one.

The Council of the Isles received its launch in London in December 1999 following the establishment of the devolved Northern Irish assembly. Tony Blair described its inaugural session "as an extraordinary and historical event that we have all the people of these islands finally coming together and saying we share certain things in common, we can resolve our differences. The British and the Irish people feel closer together now than at any time in their lifetime" (Tran 1999). Writing in the *Guardian*, Michael White wrote that the Council would probably not "matter a stuff," but likewise conceded that taken as a whole New Labour's efforts at constitutional reform were "taking us into deep, uncharted waters" (1999). Its first meeting was greatly delayed as a result of the various snags over IRA disarmament, and it was only held in November 2001 following one of many breakthroughs regarding that issue. It is expected that the Council will be concerned with several issues: the environment, tourism, transport, organized crime, and e-commerce. Although Northern Ireland has returned to direct rule, the Council of the Isles still functions.

It is unclear what role the British-Irish Council will have in the governance of the archipelago, whether, for instance, it will implement policy or whether it will function as a coordinating body between different participants. In addition, the Good Friday Agreement leaves open the possibility of members of the group reaching agreements among themselves without approval by the entire Council. Yet several constituencies appear to have a stake in keeping the Council of the Isles alive. For the New Labour government, the Council is one more plank in its federalist strategy of a revived Britain, and it foresees the Council providing a regional Isles voice with regard to the EU. For the devolved Scottish Parliament, the Council of the Isles provides another venue for expression of its autonomous identity, as well as strengthening ties with the Republic of Ireland. Northern Irish Unionists regard the Council as providing a counterbalance to the North-South Ministerial Council and bringing the Republic of Ireland into a more intimate relationship to the Union. As Graham Walker argues (Walker 2001), these interests appear to be nationalist rather than postnationalist in inspiration. But it should be recalled that nationalism and postnationalism are not necessarily incompatible. Rather, postnationalism extends nationalisms (as national identities) into regional and transnational arenas, transforming them in the process.

However it is finally judged, the symbolic importance of the Council of the Isles is undeniable. It accords a new legitimacy to both the Scottish Parliament and the Welsh Assembly, and it puts another nail in the coffin of English dominance masked as British nationalism, although the fact that the English are the only group in the Council not to have representation reminds us of that legacy. Linda Colley observed in a speech on Britishness, given at Downing Street in December 1999, that the resolution of the Irish crisis could well mean that "these islands may actually move closer together in the next century" (1999). Perhaps when we look back a century from now we will see this moment as the beginning of postnationalism in the Isles.

If we do, I suspect that we will see Nairn and Kearney, as well as others that I have discussed, as having contributed to shifting the political discourse. At the very least, they have played a role in problematizing the imagined communities of Britishness and Irishness and have thought in terms of alternatives and potentialities. To my mind, this recalls *Eureka Street*, where a shadowy male figure in the dead of night covers the walls of Belfast with the letters "OTG." At first it is almost indistinguishable from the city's overabundance of graffiti—UVF, IRA, UFF, and the like. But as the novel progress, OTG comes to represent some indefinable space that is beginning to take hold but cannot be defined. As Chuckie's best friend Jake concludes: "You know what OTG means? Almost everything. That was the point. All the other letters written on our walls were dark minority stuff. The world's grand, lazy majority will never be arsed writing anything anywhere and, anyway, they wouldn't know what to write…. That's why OTG was written for them" (Wilson 1999). At least one reading of OTG is that it represents the imaginative space beyond the sectarianism of the Troubles: the identity possibilities that have been continually suppressed but are crying out to find out expression, however amorphous. At a theoretical level, the writers whom I have discussed have attempted to produce this same open-ended space in the Isles as a whole.

Works Cited

Alibhai-Brown, Yasmin. 2000. *Imagining the New Britain*. London: Allen Lane: Penguin Press.

Anderson, James, and Douglas Hamilton. 1998. "Council of the Isles," *Irish Times*, Feb. 13.

Bragg, Billy. 2002. *Take Down the Union Jack*. Beverly Hills, Calif.: Electra Entertainment Group.

Britain, Commission on the Future of Multi-Ethnic. 2000. *The Future of Multi-ethnic Britain: The Parekh Report*. London: Profile Books.

Colley, Linda. 1992. *Britons: Forging the Nation, 1707–1837*. New Haven: Yale University Press.

———. *Britishness in the 21st Century*. 10 Downing Street Magazine 1999 [cited Feb. 24, 2002].

Davies, Norman. 1999. *The Isles: A History*. Oxford: Oxford University Press.

Deane, Seamus, ed. 1985. *Ireland's Field Day*. London: Hutchinson.

Deane, Seamus, Andrew Carpenter, and Jonathan Williams, eds. 1991. *The Field Day Anthology of Irish writing*. 3 vols. Derry, Northern Ireland: Field Day Publications.

Douglas, Neville. 1997. "Political Structures, Social Interaction and Identity Change in Northern Ireland," in *In Search of Ireland: A Cultural Geography*, ed. B. Graham. London: Routledge.

Foster, R. F. 1993. *Paddy and Mr. Punch: Connections in Irish and English History*. 1st ed. London and New York: A. Lane, Penguin Press.

Hall, Stuart. 2000. "Comment: A Question of Identity (II)," *Guardian*, Oct. 15.

Johnston, Philip. 2000. "Piece of Political History Catches Up with Straw," *Telegraph*, Dec. 12.

Kearney, Hugh F. 1989. *The British Isles: A History of Four Nations*. Cambridge: Cambridge University Press.

Kearney, Richard. 1997. *Postnationalist Ireland: Politics, Culture, Philosophy*. London: Routledge.

Kearney, Richard, and Simon Partridge. 1998. "Council of the Isles," *Irish Times*, March 2.

———. 1998. "How the Nordic Countries Resolved Conflict," *Irish Times*, Jan. 15.

Lyons, F. S. L. 1979. *Culture and Anarchy in Ireland, 1890–1939*, Ford Lectures, 1978. Oxford: Clarendon Press.

Marr, Andrew. 2000. *The Day Britain Died*. London: Profile Books.

McCrone, David. 2001. "Scotland and the Union: Changing Identities in the British State" in *British Cultural Studies*, ed. D. Morley and K. Robins. Oxford: Oxford University Press.

Mulhern, Francis. 2000. "Britain after Nairn," *New Left Review* (5):53–66.

Nairn, Tom. 1977. *The Break-Up of Britain*. London: NLB.

———. 2000. *After Britain: New Labour and the Return of Scotland*. London: Granta.

———. 2001. "Farwell Britannia: Break-Up or New Union?" *New Left Review* (7):55–74.

———. 2002. *Pariah: Misfortunes of the British Kingdom*. London: Verso.

Paxman, Jeremy. 1998. *The English: A Portrait of a People*. London: M. Joseph.

Regan, Stephen. 1992. "Ireland's Field Day," *History Workshop Journal* (33):25–37.

Shirlow, Peter. 1997. "Class, Materialism and the Fracturing of Traditional Alignments" in *In search of Ireland: A Cultural Geography*, ed. B. Graham. London: Routledge.

Tran, Mark. 1999. "Blair Hails Historic Step for Northern Ireland Peace as British-Irish Council Meets," *Guardian* Dec. 17.

———. 2000. "Straw Calls for 'Rounded' Sense of Englishness," *Guardian,* Jan. 11.

Travis, Alan. 2000. "Be Proud to Be British, Straw Tells Left," *Guardian,* Oct. 12.

Walker, Graham. 2001. "The British-Irish Council" in *Aspects of the Belfast Agreement,* ed. R. Wilford. Oxford: Oxford University Press.

White, Michael. 1999. "Rebranding the Kingdom," *Guardian,* Dec. 17.

Wilson, Robert McLiam. 1999. *Eureka Street: A Novel of Ireland Like No Other.* New York: Ballantine Books.

The Persistence of the Palestinian Question[*]

JOSEPH MASSAD

Predictions that the Palestinian Question would be resolved have foundered in the last one hundred years. Some, like Theodor Herzl, thought that the Palestinians would welcome the civilizing efforts of colonizing Jews and thus the Palestinians would not even become a Question.[1] Others later thought that had the Palestinians accepted the Zionist colonial conquest of much of their country, legitimated by the 1947 UN Partition Plan, and set up a small state on the remaining land, their Question would have been resolved. Still later, others thought that had the Arab states absorbed the Palestinian refugee population after 1948, the Question would have surely been resolved then. An impatient and exasperated world breathed a sigh of relief when Yasir Arafat and the Israeli government signed the Oslo agreement in 1993 that transformed Arafat from a Nelson Mandela into a Mangosuthu Gatsha Buthelezi, but the Question was still not resolved. Finally, some thought that if the Arab states would only accept Israel's right to be a Jewish state, that is, a state that has the right to discriminate racially and religiously against its non-Jewish citizens by law and practice (which they did at their Beirut Summit in March 2002), the Palestinian Question would have been resolved. But the Palestinian Question persisted and still persists. A decade after Oslo, it is as intransigent as it was in 1917 when the Balfour Declaration was issued. What, then, makes the Palestinian Question persist in the face of so many expectations and desires that it be resolved?

Anti-Semitism

In the last century and a half, many have tried to explain the persistence of the Jewish question, which had always been entangled with the persistence of anti-Jewish sentiment

---

[*] This article was published in *Cultural Critique,* no. 59 (Winter 2005).

1. This view is elucidated by Herzl in his futurist novel *Altneuland* whose Palestinian character Rechid Bey welcomes Jewish colonization. See Theodor Herzl, *Old New Land,* trans. Lotta Levensohn (Princeton: Markus Wiener Publishers, 1997), 122–23.

across Western history.[2] This sentiment, whether based on religious, social, ethnic (geographic and linguistic origins), or racial grounds, clustered together in the nineteenth century in a full-fledged othering ideological edifice that came to be known as anti-Semitism. In the nineteenth century, Karl Marx postulated that the Jewish Question would be resolved alongside human emancipation, which required the ending of the division between humans as "egotistical" beings inhabiting civil society and humans as "abstract" citizens in the realm of the state.[3] As such emancipation failed to materialize, twentieth-century authors, with as widely differing views as Sigmund Freud, Hannah Arendt, Theodor Adorno, Max Horkheimer, Isaac Deutscher, Abram Leon, and Jean Paul Sartre, attempted to analyze the basis of this anti-Jewish sentiment across the ages, with most concentrating on the new ideology of anti-Semitism that emerged within the belly of Romantic modernity. Their answers ranged from psychosexual explanations to socioeconomic ones. Adorno and Horkheimer argued in the *Dialectic of Enlightenment* that Enlightenment had done away with the dialectic and posited itself as the end of history and then sought to control everything totalistically. In so doing, Jews were posited and projected by anti-Semites as a "negative principle." Thus Enlightenment transformed itself into the nightmare of Nazism and a mediocritizing capitalism.[4] Abram Leon turned to Marxian economics and posited historical Jews as a people-class made necessary by Christian European economics.[5] Sigmund Freud, among other things, identified the horror felt by Christian boys when they hear of the circumcision of Jewish boys, which they interpret as castration, as one of the reasons for the contempt they feel for Jewish men.[6] Others saw the very basis of gentile identity as necessitating the hatred of the Jew, wherein, Jean Paul Sartre's thesis that "if the Jew did not exist the anti-Semite would invent him"[7] tops the list. Notwithstanding Sartre's reduction of the Jew to an object of gentile hatred lacking agency, his important thesis linked the persistence of the Jewish question to the persistence of anti-Semitism.

The European renaissance had been predicated on a hatred of the recent European barbarism, which motivated Enlightenment thinkers to attempt to invent a heroic glorious past by appropriating Greek civilization and incorporating it into the recently invented Europe—a process that was parallel to Protestantism's appropriation of the Hebrew bible in ways that the Catholic Church had previously shunned. European colonialism, having learned the lessons of the Enlightenment, was going to impart to all the colonized a sim-

---

2. See, for example, Maxime Rodinson's collected essays in his *Cult, Ghetto and State: The Persistence of the Jewish Question* (London: Al Saqi Books, 1983).

3. Karl Marx, "On the Jewish Question" (1843) in Robert Tucker, *The Marx–Engels Reader* (New York: Norton, 1978), 26–52.

4. See Max Horkheimer and Theodor Adorno, *Dialectic of Enlightenment* (New York: Continuum, 1972), especially their section "Elements of Anti-Semitism, the Limits of Enlightenment," 168–208.

5. Abram Leon, *The Jewish Question: A Marxist Interpretation* (New York: Pathfinder Press, 1970).

6. Sigmund Freud, "Analysis of a Phobia in a Five-Year-Old Boy," in *The Standard Edition of the Complete Psychological Works of Sigmund Freud* (London: Hogarth Press, 1953–1974), v 10:36f.

7. Jean-Paul Sartre, *Anti-Semite and Jew* (New York: Schocken, 1965), 13. See also Hannah Arendt's intelligent and provocative analysis of the historiography of anti-Semitism and Jew-hatred in her introductory remarks in "Preface to Part One: Antisemitism," in her classic *The Origins of Totalitarianism* (New York: Harcourt Brace Jovanovich, 1973), xi–xiii. The book was first published in 1951.

ilar cultural self-hatred, calling for the adoption of enlightened European Christian culture as model. While colonialism began to rule over peoples and cultures it had othered a priori, Jews living in Europe had experienced this othering for a much longer time, albeit intermittently. The Jewish *Haskala* emerged within this European history of self-rejection as an assimilationist project seeking to transform Jewish culture from something identified by post-Enlightened Europe as non-European, if not un-European, into something more in line with the newly invented image of Europe and its enlightenment. The rejection of things Jewish in favor of things European defined much of the *Haskala* project, which saw in assimilation the final integration of an othered Jewry into the new European self.[8] While the project seemed successful in a number of ways, especially in Germany and France and less so in "un-enlightened" Eastern Europe, it ultimately led to official Christianization through formal conversions. Indeed, Theodor Herzl himself, a mere three years before launching the Zionist project, which was to serve as a mild corrective to the *Haskala,* had proposed the mass baptism of European Jews to Catholicism in a now famous proposal to the Pope.[9]

Zionism, like the *Haskala,* adopted European, especially German, Enlightenment thought as its evaluative mode of assessing Jewishness and Judaism and sought their transformation into European enlightenment. It was not that the anti-Semites were wrong that Jews had "bold, misshapen noses; furtive and cunning eyes" as Theodor Herzl described French Jews for example,[10] or that they spoke a debased German that was nothing less than "the stealthy tongues of prisoners" as Herzl described in *Der Judenstaat,*[11] but rather that the anti-Semites did not offer a solution to this despicable Jewish condition. Zionism, which espoused these views of Jews while conscious of their anti-Semitic pedigree, simply wanted to rid Jews of such traits and teach them how to be Europeans. While Zionism espoused the goals of the *maskilim* and other Jewish assimilationists in its understanding that the mark of Jewish otherness had to be removed, it differed from both in affirming that the attempt by Jews to prove that they could become Europeans inside Europe would not be allowed by European Christians. The solution seemed self-evident: Zionism, in Herzl's words, would set up a state for the Jews that would constitute "the portion of the rampart of Europe against Asia, an outpost of civilization as opposed to barbarism."[12] This state, as Herzl's novel *Altneuland* uncovered, would outdo the Europeans at their own game of civilization. The settler colony was going to be the space of Jewish transformation. To become European, Jews must exit Europe. They could return

---

8. On the *Haskala*'s relationship to Jewish culture, see Michael Selzer's *The Wineskin and the Wizard* (New York: Macmillan, 1970) and his *The Aryanization of the Jewish State* (New York: Blackstar, 1967), 9–50.

9. On Herzl's letter, see Walter Laqueur, *A History of Zionism* (New York: Holt, Rinehart and Winston, 1972), 88–89.

10. Theodor Herzl, *The Complete Diaries of Theodor Herzl,* ed. Raphael Patai, trans. Harry Zohn (New York: Herzl Press and Thomas Yoseloff, 1960), 2:11.

11. Theodor Herzl, *The Jewish State* (New York: Dover Publications, 1988), 146.

12. Theodor Herzl, *The Jewish State: An Attempt at a Modern Solution to the Jewish Question* (London: H. Porders, 1972), 30.

to it and become part of it by emulating its culture at a geographical remove. If Jews were Asians in Europe, in Asia, they will become Europeans.[13] Herzl affirms that it is not a question of taking Jews away "from civilized regions into the desert," but rather that the transformation "will be carried out in the midst of civilization. We shall not revert to a lower stage, we shall rise to a higher one."[14] In the new settler colony, Jews would no longer be "dirty," "cunning," "parasitical," "lazy," "superstitious," "weak," "effeminate," as anti-Semitism and Zionism posited them, but would become hardworking, scientifically minded, strong, rational, clean, and civilized—in short, European.[15]

Upon encountering the Palestinian Arabs, Zionism's transformative project expanded. While it sought to metamorphose Jews into Europeans, it set in motion a historical process by which it was to metamorphose Palestinian Arabs into Jews in a displaced geography of anti-Semitism. We will see how the persistence of this anti-Semitic impulse in European Christian thought in the nineteenth century, transmitted to and internalized by Jewish Zionism, will organize much of Zionism's cultural outlook and the political projects attendant to it in the next century.[16] The ultimate project of cultural transformation that Zionism embarked upon, then, was the metamorphosis of the Jew into the anti-Semite, which Zionism understood correctly to be the ultimate proof of its Europeanness. The Jewish holocaust only served to strengthen this belief by Zionism, which insisted that only those Jews who answered its transformative call in its settler colony escaped the fate that befell Jews who insisted on their diasporic/Jewish condition. Herein lies Zionism's contempt for the diaspora and holocaust victims.[17] But Zionism's project proved to be two-fold: In transforming the Jew into the anti-Semite, it became necessary to transform the Palestinian Arab into the disappearing European Jew.

Settler Colonialism

In order to transform Jews into Europeans in Asia, Zionism sought to make available to them a battery of professions denied them intermittently during their residence in Europe, namely in the fields of agriculture and soldiery, thus making them productive laborers and manly conquering sabras in one sweep. What would afford them these opportunities was an Asiatic land "reclaimed" by Zionism as the inheritance of modern Jews from what it posited as their "Hebrew forefathers." Excavating the Hebrew past in order to serve as the basis for the Jews' future would become a central task of the Zionist project.[18]

---

13. See Herzl, *Old New Land*.

14. Ibid., 82.

15. On the transformation of Jews into tough masculine men, see Paul Breines, *Tough Jews: Political Fantasies and the Moral Dilemma of American Jewry* (New York: Basic Books, 1991).

16. On the gentile history of Zionism, see Regina Sharif, *Non-Jewish Zionism: Its Roots in Western History* (London: Zed Press, 1983).

17. On Zionism and Israel's relationship to the Jewish holocaust, see Tom Segev, *The Seventh Million: The Israelis and the Holocaust,* trans. Haim Watzman (New York: Hill and Wang, 1993); Hannah Torok-Yablonka, "The Recruitment of Holocaust Survivors During the War of Independence," *Studies in Zionism* 13, no. 1 (1992), 43-56; Peter Novick, *The Holocaust in American Life* (New York: Houghton Mifflin, 1999); Lenni Brenner, *Zionism in the Age of the Dictators: A Reappraisal* (Westport, Conn.: Lawrence Hill and Co., 1983); and Norman Finkelstein, *The Holocaust Industry* (New York: Verso, 2000).

18. On the ideological basis and the actual practice of Israeli archaeology, see Nadia Abu El-Haj, *Facts on the Ground: Archaeological Practice and Territorial Self-fashioning in Israeli Society* (Chicago: University of Chicago Press, 2001).

Zionism understood well that for Jews to become European, they could not remain identified in tribal or religious terms, but rather in terms of nationhood. It is in this context that the religious origins of Judaism are transformed into national origins and ancient Hebrew kings become the progenitors of modern Jews. The European nationalist principles of *blut und boden* would guide Zionism's invention of Jews as a nation with its own land. To bring this about, the first item on their agenda was to colonize and settle such land. This "nahalat avot," or the land of the forefathers, the Jewish settlers were going to transform from a "desolate" and "neglected" Asiatic desert into a blooming, green European terrain full of forests and trees—a persistent point of pride for Israeli Jews. Not only did Theodor Herzl's futurist novel *Altneuland* serve as a fantastical blueprint for this effort, but also the very image of the Jew as carrier of European gentile civilization to a barbaric geography was definitional of Zionist political argumentation. Thus in 1930, Chaim Weizmann articulated the project thus: "[w]e wish to spare the Arabs as much as we can of the sufferings which every backward race has gone through on the coming of another, more advanced nation."[19] As the Palestinians decided to resist this *mission civilisatrice*, Weizmann, who was to become Israel's first president, characterized the tasks before Zionism in quashing such resistance as follows: "On one side, the forces of destruction, the forces of the desert, have arisen, and on the other side stand firm the forces of civilization and building. It is the old war of the desert against civilization, but we will not be stopped."[20] Indeed they were not. They went on to destroy much of Palestinian society and expel the majority of its population. Much anxiety, however, remained constitutive of Zionism regarding the remaining signifying traces of the Palestinians and the purported traces of the Hebrews that Zionism insisted could be excavated. Thus Moshe Dayan's now famous words about what befell Palestinian towns tell us not only about the destruction of the non-Jewish past of Palestine, but also about the production of a Jewish past that Zionism collapsed into Hebrewness:

> Jewish villages were built in the place of Arab villages. You don't even know the names of these Arab villages, and I don't blame you, because these geography books no longer exist. Not only do the books not exist, the Arab villages are not there either. Nahalal arose in the place of Mahlul, Gvat in the place of Jibta, Sarid in the place of Haneifa, and Kfar-Yehoshua in the place of Tel-Shaman. There is not one single place built in this country that did not have a former Arab population.[21]

This palimpsestic operation was not at all arbitrary, but rather was well-planned, from the beginning of colonization with the establishment of the Jewish National Fund's

---

19. Quoted in Simha Flapan, *Zionism and the Palestinians* (London: Croomhelm, 1979), 71.

20. Colonial Office [CO] 733/297/75156/II/Appendix A, extract from Weizmann's speech, April 23, 1936, Great Britain, Peel Commission Report, pp. 96–97, cited in Philip Mattar, *The Mufti of Jerusalem: Al-Hajj Amin-al-Husayni and the Palestinian National Movement* (New York: Columbia University Press, 1988), 73.

21. *Ha'Aretz* (April 4, 1969), cited in David Hirst, *The Gun and the Olive Branch: The Roots of Violence in the Middle East* (London: Faber and Faber, 1984), 221.

"Place-Names Committee,"[22] which was itself renamed, after 1948, the "Israel Place-Names Committee." Zionist renaming continued unabated upon Israel's occupation of the West Bank and the Gaza Strip.[23] The new names persisted after the Oslo agreement. Thus, the West Bank still carries its excavated Zionist names, Judea and Samaria, names that are used in government and journalistic parlance, by Likud and by Labor leaders and followers alike.

Not only have the new excavated names persisted, but also the very colonial project that was the originary driving force of Zionism has not abated either. Since 1948, Zionist colonial settlement transformed Palestine's terrain by erecting new towns and cities on the ruins and traces of Palestinian lives. European Jewish colonists inhabited those Palestinian spaces that they did not destroy by converting them into European Jewish locales. In his discussion of the early colonization efforts of holocaust survivors upon arriving in Palestine, the Israeli historian Tom Segev had the following to say:

> [T]he War of Independence broke out, and tens of thousands of homes were suddenly available... Hundreds of thousands of Arabs fled, and were expelled from their homes. Entire cities and hundreds of villages left empty were repopulated in a short order with new immigrants. In April 1949, they numbered 100,000, most of them Holocaust survivors. The moment was a dramatic one in the war for Israel, and a frightfully banal one, too, focused as it was on the struggle over houses and furniture. Free people—Arabs—had gone into exile and become destitute refugees; destitute refugees—Jews—took the exiles' places as a first step in their new lives as free people. One group lost all they had, while the other found everything they needed—tables, chairs, closets, pots, pans, plates, sometimes clothes, family albums, books, radios, and pets. Most of the immigrants broke into the abandoned Arab houses without direction, without order, without permission. For a few months the country was caught up in a frenzy of take-what-you-can, first-come, first-served. Afterwards the authorities tried to halt the looting and take control of the allocation of houses, but in general they came too late. Immigrants also took possession of Arab stores and workshops, and some Arab neighborhoods soon looked like Jewish towns in pre-war Europe, with tailors, shoemakers, dry-goods merchants—all the traditional Jewish occupations.[24]

Zionism would transform these towns further into purely European locales with a Hebrew flavor, which it conflated with the new Jewish identity. Not only did Zionism reappropriate the secular and religious history of the Hebrews from a European Protestantism intent on appropriating the Hebrews' religious philosophy, it also adopted lock, stock, and barrel Europe's suspect Greek heritage as its own as well, on account of its European civilizational commitments. It is in this spirit that the schismatic divide between

---

22. See Saul Cohen and Nurit Kliot's "Israel's Place-Names as Reflection of Continuity and Change in Nation Building," *Names: Journal of the American Name Society* 29 (Sept. 1981), 3. The Jewish National Fund was and is the Zionist organization that owns all Jewish-"acquired" lands in Palestine.

23. See Saul Cohen and Nurit Kliot's "Place-Names in Israel's Ideological Struggle over the Administered Territories," *Annals of the Association of American Geographers* 82 (1992), 4.

24. Tom Segev, *The Seventh Million: The Israelis and the Holocaust,* trans. Haim Watzman (New York: Hill and Wang, 1993), 161–62.

Jewish and Christian ethics was unified after World War II as the so-called Judeo-Christian ethical legacy common to all the civilized.[25]

The Palestinian Question persisted throughout Zionism's pre-State history as the national question, as well as the land question. Israel's establishment in 1948 set in motion an uninterrupted process of colonization, with its 1967 conquest of the West Bank and the Gaza Strip marking an intensified effort that was given an even stronger push since the Oslo agreement was signed, as the number of Jewish colonial settlers in the still-occupied territories have doubled since 1993. Since September 11, whatever limitations the United States had placed on Israeli violence against the Palestinians and confiscation of their lands were simply removed. Indeed, Israeli leaders drew immediate parallels between the new US war on terrorism and their war against the Palestinians. If September 11th marks a new era for the rest of the world, for the Palestinians it marks no breaks at all. For Israel, September 11 and the subsequent US invasion of Iraq simply mark another opportunity to legitimate its continued colonization of Palestinian lands, its construction of colonial settlements, and its murder of the Palestinian people, none of which has abated after September 11th any more than it did before that date. But as Zionism's colonization continues, so does Palestinian resistance. The Palestinian Question, therefore, persists as long as Zionism's colonial venture persists.

Racism

As Zionism was metamorphosing Palestine into the land of the ancient Hebrews, which would then be repackaged as the land of modern and future Jews, Zionism also set its cultural production in motion. Zionism's objective was to ensure Israel's Europeanness and its non-Asianness, or, in Zionist parlance, its non-"levantineness." The possible levantinization of Zionism's new Asian-turned-European geography was blamed not solely on the persistence of Palestinian traces and bodies within the newly declared Euro-Jewish space, but more terrifyingly on Zionism's abduction of Arab Jews into the heart of its project. The anxiety that the Arab Jews caused was as great as that caused by the Palestinians, added to which were the "hordes" of Arabs surrounding this new oasis of European culture—what Israeli Jews call today their "tough neighborhood."[26] This, however, never stopped Zionism from appropriating the fruit of the land that Palestine's peasants produced. It is in this vein that Zionism appropriated Palestinian and pan-Syrian food like hummus, falafil, tabbulah, maftul (increasingly known in the United States and Europe as "Israeli couscous"), and finely diced Palestinian rural salad (now known in New York delis as "Israeli salad") as its own national dishes.

---

25. On the origins of the neologism "Judeo-Christian tradition," see Novick, *The Holocaust*, 28.

26. The "tough neighborhood" description is a favorite of Israeli former (and possible future) Prime Minister Benjamin Netanyahu. See for example his discussion with US Secretary of State Madeleine Albright on November 14, 1997, in London where he told her that "we live in a tough neighborhood." The transcript of the meeting is available at the website of the US embassy in Israel at www.usembassy-israel.org.il/publish/peace/archives/1997/me1114b.html viewed on Nov. 20, 2002.

Palestinians have figured in different, albeit related, ways to the chain of Zionist ideologues from Herzl to Menachem Begin and Ariel Sharon. While Herzl saw them as a "dirty" people who looked like "brigands,"[27] Menachem Begin was to see them as "two-legged beasts."[28] Note the complete congruence between anti-Semitic adjectives used against Jews and their adoption by Zionism to describe the Palestinians. While Herzl sought to "transfer the penniless population" to the surrounding countries, Ben Gurion and the Zionist leadership carried out that task successfully in 1948 when they expelled the majority of the Palestinian population, and less successfully in 1967 when they expelled only a few hundred thousands. The tolerance of Israeli Jews of "dirty foreigners" among them has its limits. According to recent Israeli polls, 46 percent of Israeli Jews believe that all remaining Palestinians inside Israel and the Occupied Territories should be expelled.[29] This is a key practice in Zionism's program of transforming the Palestinian into the Jew. Through the mechanism of expulsion, the land-based Palestinian is metamorphosed overnight into the landless wandering diaspora Jew for whom Zionism has only contempt. While the adoption of anti-Semitic epistemology in viewing the Palestinians organized Zionism's overall encounter with this mostly peasant population, physical expulsion became the principal instrument at the disposal of Zionism and Israel to effect this metamorphosis.

But despite Zionism's valiant efforts, it was unable to expel all Palestinians. It transformed those who remained inside Israel into foreigners in their own land and subjected them to a military, racialist system of rule from 1948 until 1966 that was reminiscent of the life of German Jews under the worst period of the Nuremberg laws from 1937 to the start of World War II[30]—here the 1956 massacre of Kafr Qasim, in which forty-seven Palestinian Israeli citizens (all of them unarmed civilians) were gunned down by Israeli soldiers[31] is analogous to, although not symmetrical with, Kristallnacht. Since 1966 to the present, this population has lived under a civilian, racialist system of rule reminiscent of the less extreme experiences of German Jews in the earlier period of the Nuremberg laws (from 1934 to 1937).[32] As for the Palestinian population of the West Bank and Gaza whom Israel captured in 1967, it transformed their lands and homes into the besieged Warsaw Ghetto. If anti-Semitic Jews could make the Palestinian "desert" bloom, evidence of Palestinian agriculture had to be erased. It is in this vein that Jewish Israel has undertaken the desertification of Palestinian Lands. Israeli military and Jewish settlers' uprooting of hundreds of thousands of Palestinian olive trees in the West Bank and Gaza Strip as well as the Israeli military's razing of four million square meters of cultivated land are

---

27. Herzl, *Old New Land,* 42.

28. Menachem Begin, speech to the Knesset, quoted in Amnon Kapeliouk, "Begin and the 'Beasts,'" *New Statesman,* June 25, 1982.

29. This poll was taken on March 22, 2002, by the Israeli Jaffee Center for Strategic Studies.

30. See Sabri Jiryis, *The Arabs in Israel* (New York: Monthly Review Press, 1976).

31. See Hirst, *The Gun and the Olive Branch.*

32. See Uri Davis, *Israel: An Apartheid State* (London: Zed Press, 1987).

engineered, among other things, to prove that Palestinians would only be allowed to live in a desert.[33] Only anti-Semitic Jews can live in a European simulacrum of green hills and meadows. The Judaized Palestinian shall live in the desert, if allowed to live at all.

Israel was able to replicate the different conditions under which European Jews suffered under extreme anti-Semitic conditions by imposing those same conditions on the different sectors of the Palestinian people, with one important twist. It is now Jews who are the anti-Semitic enforcers of oppression against a recently Judaized population. Indeed, the expelled Palestinians have experienced life in ways that are uncanny in their similarity to the situation of European Jews in the Europe of the nineteenth and part of the twentieth century. In those countries where Palestinians are granted equal legal rights, as in Jordan, they face unofficial discrimination at every level of government with political campaigns by extremists calling for their expulsion or "repatriation"—a term not lost on those who know the history of anti-Semitic campaigns to expel Jews from Europe.[34] In those countries that refused to grant them equal rights, such as Lebanon, they have been languishing in refugee camps for fifty-four years with no rights and constant police harassment and militarized campaigns to massacre them and "repatriate" them.[35] Even those diaspora Palestinians seeking assimilation in their new homes are prevented from doing so on a regular basis in much of the diaspora. The transformation of Palestinians into Jews is located precisely in these parallels. The fact that the anti-Semitic epithet "dirty Jew" has metamorphosed into the favorite Jewish insult against Palestinians, namely "dirty Arabs" or "Aravim milukhlakhim," encapsulates this process perfectly.

But turning Palestinians into Jews does not mean that they can have access to their own Palestinian Hebrew ancestors. On the contrary, it is precisely through Zionism's appropriation of the history of the Palestinian Hebrews as the ancestors of the European-Jews-turned-anti-Semites that the Palestinian Arabs lose any connection to their Hebrew ancestry. While neighboring Egyptians, Jordanians, Lebanese, and Iraqis can narrate a national history that extends to the Pharaohs, the Nabateans, the Phoenicians, and the Babylonians, Palestinians cannot lay any national claims to Palestine's past. As recent converts to landless Jewishness, they cannot access the past of a land colonized by anti-Semitic Hebraic Jews, nor can they claim ancestors uncovered by Zionists to be their own exclusive progenitors. This is not so unlike the process through which the Hebrew prophets were abducted from the Jewish tradition into Chritianity.

These constants of Zionist thought persist uninterrupted, from Herzl's *Der Judenstaat* to a living and prospering *Medinat Yisrael* that hopes to become once and for all *Palästi-*

---

33. The Palestinian Ministry of Agriculture cited the number of 374,000 uprooted trees in the first eight months of the intifada that broke out in September 2000. Other sources like the Palestinian Initiative for the Promotion of Global Dialogue and Democracy put the number at 227,995 trees, posted on website at www.miftah.org/report.cfm.

34. On Palestinians in Jordan, see Chapter 5 of my *Colonial Effects: The Making of National Identity in Jordan* (New York: Columbia University Press, 2001).

35. On Palestinian refugees in Lebanon, see Wadie Said, "The Obligation of Host Countries to Refugees under International Law: The Case of Lebanon," in *Palestinian Refugees: The Right of Return*, ed. Naseer Aruri (London: Pluto Press, 2001).

nenser-rein. Evidently, this Zionist desire for national, racial, and religious purity uncontaminated by an other hardly deviates from European anti-Semitic nationalist precedents.

The Europeanness of the state was a clear goal at the outset. Herzl saw the state as adopting German for its language, as well as for the name of its cities. In his novel, he proposed "Neudorf" as one such city name. He rejected Yiddish as the language of the settler colony owing to its being a "ghetto" language and a "miserable stunted jargon."[36] The East European Zionist Hebraists showed a better understanding of Europeanness than the West European Herzl, who sought blind emulation, for they insisted on an ancient language in an ancient land, echoing the European nationalist principles of *Blut und Boden*. While the Hebraists insisted that a new secular Hebrew could better serve as the language of the new redeemed Jews, thus further conflating the ancient Hebrews with modern Jews, they worried about Hebrew's pronunciation. In this vein, Vladimir Jabotinsky, the founder of revisionist Zionism, insisted in his 1930 essay "The Hebrew Accent" that "there are experts who think that we ought to bring our accent closer to the Arabic accent. But this is a mistake. Although Hebrew and Arabic are Semitic languages, it does not mean that our Fathers spoke in [an] 'Arabic accent'… We are European and our musical taste is European, the taste of Rubinstein, Mendelssohn, and Bizet."[37] He had already affirmed in 1926 that "Jews, thank God, have nothing in common with the East. We must put an end to any trace of the Oriental spirit in the [native] Jews of Palestine."[38]

Expressing his anxiety about Moroccan Jews' weakening the cultural metamorphosis of Ashkenazi Jews into Europeans, David Ben Gurion stated that: "We do not want Israelis to become Arabs. We are in duty bound to fight against the spirit of the Levant, which corrupts individuals and societies, and preserve the authentic Jewish values as they crystallized in the [European] Diaspora."[39] The newspaper *Ha'Aretz* worried in 1949 that some of the Arab Jews were "at an even lower level than what we knew with regard to the former Arabs of Eretz Yisrael."[40] A whole cultural operation of civilizing non-European Jews was devised, however unsuccessfully, to "develop" them.[41]

As Michael Selzer has shown in his classic book, *The Aryanization of the Jewish State*, German anti-Semitism started a domino effect that began in Germany and ended in Palestine. If German anti-Semitism saw German Jews as dirty and cunning, medieval, and effeminate, German Jews would project such images on the Ostjuden—East European Jews—in much of their descriptions. Now it was the turn of the Ostjuden to use such adjectives in describing Arab Jews.[42] While Selzer did not carry his argument fur-

---

36. Herzl, *Jewish State*, 146.

37. Vladimir Jabotinsky, *The Hebrew Accent* (Tel Aviv: HaSefer, 1930), 4–9, cited by Ella Shohat, *Israeli Cinema: East/West and the Politics of Representation* (Austin: University of Texas Press, 1989), 55.

38. Vladimir (Ze'ev) Jabotinsky, "Jews of the East" (1919), quoted in *Ha'Aretz*, July 22, 1983.

39. Sammy Smooha, *Israel: Pluralism and Conflict* (Berkeley: University of California Press, 1978), 86–88.

40. Aryeh Gelblum, *Ha'Aretz*, April 22, 1949.

41. See Ella Shohat, "Sephardim in Israel: Zionism from the Standpoint of Its Jewish Victims," *Social Text* 19/20 (fall 1988), 1–35, and my "Zionism's Internal Others: Israel and the Oriental Jews," *Journal of Palestine Studies* 100 (summer 1996), 53–68.

42. Selzer, *Aryanization*. 86.

ther to include the Palestinians, they were to become the ultimate object of such displacement. In a short time following their absorption in the settler colony, the Jewish population, regardless of ethnic origins, would internalize this anti-Semitic epistemology in describing the Palestinians.

This is not simply a superstructural neurosis that has afflicted Zionism; it is rather the epistemological foundation on which it rests. If Zionism proceeded from a rejection of all things Jewish in favor of European culture, then its pedagogical mission was to transform all Jews into that model. To justify its colonization efforts of Palestine to a gentile European world, Zionism would present Jews as carriers of European civilization to a land burdened by a barbaric, parasitical population who neglected it and transformed it into a desert. Much of what anti-Semitism projected onto European Jews would now be displaced onto Palestinian Arabs, who were seen to embody the attributes that both Zionism and anti-Semitism insisted had been previously embodied by diaspora Jewry.

Even when the parallels between anti-Semitic and Zionist practices would correspond fully to each other, Zionism and Israel showed, and still show, no embarrassment. If anything, as the following will demonstrate, Israeli Jewish soldiers today are willing disciples of all anti-Semites, including the Nazis. This is not a new development, but harks back to the primal scene of Jewish Zionism's marriage to anti-Semitism.

Theodor Herzl, who later went to foster alliances with the anti-Semites of his day, wrote in his diaries in 1895 that anti-Semitism was "more than understandable," and that it was "salutary" and "useful to the Jewish character." He went further to explain that anti-Semitism constituted an "education of a group by the masses." He would predict that with "hard knocks," "a Darwinian mimicry will set in."[43] His rationale would persist to the present. Israeli soldiers, engaged in putting down the second Palestinian uprising against Israeli military occupation, found pedagogical inspiration in an anti-Semitic precedent, namely the Nazi assault on the Warsaw Ghetto during World War II. According to the Israeli newspaper *Ha'Aretz*:

> In order to prepare properly for the next campaign, one of the Israeli officers in the territories said not long ago, "it's justified and in fact essential to learn from every possible source. If the mission will be to seize a densely populated refugee camp, or take over the casbah in Nablus, and if the commander's obligation is to try to execute the mission without casualties on either side, then he must first analyze and internalize the lessons of earlier battles—even, however shocking it may sound, even how the German army fought in the Warsaw ghetto." The officer indeed succeeded in shocking others, not least because he is not alone in taking this approach. Many of his comrades agree that in order to save Israelis now, it is right to make use of knowledge that originated in that terrible war, whose victims were their kin.[44]

---

43. Herzl, *Complete Diaries*, 1:10.
44. Amir Oren, "At the Gates of Yassergrad," *Ha'Aretz*, Jan. 25, 2002.

The more recent practice of writing numbers on the arms of thousands of Palestinians that have been crammed in Israeli detention camps since February 2002 to the present further demonstrates the Nazi system as a pedagogical model for the Israeli army.[45]

The racism of Zionism clearly derives from a prior anti-Semitism whose object has simply been exchanged. The persistence of the Palestinian Question therefore is organically linked to the persistence of the Jewish Question, whose Zionist resolution was accomplished through displacement. Zionism was not entirely convinced that its colonial settler project would be sufficient to transform Jews into Europeans. Its higher objective was that Jews would be normalized only when they have become European anti-Semites, when they began to view diaspora Jewishness through the eyes of anti-Semitism. Examples of this abound. In line with Zionism's contempt for the Jewish diaspora, as well as for Jewish victims of the holocaust as passive weaklings, is the popular modern Hebrew term for "sissy": the word "sabon" or soap. The term appeared in the wake of World War II when stories circulated about Jews being turned into soap by the Nazis.[46] Even holocaust survivors were seen through the spectacles of anti-Semitism. Ben Gurion himself saw survivors as a "people who would not have survived if they had not been what they were—hard, evil, and selfish people, and what they underwent there served to destroy what good qualities they had left."[47] In this context, Zionism's achievement was precisely this metamorphosis of the Jew into the anti-Semite. The persistence of anti-Semitism within Zionism as a guiding epistemology accounts, then, for much of the persistence of the Palestinian Question.

Nationalism

Zionism is first and foremost a nationalist ideology in the European Romantic tradition, albeit a late comer to that tradition. The influence of German romanticism, the German youth movement, as well as fin-de-siècle evolutionist thought and theories of race and degeneration inform much of its ideological makeup. Indeed, Max Nordau, the theorist of degeneration par excellence, was one of Zionism's philosophical fathers, calling for the regeneration of the degenerated Jews.[48] Nordau was careful to emphasize that "We shall not become Asians there [in Palestine], as far as anthropological and cultural inferiority are concerned, any more than the Anglo-Saxons became Indians in North America, Hottentots in South Africa, or members of the Papua tribes in Australia."[49]

---

45. Gideon Alon and Ori Nir, "Mofaz: IDF Will Stop Writing Numbers on Prisoners' Arms," *Ha'Aretz*, March 13, 2002.

46. See Beit-Hallahmi, *Original Sins: Reflections of the History of Zionism and Israel* (London: Pluto Press, 1992), 128–29.

47. Quoted in Peter Novick, *The Holocaust in American Life* (Boston: Houghton Mifflin, 1999), 69.

48. In this regard, see his important essay "Jewry of Muscle," a translation of "Muskeljudentum," *Juedische Turnzeitung* (June 1903), in *The Jew in the Modern World: A Documentary History,* eds. Paul Mendes-Flohr and Jehuda Reinharz (Oxford: Oxford University Press, 1980), 434–35.

49. Yosef Gorny, *The Arab Question and the Jewish Problem* (Tel Aviv: Am Oved, 1985), 39.

Like all nationalisms, Zionism is founded on a binary of self and other for its identitarian project. What is noteworthy in this regard is how it is the anti-Semite, not the Jews, who constitutes the self for Zionism, with the Jew being the other against whom the new self must be based. In internalizing anti-Semitic subjectivity, Zionism adopts its epistemology lock, stock, and barrel, thus seeing the Jew as everything the new Zionist identity is not. In Zionist lingo, this is translated into a forsaking of the diaspora Jew for the benefit of the new land-based Israeli Jew who is modeled after the anti-Semite in opposing the very existence of the diaspora Jew. If the anti-Semite seeks the physical expulsion and annihilation of the diaspora Jew, the Israeli Jew is committed to a similar project. The "assistance" rendered by Zionism to anti-Jewish regimes in expelling their Jews to Israel is now the stuff of history, but equally important is Zionism's commitment to the annhilation of the diaspora Jew ontologically, if not physically. The new Zionist Jew is then ontologically constituted in opposition to all things diasporically Jewish (and that was for the most part much of Jewish existence when Zionism emerged) which are viewed through the spectacles of anti-Semitism. By attempting to repress the diaspora Jew within its new subjectivity, Zionism is always ill at ease and fears the return of the repressed. By externalizing its anxiety onto the Palestinians as the new diaspora Jews, it ensures the continued stability of its new subjectivity by repressing them. Thus, the persistence of Zionism's oppression of the Palestinians is necessary for Zionism's ability to maintain the ontological structure of its new identity, without which, it fears, the diaspora Jew within might return to haunt it.

Zionism is also a colonial movement made possible by a European colonizing world that it hoped it could both assist and extend. The end of formal colonialism, which culminated in the liberation of Algeria in 1962 and the independence of Portugal's African colonies (including Angola and Mozambique in 1975), left Israel battling alongside Rhodesia and South Africa as the only remaining settler colonies in Asia and Africa. Being the last settler-colony since 1994 has not been a reassuring status for Israel. The jingoistic nationalism of Israeli society, its high militarization, and its racially supremacist ideology mask an increasing anxiety about its place in the world. Zionism's transformation of the Jew into the European anti-Semite, however, is the reassuring element in its persistent strategy of garnering continued support.

Israel's packaging itself as an extension of Europe is what accounts for much of the support the settler-colony has received from Europe and America over the last century. Herzl understood this only too well when he predicted that the anti-Semites would be Zionism's best supporters: "[T]he Governments of all countries scourged by Anti-Semitism will be keenly interested in assisting us to obtain [the] sovereignty we want."[50] Indeed, "[n]ot only poor Jews" would contribute to an immigration fund for European Jews, "but also Christians who wanted to get rid of them."[51] Furthermore, "honest Anti-Semites…will combine with our officials in controlling the transfer of our estates."[52]

---

50. Herzl, *Jewish State,* 93.

51. Ibid., 122.

52. Ibid., 112.

The persistence of anti-Semitism in Euro-American thought today, together with its continued hatred of the figure of the Jew, is precisely what informs European and American support for the anti-Semitic Jews inhabiting Israel. It is hardly a coincidence in this regard that anti-Semitic Christian fundamentalists are Israel's strongest supporters in the United States. Zionism understands this all too well, as it had based its entire project on this correct assumption and expectation.

Palestinian resistance and demands for the end of Israeli racism and colonialism, and for the transformation of Israel into a nonracialist binational state, are registered by Zionism as "anti-Semitic." The irony of an anti-Semitic Zionism depicting the Palestinians as the real anti-Semites is not a simple rhetorical move, but instead is crucial to Zionism's fashioning of Jewish public opinion, both in Israel and on a global scale. If European anti-Semitism, and Zionism with it, targeted the Asiatic Jew of Europe, then Palestinian resistance, dubbed "anti-Semitism," is similarly targeting the Europeanized Jew in Asia. What Palestinian resistance demands is the de-Europeanization of the Jew; it calls for Zionism's abandonment of European anti-Semitism as its inspirational source. What the Palestinians are calling for is the Asianization of Israel's European Jews, with the result that they come to view themselves as not only *in* the Middle East but *of* it. In doing so, Palestinians are striking at the very heart of the Zionist project, namely the Europeanization of the Jew in an Asian milieu. The insistence of Zionist ideologues on their project is governed by their rejection of the return of the Asiatic in the Jew, which they know would result in loss of European and American support.

Zionism did not struggle for a hundred years to transform the Jew into the anti-Semite and thus become part of Europe, only to be defeated by the "new Jews." Its persistence in oppressing the Palestinians is precisely its persistence in suppressing the Jew within. American and European anti-Semitic commitments to support de-Judaized Jews in Israel lies at the heart of the Palestinian Question. *The persistence of the Palestinian Question, therefore, is the persistence of the Jewish Question.* Both questions can only be resolved by the negation of anti-Semitism, which still plagues much of Europe and America and which mobilizes Zionism's own hatred of Jewish Jews *and* of the Palestinians.

The Art of Forgetting

Xavier Rubert de Ventós

There exists a sense of identity or belonging, be it individual or collective, that is as basic as the impulse to eat or procreate. It is a self-awareness that springs to consciousness when it runs into resistance, or flies in the face of those "others" whose recognition it demands. Those others, in turn, respond as the water does to Narcissus in Wilde's fable: "If I recognize you, Narcissus, and find you pleasing, it is because in your eyes I see reflected the ripples of my waters." This play of crisscrossed narcissisms corresponds to the benign, assertive, and not imposing form of nationalism. This nationalism defends its own identity but does not pretend to convert or enlighten others with the universal principles that it incarnates, be it revealed Truth or enlightened Reason, and that those others should recognize in order to know themselves.

But how is that the ideology of the nineteenth and twentieth centuries should accept strong, expansionist nationalism and reject its weak, merely assertive, version? Convinced, at first, that soon we were going to move "from the governing of people to the administration of things," then determined to culminate history by means of free market economic planning and bureaucratic centralization, those defensive nationalisms seemed like atavistic reflexes or residual lumps soon to be dissolved. The truth, however, is that those nationalisms have proven to be as weak as…a bull. It was these weak nationalisms that inspired the revolutions of the twentieth century that offered the only resistance to the dominant empires (Algeria, Vietnam, Cuba).

How, then, do we dare to dismiss such nationalisms, saying that "they have not managed to offer any solution to the problems of the 20th century," and to suggest that they are merely "visceral responses, immature and unreliable…that channel certain aspirations of the uneducated and conceal realities that are more hazy than they might appear"? In less than one week we could read (in the *New York Times*) that it was an issue of "ambitious minorities" who for "selfish reasons"…and out of "personal interest" invent "artificial claims"…meant to agitate "xenophobic minorities"…that only aspire to "Balkanize Europe"…by means of a "fundamentalist regionalism" based on "the myth of race of bloodlines"…and "other *entropic factors (sic).*" Along the same lines, any phenomenon that might contribute to the secession or dissolution of a state—of any state, whether in Tibet or Sri Lanka—was automatically described by the newspapers in terms that tilt between hostility and condescension.

It has been said that "at the heart of nationalism understood as a 'daily plebiscite' is the *will* of men and not *natural events.*" Certainly, and this is by no means the only way in which a liberal can understand nationalism. But it just so happens that this *will* is also an event—and a stubborn one—that can no more be erased by decree than the waves of the sea can be swept with a broom. *E pur si muove.* Few things are perhaps as universal as this particularistic credo that, as M. Walzer says, "seems to have nothing going for it but its own popularity." No matter how it is defined—"collective selfishness," "mass paranoiac individualism," "malignant fantasy"—the fact is that a consciousness or perception of self as pertaining to a more or less diffuse group exists. A group that in minimalistic terms can be defined, along the lines of Durkheim or Parson, as "a communications community" (K. Deutsch) or an "existence integrated in a message system" (D. Wolton, J. A. Bastinter). This consciousness, on the other hand, can take the most diverse shapes: from the "tranquil confidence in the regular, harmonious, and simultaneous activity of people whom we do not know, but who speak like we do and who read the same newspapers more or less at the same time" (B. Anderson), to the ineffable nostalgia of the immigrant, or to the tense and xenophobic vindication of self-government by virtue of which, as Isaiah Berlin says, "men prefer to be ruled, even roughly, by members of their own nation or class than to be under the tutelage, even benevolent, of masters from another country, another class, or another medium." Be that as it may, the fact is that a community of origin, shared beliefs, and adhesion to determined goals generate a sentiment of diffuse solidarity that requires the recognition (if not the submission) of others. And that community will also need to renounce its original narcissism in order to form part of an open and cosmopolitan society in which, as Max Weber proclaims, *die Staadluft macht frei*—city air makes you free.

Still and all, a truly open and democratic society doesn't limit itself to breaking the community's bonds and conventions; rather, it recovers and uses them on its own level. Don't we always say that political democracy needs a "democratic culture" at its base: a series of tacit conventions on which to be founded?[1] Well, then, this "democratic culture" is nothing more than the reconstruction on a "political" scale of the traditional or metropolitan cohesion on which the freedom of the smallest or most homogeneous communities is founded. And such a "democratic culture" must be used by the state to compensate

---

1. This is precisely one of the elements that J. Rawls has had to add to his "Theory of Justice" in *Political Liberalism* (New York: Columbia University Press, 1993): that apolitical conception of justice is expressed in terms of certain fundamental ideas seen as implicit in the public political culture of a democratic society—what we may call its "background culture" (14).

and fill out—not to replace—that cohesion until it makes a continent of democratic liberty out of those islets of autonomy of identity.

The first denial of identity, which anthropologists associate with the very origin of civilization, is the incest taboo: the prohibition on coupling within the clan or tribe. The exchange of women—they add—favors the exchange of goods, and thus that of information in general. "The universality of commerce," wrote Weber, "thus predates that of thought which, not by chance, developed in such an intensely mercantile area as the Mediterranean." The generalization of exchange breaks the endogamy of the group by creating open societies whose identity is no longer solely defined by their membership in the clan and the religion of their ancestors.

We know how the Greeks symbolized this passage through the myth of the displacement of the *chthonic* or terrestrial gods who oversaw the cult of the ancestor (Zeus Sarapis, Aphrodite Ephesia, the Erinyes, and so on) by the new *Olympian* gods of the air, who now incarnate universal archetypes unbound by clan or ancestry. In *The Oresteiad* we witness this transmutation of tribal fidelity into poetical "nomos": the clash and consequent pact between these two principles. This pact was initiated politically by the reform of Cleisthenes in Greece and Marcus Tullius in Rome, who define the individual not by blood or origin but rather by the neighborhood (demos) or city in which he lives, and was defended by Aristotle as a *methodos* toward political democracy, "whereby one who desires to found the city must take care that the people forget their previous bonds."

This is the universalistic imperative of forgetting and *political* uprooting, to which will soon be added the *religious* uprooting predicated by Christianity (and with which the former will maintain a competitive and conflictive relationship). Like Aristotle, Saint Paul will not want any longer the existence of either Jew or Gentile. Like Clysthenes or Marcus Tullius, Luke and Matthew are also apostles of oblivion: "I have come to separate man from father and woman from mother…and he who does not reject his father, his mother, his wife, children, and brothers cannot be my disciple." Now, both the Classical and the Christian tradition try to negotiate this oblivion by presenting it as *another form* of remembrance: as a new way of belonging as the persistence of the old identity lingers in a new medium, like a pact, in fact, with the old particularist gods—with the Erinyes in the *Oresteiad*, with Yahweh in the New Testament, with the eponymous gods in the *démos*, with the archons in the Council of the Five Hundred.

This second part is precisely what has been forgotten by the tradition that (starting out from that exogamy and finding its inspiration in this Classical and Christian tradition) came up with the formulation of the *Social Contract*. This is a contract according to which the individual must be extirpated from his community of origin in order to be integrated into a new society of laws.[2] "Se me olvidó que te olvidé/yo que de nada me olvido," says the Colombian song: "I forgot that I forgot you/I who never forgets a thing."

---

2. In contrast to the Rousseauian *Contrat*, Suárez's *Pactum* did not eliminate the rights that anteceded the pact, and it authorized its retraction in the name of a "natural liberty" never negotiated or negotiable.

The West forgot that its foundation was built on forgetting, whence it pretended to found its political order on pure amnesia. From there on in, any memory of its origins could only be understood either as a pathological individual symptom or as collective atavism. Cosmopolitanism no longer appeared to be an arduous, painful, and delicate conquest, but rather the very condition of modernity. What should have been a process *in fieri* (a process of constant *reparation* by means of mourning and ritual ceremonies carried out to pacify the ancestors, the tellurian forces, the lar and penate gods) was now taken for granted as a fact *in factum esse,* even as an ideal. Many should simply and plainly forget the repression of "that field of obscure representations" that Kant himself recognized as "the greatest continent on the map of our spirit." Only a radical capacity for abstraction with regard to all familiar, ethnic, or national origin would allow for the emergence of a community that was no longer natural, but civil: a republic of citizens based on "the experience of the community of uprooting" that took on "a veil of ignorance" regarding any previous social roots.

The classical *pact of forgetfulness* is now transformed into the *forgetting of the pact* that gave rise to it. What had been a gradual and dynamic process came to look like a binary reality: a civil and progressive nation born of the social pact against parochial, atavistic, and backward nationalisms; the "republican" people against a "merely natural or geographical" population. And, what is worse, for it has ended up confusing all the theories to date: mixing up, in its definition of this civil and republican nationalism (1) *natural* or primary elements, (2) elements that would *induce* or *produce* the new nationalism, (3) elements *induced* by or *derived* from it, and even (4) elements *reactive* to it.

No more talk, be it pro or contra, of nationalism as a *totum revolutum* in which the ingredients are blended to the taste of the consumer. I would like to take on the phenomenon in a clear, distinct, and systematic way. A way that will allow us to distinguish the "common fabric" and the "specific difference" within the phenomena that we vaguely and imprecisely call nationalistic. And that will allow us, above all, to specify the subtle but definitive change that takes us from the *sublimation of forgetting* to the direct *constitution of the error* according to Renan's definition: "*L'oubli, je direais même l'erreur historique, est un facteur essential à la creation d'une nation.*"

This metamorphosis by which we move from the sublimation of memory to its replacement becomes evident in the teaching of language and history by the modern state: in its manufacturing of a "universal language" (Condorcet) that must purify the language of vernacular flaws and in its "invention of a tradition" as analyzed by Hobsbawm and Baroja. It is now important "not only that each citizen learn in elementary school the standardized, cultivated, centralized language, but also that he forget (or at least devalue) the dialect that is not taught in school." This is, in the final analysis, the culturicidal role of school in the national state just as Rousseau had defined it in *Émile:* "An education that should give pupils the national shape, and direct their opinions and tastes to such an extent that they will be patriots by inclination, by passion, by necessity. On opening his eyes for the first time, a child should see the image of the Nation and until his death should not see any other thing." Such is the mission of the Ministers of Public Instruction who, like the one cited by Mill in 1843, "will boast of the fact that a million children are reciting the same lesson in the same half hour in every city in France." And this is no doubt the reference of J. A. Bastinter when in the pages of *El País* he laments that "if a new vision of Spain is not transmitted to the textbooks of public education—as the French Third Republic knew so well how to do—the battle for the State will be lost." A "battle for the State" that, multiplied by twelve, has made it impossible for the European Parliament and Council to reach a consensus on a unified European history to be taught in high school.

Equally nationalistic phenomena are or have been the colonial revolution and Nazism, French grandeur and the Castilian fanaticism of unity, Arabic fundamentalism and American patriotism, nostalgic Catalan distrust and Basque irredentism, Pan-Slavism and Baltic resistance, the segregation of Pakistan and the Tamil struggle, the reinvention of Hebrew in Israel and the vindication of the *chadoor* in Bordeaux...

Added to the *conflict* that arises from the contact and overlapping of these nationalisms is the *confusion* that results from calling them all by the same name without distinguishing their specific differences, going no farther, in any case, than labeling the dominant or consolidated nationalisms as "good" and those that aspire to be recognized as "dangerous."

Let us take a look, then, in a first approach, at the four types of factors that constitute nationalism and how they take on distinct configurations with one or another dominant note.

A. *Primary factors* of "nationalistic" sentiment are the community of blood, lineage, race and ethnicity, territory, and language, as well as traditions, customs, usages, and religious beliefs.

B. *Factors that induce* or generate a broader and more diffuse nationalism (here based on participation and exchange, not only identity or affinity), which are: the development of a communications network and a mercantile economy; the formation of cities, of centralized monarchies, and of modern armies—that is, the elements that break with the prior communal or feudal order and that allow us to speak of a "nation."

C. *Induced or derived factors,* the same factors as levels A or B when they are now utilized as a superstructure directed toward the "nationalization" of a territory: centralized bureaucracy, professional army, national language, and education. Classical examples of this would be "mercantilism" in the economy, "Nebrijism" in language, and the "parallel action" of culture by means of which nationalists form the state so that the state can finish the work of forming the nation.[3]

D. *Reactive factors and effects* are those configuring the syndrome of rejection, the defensive reflexes, and the search for primordial anchors that appear in traditional societies in the face of planned modernization by what Badie has called the "exported State."

---

3. "Parallel action" is the allegory that Musil creates for the culture of the state in *The Man without Qualities,* trans. Sophie Wilkins (New York: A.A. Knopf, 1995).

The theorists on *nation-building* who explain the appearance of state nationalism as a product of modernization usually cite all at once and in a jumble factors from the first three levels—linguistic homogeneity, the strength of the central administration, the density of the network of the cities, and literacy and education—without distinguishing when they are the very producers of the nationalism in question and when they are reproduced and manipulated by it; when they make up a common identity or mentality and when they are the very producers of the nationalism in question and when they are produced and manipulated by it; when they make up a common identity or mentality and when they are products meant to shore up an identity.

My aim in the book *Nacionalismos: El laberinto de la identidad* (1994)[4] was to make a "clear and distinct" analysis of these factors. I hope that it will allow us to discuss these issues in a less emotional, more descriptive way.

---

4. Xavier Rubert de Ventós, *Nacionalismos: El laberinto de la identidad* (Madrid: Espasa Calpe, 1994).

Part II

POPULISM AND RADICAL DEMOCRACY

Queering the Nation: Some Thoughts on Empire, Nationalism, and Multiculturalism Today

JOHN BEVERLEY

Empire and Multitude

If Antonio Negri and Michael Hardt are right, and we are in something like a new Roman Empire in which there is no longer a center or periphery (for the Empire has no outside), then the central question of our times might be: Who are the Christians today? That is, who in the world today, within Empire but not *of* it, like the early Christians, carries the possibility of a logic that is opposed to Empire and that will bring about its eventual downfall or transformation?

Even for those who continue to consider themselves Marxists in some sense, it no longer seems enough to call this subject the proletariat or the working class. Hardt and Negri themselves prefer the idea of the "multitude"—which they derive from Spinoza via the Italian political philosopher Paolo Virno. I would answer the question "Who are the Christians today?" by saying instead that they are the subaltern, the "poor in spirit," in the words of the Sermon on the Mount. This would have the effect of opening up the category of the subaltern to the future, instead of seeing it, as Gramsci did, for example, as an identity shaped by the resistance of tradition to modernity.[1] Hardt and Negri have

---

1. "The encounter between South Asian subaltern studies and Latin American critiques of modernity and colonialism have one thing in common: their conception that subalternity is not only a question of social groups dominated by other social groups, but of the subalternity in the global order, in the interstate system analyzed by Guha and by Quijano. Dependency theory was clearly an early reaction to this problematic. This is no doubt a crucial and relevant point today, when coloniality of power and subalternity are being rearticulated in a postcolonial and postnational period controlled by transnational corporations and by the network society." Walter Mignolo, "Coloniality of Power and Subalternity," in *The Latin American Subaltern Studies Reader,* ed. Ileana Rodríguez (Durham and London: Duke University Press, 2001), 441.

                    John Beverley

themselves suggested Subaltern Studies as one of their inspirations. Are the categories of the subaltern and the multitude commensurate, such that one could imagine a sort of strategic convergence between the projects of the authors of *Empire* and Subaltern Studies, particularly around the critique of the nation-state?

Yes and no. There is a perhaps crucial difference between the multitude and the subaltern: the multitude, as Hardt and Negri use the term, is meant to designate a faceless or rather many-faced, hydra-headed, hybrid collective subject conjured up by globalization and cultural deterritorialization, whereas the subaltern is in the first place a specific identity as such, "whether this is expressed in terms of class, caste, age, gender and office or in any other way," to recall Ranajit Guha's classic definition.[2] It follows that the politics of the subaltern must be, at least in some measure, "identity" politics.

The problem here is that Hardt and Negri themselves go to some pains in *Empire* to argue that multicultural identity politics as they understand it (that is, as what usually is called "liberal multiculturalism") is itself deeply complicit with Empire. For if supra- or sub-national permeability is the central economic characteristic of the new global capitalism, then multicultural heterogeneity is syntonic with this permeability in some ways, exploding or reordering at the level of the ideological superstructure previously hegemonic narratives of the unified nation-state and the people (*one* language, history, territoriality, and so on).

For Machiavelli, who was in a sense the first modern thinker of national liberation struggle, "the people" (*popolo*) is the condition for the nation and, in turn, realizes itself as a collective subject in the nation. What Hardt and Negri's concept of the multitude implies is that in effect you can have "the people" without the nation. Machiavelli believed that "the people" without the nation is irremediably heterogenous and servile—like the Jews in Egyptian captivity. It is the Prince—Moses—who confers on "the people" a unity of will and identity by making them into a nation. But the appeal to the idea of the nation also stabilizes that will and identity—as, now, *a* people—around a hegemonic vision, codified in the Law and the state apparatus, of a common language, set of values, culture, interests, community, tasks, sacrifices, historical destiny: a vision that rhetorically sutures over the gaps and discontinuities internal to "the people." But it is in those gaps and discontinuities that the force of the subaltern or the subaltern-as-multitude appears.

Is, then, the transcendence of the nation-state by globalization fortuitous for the project of human emancipation and diversity? Hardt and Negri, following a tradition of Marxist antinationalism that goes back to Rosa Luxemburg, seem to think that it is. Their argument against multiculturalism in *Empire* is connected to their argument against hegemony in Gramsci's sense of "moral and intellectual leadership of the nation." They want to imagine a form of politics that would go beyond the limits of both the nation and the forms of political and cultural representation traditionally bound up with the idea of hegemony—a politics of "constituent power," as they call it. Thus, for example:

---

2. Ranajit Guha, "Preface," in *Selected Subaltern Studies,* eds. Ranajit Guha and Gayatri Spivak (New York: Oxford University Press, 1988), 35.

> The multitude is self-organization. Certainly, there must be a moment when reappropriation and self-organization reach a threshold and configure a real event. This is when the political is really affirmed—when the genesis is complete and self-valorization, the cooperative convergence of subjects, and the proletarian management of production become a constituent power. This is the point when the modern republic ceases to exist and the postmodernist posse arises. This is the founding moment of an earthly city that is strong and distinct from any divine city. The capacity to construct places, temporalities, migrations, and new bodies already affirms its hegemony through the actions of the multitude against the Empire.[3]

But where would this "capacity to construct places, temporalities, migrations, and new bodies" come from if not from subjectivities defined by (subaltern) "identity"? *Empire* seems to move at times into a postpolitical register altogether, which depends paradoxically, in the fashion of Marx and Engel's "all that is solid melts into air," on the radicalizing power of capital itself, seen as the outcome of collective labor, to both transform and transnationalize the proletariat, in the process bursting apart the integument of the nation-state and allowing for the emergence of new forms of political activity and mobilization. One of these new forms, Hardt and Negri argue, appears around the question of the population displacements produced by globalization. Mass immigration, they claim, reveals the antagonism of the multitude—the subject both engendered by and opposed to global capital—and the anachronistic system of national borders. From this it follows for them that the demand for global citizenship, founded on the general right to control one's movement, is the multitude's ultimate demand.

This is certainly a legitimate demand, as is the related demand for a universal social wage. It is hard, though, to see it as a demand—even what Trotskyists used to call a "transitional demand" (a demand for a reform that if met would produce a chain of progressively more radical demands)—that would explode the limits of global capital or its emerging political-ideological superstructure. Rather, it seems that global capital is the precondition for both making and fulfilling that demand. For Hardt and Negri, the multitude is an "expanded" way of naming the proletariat that does not limit it to the category of productive wage labor, a way of seeing the proletariat itself as a hybrid or heterogenous subject, conjured up by but always/already in excess of capitalism at its present stage. We know, of course, that the idea of the subaltern played a similar role for Gramsci in the *Prison Notebooks,* beyond its usefulness as a euphemism to placate the prison censors. But how much of the radical potential that they attribute to the multitude is, at least in part, a resistance to coming under formal or real subsumption in capitalist relations of production, that is, to becoming proletarianized? Isn't the distance or incommensurability between the "proletariat" as a category (defined by formal or real subsumption in capitalist relations of production) and the multitude—that is, between what Marx called abstract and real labor—a difference marked precisely by, or as, "identity"? If this is so, then the question of multiculturalism and "identity" moves from the status of a secondary contradiction to become the, or a, main contradiction.

---

3. Michael Hardt and Antonio Negri, *Empire* (Cambridge and London: Harvard University Press, 2000), 411.

Hardt and Negri seem to approximate a recognition of the crucial role of identity, or, as they put it, "singularity," when they write:

> The multitude affirms its singularity by inverting the ideological illusion that all humans on the global surfaces of the world market are interchangeable. Standing the ideology of the market on its feet, the multitude promotes through its labor the biopolitical singularizations of groups and sets of humanity, across each and every node of global exchange (395).

But there is an ambiguity here. Is it that Hardt and Negri are noting the emergence of new logics of the social that oppose or resist the homogenizing effects of market capitalism in the name of (previously constituted?) "singularities," which now acquire in the face of capital a force of radical negativity? Or is it that the generalization of labor power produced by the commodification of human labor is the precondition for "biopolitical singularizations of groups"? In the second case, their argument, though it appears in a postmodernist guise, is essentially similar to that of orthodox Marxism (to be specific, it resembles in some ways Karl Kautsky's idea of superimperialism). To be against capitalism, one must first have to be transformed by it. There can be no resistance to *becoming* proletarianized, only resistance from the position of being always/already subject to capital. Hardt and Negri write: "[T]he telos of the multitude must live and organize its political space against Empire and within the 'maturity of the times' and the ontological conditions that Empire presents" (407). True; but this is also to subordinate the struggle against capital to the time of capital. What the equation of the multitude and early Christianity suggests, instead, is that both new and old forms of temporality, which are not the time of capital, or Empire, need to express themselves. Because the telos of the multitude is, in the last instance, a telos opposed to the telos of Empire, even as it arises within it. If what the multitude resists is the "interchangeability" that results from the general commodification of labor and nature, then what it affirms as singularity are forms of cultural and psychic difference, time, need, and desire, which are at odds with the "ontological conditions that Empire presents."

Hardt and Negri borrow Virno's metaphor of "Exodus" to describe the detachment of the multitude from the nation-state, envisioning a movement from the "modern republic" to the "postmodernist posse." But an Exodus to where (because Exodus is also for Virno "the foundation of a Republic")?[4] If the demand for global citizenship has a slightly reformist air, there is a more militant antagonism to Empire that is revealed for Hardt and Negri in spontaneous and punctual acts of insurgency like the Los Angeles riots, the Zapatista rebellion in Chiapas, the Seattle demonstrations against the World Trade Orga-

---

4. "I use the term *Exodus* here to define mass defection from the State.… Exodus is the foundation of a Republic. The very idea of 'republic,' however, requires a taking leave of State judicature: if Republic, then no longer State. The political action of Exodus consists, therefore, in an *engaged withdrawal.* Only those who own a way of exit for themselves can do the founding; but, by the opposite token, only those who do the founding will succeed in finding the parting of the waters by which they will be able to leave Egypt." Paolo Virno, "Virtuosity and Revolution: The Political Theory of Exodus," in *Radical Thought in Italy: A Potential Politics,* eds. Paolo Virno and Michael Hardt (Minneapolis: University of Minnesota Press, 1996), 196.

nization, or the Intifada. Christians versus Rome, in other words. Yet all of these movements are deeply embedded in one form or other of identity politics. Early Christianity was an ideology—indeed, it served Althusser as the very model of ideology. As such it had to create new kinds of territoriality within the Empire (I understand *territoriality* to designate the relation between personal identity and space). What were the territorialities Christianity created? Initially the scattered "communities" of believers represented in the Epistles (Romans, Corinthians, Philippians, Ephesians…), but eventually, out of those communities, and with the breakdown of the Empire (a breakdown in part due in part to their proliferation), nations, or at least the basis for the modern European nation-states.

If we put the question of multiculturalism and the question of the limits of the nation together, it becomes apparent that without the capacity to interpellate hegemonically the nation (which could be either an actual or a *possible* nation), identity politics has no other option than to be part of "the cultural logic of late capitalism" (to use Fredric Jameson's phrase), because it simply expresses what is already the case, indeed even desirable, within the rules of the game of the world market system and liberal democracy, rather than something that is driven to contravene those rules. Its radical potential as a site for mobilization against the power and hegemony of global capital therefore depends on the nation. Outside that territoriality it becomes what Coco Fusco calls "happy multiculturalism" —that is, an aspect of the ideological superstructure of globalized capital itself.

But the same criticism could be made of the idea of the multitude. If it cannot address itself to an instance of hegemony, is the action of the multitude political at all, or simply a kind of turbulence created and tolerated by the generalization of market relations (in such a way that neoliberalism might seem a better ideological expression of the multitude's reality than communism or socialism), and in any case controllable by military and police operations? An earlier Marxism in Latin America supposed that the "Indian question" would be solved through the proletarianization and acculturation of the indigenous peoples of the continent. José Carlos Mariátegui was one of the first to argue against this conception in the 1930s, noting that the bases for socialism could also be found in both pre-Colombian and contemporary features of precapitalist indigenous Andean societies. A text like *I, Rigoberta Menchú,* similarly, forces us to recognize that the participation of indigenous groups in the armed struggle in Guatemala was directed in part against, or to limit, their proletarianization and acculturation/transculturation. As Menchu herself has explained on numerous occasions, this is not exactly the same thing as a rejection of modernity or science and technology, as it is sometimes made out to be by her critics; rather, it is an insistence that modernity come on terms that are acceptable to indigenous groups. Ideologically, therefore, their struggle required an affirmation of indigenous "identity": values, languages, customs, dress, and territoriality (especially crucial in this regard is the defense of communal land rights).

Hardt and Negri include indigenous struggles such as those represented in *I, Rigoberta Menchú* in their concept of the multitude. But then the question remains: Are what they understand by ideological dynamics of the multitude the same thing as the ideological dynamics that actually motivate these struggles? Or have they subsumed those dynamics in their concept of the multitude, which risks becoming, like the orthodox Marxist concept of the proletariat, another "universal" subject?

The Nation and Modernity

There has been some effort to revive Leninism lately—most prominently (not to say hysterically) perhaps by Slavoj Žižek. But the aspect of Lenin's thought that deserves continued attention in relation to our concerns here is not one that someone like Žižek, who shares Hardt and Negri's rejection of multiculturalism and identity politics, would approve of. That is so because it has to do with what was called in orthodox Marxism the "national question," which was at heart a question of national "identity."

To recall briefly Lenin's argument in this regard: In the stage of monopoly capitalism, based on competition for raw materials and labor supply between national capitalisms, the main contradiction shifts from the capital-labor contradiction within the territoriality of given nation-states to the conflict between dominated and dominant capitalist nations or national groups. The main form of anticapitalist struggle in turn shifts from class-based unions and parties—the organizations of the second International—to national liberation struggles, preferably led by the working class, but not limited to working class interests as such.

It could be argued that underlying the conflict between the so-called free world and communism in the Cold War was a deeper conflict between forces of globalizing capitalism, based in but no longer strictly limited to the nation-state, and those of ethnic nationalism. If that is true, then the political and strategic contradiction between capitalism and communism consisted in the fact that communism acted essentially as a proxy and a material support for nationalist struggles. A case could be made similarly that the problem of the nation and of national identity is still at the heart of global conflict, even though the nature of that conflict has shifted in the last quarter century. Especially in the light of the Anglo-American invasion of Iraq (an action Hardt and Negri regard as deeply anachronistic), it is thus perhaps best to respond to the claim underlying *Empire* that the nation-form has been, or is in the process of being, transcended by the present stage of capitalism, which no longer requires that form in the way monopoly capital did (in that competition between respective national capitals was also military and diplomatic competition between nation-states): It is too early to tell. It may be that the partial disabling of the economic autonomy of the nation-state by globalization and the sometimes disastrous consequences this produces (for example, the recent collapse of Argentina) may in some ways lend a new intensity and urgency to the national or the "local."

Lenin's argument about the "national question" represents his most original and politically charged contribution to Marxist theory, in the sense that it introduces the possibility of "cultural" determination into classical Marxism, at the same time locating that cultural determination within the parameters of a historical materialism—that is, in the particularity of the Imperialist form of capitalism (significantly, it is the aspect of Lenin's thought that Žižek all but completely passes over, preferring to dwell instead on the, for me, less original and less fortunate concepts of the vanguard party and the "dictatorship of the proletariat"). But, in the way it specifically articulates the idea of national liberation struggle, Lenin's argument is not particularly useful for taking up the question of the nation today—that is, as a question not only about what nations have been but about what they might become—in what Lenin himself would probably have agreed is a new "stage" of capitalism.

The Russian empire was, in Lenin's image, the prison-house of nations. In thinking about what constituted a nation, however, Lenin (and thence Stalin in his famous 1914 essay on the National Question) took over the conventional social-democratic idea—articulated by his mentor and rival Kautsky—that a nation was a permanent and relatively homogeneous community of language, territory, market, economy, psychology, and culture. Soviet nationalities policy followed more or less this conception, aiming at a "union" of nominally independent republics, each built around a single dominant national or ethnic group, despite evident incoherences (what to do about Soviet Jews, for example, who were a people without a specific territoriality?) and adjustments dictated by Stalinist *realpolitik* (deportation or relocation of ethnic groups deemed hostile to the Soviet project, settlement of Russian minorities in other "nations," and the like). The notion of the nation itself as "multinational"—that is, multicultural—was rejected by Lenin and the Bolsheviks as "reformist." One can see in this conception the seeds of the eventual breakup of both the Soviet Union and Yugoslavia, which showed a tendency to fracture precisely along the "national" lines affirmed in the constitution of the various republics.

The alternative position in early twentieth-century Marxism was that of the Austro-Marxist Otto Bauer in his 1907 treatise *The Question of Nationalities and Social Democracy* (Lenin commissioned Stalin to write his essay on the national question in response to Bauer). Reflecting the multilinguistic and multiethnic character of the Austro-Hungarian Empire, then in decay, Bauer was concerned with the problem of minorities that, like the Russian Jews, possessed attributes of nationhood—what Bauer called a "community of will"—but not an independent territorial state founded on those attributes. Bauer set up the following problematic in this regard:

1. National or ethnic identities—"communities of will"—are not simply ideological hallucinations or forms of false-consciousness, as the antinationalist position in Marxism and anarchism argued, but are themselves the determinate products of the impact of capitalist combined and uneven development on different populations. They amount to what in sociological terms could be characterized as a contradiction between (national-ethnic) *Gemeinschaft* versus (capitalist-modern) *Gesellschaft*.
2. In liberal-democratic states, national or ethnic multiculturalism may be tolerated in principle but in practice is always limited by the hegemony of a dominant nation or ethnic group.
3. Therefore, the same principle of self-determination that legitimizes the existing nation-state and the hegemony of the dominant national or ethnic group may

then be used by disaffected minorities to demand states where they would be a majority.

4. But should these disaffected minorities become states?

Bauer's response to this last question in particular was to seek to divorce the "community of will" of language, group experience, and psychology or "national character" from the form of territoriality defined explicitly as "national" in the sense reflected in the Kautsky-Lenin position (that is, exhibiting a community of language, language, market, and so forth). He does this by imagining democratically organized forms of relative legal, political, and cultural autonomy and self-determination for national or ethnic minorities within a larger territoriality, which, however, would also be a nation, or, to use his own term, a "multinational state" in some sense or other. As remarked by the editor of the recent republication of Bauer's book in English translation, Bauer challenges in effect the main assumptions of the contemporary world of nation-states: to wit, "that sovereignty is unitary and indivisible, that national self-determination requires the constitution of separate nation-states, and that nation-states are the only recognized national players."[5]

There is much that seems dated in Bauer's argument today; but there is also a basic impulse that is worth reconsidering. In a world marked by mass immigration or articulation of national or group identities over previous forms of territoriality, national or otherwise (Basque nationalism, involving as it does parts of both Spain and France, being one such case), Bauer's proposal has the advantage of redefining radically the problem of minority populations within or between existing nation-states, since no population group is "national" as such, nor does nationalism mean necessarily national "exclusivity" (just as the Basques are a "community of will" within Spain and France, there are non-Basque populations groups within what would become a Basque "nation"). One might see Bauer in this regard as the first theoretician of multiculturalism rather than cultural-linguistic-legal homogeneity as the basis for a nation's identity. This makes him also one of the first Marxists, after Marx himself, to think outside the framework of a normative modernity.

---

5. Otto Bauer, *The Question of Nationalities and Social Democracy,* trans. Joseph O'Donnell (Minneapolis and London: University of Minnesota Press, 2000). Hardt and Negri take up Bauer, noting that, "in the gentle intellectual climate of that 'return to Kant,' these professors, such as Otto Bauer, insisted on the necessity of considering nationality a fundamental element of modernization. In fact, they believed that from the confrontation between nationality (defined as community of character) and capitalist development (understood as society) there would emerge a dialectic that in its unfolding would eventually favor the proletariat. This program ignored the fact that the concept of the nation-state is not divisible but rather organic, not transcendental but transcendent, and even in its transcendence it is constructed to oppose every tendency on the part of the proletariat to reappropriate social space sand social wealth... The authors celebrated the nation without wanting to pay the price of this celebration. Or better, they celebrated it while mystifying the destructive power of the concept of nation. Given this perspective, support for the imperialist projects and inter-imperialist war were really logical and inevitable positions for social-democratic reformism" (*Empire,* 111–12). The identification of the position of Austro-Marxism with social imperialism is, I believe, historically incorrect. Hardt and Negri may be confusing Bauer with Kautsky, whose theory of the nation as a community of language was precisely the one taken over by Lenin and the Bolsheviks. See, e.g., E. Nimni, *Marxism and Nationalism: Theoretical Origins of a Political Crisis* (London: Pluto Press, 1994).

That is an important achievement, because in many ways the argument between capitalism and socialism that framed the Cold War was essentially an argument about which of the two systems could best carry forward the possibility of a political, scientific, cultural, and economic modernity latent in capitalism itself. The basic premise of Marxism as a modernizing ideology was that bourgeois society could not complete its own promise of emancipation and material well-being, given the contradictions inherent in the capitalist mode of production—contradictions, above all, between the social character of the forces of production and the private character of ownership and capital accumulation. Freeing the forces of production from the fetters of capitalist relations of production—so the familiar argument went—the state socialist or quasi-socialist regimes inspired by the Soviet model would soon overcome these limitations, inaugurating an era of unprecedented economic growth, which in turn would be the material precondition for socialism and eventually the transition to communism. The, at least for our time, ultimately triumphant response of capitalism was that in the long run the force of the free market would be more dynamic and efficient in producing modernity and economic growth.

What was not in question on either side of this argument, however, was the desirability of modernity as such. In turn, the various forms of nationalism shared this consensus (that is why dependency theory became the underlying political economy of nationalism). Habermas's concept of communicative rationality expresses the prospect of a society that is, or could become, transparent to itself. As Bauer realized almost a century earlier, however, what opposes transparency or the universalization of communicative rationality is not only the conflict of tradition and modernity—the "incompleteness" of modernity, to borrow Habermas's own phrase— but also the intensification of forms of social heterogeneity and difference produced in part by the very process of capitalist modernity itself. Bauer's problem was to imagine the project of the left as detached from the telos of modernity, particularly as it is incarnated in the "history" of the nation-state.

What is at stake in this question is the relationship between subalternity, narrative history, and the time of capital. Dipesh Chakrabarty formulates the problem in the following way:

> [S]ubaltern histories written with an eye to difference cannot constitute yet another attempt, in the long and universalistic tradition of "socialist" histories, to help erect the subaltern as the subject of modern democracies, that is, to expand the history of the modern in such a way as to make it more representative of society as a whole.... Stories about how this or that group in Asia, Africa, or Latin America resisted the "penetration" of capitalism do not, in this sense, constitute "subaltern" history, for these narratives are predicated on imagining a space that is external to capital—the chronologically "before" of capital—but that is at the same time a part of a historicist, unitary time frame within which both the "before" and "after" of capitalist production can unfold. The "outside" I am thinking of is different from what is simply imagined as "before or after capital" in historicist prose. This "outside" I think of, following Derrida, as something attached to the category "capital" itself, something that straddles a border zone of temporality, that conforms to the temporal code within which "capital" comes into being even as it violates that code, something we are able to see

only because we can think/theorize capital, but that also always reminds us that other temporalities, other forms of worlding, coexist and are possible.... Subaltern studies, as I think of it, can only situate itself theoretically at the juncture where we give up neither Marx nor "difference," for, as I have said, the resistance it speaks of is something that can happen only within the time horizon of capital and yet has to be thought of as something that disrupts the unity of that time. Unconcealing the tension between real and abstract labor ensures that capital/commodity has heterogeneities and incommensurabilities inscribed in its core.[6]

The equation between the nation-state and the modern rests on the fact that the problem of the state is to incorporate its population into its own modernity. The population—or sectors of it—lags behind modernity (expressed as instrumental or bureaucratic reason). What the concept of ungovernability expresses is the incommensurability between what Chakrabarty calls the "radical heterogeneity" of the subaltern and the reason of state. Ungovernability is the space of recalcitrance, disobedience, marginality, anachronism, insurgency. But ungovernability also designates the failure of formal politics and of the nation—that is, of hegemony. In this sense, like Hardt and Negri's multitude, the subject of Empire has a differential relation with the nation: It is "below" or "in excess of" the nation. It "interrupts" the "modern" narrative of the transition from feudalism to capitalism, the formation and consolidation of the nation-state, and the teleological passage through the different "stages" of capitalism (merchant, competitive, monopoly, imperialist, now global).

The privileging in postmodernist social theory of the concept of civil society might be seen as connected to this argument from Subaltern Studies, since it is founded on a disillusionment with the state's capacity to organize society and to produce modernity in either a capitalist or socialist form. But it would be a mistake to assume that the subaltern is necessarily coextensive with civil society. That is because the idea of civil society in its usual sense (Hegel's *burgerlich Gesellschaft*) is also tied, like the nation-state itself, to a narrative of "development" or "unfolding" (*Entwicklung*), which by virtue of its own requirements (formal education, literacy and scientific and technical education, nuclear family units, party politics, business, private property) excludes significant sectors of the population from full citizenship or limits their access to citizenship. That exclusion or limitation is what constitutes the subaltern.

It follows that what Chakrabarty calls the "politics of despair" of the subaltern may be driven by a resistance to, or skepticism about, not only the official nation-state but also what constitutes civil society. The equation between civil society, culture, and hegemony in Gramsci and other thinkers of modernity runs up against the problem that subaltern negativity is often directed precisely against what is understood and valued as "culture" by dominant groups. This line of thought might seem at first sight to be a variation of Gramsci's point about the possible noncoincidence between "the people" and the nation

---

6. Dipesh Chakrabarty, *Provincializing Europe: Postcolonial Thought and Historical Difference* (Princeton and Oxford: Princeton University Press, 2000), 95.

(that noncoincidence, to repeat, is what the concept of the subaltern designates). But the crisis of the nation-state is also the crisis of the solution that Gramsci sought to this problem: that is, the idea of national-popular hegemony. Hegemony itself is seen by cultural studies theorists such as Homi Bhabha or Néstor García Canclini as founded on an outmoded distinction that links subalternity to *premodern* and hegemony to *modern* forms of culture. In contemporary societies, so Canclini in particular argues, the tradition/modernity binary dissolves, and thus along with it the dichotomy subalternity/hegemony.[7]

Hardt and Negri borrow from cultural studies the idea that the category that expresses the dynamic of popular culture is hybridity more than subalternity. Hardt has written convincingly about the "end of civil society," tied as it is to the form of the nation. Cultural studies posit the emergence of a new, transnational form of civil society, based on cultural diaspora, deterritorialization, and hybridization. If hybridization is coextensive with civil society, however, the binary that is not deconstructed by cultural studies is the one that is constitutive of this normative (as opposed to descriptive) sense of hybridization as a social process: that is, the state/civil society dichotomy itself, where civil society is seen as a space of pluralism and heterogenous agency , as against the monological and homogenizing narrative of the nation-state. Thus, in seeking "democratically" to displace hermeneutic authority from bourgeois high culture to popular reception and "crossovers," cultural studies ends up in some ways legitimizing the market and globalization. The very cultural logic it represents points in the direction of assuming that hegemony is no longer a possibility, because there no longer exists a common cultural basis for forming the collective national-popular subject required to exercise hegemony. What remain are only deterritorialized identities or identities in the process of becoming deterritorialized.

Fredric Jameson explains magic realism as entailing the coexistence in a given social formation of temporalities and value systems corresponding to different modes of production that bleed through each other, in the manner of a palimpsest.[8] But the generalization of the time of capital that globalization entails tends instead toward a single, overarching temporality— that of the circulation of commodities and "the end of history"— in which other historicities continue to exist simply as elements of pastiche. For Jameson, postmodernist historicist pastiche, or *mode retro,* is possible only because history has lost its power to represent the subject and the national-popular.

------

7. "The bibliography on culture tends to assume that there is an intrinsic interest on the part of the hegemonic sectors to promote modernity and a fatal destiny on the part of the popular sectors that keeps them rooted in tradition. From this opposition, modernizers draw the moral that their interest in the advances and promises of history justifies their hegemonic position: meanwhile, the backwardness of the popular classes condemns them to subalternity.... [But] traditionalism is today a trend in many hegemonic social layers and can be combined with the modern, almost without conflict, when the exaltation of traditions is limited to culture, whereas modernization specializes in the social and economic. It must now be asked in what sense and to what ends the popular sectors [also] adhere to modernity, search for it, and mix it with their traditions." Néstor García Canclini, *Hybrid Cultures* (Minneapolis: University of Minnesota Press, 1995), 145–46.

8. Originally in *The Political Unconscious.* For a later restatement, see Jameson's essay on the Soviet film director Tarkovsky, "On Soviet Magic Realism," in *The Geopolitical Aesthetic: Cinema and Space in the World System* (Bloomington: Indiana University Press, 1992).

If there was implicit in the idea of the melting pot (or, in Latin American nationalism, *mestizaje*), a teleological narrative of the adaptation of "the people" to the state (and vice versa), a similar, albeit usually unacknowledged) postnational teleology operates in the concept of hybridity/hybridization in cultural studies, since it designates a dialectical process—seen as both inevitable and providential—of the "overcoming" of antinomies that are rooted in the immediate cultural and historical past, including the "past" of high modernism itself. Despite its gestures to postmodernism, then, cultural studies simply transfers the dynamic of modernization from the sphere of modernist high culture and the state ideological apparatuses to mass culture, now seen as more capable of producing "cultural citizenship." In this sense, cultural studies does not break with the values of modernity and does not, in itself, point beyond the limits of neoliberal hegemony. The positivist epistemology and politics (alternatively social democratic or neo-Leninist) of the "left" critics of multiculturalism and nationalism like Žižek, together with the discourse of civil society and hybridity mobilized by cultural studies in response to the "flows" of economic and cultural globalization, are two sides of the same coin: forms of the rationality of a capitalist modernity in which "traditional" identities and value systems now seen as anachronistic should disappear or be sublated in a new "mix."

A Radical Multiculturalism

We return, then, to the "radical heterogeneity" of the subaltern. Is the exteriority of the subaltern simply a function of its anachronism, or does it instead represent a contradictory alterity within modernity—"something that conforms to the temporal code within which capital comes into being while violating that code at the same time," to recall Chakrabarty (that is, different logics of the social and different modes of both experiencing and conceptualizing history and value within the time of capital and the territoriality of the nation-state)? No one doubts that in a period of conservative Restoration such as our own multicultural demands for "recognition" could lead to new, apartheid-like forms of territoriality tolerated, and in some cases even encouraged, by both local states and the international system. It was the intention of the white regime in South Africa in creating legally autonomous and "self-determined" tribal states—the *bantustans*—to avoid by this means the prospect that the majority black and colored population of the country could form a political majority. What is radical in multicultural demands, what makes them the crucial arena for the formation of "constituent power," then, is not so much people's desire for "recognition" or to have a "space of one's own," but rather the way these demands propose to redefine the identity of both the nation and the international order: that is, they are radical to the extent that they seek to *universalize* their singularity.

In Frantz Fanon's succinct definition, the nation-state is a "bourgeois contrivance," and we do well not to overlook this. But it would be a form of essentialism to argue that the idea of the nation as such is limited to only one form of class rule, and it would be shortsighted to found a political alternative to globalization on the negation of contradictions within or between nations that in one way or another are contradictions about national identity and values. That negation would amount to a postmodernist version of the now properly discredited argument that in national liberation struggles women, gays, workers, peasants, and the like must suspend their specific demands in favor of national "unity" against a common enemy. What might be envisioned in the place of both classical nationalism and "class"-based politics is a new kind of politics that interpellates "the people" as a historical bloc within the framework of an existing or possible nation or confederation of nations—not as a unitary, homogeneously modern subject but rather, in the fashion of Bauer's "communities of will," as one that is internally fissured, heterogenous, multivalent. To put this another way, the unity and mutual reciprocity of the elements of the subject that Hardt and Negri designate as the multitude depends (as the image of the Rainbow Coalition in the United States meant to symbolize) on a recognition of sociocultural difference and incommensurability—an affirmation, that is, of "contradictions among the people." Socialism would be the social and economic form of this difference and incommensurability, promoting from them the ideal of an egalitarian society, but without resolving them into a transcendent or unitary cultural or political logic.

To construct the politics of the multitude today, under conditions of globalization and in the face of the neoliberal critique and privatization of state functions, may therefore, in some circumstances, require a *relegitimization* and reterritorialization of the nation-state. But, of course, such a relegitimization would also require, at the same time, new concepts of the nation, of "national" identity and interests, of citizenship and democracy, of the "national-popular," and of politics itself.

Would a radical multiculturalism mean the end of the nation as such, or is it rather a question of "queering" the nation? Is the anxiety about multicultural heterogeneity being expressed powerfully from both the political right and left the same anxiety expressed in the idea of homosexual panic in queer theory: that is, an anxiety about something that is always/already the case?

From the Spains Defeated to the Spains Restored: Around a Map

Ernest Lluch

I

Joseba Aguirreazkuénaga gave me a photocopy of a map dividing Spain into the following four categories: uniform, incorporated or assimilated, autonomous, and colonial. The origin of the map was a mystery, which prevented us from determining what the book was saying as well as what it meant. If we could identify it, we would have a vivid memory of what Spain was like many years afterward. The map was taken, as my brother Enric ascertained, from a book by Francisco Torres Villegas.[1] This widely distributed work had as one of its four illuminated maps the one, appearing on pages 298–299 of volume I, that distinguished between the four Spains. As the legend on this map reads, "uniform or purely constitutional Spain comprises…thirty-four provinces of the Crowns of Castilla and León, equal in all their economic, juridical, civil, and military branches; incorporated or assimilated Spain comprises the eleven provinces of the Crown of Aragon, still uneven in modes of contribution and in certain points of private law; and autonomous Spain, which comprises…four autonomous or exempt provinces [Navarra, Vizcaya, Guipúzcoa, and Álava] that conserve their special regime different from the others."

The author was addressing the town councils, as attested by his earlier work, *Guía de alcaldes y ayuntamientos… en que se consignan cuantos deberes y atribuciones competen* [Guide for mayors and town councils…specifying the incumbent duties and attributes] (Madrid,

---

1. *Cartografía hispano-científica, o sea, los mapas españoles en que se representa a España en todas sus diferentes fases* (Madrid, 1852, 2 vols., 471 pp., 4h + 379 pp. 4h con 4 mapas iluminados, 2ª ed., 1857).

1847, 2 vols.). The *Cartografía* is influenced, according to the author, by the geographical ideas of Montesquieu, Bossuet, and the Bible.

The *Cartografía,* in its text, indicates that the Crown of Aragon "had epochs that were very rich due to the liberality of its government and the extent of its relationships and conquests. Under the protection of its *Cortes* and its Supreme Magistrate, it was well governed economically, personal security and ownership of properties were respected, and public offices were distributed fairly and in a timely manner…, but because it took part in the war of succession in favor of the House of Austria it was regarded as a conquered territory and lost its important privileges".[2]

Concerning autonomous Spain and, specifically, the Basque Provinces, it affirms: "They have their special regime for administration and common law and, regarding the contribution of money and blood, they avail themselves of means which they themselves regard as convenient…their union with the Spanish Monarchy was accompanied by such exemptions and privileges that they have not paid taxes except by way of voluntary donation…nor have they been subject to draft or naval levy…as if they were a country united but independent in its government".[3]

The latest version of the map was its reproduction in the work by Herrero de Miñón,[4] where, moreover, it served as inspiration for Juan Pablo Rada's splendid design for the book's title page, provoking the unjustified indignation of the neocentralists Ugarte and Elorza.

II

Why such indignation? Maps have a way of causing it, as the history of cartography demonstrates. But, additionally, in this case the indignation was exacerbated by a certain neo-Jacobinism on the part of the offended parties, who used as their pretext the fact that in Rada's design the old Kingdom of Galicia had been drawn in a color different from that of Uniform Spain.

The quite reasonable innovation of the designer—who gives notice that he is not reproducing but instead working "over" the map of Torres Villegas—corresponds, no less, to the map tacitly designed by the democratic Spanish Constitution in force at the time, as the legal historian Jon Arrieta has informed us,[5] provided that we place in relation to one another—this is what jurists call systematic interpretation—articles 3; 149, 1, 8th; Transitory 2nd and Additional 1st of the Constitution. Galicia, present-day Euskadi, and Catalonia are the only Autonomous Spanish Communities that have their "own language" (art. 3, Spanish Constitution), have their own private rights (art. 149, 1, 8th, Spanish Constitution), and voted for Statutes of Autonomy between 1932 and 1936, prior to the Constitution (Transitory 2nd), which is also a historic right. Therefore, and I return to Herrero's book,[6] it is not surprising that to them alone has the Spanish Council of

---

2. Ibid., 301-a.

3. Ibid., 302-b.

4. Miguel Herrero de Miñón, *Derechos Históricos y Constitución* (Madrid: Taurus, 1998), 16.

5. See Jon Arrieta, "Historic Rights Are Present Rights" *Talaia* 1 (October 1997), 92ff.

6. Herrero de Miñón, *Derechos Históricos,* 147.

State authorized application of the Additional First Disposition of the Constitution, which "recognizes and guarantees" preexisting Historic Rights. My recent studies regarding the Austrias and a character as crucial as Count Juan Amor de Soria convince me more and more each day that what I have termed *the Catalan alternative*[7] posits Catalonia as part of the federal project of the Crown of Aragon, extending it to all of Spain.

III

Catalonia's consciousness of belonging to the higher reality that was the Crown of Aragon is expressed in the title of what is thought to have been the first Catalanist publication, *El Vapor*. On October 22, 1854, its director, Victor Balaguer, wrote of "the democratic tendency of our rights and privileges and the blind obedience of the great kings of Aragón to the great laws of the country." The Catalonia/Crown of Aragon duality had to disappear in favor of the former with the end-of-century outbreak of Spanish nationalism, which played a crucial role in the abolition of Basque rights, causing Catalan regionalism to accentuate its positions. In a parallel manner, it is possible that this may have influenced as well the diffusion of Spanish chauvinism into Aragon. This is a dynamic complex that will have to be clarified. One of the final moments of the survival of the Crown of Aragon as a potent political idea was the pact of Tortosa, signed on May 18, 1869, by the Aragonese, Catalan, Mallorcan, and Valencian federal republicans. The pact had as its primary objectives to defend the Revolution of 1868 and to reclaim the political style of the ancient Crown of Aragon with its peculiar political organization.

Amor de Soria tried to extend the project of confederation to all the Spains. The Americanist projects of Aranda, which could have changed the destiny of the Atlantic basin, were frustrated long ago by what I have termed *Las Españas vencidas del siglo XVIII* [The defeated Spains of the 18th century].[8] To achieve them and even to understand them would require, in the face of Castilian assimilationism, that we understand and respect the "Spains restored to fullness yet plural" toward which the Austracism with so many connections to Aranda himself and his "military party" was heading. On the other hand, it cannot be doubted that Navarra, still without a preconstitutional plebiscite, is legitimizing its position on the map through its exceptional autonomous situation that is now recognized by everyone.

The result of all this is the legitimacy of Rada's design, not only for the freedom of the artist himself, who expressly acknowledges his source of inspiration, but also for his complete "fidelity to the constitution," a loyalty to what the Constitution says and implies as well as to the patent or latent history underlying it.

My friend Pedro Schwartz wrote on one occasion that the autonomic option of our democratic Constitution implied that the liberals had become Carlists. I think not, in that the Carlists were only in favor of provincial rights through opportunism, and that in their origins they were linked to the unitarism of Felipe V. But there is in Spain a permanent liberal tradition that runs from provincial rights to the State of the Autonomies.

---

7. See Ernest Lluch, *L'altelnativa catalana* (Vic: Eumo, 2000).
8. Ernest Lluch, *Las Españas vencidas del siglo XVIII* (Barcelona: Crítica, 1999).

IV

I have illustrated on other occasions the persistence of Austracist ideas in eighteenth and early nineteenth century Catalonia. Even in Aragon, the celebration of the Cortes in 1808 convened by General José de Palafox is an event almost forgotten, though significant. We do not wish to belabor the point, except to say that it is hard to imagine that the people of Aragon could once again resuscitate something defunct since June 29, 1707, if a popular and doctrinal memory had not been kept alive in Aragon for over a hundred years leading up to June 9, 1808. Only the Spanish chauvinism so dominant in our historiography is capable of undervaluing the tense and silent effort maintained for an entire century.

The kingdom of Aragon was not united absolutely under the insignia of Archduke Carlos. It was a degree of division similar to the Catalan, since, not in vain, it was not until the aforementioned June 29, 1707, that it became clear that Felipe V would repeal all the rights of the Crown of Aragon when he did so with Aragon proper and as well with Valencia. Catalan radicalism arose, precisely, from that repeal. That explains why the Aragonese Austracists took the definitive step toward exile until that became one of their most consistent, or *the* most consistent, actions, with their principal theorist, Juan Amor de Soria, among them. The degree of doubt prior to 1707 as to whether Felipe V would honor their rights explains the unfavorable reaction of many Bourbons, or "adherents of Babel," such as the archbishop of Zaragoza, when they saw with disbelief that he was indeed repealing them. Antonio Peiró Arroyo (in a book that we will be following, published in an admirable but poorly distributed edition) offers the blunt testimony of the archbishop: "[T]he despair that the abolition of freedoms, privileges, and styles they have enjoyed since birth has provoked in the Aragonese…a quite natural resentment among people accustomed to living in the free exercise of their rights." On the occasion of the repeal, Josef Sisón, a supporter of Felipe but also of the rights of the people, makes some predictions: "[T]he dissidents are pleased to see the faithful treated in this manner and believe that this will attract everyone to their party and that when they are united it will be only a matter of time before their laws and privileges will be restored, ending the oppression they have come under of late".[9]

Previously we pointed out that Aragon was the only element of the Crown that recovered its *Cortes*, even if only on that one occasion, but we should now emphasize that the survival of Aragonese civil rights beyond the crisis of 1707 was more vigorous and of longer duration than in other parts of the Crown. One explanation may be the publication during the stressful eighteenth century of a considerable number of texts.[10] The first was the compilation *Forurorum atque observantiarum Regni Aragonum Codex* by Didaco Franco de Villalba, a thick volume of more than 800 pages published in 1727 and again in 1743. In the 1740s, Francisco Carrasco wrote two manuscripts that were widely circulated and subsequently published by Francisco La Ripa—*Breve noticia de los quatro Juicios*

---

9. Antonio Peiró Arroyo, *Las Cortes Aragonesas de 1808. Pervivencias forales y revolución popular* (Zaragoza: Cortes de Aragón, 1985).
    10. Ibid., 36–40 and 64.

Privilegiados de Aragón [Brief account of the four privileges granted to Aragon] (1784; 2nd ed. 1795), and *Segunda ilustración a los quatro procesos forales de Aragón* [Second illustration of the four legal processes pertaining to the rights of Aragon] (1772; 2nd ed. 1797)—recounting the powerful legend of how the kingdom of Sobrarbe won its rights. The work regarded as most important is that of Ignacio Jordan de Asso and Miguel de Manuel, *Instituciones de Derecho Civil de Castilla* [Institutions of civil law in Castile] (1771 and several later editions, that of 1792 being reprinted in 1975), which compares Castilian and Aragonese law. A number of manuscripts on Aragonese law were circulated, and one of these, written between 1781 and 1808, was published in Zaragoza in 1842: *Manual del abogado aragonés* [Manual for the Aragonese lawyer]. Aragon, both in its history and in its language, also inspired several historical, economic, and philological works between 1780 and 1800 in a legal process parallel to that conducted in Cataluña. Peiró highlights with political acumen the *Apología de algunos escritores sobre el antiguo Reyno de Sobrarbe, sus Fueros y los de Jaca* [Apology of several writers concerning the ancient kingdom of Sobrarbe, its rights and those of Jaca] (1795; 2nd ed. 1801) by Juan Antonio Enaguila, and the *Compendio historico de los reyes de Aragon desde su primer monarca hasta su union con Castilla* [Historical compendium of the kings of Aragon from its first monarchy until its union with Castile] (1797; 2nd ed. corrected, 1848–1850, 5 vols.) by Antonio Sas.

Politically the only specific revindication of Aragonese tradition during the eighteenth century is the *Representación* presented by the four capitals of the Crown of Aragon (Barcelona, which initiated it; Zaragoza; Valencia; and Palma de Mallorca) in 1760, which were the only ones that could speak in the name of the old territories. The mere fact that the four capitals of the defeated Crown signed jointly is already significant with respect to the vivid memory of its reality by privileged, Bourbon groups, since these were the ones that held municipal power. The radical nature of some of their demands—knowledge of their own languages, modifications in the municipal regime, the elimination of discrimination based on origin for appointment to high office—suggests a more Austracist interpretation of this *Representatión* than that made by Peiró.[11]

The crucial city of Zaragoza in the war of 1808 against the French underwent a series of internal convulsions caused by popular movements that obliged the authorities to surrender their arms to the people. A trial that led to the resignation of the Captain General, in favor of his second in command, could not prevent the successful demand that General José de Palafox be appointed Captain General of Aragon. To Palafox, as well as to the general, it seemed that his appointment was *de facto* but not *de jure*. Such legitimacy could only come from the application of the "old laws" with the convocation of the Aragonese *Cortes* representative of the diverse social strata. Given the warlike situation, representation by class was reduced: ten ecclesiastics, seven noblemen, eight representatives from eight cities, and nine hidalgos. The five sessions of the *Cortes* evoked by Peiró, and their corresponding *Acts*, provide us with an adequate vision of their content. Pressures were exerted to keep the *Cortes* from being celebrated, but favorable opinion nevertheless prevailed.

---

11. Ibid., 55–57.

The *Cortes* not only had to agree on, but also to constitute, a permanent Junta to meet with the other provinces and kingdoms of Spain, so we are witness to a political decision that clearly restores the one that was repealed more than a hundred years earlier. After proclaiming Fernando VII king, José de Palafox was recognized as both Captain General and the political and military governor of Aragon. In this way, not only was his military authority legitimized, but political authority was also added to it, a political authority that had to be developed through the actions of the aforementioned permanent Junta. The war, with a great defeat in Figuerelas, placed military considerations in the foreground, although even on a date as stressful as July 27 the advisory Junta was convoked to obtain public endorsement. This endorsement was granted, with the significant stipulation that the political authority of Palafox be approved by the *Cortes* of Aragon.[12]

In the *Acts* it is possible to verify his influence over Tortosa (represented) and Lerida, as well as in other Spanish territories. The federalizing tone can be observed in point 7: "that care should be taken to maintain relations with the other kingdoms and provinces of Spain, which should form with us a single, united Family." These kingdoms and provinces were to be organized by delegations, which in the Aragonese case was understood as "Junta of Delegates of the Kingdom" of Aragon. The *Cortes* expressed their will to appoint José de Palafox y Melci their president and effective Captain General. It is not surprising that in his appearance before the *Cortes* of Cadiz the bishop of Teruel proposed those of Aragon as a model.

The rise of liberalism in Aragon was in the spirit of the memory of the institutions repealed in 1707, which were now restored. There were frequent allusions to rights and to individuals such as Juan de Lanuza and Antonio Pérez. A series of articles commemorated the Rights of Sobrarbe, and such expressions occurred outside Aragon and among liberals. It was claimed that the freedoms granted in that document were comparable to those derived from the Constitution of Cadiz.[13] Let us suggest now that the historical path to be taken by the liberals will restore not only the pre-1707 arrangement prevailing in Aragon but throughout the Crown, as we will see below in the case of Catalonia.

Now we want to show how liberalism facilitated the restoration of the rights and boundaries of the Crown of Aragon, an effect that would endure until the end of the nineteenth century, when Catalanism would be limited exclusively to Catalonia, displacing the struggle for rights that had lasted almost two centuries in the form of an expanded, incorporated Aragonism.

The journal *El Vapor,* with a significance reflected in its name, affirmed on February 14, 1835, that "we seek the prestige of the rights taken from us in our time of crisis," and reiterated one year later, on June 11, 1836, that "ultimately, no province was to become more liberal than Catalonia, since to take this path it was only necessary to recall its former splendor, and the long struggle it had to undergo in defense of its rights during the

---

12. Ibid., 55–57.

13. Antonio Peiró Arroyo, "El trienio liberal y los orígenes del aragonismo" *Rogle* 17 (1982), 16–17.

centuries of its glory and heroism. Centuries that will be revived!" At any rate, in 1835 unitarist Catalans such as F. Raull reminded people in "the conquered provinces of what Catalonia had once been." On September 20, 1835, in the same journal, he asked: "What has become of the *Cortes* of Barcelona, Monzón, Zaragoza, etc., where communal affairs were handled with such freedom and good sense? What has become of the rights enjoyed by these provinces, laws so in keeping with the character and customs of the citizens?" The answers to these questions will be blunt: "since the fatal reunion of the two Crowns it is obvious that we have counted for nothing in the world" and "how different the respect accorded to the name Catalan then and now, when we are regarded as simply residents of another Spanish province." The fact that the *Constitución catalana y Cortes de CataluÚa* [The Catalan Constitution and the *Cortes* of Catalonia] was republished in the crucial year 1835 can only be interpreted as a manifestation of political consciousness.[14]

On the other hand, progressive liberals like Antonio Ribot i Fontseré urged the reconstitution of the former Aragonese-Catalan kingdom under the scepter of undefeated General Espartero: "Come, Duke, to Zaragoza, and you will be king of Aragon," sang the *Romancero del Conde Duque*.[15] It is impressive that the term "Coronilla" [beloved Crown] and all that it implies has not vanished in all these years. A progressive radical like Toms Bertrán i Soler affirms in a speech before the General Council of Catalonia that "to the cry of 'rights' that is most soothing to Catalans…Catalonia will rise up to demand en masse…a concession granted previously to the Basques, who had no more right to it than the Catalonians." The opposition of the Carlists is radical: "What would the Crown of Aragon, and Catalonia in particular, gain from the current constitution? What would the Basques gain?"[16]

V

The situation of the Basque Country and of Navarre was quite different from that of the territories of the Crown of Aragon. Their preference for the unitarist over the separatist forces during the War of Succession guaranteed them the possession of their rights after 1714. From the point of view of general political logic, this placed them in an exceptional position, while previously, in an incorporated monarchy like that of the Spain of the Austrians, they fit in perfectly as just another province. Having seen their rights repealed, the four territories of the Crown of Aragon had a superior organization: separate and combined *Cortes*, territorial councils, and a supreme Council of Aragon. For this reason, not only did the Basque and Navarrese rights survive as an exception, but also what had con-

---

14. According to Pere Anguera, "La percepció de la catalanitat en els liberals I en els carlins durant la guerra dels set anys," in *Le discourse sur la nation en Catalogne au XIXe et XXe siècles* (Paris: Editions Hispaniques, 1995), 189–209.

15. Pere Anguera, "Catalanitat i anticentralisme a mitjan segle XIX," in *El catalanisme d'esquerres* (Girona: Cercle d'Estudis Històrics i Socials, 1997), 8.

16. J. Camps Giró, *La Guerra dels matiners i el catalanisme polític [1846–1849]* (Barcelona: Cunal, 1978), 245–248, 258, and 272.

stituted an insurmountable obstacle had been eliminated after 1707–1714 by "right of conquest." In this way the Basque and Navarrese rights prevailed, but remained isolated in a unitarist Spain by force of arms. They had ceased being the norm and were now an exception.

This led to two historical sequences with important imbalances. The first was formed by a tension between rights and challenges to them represented by the Constitution of 1812. The latter consecrated the continuity of the centralism of the Bourbons and in particular events that ensued after the Canovists. It must not be forgotten that there exists a "political autonomy" connected with the "jauntxos" as well as a "popular autonomy" that extended privileges such as fiscal exemptions or exemptions from military service to large segments of the population.

If we examine our own history we can better understand the autonomist attitude. The few municipal elections held at the beginning of the nineteenth century rarely attracted more than 10 percent of eligible voters. Jon Arrieta tells me that, based on municipal records in Guipuzcoa, already in the sixteenth century 40 percent of the population was eligible to vote and 50 percent of those actually voted. If we compare these results, we can verify from specific and real experience how ancient legislation could be contemplated, not with melancholy nostalgia, but with operative nostalgia. It would be insulting to the reader to insist that either of these formulae satisfies contemporary democratic criteria, but it is useful to recall that the ravages of despotic absolutism destroyed certain relative freedoms that the first liberalism was unable to exceed.

The latter is what Txema Portillo so astutely calls the "symbolic condition" of autonomy. From here it follows that, in a second historical sequence[17] there appears an incompatibility between the "provincial body" and the "constitutional State." The Basque case had not helped resolve it, being more historicist than rational, more applied than theoretical. In the tensions between these two historical sequences, liberal autonomy or autonomous liberalism "constituted the most serious effort, hitherto, to resolve a question that was extremely painful for Euskadi and for the whole of Spain: the inadequacy of the Basque country in and with the Spanish constitutional State".[18] A "tempered liberalism," according to the terminology of Juan Varela, that was closer to Montesquieu than to Rousseau.

Alfonso de Otazu, following Francis Bacon, points out that the revolution of 1830 brought about an interruption in the decision of Fernando VII and Calomarde to initiate the elimination of the autonomies, for which purpose they had taken the precaution of concentrating troops in Burgos under the command of General O'Donnell. In light of this, we have to accept the probability of the hypothesis: "[T]he repeal of autonomy would have been, in 1830, more beneficial than harmful for the survival of autonomous rule proper, because if it had been repealed by Fernando VII at the end of his reign, the

---

17. Miguel Herrero de Miñón, "Fuerismo liberal," in *Fausto de Otazu a Iñigo Ortés de Velasco. Cartas 1834–1841,* eds. Juan Vidal-Abarca, Federico de Verástegui, and Alfonso de Otasu (Vitoria-Gasteiz: Diputación Foral de Álava, 1995), 2:7–8.
18. Ibid., 7.

Carlists would not have been able to include its defense as part of their ideology. Autonomy would thus have been an exclusive ideological component of the autonomous liberals and, in this way, the exalted ones would not have succeeded in putting it in the bottomless sack of items they considered inherent to the Old Regime."[19]

The tension between absolutist despotism and local liberties increased during the sixteenth, seventeenth, and eighteenth centuries, with the outcome favoring the former. Therefore, and unlike what happened in the rest of the Kingdom of Spain, "in the Basque country they practiced census democracy from the sixteenth century on," which implied "a certain level of wealth that, in some cases, required the ownership of urban or rural lands or a specific level of income." Naturally, today this does not seem fully democratic to us, "but throughout the old Regime, the Basque country was the only territory of the monarchy in which such a system was established. In the nineteenth century, the liberal revolution…extended it, as if it were a great innovation, to the rest of the Kingdom, but the Spanish citizens took many years to free themselves from census democracy."[20] They delayed so long that the change did not occur until 1931, for a few years, and permanently in 1977. This all indicates that one of Otazu's favorite phrases (in this case Fausto) "autonomy, not feudalism" had attained its full meaning. As had the refusal of the absolutists and the Carlists to affirm the rights until it becomes necessary to use them as bait for the Basque-Navarrese masses.[21]

Autonomy, an invention of liberalism, was able to maintain "peace and rights," and to move toward autonomous provincialism and greater coordination during the period 1839–1878. This permanence of Basque autonomy "is due in large measure to this coincidence between autonomy and moderation."[22] The repeal of rights left autonomist liberalism with no ground to stand on. Some moved toward Carlism, others toward the newly emerged Basque nationalism—one that was *born* radical, just as the preceding and more powerful Spanish-ist nationalism was radical. In fact one element of moderation and permanent tension was the entry of autonomist liberals into the Basque Nationalist Party. One of them, Ramón de la Sota, left a permanent impression to the point of becoming a "soul" even to this day, as Joseba Arregui has affirmed. An influence so lasting that it allows us, then and now, to speak of "two souls," one independent and another autonomist, in the tradition of the PNV.

Other autonomist liberals moved further to the left. Not in vain has the most distinguished Basque socialist, Indalecio Prieto, pronounced as creed and flag his insistence that "he was a socialist because he was a liberal." A progressive liberalism that included rights even as it declared itself on the margin of nationalism. Thus he expressed it clearly on May 2, 1931: "but do not forget, Basque autonomist liberals, that the Statute by which this country will be ruled from this day forth, *conjoining all of the liberal principles beating at the heart of its ancient privileges*, must be the work that emerges from the constitutional *Cortes*, from the constituent Assembly, formed freely by the will of all Spain."[23] Other

---

19. Alfonso Otazu, "Introducción," to Herrero de Miñón, *Fausto de Otazu a Iñigo Ortés de Velasco*, 1:109.
20. Ibid., 159.
21. Herrero de Miñón, *Fausto de Otazu a Iñigo Ortés de Velasco*, 11.
22. Ibid., 13.
23. Alfonso Carlos Saiz Valdivieso, *Indalecio Prieto y el Nacionalismo Vasco* (Bilbao: Laida, 1989), 63; italics mine.

socialists, like Tomas Meabe, fought to adopt the liberal "Gernikako arbola" as their own or, like Tomás Echeverría, make the autonomous tradition of the Basque country their own.[24]

As late as August 1998 Ramón Jáuregui took from a good Basque historian the thesis of the autonomies as "assemblies of farmers." It is surprising that he interprets "farmer" pejoratively, when that was the primary occupation of those who worked, because of which others regarded it as a term of praise. Praise that, unfortunately, cannot be full, since not all participate, although perhaps a greater proportion participated than in the simultaneous liberal municipal elections. Not in vain, in 1839, did those who regarded the autonomies critically underscore, negatively, the fact that the "aristocrats" with their influence participated excessively, limiting popular participation. This is an interpretation of Fusi Aizpurúa, more doctrinal Jacobin than liberal, leading to a somewhat unfavorable assessment of autonomous rights, contrary to the positive opinion of Karl Marx concerning the value of medieval freedoms, at least as a valid reminder at the beginning of the nineteenth century.

VI

The matters discussed above reveal basically certain unexpected facts, based on the clear continuity of historical events. Autonomism contained degrees of freedom that the absolute despotism of the Old Regime reduced appreciably. This despotism proper to the formative stage of nation-states is the unitarism that passed into the French Revolution and into strict liberalism, as Alexis de Tocqueville taught it. In the Crown of Aragon as well as in the Basque country and Navarre, liberals (or some of them with an advanced orientation in the stages of census democracy) managed to discern the most libertarian seam present in the ancient privileges. They saw too that communities formed over long periods of time inherently possessed ways of defending their "body politic." History written substantially from the perspective of the Spanish chauvinism (but also by Catalan or Basque nationalism) has concealed, ignored, or undervalued the facts that we have noted here—facts suggesting a history that must be and can be constructed from perspectives already existing and that can be outlined in our future constitutional journey.

That alternative historiography is also evident in the current attitude toward the possibilities inherent in the 1978 constitution, still in force, which in so many aspects seems like an echo of the Austracist illusion, to which it is united after two centuries by the ideas we have described.

In the "Spains restored," for which the Crown of Aragon could serve as a paradigm, the agonizing Basque problem may find its solution. The parallelism indicated by Jon Arrieta[25] between two classic authors of the Basque and Catalan-Aragonese world, Salazar de Fontecha and Crespi de Valldaura, respectively, might in this way prove to have renewed validity.

---

24. Ibid., 24.
25. *Initium. Revista Catalana d'Història del Dret* I, (1996), 207ff.

Populism: What's in a Name?

Ernesto Laclau

Any definition presupposes a theoretical grid giving sense to what is defined. This sense—as the very notion of definition asserts—can only be established on the basis of differentiating the defined term from something else that the definition excludes. This, in turn, presupposes a *terrain* within which those differences as such are thinkable. It is this terrain that is not immediately obvious when we call a movement (?), an ideology (?), a political practice (?) *populist*. In the first two cases—movements or ideologies—to call them populist would involve differentiating that attribute from other characterizations at the same defining level, such as "fascist," "liberal," "communist," and so on. This engages us immediately in a complicated and ultimately self-defeating task: finding that ultimate redoubt where we would find "pure" populism, irreducible to those other alternative characterizations. If we attempt to do so we enter into a game in which any attribution of a social or ideological content to populism is immediately confronted with an avalanche of exceptions. Thus we are forced to conclude that when we use the term some actual meaning is presupposed by our linguistic practices, but that such a meaning is, however, not translatable into any definable sense. Furthermore, we can even less, through that meaning, point to any identifiable referent (which would exhaust that meaning).

What is it that happens when we move from movements or ideologies as units of analysis, to political practices? Everything depends on how we conceive of that move. If it is governed by the unity of a subject constituted at the level of the ideology or the political movement, we have not, obviously, advanced a single step in the determination of what is specifically populist. The difficulties in determining the populistic character of the subjects of certain practices cannot but reproduce themselves in the analysis of the practices as such, as far as the latter simply *expresses* the inner nature of those subjects. There is, however, a second possibility—namely, that the political practices do not *express* the nature of social agents but, instead, *constitute* those agents. In that case the political practice would have some kind of ontological priority over the agent—the latter would merely be the historical precipitate of the former. To put it in slightly different terms: Practices would be more primary units of analysis than the group—that is, the group would only be the result of an articulation of social practices. If this approach is correct, we could say that a movement is not populist because in its politics or ideology it presents actual *contents* identifiable as populistic, but rather because it shows a particular *logic of articulation* of those contents—whatever they may be.

A last remark is necessary before we enter into the substance of our argument. The category of "articulation" has had some currency in theoretical language over the last thirty or forty years—especially within the Althusserian school and its area of influence. We should say, however, that the notion of articulation that Althusserianism developed was mainly limited to the *ontic* contents entering into the articulating process (the economic, the political, the ideological). There was some *ontological* theorization as far as articulation is concerned (the notions of "determination in the last instance" and of "relative autonomy"), but as these formal logics appeared as necessarily derived from the ontic content of some categories (e.g., the determination in the last instance could *only* correspond to the economy), the possibility of advancing an ontology of the social was strictly limited from the very beginning. Given these limitations, the political logic of populism was unthinkable.

In what follows, I will advance three theoretical propositions: (1) that to think about the specificity of populism requires starting the analysis from units smaller than the group (whether at the political or the ideological level); (2) that populism is an ontological and not an ontic category (i.e., its meaning is not to be found in any political or ideological content entering into the description of the practices of any particular group, but rather in a particular *mode of articulation* of whatever social, political, or ideological contents may exist); and (3) that that articulating form, apart from its contents, produces structuring effects that primarily manifest themselves at the level of the modes of representation.

Social Demands and Social Totality

As I have just asserted, our starting point should be the isolation of smaller units than the group and the consideration of the social logics of their articulation. Populism is one of those logics. Let us say, to start with, that our analysis postulates an asymmetry between the community as a whole ("society") and whatever social actor operates within it. That is, there is no social agent whose will coincides with the actual workings of society conceived as a totality. Rousseau was perfectly aware that the constitution of a general will—which was for him the condition of democracy—was increasingly difficult under the conditions of modern societies, whose very dimensions and heterogeneity make imperative the recourse to mechanisms of representation; Hegel attempted to address the question through the postulation of a division between civil and political society, where the first represented particularism and heterogeneity (the "system of needs") and the second the moment of totalization and universality; and Marx reasserted the utopia of an exact overlapping between communitarian space and collective will through the role of a universal class in a reconciled society. The starting point of our discussion is that no attempt to bridge the chasm between political will and communitarian space can ultimately succeed, but instead the attempt to construct such a bridge defines the specifically political articulation of social identities.

We should add, to avoid misunderstanding, that this nonoverlapping between the community as a totality and the actual and partial wills of social actors does not lead us to adopt any kind of methodologically individualistic approach to the question of agency. The latter presupposes that the individuals are meaningful, self-defined totalities; it is only one step from there to conclude that social interaction should be conceived of in terms of negotiations between agents whose identities are constituted around clear-cut interests. Our approach is, on the contrary, entirely holistic, the only qualification being that the promise of fullness contained in the notion of an entirely self-determined social whole is unachievable. So the attempt at building communitarian spaces out of a plurality of collective wills can never adopt the form of a contract—the latter presupposing the notions of interests and self-determined wills that we are putting into question. The communitarian fullness that the social whole fails to provide cannot be transferred either to the individuals. Individuals are not coherent totalities but merely referential identities that have to be split up into a series of localized subject positions. And the articulation between these positions is a social and not an individual affair (the very notion of "individual" does not make sense in our approach).

So what are these smaller units from which our analysis has to start? Our guiding thread will be the category of "demand" as the elementary form in the building up of the social link. The word "demand" is ambiguous in English: it has, on the one hand, the meaning of *request* and, on the other, the more active meaning of *imposing* a request—a claim—on somebody else (as in "demanding an explanation"). In other languages, like Spanish, there are different words for the two meanings: the word corresponding to our second meaning would be "*reivindicación.*" Although when in my analysis I use the term "demand" I clearly put the stress on the second meaning, the very ambiguity between both is not without its advantages, because the theoretical notion of demand that I will employ implies a certain undecidability between the two meanings—in actual fact, as we will see, they correspond to two different forms of political articulation. Let me also add that a common hidden assumption underlies both meanings: namely that the demand is not self-satisfied but has to be addressed to an instance different from that within which the demand was originally formulated.

Let us give the example of a straightforward demand: a group of people living in a certain neighborhood want a bus route introduced to transport them from their places of residence to the area in which most of them work. Let us suppose that they approach the city hall with that request and that the request is satisfied. We have here the following set of structural features: (1) a social need adopts the form of a *request*—i.e., it is not satisfied through self-management but rather through the appeal to another instance that has the power of decision; (2) the very fact that a request takes place shows that the decisory power of the higher instance is not put into question at all—so we are fully within the first meaning of the term *demand;* (3) the demand is a punctual demand, closed in by itself—it is not the tip of an iceberg or the symbol of a large variety of unformulated social demands. If we put these three features together we can formulate the following important conclusion: Requests of this type, in which demands are punctual or individually satisfied, do not construct any chasm or frontier within the social. On the contrary, social actors are accepting, as a nonverbalized assumption of the whole process, the legitimacy of each of its instances: Nobody puts into question either the right to present the request or the right of the decisory instance to take the decision. Each instance is a part (or a differential point) of a highly institutionalized social immanence. Social logics operating according to this institutionalized, differential model I will call *logics of difference.* They presuppose that there is no social division and that any legitimate demand can be satisfied in a nonantagonistic, administrative way. Examples of social utopias advocating the universal operation of differential logics come easily to mind: the Disraelian notion of "one nation," or the Welfare State, or the Saint-Simonian motto "from the government of men to the administration of things."

Let us now go back to our example. Suppose that the request is rejected. A situation of social frustration will, no doubt, derive from that decision. But if it is only *one* demand that is not satisfied, that will not alter the situation substantially. If, however, for whatever reason, the variety of demands that do not find satisfaction is very large, that multiple frustration will trigger social logics of an entirely different kind. If, for instance, the group of people in that area who have been frustrated in their request for better transportation find that their neighbors are equally unsatisfied in their claims at the levels of security, water supply, housing, schooling, and the like, some kind of solidarity will arise between them all: All will share with one another the fact that their demands remain unsatisfied. That is, the demands share a *negative* dimension beyond their positive differential nature.

A social situation in which demands tend to reaggregate themselves on the negative basis that they all remain unsatisfied is the first precondition—but by no means the only one—of that mode of political articulation that we call populism. Let me enumerate those of its structural features that we can detect at this stage of our argument: (1) While the institutional arrangement previously discussed was grounded on the logic of difference, we have here an inverse situation, which can be described as a *logic of equivalence*—that is, one in which all the demands, in spite of their differential character, tend to reaggregate themselves, forming what I will call an *equivalential chain.* This means that each individual demand is constitutively split: On the one hand it is its own particularized self; on the other it points, through equivalential links, to the totality of the other demands. Returning to our image: Each demand is, actually, the tip of an iceberg because although it only shows itself in its own particularity, it presents its own manifest claim as only one among a larger set of social claims. (2) The subject of the demand is different in our two cases. In the first, the subject of the demand was as punctual as the demand itself. The subject of a demand conceived as differential particularity we will call *democratic subject*. In the other case the subject will be wider, for its subjectivity will result from the equivalential aggregation of a plurality of democratic demands. A subject constituted on the basis of this logic I will call *popular subject*. This shows clearly the conditions for either the emergence or the disappearance of a popular subjectivity: The more that social demands tend to be differentially absorbed within a successful institutional system, the weaker the equivalential links will be and the more unlikely will be the constitution of a popular subjectivity; conversely, a situation in which a plurality of unsatisfied demands and an increasing inability of the institutional system to absorb them differentially coexist, creates the conditions leading to a populist rupture. (3) It is a corollary of the previous analysis that there is no emergence of a popular subjectivity without the creation of an internal frontier. The equivalences are only such in terms of a lack pervading them all, and this requires the identification of the source of social negativity. Equivalential popular discourses divide, in this way, the social into two camps: power and the underdog. This transforms the nature of the demands: They cease to be simple requests and become fighting demands (*reivindicaciones*)—i.e., we move to the second meaning of the term *demand*.

Equivalences, popular subjectivity, dichotomic construction of the social around an internal frontier—we now have apparently all the structural features to define *populism*. Not quite so, however. A crucial dimension is still missing, which we have now to consider.

Empty and Floating Signifiers

Our discussion so far has led us to recognize two conditions—which structurally require each other—for the emergence of a populist rupture: the dichotomization of the social space through the creation of an internal frontier and the construction of an equivalential chain between unfulfilled demands. These, strictly speaking, are not two conditions but rather two aspects of the same condition, for the internal frontier can only result from the operation of the equivalential chain. What is important, in any case, is to realize that the equivalential chain has an *anti-institutional* character: It subverts the particularistic, differential character of the demands. There is, at some point, a short circuit in the relation between demands put to the "system" and the ability of the latter to meet them. What we have to discuss now are the effects of that short circuit on both the nature of the demands and the system conceived as a totality.

The equivalential demands confront us immediately with the problem of the representation of the specifically equivalential moment. For, obviously, the demands are always particular, while the more universal dimension linked to the equivalence lacks any direct, evident mode of representation. It is my contention that the first precondition for the representation of the equivalential moment is the totalization (through signification) of the power that is opposed to the ensemble of those demands constituting the popular will. This should be evident: For the equivalential chain to create a frontier within the social, it is necessary that it somehow represent the other side of the frontier. There is no populism without discursive construction of an enemy: the Ancien Régime, the oligarchy, the Establishment, or whatever. I will later return to this aspect. What I will now concentrate on is the transition from democratic subject positions to popular ones on the basis of the frontier effects deriving from the equivalences.

So how does the equivalence *show* itself? As I have asserted, the equivalential moment cannot be found in any positive feature underlying all the demands, for—from the viewpoint of those features—they are entirely different from each other. The equivalence proceeds entirely from the opposition to the power beyond the frontier, which does not satisfy any of the equivalential demands. In that case, however, how can the chain as such be represented? As I have argued elsewhere,[1] representation is only possible if a particular demand, without entirely abandoning its own particularity, starts also functioning as a signifier representing the chain as a totality (in the same way as gold, without ceasing to be a particular commodity, transforms its own materiality into the universal representation of value). This process by which a particular demand comes to represent an equivalential chain incommensurable with it is, of course, what we have called *hegemony*. The demands of Solidarnosc in Poland, for instance, started by being the demands of a particular working class group in Gdansk, but as they were formulated in an oppressed society, where many social demands were frustrated, they became the signifiers of the popular camp in a new dichotomic discourse.

Now there is a feature of this process of constructing a universal popular signification that is particularly important for understanding populism. It is the following: The more the chain of equivalences is extended, the weaker will be its connection with the particularistic demands that assume the function of universal representation. This leads us to a conclusion that is crucial for our analysis: The construction of a popular subjectivity is only possible on the basis of discursively producing *tendentially* empty signifiers. The so-called "poverty" of the populist symbols is the condition of their political efficacy—as their function is to bring to equivalential homogeneity a highly heterogeneous reality, they can only do so on the basis of reducing to a minimum their particularistic content. At the limit, this process reaches a point where the homogenizing function is carried out by a pure name: the name of the leader.

There are two other important aspects that, at this point, we should take into consideration. The first concerns the particular kind of distortion that the equivalential logics introduces into the construction of "the people" and "power" as antagonistic poles. In the case of "the people," as we have seen, the equivalential logic is based on an "emptying" whose consequences are, at the same time, enriching and impoverishing. Enriching: The signifiers unifying an equivalential chain, because they must cover all the links integrating the latter, have a wider reference than a purely differential content that would attach a signifier to just one signified. Impoverishing: Precisely because of this wider (potentially universal) reference, its connection with particular contents tends to be drastically reduced. Using a logical distinction, we could say that what it wins in *extension* it loses in *intention*. And the same happens in the construction of the pole of power: That pole does not sim-

---

1. Ernesto Laclau, "Why do empty signifiers matter to politics?" in *Emancipation(s)* (London: Verso, 1996).

ply function through the materiality of its differential content, for that content is the *bear-er* of the negation of the popular pole (though the frustration of the latter's demands). As a result, an essential instability that permeates the various moments that we have isolat-ed in our study. As far as the particular demands are concerned nothing anticipates, in their isolated contents, the way in which they will be differentially or equivalentially artic-ulated—that will depend on the historical context—and nothing anticipates either (in the case of the equivalences) what the extension will be or the composition of the chains in which they participate. And as for the two poles of the people/power dichotomy, their actu-al identity and structure will be equally open to contestation and redefinition. France, for example, has experienced food riots since the Middle Ages but these riots, as a rule, did not identify the monarchy as their enemy. All the complex transformations of the eigh-teenth century were required to reach a stage in which food demands became part of rev-olutionary equivalential chains embracing the totality of the political system. And the American populism of farmers, at the end of the nineteenth century, failed because the attempt at creating chains of popular equivalence unifying the demands of the dispos-sessed groups found a decisive obstacle in a set of structural *differential* limits that proved to be stronger than the populist interpellations: namely, the difficulties in bringing togeth-er black and white farmers, the mutual distrust between farmers and urban workers, the deeply entrenched loyalty of Southern farmers to the Democratic Party, and so forth.

This leads us to our second consideration. Throughout our previous study, we have been operating under the simplifying assumption of the *de facto* existence of a frontier sep-arating two antagonistic equivalential chains. This is the assumption that we have now to put into question. Our whole approach leads us, actually, to this questioning, for if there is no a priori reason why a demand should enter into some particular equivalential chains and differential articulations rather than into another, we should expect that antagonistic political strategies would be based in different ways of creating political frontiers, and that the latter would be exposed to destabilizations and transformations.

If this is so, our assumptions must, to some extent, be modified. Each discursive ele-ment would be submitted to the structural pressure of contradictory articulating attempts. In our theorization of the role of the empty signifiers, their very possibility depended on the presence of a chain of equivalences that involves, as we have seen, an internal fron-tier. The classical forms of populism—most of the Latin American populisms of the 1940s and 1950s, for instance—correspond to this description. The political dynamic of populism depends on this internal frontier being constantly reproduced. Using a simile from lin-guistics we could say that while an institutionalist political discourse tends to privilege the syntagmatic pole of language—the number of differential locations articulated by relations of combination—the populist discourse tends to privilege the paradigmatic pole—i.e., the relations of substitution between elements (demands, in our case) aggregated around only two syntagmatic positions.

The internal frontier on which the populist discourse is grounded can be, however, sub-verted. This can happen in two different ways. One is to break the equivalential links between the various particular demands, through the individual satisfaction of the latter. This is the road to the decline of the populist form of politics, to the blurring of the internal frontiers, and to the transition to a higher level of integration into the institutional system—a transformist operation, as Gramsci called it. It corresponds, broadly speaking, to Disraeli's project of "one nation" or to the contemporary attempts by theoreticians of the Third Way and the "radical center" at substituting politics by administration.

The second way of subverting the internal frontier is of an entirely different nature. It does not consist in *eliminating* the frontiers but instead in *changing their political sign*. As we have seen, as the central signifiers of a popular discourse become partially empty, they weaken their former links with some particular contents—those contents become perfectly open to a *variety* of equivalential rearticulations. Now, it is enough that the empty popular signifiers keep their radicalism—that is, their ability to divide society into two camps—while, however, the chain of equivalences that they unify becomes a different one, for the political meaning of the whole populist operation to acquire an opposite political sign. The twentieth century provides countless examples of these reversals. In America, the signifiers of popular radicalism, which at the time of the New Deal had a mainly left-wing connotation, are later reappropriated by the radical right, from George Wallace to the "moral majority." In France the radical "tribunicial function" of the Communist Party has, to some extent, been absorbed by the National Front. And the whole expansion of Fascism during the interwar period would be unintelligible without making reference to the right-wing rearticulation of themes and demands belonging to the revolutionary tradition.

What is important is to grasp the pattern of this process of rearticulation: It depends on partially keeping in operation the central signifiers of popular radicalism while inscribing within a different chain of equivalences many of the democratic demands. This hegemonic rearticulation is possible because no social demand has abscribed to it, as a "manifest destiny," any a priori form of inscription—everything depends on a hegemonic contest. Once a demand is submitted to the articulatory attempts of a plurality of antagonistic projects it lives in a no-man's-land vis-à-vis the latter—it acquires a partial and transitory autonomy. To refer to this ambiguity of the popular signifiers and of the demands that they articulate, I will speak of *floating signifiers*. The kind of structural relation that constitutes them is different from the one that we have found operating in the empty signifiers: While the latter depend on a fully fledged internal frontier resulting from an equivalential chain, the floating signifiers are the expression of the ambiguity inherent in all frontiers and of the impossibility of the latter's acquiring any ultimate stability. The distinction is, however, mainly analytic, for in practice empty and floating signifiers largely overlap: There is no historical situation where society is so consolidated that its internal frontier is not submitted to any subversion of displacement, and no organic crisis so deep that some forms of stability do not put limits on the operativity of the subversive tendencies.

Populism, Politics, and Representation

Let us put together the various threads of our argument so as to formulate a coherent concept of populism. Such a coherence can only be obtained if the different dimensions entering into the elaboration of the concept are not just discrete features brought together through simple enumeration, but part of a theoretically articulated whole. To start with, we only have populism if there is a series of politico-discursive practices constructing a popular subject, and the precondition of the emergence of such a subject is, as we have seen, the building up of an internal frontier dividing the social space into two camps. But the logic of that division is dictated, as we know, by the creation of an equivalential chain between a series of social demands in which the equivalential moment prevails over the differential nature of the demands. Finally, the equivalential chain cannot be the result of a purely fortuitous coincidence, but has to be consolidated through the emergence of an element that gives coherence to the chain by signifying it as a totality. This element is what I have called "empty signifier."

These are all the structural defining features that enter, in my view, into the category of populism. As can be seen, the concept of populism that I am proposing is a strictly *formal* one, for all its defining features are exclusively related to a specific mode of articulation—the prevalence of the equivalential over the differential logic—independent of the actual *contents* that are articulated. That is the reason why, at the beginning of this essay, I asserted that "populism" is an ontological and not an ontic category. Most of the attempts at defining populism have tried to locate what is specific to it in a particular ontic content and, as a result, they have ended in a self-defeating exercise whose two predictable alternative results have been either to choose an empirical content that is immediately overflowed by an avalanche of exceptions, or to appeal to an "intuition" that cannot be translated into any conceptual content.

This displacement of the conceptualization, from contents to form, has several advantages (apart from the obvious one of avoiding the naïve sociologism that reduces the political forms to the preconstituted unity of the group). In the first place, we have a way of addressing the recurrent problem of dealing with the ubiquity of populism—the fact that it can emerge from different points of the socioeconomic structure. If its defining features are found in the prevalence of the logic of equivalence, the production of empty signifiers, and the construction of political frontiers through the interpellation of the underdog, we understand immediately that the discourses grounded in this articulatory logic can start from *any* place in the socioinstitutional structure: clientalistic political organizations, established political parties, trade unions, the army, revolutionary movements, and so on. "Populism" does not define the actual politics of these organizations but rather is a way of articulating their themes—whatever those themes may be.

Secondly, we can grasp better, in this way, something that is essential for an understanding of the contemporary political scene: the circulation of the signifiers of radical protest between movements of entirely opposite political signs. I have made reference before to this question. To give just one example: the circulation of the signifiers of Mazz-

inianism and Garibaldianism in Italy during the war of liberation (1943–1945). These had
been the signifiers of radical protest in Italy, going back to the Risorgimento. Both fascists and communists tried to articulate them to their discourses and, as a result, they
became partially autonomous vis-à-vis those various forms of political articulation. They
retained the dimension of radicalism, but whether that radicalism would move in a Right
or in a Left direction was at the beginning undecided—they were floating signifiers, in the
sense that I have discussed. It is obviously an idle exercise to ask oneself which social
group expresses itself through those populist symbols: The chains of equivalence that they
formed cut across many social sectors, and the radicalism that they signified could be
articulated by movements of entirely opposite political signs. This migration of signifiers
can be described if populism is conceived as a formal principle of articulation, but not if
that principle is concealed behind the particular contents that incarnate it in different political conjunctures.

Finally, approaching the question of populism formally makes it possible to address
another, otherwise intractable issue. To ask oneself if a movement *is* or *is not* populist is,
actually, to start with the wrong question. The question that we should, instead, ask ourselves, is the following: *To what extent* is a movement populist? As we know, this question
is identical to this other one: To what extent does the logic of equivalence dominate its discourse? I have presented political practices as operating at diverse points of a continuum
whose two *reductio ad absurdum* extremes would be an institutionalist discourse dominated
by a pure logic of difference and a populist one, in which the logic of equivalence operates
unchallenged. These two extremes are actually unreachable: Pure difference would mean
a society so dominated by administration and by the individualization of social demands
that no struggle around internal frontiers—i.e., no politics—would be possible; and pure
equivalence would involve such a dissolution of social links that the very notion of "social
demand" would lose any meaning—this is the image of the "crowd" as depicted by the
nineteenth-century theorists of "mass psychology" (Taine, Le Bon, Sighele, and others).

It is important to realize that the impossibility of the two extremes of pure difference
or pure equivalence is not an empirical one—it is logical. The subversion of difference by
an equivalential logic does not take the form of a total elimination of the former through
the latter. A relation of equivalence is not one in which all differences collapse into identity but one in which differences are still very active. The equivalence eliminates the *separation* between the demands, but not the demands themselves. If a series of demands—transport, housing, employment, and the like, to go back to our initial example—are unfulfilled,
the equivalence existent between them—and the popular identity resulting from that equivalence—requires very much the persistence of the demands. So equivalence is still definitely
a particular way of articulating differences. Thus between equivalence and difference
exists a complex dialectic, an unstable compromise. We will have a variety of historical
situations that presuppose the *presence* of both, but at the same time their *tension*. Let us
mention some of them:

1. An institutional system becomes less and less able to differentially absorb social demands, and this leads to an internal chasm within society and the construction of two antagonistic chains of equivalences. This is the classical experience of a populist or revolutionary rupture, which results generally from the type of crisis of representation that Gramsci called "organic crises."

2. The regime resulting from a populist rupture becomes progressively institutionalized, so that the differential logic starts prevailing again and the equivalential popular identity increasingly becomes an inoperative *langue de bois,* governing less and less the actual workings of politics. Peronism, in Argentina, attempted to move from an initial politics of confrontation—whose popular subject was the "descamisado" (the equivalent of the *sans-culotte*) to an increasingly institutionalized discourse grounded in what was called "the organized community" (*la comunidad organizada*). We find another variant of this increasing asymmetry between actual demands and equivalential discourse in those cases in which the latter becomes the *langue de bois* of the state. We find in them that the increasing distance between actual social demands and dominant equivalential discourse frequently leads to the repression of the former and the violent imposition of the latter. Many African regimes, after the process of decolonization, followed this pattern.

3. The attempts by some dominant groups to constantly re-create the internal frontiers through an increasingly anti-institutional discourse. These attempts generally fail. Let us just think of the process, in France, leading from Jacobinism to the Directoire and, in China, the various stages in the cycle of the "cultural revolution."

A movement or an ideology—or, to put both under their common genus, a discourse—will be most or least populistic depending on the degree to which its contents are articulated by equivalential logics. This means that no political movement will be entirely exempt from populism, because none will fail to interpellate to some extent "the people" against an enemy, through the construction of a social frontier. That is what its populist credentials will be shown to be, in a particularly clear way, at moments of political transition when the future of the community lies in the balance. The degree of "populism," in that sense, will depend on the depth of the chasm separating political alternatives. This, however, poses a problem. If populism consists in postulating a radical alternative within the communitarian space, a choice in the crossroads on which the future of a given society hinges, does not *populism* become synonymous with *politics?* The answer can only be affirmative. Populism means putting into question the institutional order by constructing an underdog as a historical agent—i.e., an agent that is an *other* in relation to the way things stand. But this is the same as politics. We only have politics through the gesture that embraces the existing state of affairs as a system and presents an alternative to it (or, conversely, when we defend that system against existing potential alternatives). That is why the end of populism coincides with the end of politics. We have an end of politics when the community (conceived as a totality) and the will (representing that totality) become indistinguishable from each other. In that case, as I have argued throughout this essay, politics is replaced by administration and the traces of social division disappear. Hobbes's Leviathan as the undivided will of an absolute ruler, or Marx's universal subject of a classless society represent parallel ways—although, of course, of an opposite sign—of the end of politics. A total, unchallengeable state or the withering away of the state are both ways of canceling out the traces of social division. But it is easy, in that sense, to see that the conditions of possibility of the political and the conditions of possibility of populism are the same: They both presuppose social division; in both we find an ambiguous *demos* that is, on the one hand, a section within the community (an underdog) and, on the other hand, an agent presenting itself, in an antagonistic way, as *the whole* community.

This conclusion leads me to a last consideration. As long as we have politics (and also, if my argument is correct, its derivative, which is populism), we are going to have social division. A corollary of this social division is that a section within the community will present itself as the expression and representation of the community as a whole. This chasm is ineradicable as far as we have a *political* society. This means that "the people" can only be constituted in the terrain of the relations of representation. We have already explained the representative matrix out of which "the people" emerges: a certain particularity that assumes a function of universal representation; the distortion of the identity of this particularity through the constitution of equivalential chains; the popular camp resulting from these substitutions presenting itself as representing society as a whole. These considerations have some important consequences. The first is that "the people," as operating in populist discourses, is never a primary datum but a construct—populist discourse does not simply *express* some kind of original popular identity; it actually *constitutes* the latter. The second is that, as a result, relations of representation are not a secondary level reflecting a primary social reality constituted elsewhere; they are, on the contrary, the primary terrain within which the social is constituted. Any kind of political transformation will, as a result, take place as an internal displacement of the elements entering the representation process. The third consequence is that representation is not a second best, as Rousseau would have had it, resulting from the increasing chasm between the universal communitarian space and the particularism of the actually existing collective wills. On the contrary, the asymmetry between community as a whole and collective wills consists of that exhilarating game that we call politics, from which we find our limits but also our possibilities. Many important things result from the impossibility of an ultimate universality—among others, the emergence of "the people."

Nourishment by the Negative: National Subalternity, Antagonism, and Radical Democracy

Joseba Zulaika

> No social movement can, in fact, enjoy its status as an open-ended, democratic political articulation without presuming and operationalizing the negativity at the heart of identity.
>
> — J. Butler, E. Laclau, and S. Žižek

Now that proper states are disappearing in Europe and elsewhere, the task of rethinking the hegemonic strategies of nation-states and stateless nations has become more urgent than ever. The goal is to open up fresh theoretical fields in which old national antagonisms between dominant and subaltern nationalisms allow for new articulations. The unreachable gap between the necessity and impossibility of national sovereignty has never been starker. It is in this context that the ideas about contingency, hegemony, and universality recently discussed by Judith Butler, Ernesto Laclau, and Slavoj Žižek, following Ernesto Laclau and Chantal Mouffe's pathbreaking *Hegemony and Socialist Strategy*, provide critical theoretical help. The commitment of these thinkers to "radical democracy" makes their work politically relevant to provide solutions to conflicts emerging from the new historical conditions of contemporary societies.

As deployed by Laclau and Mouffe, the subversive Gramscian notion of "hegemony" promises to be of crucial relevance. With Europeanization and globalization moving in one direction, and the reemergence of substate-level nationalisms in another, historical hegemonic relations are being challenged and new hegemonic formations are in the process of being created. A clear understanding of antagonistic relations can help transform them into new hegemonic articulations that would benefit both sides. Hegemonic relations are characterized thus by Laclau:

1. Unevenness of power is constitutive—
2. There is hegemony only if the dichotomy universality/particularity is superseded; universality exists only if it is incarnated in—and subverts—particularity but, conversely, no particularity can become political without becoming the locus of universalizing effects—
3. Hegemony requires the production of tendentially empty signifiers which, while maintaining the incommensurability between universal and particulars, enables the latter to take up the representation of the former—
4. The terrain in which hegemony expands is that of the generalization of the relations of representation as a condition of the constitution of a social order (Butler, Laclau, and Žižek 2000:207).

The crucial point about this view of hegemony is that it always alludes to an absent totality, a contingency that has to be confronted, a fault that needs filling, a negative that has to be overcome.

Theory is confronted with the following challenge: Could progressive thinkers situated on the various sides of the violent antagonism open up a discourse of "radical and plural democracy" that would allow for a new political articulation, one that could make inroads in turning the entrenched political antagonisms into autonomous and yet interconnected hegemonic spaces? This amounts to creating a language that will provide the element of universality, always subverted by particularity, to allow for the expansion of equivalential links among the various democratic struggles against forms of subordination.

Nourishment by the Negative: Mythic Food

Hegemonic struggles imply that social identities are never fully constituted. Since identity claims are at the core of stateless nationalist movements, a critical aspect of the theoretical task envisioned here has to do with the study of such always incomplete constitution of identity, as distinct from its various identification processes. Here the consideration of the Negative at the heart of identity takes center stage. Antagonism is the political category that articulates that negativity.

Basque culture is illustrative of the centrality of the Negative in both identity and politics. It can serve as an exemplar to test the issue of the sociocultural matrix in which these theoretical "universals" ("negative," "subject," "hegemony") take place. The debate between Laclau and Butler over the opposition structural determination/cultural specificity of such hegemonic relations is a case in point.[1]

---

1. The gist of this debate can be gathered from Laclau, who approvingly quotes Butler's comment on Hegel's notion of universality in the sense that "it will have to become a universality forged through the work of cultural translation." And Laclau adds: "It means that the universal—or the abstract—should not be discarded in the name of historical specificity, but should itself be considered as a specific historical construct." A follow-up to this is Butler's remark that "no notion of universality can rest easily within the notion of a single 'culture,' since the very concept of universality compels an understanding of culture as a relation of exchange and a task of translation." It is such "contamination" between the particular and the universal that proves for Laclau that "there is no universality which is not a hegemonic universality." (Butler, Laclau, and Žižek, 192–93).

Basque traditional mythology confronts the observer with a most cryptic conceptual sustenance: the flying witch Mari, Queen of Basque mythology, who together with all the mythical sirens is said to be nourished by *eza* (negation).[2] To the question "What is your subsistence?," mythology reports that Mari's flat and repeated response has been "eza." In one tale, for instance, she offered a shepherd excellent cider. He asked, "What kind of apples did you use to make this cider?" Her reply was, "With those given to negation." In another tale, when asked about her friends' whereabouts, Mari replies that "They are searching for negation." Although there is never a narrative in which she lives on affirmation alone, in one report she is said to have been fed "with the no and the yes." In six out of seven tales recorded by Arrinda Albisu (1965:191–93), Mari subsists on negation alone. Barandiaran remarks, "It is common to say that Mari supplies her food store both at the expense of those who *deny what is* and those who *affirm what is not*" (1972:166). In either denying what is or affirming what is not, the end result is a statement of the negative *eza*.

The polar opposite of *ez* (no) is *bai* (yes). *Bai* also means "sieve,"[3] and again, under the image of the sieve, *bai* is a conspicuous theme in Basque mythology. On various occasions the Devil punishes his unfortunate captives by ordering them to perform with a sieve "interminable tasks," such as carrying water with a bucket whose bottom is a sieve, or separating white flour from bran flour by sifting them—sheer impossibilities. These endless tasks attached to the affirmative *bai* clearly speak of a threshold that fails to sort out two different kinds of things or of a container that lacks the compactness needed to hold liquid substance within. As we shall see below, *bai* stands for a syntax of indeterminate series with no possibility of classification and order, its inevitable consequence being paradox.

Negative and Affirmative: The Syntax of Hegemony

Hegemony emerges in the field of articulatory practices of relations of power. There is no place for hegemonic formations in a completely closed system. It is the "logic of the contingent" and the open nature of the social that causes hegemony always to be a contested field. In the end, "Hegemonic relations are syntactic relations founded upon morphological categories which precede them" (Laclau and Mouffe 1985:134).

Continuing with our test about the extent to which these hegemonic formations are embedded in a cultural matrix, I have insisted in my own ethnographic work that Basque violent practices are articulated in part by the negative/affirmative polarity in cultural semantics (Zulaika, 1988, Chapter 13). That is, the mythical elaboration of the affirmative/negative reflects a tension that is present in other areas of the culture as well, syntactical grammar being a crucial field. There is a most significant syntactical use of the

---

2. The adverbial form of the negative is *ez* "no"; the substantive form is *eza* "the no."

3. Etymologically *bai* (sieve) is generally believed to derive from *bane*, whence the Romance *van* and the older Basque *bahe* (Michelena 1976:143).

affirmative *bai* (yes): In Basque syntax, causals and conditionals, as well as classically all sorts of subordinate clauses, are formed with *bai* or its derivatives *bait-* and *ba-*.[4] From this sameness of bai and *ba-/bait-* it follows that *bai* statements can be both assertive and hypothetical for the Basque speaker. When they are part of a longer sequence, *bai* statements are syntactically subordinate and never complete in themselves. The syntactical meaning of affirmation is therefore one of asserting hypothesis, conditionals, causals—all of them subordinate and indeterminate clauses. Aversive relationship is produced with *baina* (but), and again Schuchardt recognizes the kinship between *baina* and *bai*. Thus, the *baina* particle is also perceived as expressing derivative and dependent clauses in consistency with *bai*'s syntactical meanings. As the mythical *bai* (sieve) generates indeterminate series that can never be completed, so does the syntactical *bai* generate inconclusive subordinate affirmation.[5] In sum, the affirmative is represented mythically by the metaphor of the sieve prompted by the homonymy between *bai* "yes" and *bai* "sieve."

That the cultural implications of syntax are a chain of "affirmative" equivalences is relevant for the workings of the logics of hegemony, to the extent that hegemonic relations are syntactical, and that the political and social realities are embedded in the language of the group. We might say that hegemony requires yes-saying, while antagonism to it relies fundamentally on no-saying. That is, if the affirmative is lacking in the notion of definite limit and therefore results in caverns of indeterminacy, paradox, and subalternity, the negative provides in culture the fundamental concept of limit, whether material, psychological, or logical, as well as liberation from the labyrinthine consequences of the affirmative. No wonder, then, that the mythical hero Mari is nourished by the No. How else could she protect culture from the chaotic effects deriving from indeterminate—and hegemonically subalternistic—affirmation?

A basic paradigm of order is thus established in cultural semantics by the mythical opposition between the affirmative and the negative. This order not only pervades language but it offers as well the basic matrix to understand the social and to serve as the model of hegemonic articulations. As I have described elsewhere (Zulaika 1988:300–06), personal identity and the political attitudes of the youth are key domains in which we can

---

4. The linguist Lafon has made this point most explicit when he writes in a summarizing statement: "Thus, the two verbal prefixes of syntactic value in Basque, *ba-* 'yes' and *bait-* mark of dependency, repose on two affirmative particles of which the second derives from the first" (1966:224). Schuchardt had made the same point earlier: "*Bai* and *ba* are in any case a single word; *ba* is an alternated form of the former. The Basque we are studying here does not have a *ba* with the sense of 'yes'; it only appears in connection with verbal forms, and then with double use" (1947:72).

5. From a logical point of view there is nothing surprising about the double nature of *bai* as assertive and hypothetical particle, for conditionals and causals are, in a sense, affirmative sentences (see Ryle 1971:235). What differentiates them is that *bai* hypotheticals are part of a longer sentence, whereas *bai* assertoric sentences are not. As Geach puts it, "the assertoric force of a sentence is thus shown by its not being enclosed in the context of a longer sentence" (1965:456; his emphasis). It is the sense of an interrogative or the possibility of a hypothetical or the affirmative response to an implicit or explicit question that is asserted by *ba-*. In brief, the subordinating *bai* asserts but does not determine the sense of hypothetical-causal sentences; for this the complete sentence is needed. But in indeterminacy, syntax rules out the assertoric force of individual sentences. The syntactical *bai*'s inability to determine the sense of an interrogative, hypothetical, or categorical statement is analogous to the mythical *bai*'s inability to dissociate white flour from bran flour.

perceive the full impact of the negative at work. Thus, the most typical definitions of "being Basque" have consisted in "*not* being Spanish" or "*not* being French," while the most enlarged and most profusely used word in political graffiti in the Basque Country is overwhelmingly EZ ("No"). EZ becomes a mantra, a kind of verbal amulet in extreme situations such as torture when all other language and resistance has been destroyed.[6] In political discourse the very concept of "negotiation," central to hegemonic practices, and which has been described by Fisher and Ury (1981) as a strategy of "getting to yes," entails affirmative indeterminacy and has been frequently stigmatized as "treason."

Negative Equivalence and Antagonism

Equivalence is the key relationship for the understanding of hegemonic articulations and subversions. What the logic of equivalences does is dissolve the specificity of each position. Thus, in a situation of political repression, the repressive power's various institutions (military, law, media, education, and the like) lose their differential contents: "[T]he differences cancel one other out insofar as they are used to express something identical underlying them all" (Laclau and Mouffe 1985:127). The element common to the equivalential chain can only be expressed in reference to something external, that is, something that, having dissolved all positivity, each of the contents *is not*. To say that this purely negative identity can only be expressed by such equivalence is like saying that the contingent is always subverting the full constitution of the social as necessary. This limit of the social is precisely the formula of antagonism. The point is not that being something is not being something else but "that certain discursive forms, through equivalence, annul all positivity of the object and give a real existence to negativity as such" (1985:128–29). Peripheral violent nationalisms, in their unending antagonism, provide clear examples in which objectivity and negativity, by reciprocal subversion, become constitutive of the political situation.

It is most relevant to point out that, much as the society is never transparent, neither is antagonism transparent. In fact, the effect of the equivalential logic imposed by antagonism has the effect of reducing the differences and typically simplifying the political space into two opposing factions. Such division of the political into two fields, with a single and clearly defined enemy, provides a different context from a politics in which the issues are not delimited antagonistically in a bipolar field. Laclau and Mouffe characterize the bipolar field as "popular subject position" and the multipolar field as "democratic subject position" (1985:131). It is not mere linguistic coincidence that in the Spanish/Basque struggle,

---

6. Basic to Freud's theories is that there is not a "no" in the unconscious, but rather that a recognition of the unconscious is expressed in a negative formula. What negation accomplishes is that "The subject-matter of a repressed image or thought can make its way into consciousness on condition that it is *denied*" (Freud 1925:182; his emphasis). A historically consequential instance of this logic can be found in the life of Martin Luther as a young man; he is reported to have suffered a fit in the choir in which he roared "I am *not!*" Erikson considers the incident decisive in determining Luther's career; he views the fit as part of a severe identity crisis "in which the young monk felt obliged to protest what he was *not* (possessed, sick, sinful), perhaps in order to break through to what he was or was to be" (1958:36; emphasis in original).

the Spanish party in power is named "Popular Party" and the now outlawed pro-ETA Basque organization has been called "Popular Unity." In their programmatic statements and daily practices they have both made clear that, while invoking "democracy" as their political horizon, their positions are in fact nothing *but* bipolar and therefore "popular."

The presence of such bipolar frameworks forces on us the study of antagonism. A theoretical understanding of antagonism must grasp the central point that it "does not have an objective meaning, but it is that which prevents the constitutions of objectivity itself" (Laclau 1990:17). While authority attempts to establish an objective order of social relationships, antagonism subverts authority because it has no definitive ground. Antagonism does not allow for something to be what it is insofar as this something depends for its existence on an external reality. Antagonism arises when this relation is shown to be contingent. Žižek points to two kinds of antagonism: as the relation between antagonistic subject-positions, but also, in its radical form, as a limit of the social. He adds the following critical observation: "[T]he notion of antagonism involves a kind of metadifference: the two antagonistic poles differ in the very way in which they define or perceive the difference that separates them... The consequences of this misreading are far-reaching" (Butler, Laclau, and Žižek 2000:215).

Antagonism as "the limit of all objectivity" needs to be carefully distinguished from both "real opposition" (in which real objects have a life of their own independent of the opposition) and "logical contradiction" (in which each term has its own reality independent of the relation). Oppositions and contradictions do not necessarily imply antagonism, although they provide the conditions for it. What typifies an antagonistic situation is that "the presence of the 'Other' prevents me from being totally myself" (Laclau and Mouffe 1985:125). Thus, antagonisms are "external" to society.[7]

It is crucial to understand the nature of antagonism if we are to grasp the full complexity of the personal and political dilemmas and fantasies of the "nourishment of the negative." The meaning of the negative resides initially in logical contradictions and real oppositions, but it is when it becomes the foundation of antagonism that its reality becomes deeply symbolic. Laclau and Mouffe's analysis provides the link:

> Insofar as there is antagonism, I cannot be a full presence to myself. But nor is the force that antagonizes me such a presence: its objective being is a symbol of my non-being and, in this way, it is overflowed by a plurality of meanings which prevent its being fixed as full positivity. Real opposition is an objective relation—that is, determinable, definable—among things; contradiction is an equally definable relation among concepts; antagonism constitutes the limits of every objectivity, which is revealed as partial and precarious objectification. If language is a system of differences, antagonism is the failure of difference: in that sense, it situates itself within the limits of language and can only exist as the disruption of it—that is, as metaphor. We can thus understand why sociological and historical narratives

---

7. Antagonisms are "internal" only when we conceive of "society" either as a group of physically existing agents or as an empirical totality. The view of society as always incomplete and never able to fully constitute itself discards these premises.

must interrupt themselves and call upon an "experience," transcending their categories, to fill their hiatuses: for every language and every society are constituted as a repression of the consciousness of the impossibility that penetrates them. Antagonism escapes the possibility of being apprehended through language, since language only exists as an attempt to fix that which antagonism subverts. (125; italics in original)

Such incompatibility between antagonism and language, and consequently the links between antagonism and "symbol" and "metaphor," as well as "ritual," has been central to my own work on political violence, according to which, following Kenneth Burke, the Tribal No cannot be spoken or imagined but only acted out (Zulaika 1988:311–12). It was Burke (1966) who, in his "Definition of Man," characterized the symbol-using animal by the clause "Inventor of the negative"; or perhaps it might be better to say, he added, that the negative "invented" man. The theory of antagonism provides new ground to articulate these fundamental relationships.

Universalizing the Negative

Elsewhere I have analyzed at length the negative logic of ritual form and image in Basque traditional culture (Zulaika 1987, 1988: Chapter 13). Following Rappaport (1979) and Turner (1977), I compared ritual—as a mechanism for bringing about a transition, as in rites of passage, between two indeterminate states—to a cybernetic system in which information is quantified in negative terms (Bateson 1972:399). That is to say, ritual becomes a kind of *reductio ad absurdum* after alternative possibilities that did not occur have been considered as well. Ritual thus becomes a kind of thermostat whose feedback system regulates social life. Various performative models of such reduction of alternatives have been described by ethnographers in the fields of folk medicine, popular games, and political action. If a rational-instrumental behavior operates *positively* by means/ends causal linkages, ritual behavior is efficient in terms of cultural conventions and in formal terms works *negatively* by means of exclusions and reductive processes. Erikson points out that "We suspect that in man the *overcoming of ambivalence* as of ambiguity is one of the prime functions of ritualization" (1966:339). Thus ritual appears to be an effective way to rule out verbal ambiguity and deception. Similarly, in situations in which political verbosity and theatrics become intolerably ambiguous, the military's factitive messages of ritual acting out (to give only one example) are to be preferred.

This formally negative character of ritual can be observed as well in the ways in which it affects images. It again underscores how cultural semantics can lead to an *expansive process* or alternatively to a *reductive process* of "empty" signifiers. Burke, who discerns the specific nature of human language in the ability to master the negative, offers a key remark: "the negative is not picturable, though it can be *indicated*—as by a headshake, or the mathematical mark for minus, or the word *no*. It is properly shown by a *sign*, not by an *image*" (1966:430; his emphasis). In the traditional mythology mentioned above, the conceptual negative can be pictured as well by the negative "image" of an empty container. Thus we find in mythical Basque imagery that not only is Mari nourished by *eza* ("the no"), but her underground caves are also filled with *huts* (empty) objects such as cups, canteens, and candlesticks. A clearly imageless quality attaches to such imagery of containers, for what they depict is not a separate image but instead a relationship of inclusion.

Bateson has speculated on the step from animal to human communication as a shift from iconic to verbal signaling (1972:411–25). In his analysis, the key factor for such a primary step is the formation of the simple negative. An animal can communicate the message "don't" only if the other animal can iconically propose the pattern of action that is not to be followed. But there still remains a great step from "don't" to the verbal simple negative "not," which is essential to create the separateness between signal and referent necessary for naming. At the level of image a parallel negative appears to be granted by *huts*, a superconcept in Basque semantics that means simultaneously "void," "empty," "pure," "simple," "absence," "fault," and so forth. The predicative function of *huts* consists in creating a field of exclusion, a frame of "nothing but" or negative information: When applied to primary or secondary qualities, exclusion means that they are "only, completely" that quality; if applied to objects such as containers or bodies, exclusion means "absence, emptiness" of material elements; and the field of exclusion turns concepts of higher order into "simply, absolutely" those abstractions.[8] In brief, the formal necessity for simplicity, essential to any conceptual system, in the Basque language is resolved by the field of exclusion provided by *huts*.[9] By creating a field of discontinuity or exclusion, a definiteness of sense essential for naming and imaging is thus achieved.

What is significant in relation to the main argument of this paper is the opposition between the *reductive form* of ritual process and the *expansive form* of hegemonic equivalences. That is to say, cannot this same semantics of the "void"—as "a field of exclusion" that formally grants simplicity to objects that, depending on their logical hierarchy, "simply" or "totally" or "purely" or "only" or "by default" possess that quality—be made to represent as well the inclusive field by which the equivalential logic produces universality? That is, the "non-place," the "empty placeholder" by which the chain of equivalences works is, in folk semantics, simply an "empty" container.

Regarding the relationship between universality and negation, this is how Butler summarizes Hegel's position: "[Universality is] that which has negation as its essential activity, and is itself also subject to negation" (Butler, Laclau, and Žižek 2000:23). As to the logic of equivalences, this is how Laclau, commenting on Butler's notion of "translation"[10] describes it: "[T]he equivalential moment is there anyway, producing its effect, whose

---

8. Not surprisingly, *huts* has given origin to metaphysical interpretations that obscure the formal nature of the concept. Goenaga applies to it the Heideggerian dialectics between "being" and "nothingness:" "The *uts* is the *no*, but the no of a something. The being is the *yes*" (1975:145).

9. It is important to note that the primary-process thinking of dreams or myths is characterized by the absence of partial negatives that permit metacommunicative statements such as "This is *only* a dream" or "This is *only* a myth." In Basque language, *huts* provides that partial negative.

10. In translation the deterritorialization of a certain content is achieved by adding something outside the original context that universalizes it; thus, for instance, by multiplying the positions of enunciation, a feminist discourse can claim women's rights in the name of human equality.

name is *universality*. The only status I am prepared to grant to universality is that of being the precipitate of an equivalential operation, which means that the 'universal' is never an independent entity, but only the set of 'names' corresponding to an always finite and reversible relation between particularities." (Butler, Laclau, and Žižek 2000:194; authors' emphasis). A folk visual form of such an "empty" placeholder that is universality is the container/content dialectics of traditional mythologies (Lévi-Strauss 1963).

In their "contemporary dialogues on the left," Butler, Žižek, and Laclau are concerned with the elaboration of an emancipatory discourse that keeps a universal dimension alive. They find no progressive politics of pure particularity. All particularistic demands are made in terms of something that transcends particularity. "The central point [is] that for a certain demand, subject position, identity, and so on, to become political means that it is *something other* than itself, living its own particularity as a moment or link in a chain of equivalences that transcend and, in this way, universalize it" (Butler, Laclau, and Žižek 2000:209–10). The main task of the Left is therefore the construction of languages providing that element of universality that makes possible the establishment of equivalential links.

Thus, universalism (the moment of articulated totality) and particularism are not two opposed notions, but rather have to be conceived of as the two different moves that shape a hegemonic, articulating totality. The logic of equivalence; assumption by a particularity of a function of universal representation; and the logic of difference that separates the links of the equivalential claims are, for Laclau, the three hegemonic operations. The only status of universality is that of being the precipitate of an equivalential operation, which means that the "universal" is never an independent entity, but only the set of "names" corresponding to an always finite and reversible relations between particularities.

Laclau sees in the unsolvable paradox between universality and particularism—the universal is incommensurable with the particular, yet it cannot exist with the particular—the very precondition for democracy. The possibility of democracy is due to the fact that, since the universal has no necessary body or content, various groups compete among themselves to temporarily give to their particularisms the function of universal representation. It is the failure of any society—or difference—to constitute itself permanently as a society that renders impossible the attempts of its bridging the particular and the universal, once and for all; this impossibility both allows and forces the need for democratic interaction.

The theoretical abyss between the universal and the particular—by which the universal is nothing but a particular that has become dominant, while the pure particular with no appeal to the universal is a self-defeating project—may serve as the ground for rethinking the relations between the suprastate formations, nation-states, quasi-states, historical stateless nations, regions, transnational corporations, particular groups, and the like. Particularistic claims, such as self-determination, in the end appeal to universal principles. Moreover, particularistic interests, if they are not to be merely relational or differential, end up conflicting with other antagonistic interests in a field of power relations, leading usually to subordination and exclusion. Unless it is stated as mere particularity, the affirmation of the particular will end up questioning the basic framework of power. The basic point, according to Laclau, is the following: We cannot affirm a differential identity without distinguishing it from a context, the establishment of this distinction being at the same time an affirmation of the context. Or alternatively: We cannot destroy a context without destroying at the same time the identity of the particular subject that is carrying out the destruction. History shows that oppositional identities have a relation of both antagonism to and dependence from the status quo from which identity is derived; confronted with the prospect of ending the hated status quo, those oppositional identities tend to feel ambivalence toward a destruction that will imply their own end as well. The relation between ETA and the Spanish state as one of mutual reinforcement is widely acknowledged among Basques. This shows the ambiguity inherent in all forms of radical opposition by which exclusion itself becomes a particular form of affirmation. True change will require not only a rejection of that which denies its own identity but also a rejection of this oppositional identity as well. There is no easy solution to the paradox of having to radically deny a power system upon which one secretly depends. The politics of the so-called "Basque radical left" are very much immersed in this paradox.

Yet, even if the antagonistic dimension were to be eliminated in the affirmation of a completely realized difference (say, the achievement of a nation-state), the universal would soon be calling at the door. The price to pay would be total integration into the new context of the nation-state. One only has to watch the European Union today to realize how besieged the European states are by "the universal." In sum, the universal is part of any identity, to the extent that *everyone's* identity is besieged by a constitutive absence.

One doesn't, of course, need the state to postulate this universality. It arises, in Gramscian terms, from civil society, which Antonio Gramsci turned into the focal point of social analysis. This moment of universality is a political moment. The only universality that can be achieved for Gramsci is one contaminated by particularity, that is, hegemonic universality.

If anything, this "non-place" of universality is therefore a site of contest, in Foucault's term an "emergence"—that is, "a pure distance, which indicates that the adversaries do not belong to a common space. Consequently, no one is responsible for an emergence: not one can glory in it, since it always occurs in the interstice" (quoted in Butler, Laclau, and Žižek 2000:37–38).

Subalternity, Negation, and Ideological Fantasy

Statelessness continues to be the ultimate political subalternity for historical nations that failed to achieve statehood. As commented earlier, with the increasing Europeanization and globalization of markets and politics, on the one hand the very autonomy of the classical European nation-states has been eroded, while on the other hand there are in Europe today a variety of stateless nations for whom their own subaltern status vis-à-vis the classical nation-states that rule them has become a newly contested territory. The new "war of terrorism" led by the United States is underscoring Europe's political and military irrelevancy in current international politics. In brief, a new hierarchy of subalternities is being reconfigured on a world scale.

"For Guha, as for Lacan," comments Beverley, "the category that defines subaltern identity or 'will' is Negation" (1999:26). In situations of political subalternity such as the Basque, entire sociological books have been dedicated to the "negations" inflicted by the hegemonic nation-state, endlessly nourishing political antagonism (Letamendia 1979; Núñez 1980). But in the new globalized world context, the classical antagonisms between subaltern nationalisms and the state also need radical rethinking—antagonisms that in the end point to the need for a new type of state. However we want to characterize this new state, assessing its relevance (or irrelevance) requires that we examine the nodal points in the hegemonic global order.

A key tenet of subaltern studies is that if the subaltern could speak then it wouldn't be subaltern (Spivak 1988). Rather than engaging in discursive responses, faced with the everlasting Negative the subaltern's only chance is frequently to act it out. Burke put it best: "Yet the Tribal No resides basically in the realm not of sensory image, but of supersensory idea. If sensation is the realm of motion, idea is the realm of action" (1966:430). Traditional mythology as well as contemporary politics are both nourished by this Tribal No. The No "of the rational-tribal idea" gets confused with "the essential nolessness of image" (ibid.). Since the Negative can neither be imagined nor articulated in hegemonic structures, it can only be acted out in ritual action. This is a central dimension of terrorism as a response to political subalternity. In the end it implies a determined denial of all politics and morality. It is an explicit repudiation of the entire field of hegemonic articulations and democratic practices of the European nation-states as being fundamentally unjust in that they deny the sovereignty of subaltern nations. In brief, considering that speaking out is nothing but belonging to the chorus of subaltern voices permitted in the name of democracy but with no real power to effect the needed changes, the very refusal to speak becomes the subaltern's ultimate denial of subalternity.

In the end, if no-saying, no response, and denial become the main field of engagement with the hegemonic force, the subaltern gets caught in the game of power it opposes; his identity may turn out to be nothing but such denial; and the denial itself may become for the hegemonic force the one message it wants to hear from the subaltern as a sign of his unending subordination. Alternative solutions, by which subalternity would be denied—not primarily by radical antagonistic no-saying and struggle, but, for example, by not acknowledging the relationship of dependence, or by pledging allegiance to a different hegemonic force, or by defining a hegemony of one's own according to political and cultural parameters—might be far more damaging to the hegemonic force.

National subalternity consists, obviously, in the feeling of double-binding entrapment vis-à-vis the hegemonic state. Double binds are formally the result of two contradictory injunctions: If you do A—say, obey—you will be punished; if you do the opposite, B—say, rebel—you will also be punished; plus a third injunction by which one cannot overcome that relationship (in situations such as child/parent, master/subordinate, and so forth) (Bateson 1972:242–49). It is the closure of the third injunction—nation-states as having the entrapping power to control the economies and politics of stateless nations—that is increasingly questionable. The theory's promise is one of helping redefine and resolve such double binds between national subalternity, negation, and global hegemony.

It is time we address the issue of ideological fantasy. The cultural ideology of stateless nations as well as entire third world regions being nourished by the oppositional negative pose a folk version of Laclau's dictum that Society is impossible. Žižek observes a double impossibility in Laclau's notion of antagonism:

> [N]ot only does "radical antagonism" mean that it is impossible adequately to represent/articulate the fullness of Society—on an even more radical level, it is also impossible adequately to represent/articulate this very antagonism/negativity that prevents Society from achieving its full ontological realization. This means that ideological fantasy is not simply the fantasy of the impossible fullness of Society: not only is Society impossible, this impossibility itself is distortedly represented—positivized within an ideological field—that is the role of ideological fantasy (say, of the Jewish plot). When this very impossibility is represented in a positive element, inherent impossibility is changed into an external obstacle. "Ideology" is also the name for the guarantee that the negativity which prevents Society from achieving its fullness does actually exist, that has a positive existence in the guise of a big Other who pulls the strings of social life, like the Jews in the anti-Semitic notion of the "Jewish plot." In short, the basic operation of ideology is not only the dehistoricizing gesture of transforming an empirical obstacle into the eternal condition (women, Blacks…are by nature subordinated, etc.), but also the opposite gesture of transposing the a priori closure/impossibility of a field into an empirical obstacle. Laclau is well aware of this paradox when he denounces as ideological the very notion that after the successful revolution, a non-antagonistic self-transparent society will come about" (Butler, Laclau, and Žižek 2000:100–101; authors' emphasis).

For stateless nations fighting for "sovereignty," such fullness of Society tends to get identified with obtaining an independent state, whose spectral nature has been brilliantly analyzed by Aretxaga (2000a, 2000b). The negativity that prevents such nations from obtaining their fullness gets translated into the form of nation-states as the Lacanian big Other, the central locus of ideological antagonism and political fantasy. Ideological fantasy has to grind the panoply of paradoxes, dependencies, and epistemological confusions that are continually generated by this collusion of domains between the impossibility of the fullness of Society and the impossibility of the historical obstacles. One is reminded here of Kant's implicit theory of "ghosts" invoked by Žižek "in order to fill in this gap between necessity and impossibility which is constitutive of the human condition" (Butler, Laclau, and Žižek 2000:235). In Žižek's view on antagonism as "metadifference" mentioned earlier, the two antagonistic poles perceive differently the very difference that separates them.

The "big Other" of the state turned into the all-encompassing guarantor of political Power, Truth, legitimacy, and transference becomes the source of the "constitutive *alienation*" of the subaltern national identity. "In short, this 'big Other' is the name for the social Substance, for all that on account of which the subject never fully dominates the effects of his acts" (Butler, Laclau, and Žižek 2000:253). As counterpoint to alienation Lacan poses *separation*. In Žižek's commentary, "Separation takes place when the subject realizes how the big Other is in itself inconsistent, purely virtual, 'barred,' deprived of the Thing—and fantasy is an attempt to fill out this lack *of the Other, not of the subject*: to (re)constitute the consistency of the big Other. For that reason, fantasy and paranoia are inextricably linked" (ibid.).

The question is why, despite the Europeanization and globalization processes that have largely made a mockery of the nation-states' economic, military, political, or informational autonomy, why do stateless nationalisms still feel that the states are the true "big Other," absolutely conditioning their national identities? For example, why is the era of Franco's "alienation" still intact for pro-ETA Basque nationalism? What maintains the preference for keeping that "alienation" rather than forcing a historically definite "separation" from it?

In the psychological equivalents of *guilt* and *anxiety,* according to which "the subject experiences guilt before the big Other, while anxiety is a sign that the Other itself is lacking, impotent" (Žižek, 2000:255), why do such stateless nationalisms prefer the "guilt" of murderous violence to the "anxiety" that the big Other of the state is no more real? The Lacanian conclusion that "Guilt masks anxiety" seems to capture perfectly the present Basque political situation. Those who murder and support the murderers have to endure the guilt of their patriotism; those who vehemently disagree with murder and are likely to participate in pacifist movements suffer the "metaguilt" of their innocence (such proclaimed innocence on the part of those opposed to the violence makes the guilty party *doubly* guilty, as compared to the situation when everybody was united in the condemnation of a dictatorial regime).

Žižek illustrates this logic with the Stalinists' trials in which "the Party leaders needed the accused's confession of *guilt* in order to avoid the unbearable *anxiety* of having to admit that 'the big Other does not exist,' that the historical Necessity of the Progress to Communism is an inconsistent phantasmatic fake" (2000:256).

Translated into the Spanish/Basque antagonism, for Basques, this results in a situation where the anxiety produced by the increasing realization that their arch-enemy the Spanish state is the big Other that no longer exists, and also the awareness that the mimetic desire for reproducing the big Dream of the European state is nothing but a "phantasmatic fake," is more unbearable than the guilt of continuing the struggle against the big Other. While one persists in the guilt, the far more lethal anxiety of having to admit "the collapse of the big Other" (Žižek 1993:237) is kept at bay. For the Spaniards, similarly, maintaining the historic guilt of military and political oppression against the Basques, now translated as the fight against terrorism, is a way of masking the anxiety that the endless history of civil wars and the grandiose universalistic discourses for the big Other of "Spain, one, great, free" were all in vain. While there is war and guilt, the fiction of the big Other can be sustained in the name of either Democracy or Freedom –anything in order to avoid the anxiety of having to admit "the terrifying abyss of the subject's ultimate and radical *freedom,* the freedom whose space is sustained by the Other's inconsistency and lack" (Butler, Laclau, and Žižek 2000:258).

The Positivization of the Negative: Competing Universalities Between "Popular" and "Democratic" Struggles

> What is a rebel? A man who says no: but whose refusal does not imply a renunciation. He is also a man who says yes as soon as he begins to think for himself.
>
> —Camus, The Rebel

As emphasized in the debate between Butler, Laclau, and Žižek, the only democratic society is one that permanently shows the contingency of its foundations by keeping the gap between the ethical moment and the normative order. The democratic transformation of a society rests on the limitation of the ethical by the normative as well as the subversion of the normative by the ethical. *Hegemony* is the name for that unstable relation between the ethical and the normative. Laclau (Butler, Laclau, and Žižek 2000:82) characterizes the ethical, first, as that aspect of the decision that is not predetermined by an existing normative framework; secondly, any normative order is nothing but the sedimented form of an initial ethical event. This implies the rejection of universalistic ethics, as well as of pure decisionism a priori (the ensemble of sedimented practices that constitute the normative framework of a certain society are the limits beyond the purely aprioristic).

Hegemonic practices imply the articulatory logics of society's incomplete and open character. But such an articulatory moment is not in itself sufficient. Hegemony implies also "confrontation with antagonistic articulatory practices," and this presupposes, in the language of Laclau and Mouffe, the language of equivalences and frontier effects and the Gramscian concept of "war of position." This concept recalls the impossibility of any closure of the social that thus becomes affected by ambiguity and "prevents it from being fixed in any transcendental signified" (Laclau and Mouffe 1985:137). An illegitimate presupposition to the concept of "war of position" is the division of the social into two camps. The work of hegemonic articulation consists in the moving frontier between the two. Such tendency to construct society in two opposing fields is the mark of Gramsci's "popular" struggles, whereas "democratic" struggles imply a plurality of political spaces.

In the context of this paper, another expression for this hegemonic agenda is "the positivization of the negative" as a dominant cultural strategy. This, for Laclau, consists in "the production of tendentially empty signifiers, which is the very condition of politics and political change. They are signifiers with no *necessary* attachment to any precise content, signifiers which simply name the positive reverse of an experience of historical limitation"

(Butler, Laclau, and Žižek 2000:185). "Justice," "order," "solidarity" are instances. "Freedom" is another name for such a "negative" of the unconditional in an entirely conditioned universe (Žižek 1997).

The negative logic of ritual reductionism works in the opposite direction. Its tendency is to continuously lead into a sort of degree zero of politics, that is, the search for the most simplified structural opposition and antagonism in the existing order. Thus, in the case of stateless nationalisms, the many contradictions internal to society become simplified to the one single structural difference of having or not having a state. Such a discursive formation reduces all "articulation," characterized by Laclau and Mouffe (1985:105) as "a relation among elements such that their identity is modified as a result of the articulatory practice," to a basic oppositional structure that tends to forget the relational nature of that very identity as Negation. This is the source of the essentialism that ensues. The Negative becomes a sort of transcendental signified, an ultimate fixity, the origin and center of all discourse. There is a place left for a field of discursivity that denies the existence of such an ultimate meaning. The power of antagonism consists in its capacity to negate and limit any existing social order, whereas its failure derives from the impossibility of any political articulation associated with absolute opposition.

The danger with such a negative is that anything that escapes structural determination (say, a terrorist group, an unstructured party, or an unregulated social movement) becomes the negative reverse of what it opposes (an army, an elected Parliament, a legal party, a social movement). But the dualisms that plague this type of politics are in the end spurious because they oppose terms that are not at the same level of formality and representation.

This degree zero of opposition implies that the identity of the opponents is forever fixed; it does not allow for any transformation in the very nature of "the enemy" for the simple reason that it requires a correlative changing of oneself. It is the opposite of Gramsci's "war of position," which "involves the progressive disaggregation of a civilization and the construction of another around a new class core" (Laclau and Mouffe 1985:70). Above all, it does not allow for the dissolving of "the enemy," since this would imply the end of one's own antagonistic identity. Such oppositional fixity forces the contenders to become blind to the massive changes happening in the world around them. Once the dominant denial of subalternity is defined as no-saying, the identity of what is denied per se is secondary to its role as oppositional identity against the dominant order.

The opposite result of Negation eliminating discourse is that it will not allow for partial fixations or "nodal points." A discourse unable to create any fixity of meaning is, naturally, the discourse of the psychotic. Mere no-saying can turn into an expression of such denial of any nodal point in the hegemonic discourse. It is the openness of the social that provides such partial nodal points in the unlimited field of discursivity.

In such a cultural system the category of the "subject" is, of course, permeated by the negative. The definition of being a person as equivalent to the power to say no is its simplest ethnographic expression. The unflinching position of the "everlasting No" runs directly against the current awareness of the discursive character of various "subject positions." The last thing for such a negative identity, in which persistence in the No is the condition of survival, is the open prospect of partaking of the multiple positions of any discourse. In the difference established earlier between the "popular" and the "democratic" subject positions, the paradigmatic shift from the first to the second requires the type of theoretical groundwork we are advocating here, that is, the expansion of equivalential chains and the diversity of subject positions provided by the theory of hegemony. Otherwise, the merely antagonistic subject blandishes its negation to point out the irrelevance of all the other subject positions within the social field of discursivity.

A crucial implication of this hegemonic logic, by which it is no longer possible for identity to remain unchanged, is that frontal opposition, far from being an external threat to the system it opposes, becomes simply an internal contradiction, another difference, and that it may even serve as a necessary underpinning of the entire system. This happens when the opposing force accepts the basic articulations of the hegemonic formation, that is, when "the *place of the negation* is defined by the internal parameters of the formation itself" (139). Thus terrorism, far from posing a real "external" threat, in most cases is well within the internal parameters of the power it opposes and ends up being co-opted by it to advance its otherwise most unsavory plans.

According to the perception of most Basques, this is certainly the case with ETA. Its inability to perceive its own role in underpinning Spain's domination derives from its definition of the Spanish hegemonic formation as constituted around a single, all-encompassing center: the military. During Franco's forty years of dictatorship there was no question that the regime relied on the military as its foundational base. Today, after more than twenty years of democracy in post-Franco Spain, the political obsolescence of ETA consists in its inability to change its premise that Spanish hegemony over the Basques still relies essentially on that single core of military power. Once defined in those terms, what count for nothing are massive transformations in the status and organization of Spanish military, such as now being subordinated to a democratic system, or now being integrated into the NATO alliance (and therefore being subject to an external command structure and becoming thoroughly dependent on outside technology), or no longer having universal conscription. As a result, if during the Francoist period armed military opposition implied frontal opposition to a military regime, during the democratic period (with Basques themselves having an autonomous government, Parliament, and police) the same military tactics possess an entirely different character—the frontal assault against the Spanish and Basque democratic society becomes "internalized," and its former military "enemy" no longer holds the center of the new hegemonic formation in a democratic order. The tragic shortsightedness of ETA's politics of military antagonism can be described as the inability to understand that "Hegemony is, quite simply, a political *type of relation*, a *form*, if one wishes, of politics; but not a determinable location within a topography of the social" (Laclau and Mouffe 1985:139). A similar criticism could be made of a nationalist politics that perceives the state as an autonomous entity in the hegemonic formation and that posits the formation of such a state of its own as the ultimate condition of its own hegemony.

This brings us back again to key concerns in our argument: how the moment of universality emerges in politics, and which "practices of translation" to establish among competing notions of universality. It is worth recalling Butler's position:

> [I]n those cases where the "universal" loses its empty status and comes to represent an ethnically restrictive conception of community and citizenship (Israel), or becomes equated with certain organizations of kinship (the nuclear, heterosexual family), or with certain racial identifications, then it is not just in the name of the excluded particulars that politicization occurs, but in the name of a different kind of universality (Butler, Laclau, and Žižek 2000:166).

This confirms Laclau's position that "there is no politics of pure particularity. Even the most particularistic of demands will be made in terms of something transcending it" (Butler, Laclau, and Žižek 2000:305).

While trying to apply this theoretical perspective to cases of terrorism, I find compelling Laclau's conclusion that "There is no future for the Left if it is unable to create an expansive universal discourse, constructed out of, not against, the proliferation of particularisms of the last few decades" (Butler, Laclau, and Žižek 2000:306). Such "implicit and undeveloped universality," translated into the project of a radical and plural democracy, is the only theoretical horizon that could articulate the antagonisms and subvert the present political stalemate.

Hegemonic Autonomy in a Radical and Plural Democracy

Post-Franco Spain decided to define itself as a "State of Autonomies," in which seventeen regional autonomies are articulated within the overarching state. This was in itself a clever hegemonic move, termed "coffee for everybody," by which the classical nationalisms of Catalonia, the Basque Country, and Galicia were bundled together and the specificity of their "national" claims dissolved amid other regions and provinces of Spain. In such a political context the very meaning of "autonomy" is obviously one of being a thoroughly subordinated and nonspecific region of Spain. Basque separatists deride the very meaning of "autonomy" as being one of complete subservience to the state.

The notion of "autonomy" has become so problematic in the Basque case that the nationalist party in power embodying those autonomous institutions decided three years ago to no longer even support the project of Basque Autonomy, thus leaving its own institutions in a constitutional vacuum. In fact, nothing expresses better the open-ended and antagonistic relations between the Spanish state and the Basque autonomous institutions than the fact that the Spanish Constitution was approved by only 33 percent of Basque votes (the Statute of Autonomy that derives from it was approved by a bare majority). Leaving aside the technicalities of the Constitution's approval, the Basque nationalist position is that the Spanish Constitution lacks legitimacy on the basis of that percentage. The Basque nationalist forces that hold the power in the region allege that not all of the Constitution's negotiated "transferences" of power have been granted yet and further that it has been devalued because of the constant challenges it has suffered from the Spanish courts, and such forces are now contesting even the validity of the Statute of Autonomy. This is the basic background of the struggle for hegemony taking place between Spanish and Basque nationalisms at the moment.

In this hegemonic struggle both Spain and the Basque Country claim to have a *foundational* status of their own. It is easy to understand how Spain as a nation-state assumes that it is an unquestionable historical reality, possessing all the legitimacies of law and military might. But the Basques too lay claims to an original sovereignty that, since the Middle Ages, has contractually been negotiated with the Spanish kings but never dissolved (Herrero de Miñón 1999). The present strategy by moderate nationalism, caught between the constitutional legitimacy and military power of the Spanish state on the one hand and the frontal antagonism of ETA's terrorism on the other, is to attempt a renegotiation of such allegedly original sovereignty within the new realities of a suprastate European Union. In doing so, the Basques are stating that Spanish hegemony is, after all, historical and modifiable.

The key issue for stateless nations here is: "How does one move from the negativity of subaltern consciousness to hegemony?" (Beverley 1999:133). In the theoretical perspective we are embracing here, a viable Basque hegemony hinges precisely on its *not* relying on claims to such foundational power but rather on using a different type of hegemonic formation based on "nodal points," or partial concentrations of power required for articulating a progressive Basque social order. While "the struggle for a maximum autonomization of spheres" needs to be recognized as primary to a radical and plural democracy, the challenge is how to constitute a formation that will avoid the negativities and antagonisms of a totalizing social order that relies in the end on the limits of what *is not*. In the present global world this requires a view of Basqueness that should be able to replace the closures of its geographic and social limits with the open frontiers of an international Basque network of economic, informational, and political interests.

A new imaginary is required if it is to overcome the radical antagonisms that keep societies such as the Basque in an endemic political stalemate. This new worldview can only come from rejecting privileged points of rupture, such as those emanating from nationality, anthropology, or linguistic insularity, as well as from the clear acceptance of the plurality of the social. That is, such a culture can only reside in a radical democracy that will combat inequality. The existence of social conflict or a general anthropological substratum does not in itself make inevitable the resistance to diverse forms of subordination. What needs to be explained is how relations of subordination turn into relations of oppression. This requires the presence of an external, further-reaching discourse that, by subsuming previous antagonisms, can turn the relations of subordination into relations of oppression. In the Basque case, democracy is the one discourse invoked by all sides to resolve the political impasse, and only by radicalizing the subversive implications of the democratic principles of liberty and equality can the various types of perceived injustice and inequality be illuminated and ultimately resolved.

The various parties in this political impasse accuse each other of "democratic deficit"—Basque nationalists accuse Madrid of not allowing Basques full democratic rights such as self-determination, while Spain, believing herself to be a full democracy, accuses the Basques of unwillingness to accept the democratic rules that apply to the entire state and considers any form of political antagonism as being nothing but justification of ETA's terrorism. The theoretical task consists in articulating the implications of a radical democratic culture to the point that it would allow for the emergence of new political subjects bridging the entrenched antagonisms within a larger social hierarchy. The first requirement in such an agenda should be to bring to the fore and examine the actual antagonisms of the situation. The emerging opportunities provided by the creation of new suprastate institutions in the European Union, plus the transformation of the very idea of "citizenship" in such a supranational context, should help in devising new formulas to undermine and resolve such antagonisms.

The principle that should guide this theoretical task is stated thus by Laclau and Mouffe: "[T]he project for a radical and plural democracy, *in a primary sense,* is nothing other than the struggle for a maximum autonomization of spheres on the basis of the generalization of the equivalential-egalitarian logic" (1985:167). This requires that subject positions cannot rely on a unitary founding principle, such as the state, or ethnicity, or social class, or linguistic difference. At the same time, radical pluralism implies that "each term of the plurality of identities finds within itself the principle of its own validity, without this having to be sought in a transcendent or underlying positive ground" (ibid.). Therefore we should not think of a universal working class, or a foundational national origin, or an essential gender class that will arbitrarily group together different subject positions, if we really want to advance the interests of the workers, women, or natives, who are better served by recognizing the plurality of antagonisms within their own class. These antagonisms are polysemic; the form they will acquire is not predetermined but responds to other elements in the social formation; and their meaning depends on hegemonic articulations.

The "statist" hegemonic interpretation given to the Basque problem by post-Franco democratic Spain has consisted in opposing "democracy" to "terrorism." On the other side, ETA's rendering of the antagonism is one of opposing the rights of Basques for political sovereignty that a "true democracy" would favor against Spanish military oppression, now masked as a constitutional democracy. That is, from both ends, the equivalential chain associated with the Other is one of "terrorist" or "military"—and charged as "non-democratic."

The intellectual task is one of formulating the hegemonic articulations of such radical and plural democracies in the present European context of state nationalisms as well as stateless nationalisms. Theoretically, to create a different and more expansive system of equivalences, this should start by recognizing that the terms of their antagonisms are

in no way fixed by past history or present political convenience. The danger of aprioristic essentialism[11] tends to take the forms of historicism, statism, classism, and nationalism. In the new European context, in which states have lost much of their sovereignty yet
"the nation-sate is not yet in the position to allow civil society to be itself" (Beverley
1999:123), new formulations are urgently needed. If "hegemony still has to *pass through*
the nation-state at some point or another," as argued by Beverley (1999:152), should the
project of the Left "be posed paradoxically as a *defense* of the nation-state, rather than as
something that is 'against' or 'beyond' the nation-state" (ibid.:153)? From Catalonia a similar argument has been audaciously elaborated for stateless nations by Rubert de Ventós
(2000), who sees the state as a fluid convergence of historical flows. What should this
"new kind of state" be, in any case?

The demand for *equality* implied by the logic of democratic equivalence is not sufficient; the demand for *liberty*, which makes a democracy actually plural, is also required.
This is implied by the principle of the separation of spaces. That is, a democracy based
on one single space of equality could be radically egalitarian but not plural if it failed to
recognize the plurality of spaces. Such democratic plurality derives from the demand of
liberty that is inherent as well in the logic of liberalism. We are not saying that these "democratic rights" are based on something like "natural rights" prior to the social rights, or
"collective rights" prior to the individual. The liberty of the individual, however, cannot be
defined in isolation; the various subject positions take place in the context of social relations. Therefore, the democratic rights, which imply equal rights for others, are exercised
collectively. The principle of democracy's plurality derives from the variety of existing
social spaces.

The incompatibilities between the principle of democratic equivalence and that of plurality arise only in the context of a closed system. It is when a space of equivalences is
no longer considered as *one* political space among others, but as the center with its own
unifying principle attempting to reduce all other differences to moments internal to itself,
that the principle of autonomy is eliminated in the name of democracy and the various
social spaces become incompatible. In this manner the logic of totalitarianism can take
root in the very terrain of democracy. In a democratic culture in which power and laws
are immanent and always subject to a process of questioning and revision, in which there
is no longer a transcendent guarantor that will provide an ultimate foundation for the
social, and in which unity will no longer erase social division, totalitarian forms typically
seek to deny internal social division as well as division between the state and society, by
assuming to represent *unitary* people. Thus, instead of the product of hegemonic and
always partial articulation, unity is assumed to be total and forever. This has been the
classical formulation by nation-states.

It is because there is no longer a transcendent order that hegemonic articulations, in
their partiality and contingency, are needed to unify certain political spaces. This leads us

---

11. A debate is ongoing on "essentialism" and "strategic essentialism" in which Žižek, Beverley, as well as Paine and
Douglass have participated and which is relevant here.

to the relationship between democracy and hegemony, and to the disturbing fact that the logic of democracy, which seeks to eliminate subordination and inequality, is per se "incapable of founding a nodal point of any kind around which the social fabric can be reconstituted," and that in the end "[democracy] is not sufficient for the formulation of any hegemonic project" (Laclau and Mouffe 1985:188). The consequences of this are far-reaching.

Confronted with the incompatible demands of opposing interests, what is needed in the end, besides the "democratic equivalence," is "the construction of a new 'common sense' which changes the identity of the different groups" (Laclau and Mouffe 1985:183). That is, the democratic equivalence should ensure that one party's gain also benefits the other, since the elimination of violent antagonism increases both parties' freedom. This "common sense" can only be achieved if the opposing parties do not consider their identities and positions as totally fixed in advance. There can be no libertarian conception of politics as long as one party tries to dominate the other side intellectually or politically by holding onto an ultimate foundation of the social. "Nourishment by the negative" will always be the starting point for such a political project—as negation is the primary step in the creation of a new process.

Works Cited

Aretxaga, B. 2000a. "A Fictional Reality: Paramilitary Death Squads and the Construction of the State." In *Death Squad: The Anthropology of Terror*, ed. J. Sluka. Philadelphia: University of Pennsylvania Press.

———. 2000b. "A Hall of Mirrors: On the Spectral Character of Basque Violence." In *Basque Politics and Nationalism on the Eve of the Millennium*, eds. W. Douglass, C. Urza, L. White, and J. Zulaika. Reno: Center for Basque Studies.

Arrinda Albisu, A. 1965, *Religión Prehistórica de los Vascos*. San Sebastián: Auñamendi.

Barandiaran, J. M. 1972. *Diccionario ilustrado de mitología vasca. Obras Completas*, vol. 1. Bilbao: La Gran Enciclopedia Vasca.

Bateson, G. 1972. *Steps to an Ecology of Mind*. New York: Ballantine Books.

Beverley, J. 1999. *Subalternity and Representation: Arguments in Cultural Theory*. Durham: Duke University Press.

Burke, K. 1966. *Language as Symbolic Action*. Berkeley: University of California Press.

Butler, J., E. Laclau, and S. Žižek. 2000. *Contingency, Hegemony, Universality: Contemporary Dialogues on the Left*. London: Verso.

Erikson, E. H. 1958. *Young Man Luther*. New York: W. W. Norton and Co.

———. 1966. "Ontogeny of Ritualization in Man." In *A Discussion of Ritualization of Behaviour in Animals and Man*, ed. J. S. Huxley, series B, vol. 251. London: Royal Society.

Fisher, R., and W. Ury. 1981. *Getting to Yes: Negotiating Agreement without Giving In.* Boston: Houghton Mifflin.

Freud, S. 1925. "Negation." *International Journal of Psycho-Analysis* 6:367.

Geach, P. T. 1965. "Assertion." *Philosophical Review* 74(4):449–65.

Goenaga, A. 1975. *Uts: La negatividad vasca.* Durango: Leopoldo Zugaza.

Herrero de Miñón, M. 1999. "Qué son y para qué sirven los Derechos Históricos." *RIEV,* 44(2):309–22.

Laclau, E. 1990. *New Reflections on the Revolution of Our Times.* London: Verso.

Laclau, E., and C. Mouffe. 1985. *Hegemony and Socialist Strategy: Towards a Radical Democratic Politics.* London: Verso.

Lafon, R. 1966. "La Particle *bait* en Basque: Ses emplois morphologiques et syntaxiques." *Bulletin de la Societe de Linguistique de Paris* 61:217–48.

Letamendia, F. "Ortzi." 1979. *El no vasco a la reforma.* 2 vols. San Sebastián: Txertoa.

Lévi-Strauss, C. 1963. *Structural Anthropology.* New York: Basic Books.

Michelena, L. 1976. *Fonetica Historica Vasca.* San Sebastián: Seminario Julio de Urquijo.

Núñez, L. C. 1980. *Euskadi sur electoral.* San Sebastián: Ediciones Vascas.

Rappaport, R. A. 1979. *Ecology, Meaning, and Religion.* Richmond: North Atlantic Books.

Rubert de Ventós, X. 2000. *De la identidad a la independencia.* Barcelona: Anagrama.

Ryle, G. 1971. *Collected Papers.* Vol. 2. New York: Barnes and Noble.

Schuchardt, H. 1947. *Primitiae Linguae Vasconum.* Ed. A. Yrigaray. Salamanca: Colegio de la Universidad.

Spivak, G. 1988. "Can the Subaltern Speak?" In *Marxism and the Interpretation of Culture,* eds. C. Nelson and L. Grossberg (Urbana: University of Illinois Press).

Turner, T. S. 1977. "Transformation, Hierarchy and Transcendence: A Reformulation of Van Gennep's Model of the Structure of *Rites de Passage.*" In *Secular Ritual,* eds. S. F. More and B. G. Myerhoff. Assen, Netherlands: Van Gorcum.

Žižek, S. 1993. *Tarrying with the Negative: Kant, Hegel, and the Critique of Ideology.* Durham: Duke University Press.

———. 1997. *The Abyss of Freedom/Ages of the World.* Ann Arbor: University of Michigan.

Zulaika, J. 1987. *Tratado Estetico-Ritual Vasco.* San Sebastián: Baroja.

———. 1988. *Basque Violence: Metaphor and Sacrament.* Reno: University of Nevada Press.

A Basque Referendum: Resolution of Political Conflict or the Promised Land of Error?

WILLIAM A. DOUGLASS and PEDRO IBARRA GÜELL

A. Prolegomena

Our subject, which, *grosso modo,* is the present status and future prospects of the Basque political conflict, is intrinsically a work in progress. Any attempt to freeze its dynamics for the purposes of depiction and analysis is akin to trying to portray the action of a soccer match through the medium of a still photograph. Furthermore, it is our intention to think outside the box, as it were, and to thereby question a political discourse that, through constant repetition by the political actors themselves, their journalistic interlocutors, and their academic interpreters, has become conventional when not downright stale. We suspect, indeed hope, that at least some of our speculation will strike many observers of Basque politics in particular, and of confrontational (even violent) politics within democratic settings in general, as truly provocative.

Our first step along these lines is to challenge the very language of the dialogue and debate concerning Basque politics. For example, in referring to ETA's violence, or for that matter the State's response to it, we will not employ the concept of "terrorism." Nor will we have recourse to the terminology that pervades the mutual accusations of the contending forces, such as "fascist" for the depiction of one's opponent's "antidemocratic" thinking that more often than not merely glosses difference of opinion. In short, we believe that terms such as *terrorist* and *fascist* have been abused and then misused within Basque political discourse to the point of banality. They are currently devoid of any analytical, or even referential, value and are now only capable of closing avenues of genuine inquiry.

Similarly, we will eschew the common journalistic distinction between "nacionalistas" and "no nacionalistas" in reporting Basque politics as both obfuscatory and inaccurate.

Obfuscating because it immediately relegates (Basque) nationalists to that murky realm of the purportedly irrational political radicalism of stateless peoples threatening, with their ethnonationalist claims and demands, the stability of the present world order of constituted states, while somehow elevating their opponents to the status of reasonable universalists.[1] Inaccurate because, in our view, nationalism never exists in a political vacuum. The foils of Basque nationalism were, are, and will be Spanish and French nationalism (in this discussion we will only be dealing with the Basque-versus-Spanish-nationalist dimension of the larger political equation).

Consequently, for our purposes, Basque nationalists are those who advocate Basque political sovereignty—ranging from the present autonomic configuration within the Spanish State to the outright political independence of the Basques. Spanish nationalists are those who oppose that which undermines the national unity of Spain. The latter may include proponents, or at least acceptors, of the present Basque autonomic configuration (seeing it as capable of being accommodated *within* Spanish national unity) to those who would diminish or destroy the present autonomic order in the name of Spain.[2]

It is necessary to qualify and contextualize our subsequent discussion of Basque nationalism. Neither is there the time nor is this the proper space in which to elaborate a comprehensive history of it. For our purposes, a broad-stroke treatment of some of its relevant characteristics and certain salient events will suffice. We recognize, however, that this is an exercise in gross oversimplification.

Finally, a word is in order about the several political parties constitutive of the Basque (democratic) political system. Gerald Brenan (1943) gave the title *The Spanish Labyrinth* to his magisterial treatment of the Spanish Civil War, thereby alerting his English readers to the extreme complexity of Spanish politics. *Labyrinthine* is an appropriate adjective with which to describe the post-Franco Basque political scene. To aid the less-informed voyager to navigate the following arguments, we offer a brief guide.

Since 1979, the three traditional Basque regions of Bizkaia, Gipuzkoa, and Araba constitute Euskadi, one of the seventeen autonomous regions that make up Spain today. The fourth "Spanish Basque" territory, Navarra, opted to become its own region independent of Euskadi. The four Basque territories are referred to collectively as Hegoalde. The overarching term for Hegoalde and Iparralde is Euskal Herria ("Basque Country"). The

---

1. Spaniards are prone to regard the unity of Spain to be a given part of the "natural" order. Like the flag-displaying American who would reject being called a (nasty) nationalist, the loyal Spaniard is simply being a "patriot." Within the Spanish context, there is a particularly sour legacy of the terms *nationalist* and *nationalism* since they were embraced and employed self-referentially by Franco and the Falange Party. This very legacy, of course, enhances the value of such terminology as a rhetorical ploy in the exercise of demonizing (in order to dismiss or even exterminate) one's political opponents.

2. Thus the categories of Basque nationalist and Spanish nationalist need not be discrete and implacably confrontational. A segment of each accepts the present autonomic framework as both beneficial and nonthreatening. It is also not inconceivable that a confirmed Spanish nationalist might view Spain as "better off" without the Basques, just as a committed Basque nationalist can harbor doubts about the wisdom of attaining an independent Basque state that would then be "on its own."

"French Basque" area, Iparralde, remains an integral part of France with minimal regional juridical character and distinctiveness.

Euskadi (as does Navarra) has its own autonomous government, Eusko Jaurlaritza, complete with a president, Parliament, and several ministries. Eusko Jaurlaritza wields considerable control over local (regional) matters, which include most aspects of the economy (including taxation), physical infrastructure (ports, highways, and the like), the educational system, social and cultural programs, and the police force. In foreign affairs Euskadi is represented by Madrid. This means that most of the region's articulation with the European Union is mediated by Spain.[3]

Basque electoral politics are currently dominated by two Spanish national parties and three Basque nationalist ones. The former include the Partido Popular (PP), or Popular Party, that of current Spanish President José María Aznar. It is conservative in its politics and neoliberal in its economics.[4] The PP's main adversary within Spanish national politics is the PSOE, the Spanish Socialist Workers' Party. Under Felipe González, the PSOE was in power for a considerable span of the post-Franco era. The PP and PSOE both contest elections in the Basque Country at all governmental levels—municipal, provincial, and autonomic.

Of the two Spanish nationalist parties, it is the PSOE that has manifested the greater degree of tolerance of Basque nationalist (or at least culturalist) aspirations. A perennial near-gridlock in Basque autonomic politics at the parliamentary level has meant that in the aftermath of elections, in which no one political party has ever gained an absolute majority, it is necessary to negotiate an interparty compromise government. On occasion the PSOE has entered into such coalitions with Basque nationalists; the PP never has. Similarly, the PSOE at times incorporates rhetoric sympathetic to Basque political autonomy into its electioneering; the PP is critical, when not downright condemnatory, of Basque autonomist (i.e., the desire for broader powers within the Spanish political framework), let alone separatist, demands.

Arrayed against the two Spanish nationalist parties are two liberal Basque ones—the PNV (or Basque Nationalist Party) and the EA (Eusko Alkartasuna, or Basque Togetherness)—and (until recently) one leftist one, Batasuna (Oneness). EA resulted from an intraparty squabble within the PNV in the 1980s and is not highly distinguishable from the latter at present. Despite their dodgy history, they tend to work together when the chips are

---

3. It should be noted that the ostensible limits of the arrangement are regularly tested by Eusko Jaurlaritza. It has a Ministry of Foreign Affairs that maintains strong ties with the Basque emigrant diasporas of North and South America, as well as Oceania. Basque presidents, members of Parliament, and ministers frequently travel abroad to conduct "state" business. Eusko Jaurlaritza sends out trade missions, particularly to Latin America. It also maintains a "foreign aid" program in several underdeveloped countries. Similarly, Eusko Jaurlaritza staffs an "embassy" and diplomatic mission in Brussels, partly for their symbolic value and partly for the purpose of furthering Basque interests within those (somewhat limited) circles of the European Union that are configured along regional or ethnic lines rather than the dominant state ones.

4. For some commentators it is the heir to the Falange Party, which was the only legal one under Franco's dictatorship. While many adherents of the PP would reject such a designation, it is somewhat reinforced by the lack of an ultra-conservative party to the right of the PP in post-Franco Spanish politics, at least to date.

down. Batasuna is the most recent incarnation of what began as HB (Herri Bata-suna—The People United) and then became, if briefly, EH (Euskal Herritarrak—Basque Citizens). HB/EH/Batasuna has played a role within Basque politics similar to that of Sinn Fein within those of Northern Ireland. Spanish nationalists, and many Basque ones as well, regard HB/EH/Batasuna as ETA's political arm. At the very least, it has rarely condemned ETA's violence, and indeed frequently justifies and defends it.[5]

The PNV regularly garners the greatest support of any single party in the auto-nomic elections and has been the single most influential force within every Basque gov-ernment formed in the post-Franco period. In the interest of clarity, we will subsequently use the PNV acronym to refer to moderate Basque nationalism and the HB one when referencing its radical-left counterpart/challenger.

B. Basque Nationalism: From Origins Through Franco

Modern Basque nationalism was configured in the city of Bilbao during the last decade of the nineteenth century by the movement's founder, Sabino de Arana y Goiri, with a small group of followers. Key for our purposes, among the many factors informing the effort, were the following:

1. The disappointment (and consequences) of defeat in the recent Carlist Wars that had stripped the Basques of a preexisting modicum of political autonomy assured to them under charters, or *fueros,* dating from at least the Middle Ages. Hence-forth, the Basques were to have the same privileges and responsibilities of every Spanish citizen.
2. An ethnicist concern for the very survival of Basque and the language given a massive in-migration of non-Basque Spaniards seeking employment in the facto-ries of an industrializing Bizkaia, and exacerbated by the belief of some Basques that they were racially superior to the newcomers.
3. A moral concern over the continued viability of (deep-seated) Basque Catholicism in the light of the secular humanism introduced by the socialist doctrines of the working class.
4. The demonstration effect of the several nineteenth-century European nationalist movements and the specific ethnonationalist example within Spain provided by the Catalans.[6]

At the turn of the twentieth century, Arana's political party, the PNV, was contest-ing successfully municipal and provincial elections. By the time of the Spanish Republic of the early and mid-1930s, Basque nationalism had matured into a formidable political force with representation in the Spanish Parliament. When the Spanish Civil War erupted in

---

5. In August 2002, Batasuna, like its predecessor Herri Batasuna, was declared illegal by the Spanish courts. Since it is banned from contesting elections, about 10 percent of the Basque electorate is currently disenfranchised.

6. During the 1880s, Sabino was himself a university student in Barcelona, where he would later publish his Basque grammar.

1936, cutting off the Basque Country from most of the rest of the Republic, PNV leader Jose Antonio Aguirre was elected by a coalition of Basque nationalist, Spanish republican and leftist parties as president of a newly declared Euskadi (de facto in control only of Bizkaia and Gipuzkoa).

For a brief nine months, Euskadi functioned as a state, fielding an army, coining a currency, and issuing passports. Faced with defeat at the hands of Franco's forces, the Basque government organized the evacuation of thousands of refugees and then went into exile. Throughout the Franco years, the Basque government-in-exile became practically synonymous with the PNV. As mortal foes of Franco, and hence the Axis, Aguirre and his circle were enthusiastic supporters of the Allies.

After World War II, Aguirre settled in New York to press the Basque claim to political sovereignty within the forum of a nascent United Nations. It seemed but a matter of time before the internationally ostracized Franco would fall or be removed from power. However, in 1952, and as part of its Cold War strategy, the United States negotiated an agreement with Madrid that established American military bases in Spain. Aguirre's complete faith in the international order had proven to be ill advised.

Basque nationalism was now locked into a waiting game with Francoism in which the time frame and the outcome were far from clear. Over the short term, the PNV/Basque-government-in-exile partnership was reorganized, both in the Basque centers of the diaspora (particularly Latin America) and clandestinely within the Basque homeland itself. Enter ETA.

By 1959, a group within EKIN (the PNV's youth branch) became disillusioned with the party's inactivity and seeming temerity. In the main university students, they were also sympathetic to the other clandestine challengers of the dictatorship—the Spanish Left. The dissidents established ETA (Euzkadi ta Askatasuna or "Basque Homeland and Liberty") and initiated a series of acts (*ekintzak*) that escalated from the circulation of clandestine literature and painting of political graffiti to vandalism and the destruction of public symbols such as monuments. Eventually, ETA would rely upon armed robberies, ransoms, and the exaction of a "revolutionary tax" from wealthy Basque businessmen to fund its activities.

In 1968, ETA received and then dealt out its first fatality. ETA's victim was Melitón Manzanas, the chief Spanish police interrogator in Gipuzkoa and an alleged torturer. Two years later, sixteen defendants were tried for the killing by a military tribunal (in what came to be known as the infamous Burgos Trial), and six received death sentences. In the face of strident international protest, which included personal appeals to Franco by the pope and several heads of state urging clemency, the death sentences were commuted—possibly the first tangible sign of weakening of a dictatorship then entering its twilight years.

In 1973, ETA perpetrated what was without doubt its single most efficacious act. On December 20, Luis Carrero Blanco, Franco's handpicked successor, was assassinated, along with his chauffeur, in a Madrid car bombing. At a stroke, ETA had created a void at the pinnacle of Spanish State power, a condition from which the dictatorship proved to be incapable of recovering. The door was open for Spain's subsequent transition to democracy after Franco's death in 1975.

C. Considering ETA

While we (and most commentators) speak of ETA in monolithic terms, there has actually been considerable tension within its ranks that on occasion has proven capable of producing outright schism. Not surprisingly, the two prominent axes of fissure are goals and tactics. We have mentioned the organization's early socialist sympathies, which means that ETA was embroiled from the outset in a classic Marxist tension between the class and national questions.[7] By 1970, a schism over this issue produced two ETAs—ETA-V, which privileged the national struggle, and ETA-VI, which emphasized the class one. The former continued to espouse the use of violence as the only effective means of producing political concessions by the Spanish State, while it seems fair to say that members of the latter (who were in the large majority) had lost their stomach for it, and their faith in its efficacy as well.

In point of fact, ETA-VI disappeared almost immediately, its members either abandoning political action altogether or passing into the ranks of the Spanish Left (primarily as Trotskyites and Maoists). In 1974, renewed schism within the ranks of ETA-V produced subspecies ETA-m (ETA militar) and ETA-pm (ETA político-militar). The former continued to privilege both the national goal and the use of violence to attain it; the latter believed that the quest for social justice should take precedence over Basque independence and that, without eschewing the possibility of renewed violence as a last resort, participation in the (anticipated) Spanish/Basque democratic political process should be given a try.

Once again the minoritarian hardliners would be the only survivors. Many ETA-pm supporters quickly abandoned the political struggle, while the remainder organized Euskadiko Ezkerra (EE), or the Basque Left, which operated for only a few years in the late 1970s and early 1980s before disbanding. Its remaining dedicated political activists joined the ranks of the PSOE for the most part. In short, the ETA that continues to operate has been forged in the crucibles of both external antipathy/repression and internal dissent. Its members are the hardcore precipitate of an unrelenting process of elimination. Today's ETA is truly hard line in its commitment to *both* Basque independence (defined broadly to include Navarra and Iparralde) *and* violence as the only means to attain it, should the demand for serious negotiations continue to go unheeded.

In contrast to the constituted political parties (Spanish and Basque nationalist) configuring the Basque political system, ETA is as much a concept as it is a political organization (Douglass and Zulaika 1990). Indeed, ETA's status and structure are as shadowy as its actions; and the interpretation of ETA differs greatly depending upon one's position

---

7. The details of the several tendencies within ETA and their tensions during the late 1960s and 1970s are beyond our scope. For fuller treatment see Ibarra Güell 1989.

within (or without, for that matter) the spectrums of the respective Spanish and Basque polities. For the Spanish government and Spanish political parties alike, in virtually all the Spanish media and in most of the international press as well, ETA is depicted as a criminal organization—a police matter to be dealt with solely by the criminal justice system. Similarly, ETA's violence is far from defended or justified by a majority of Basque nationalists (however much Spanish nationalists would like to argue to the contrary). Particularly in recent years, ETA's support within Basque society has eroded palpably.

ETA's "legitimacy"—its claim to political protagonism and its public support—is a complex, mercurial, thorny, and opaque issue that proves most difficult to measure.[8] It seems fair to conclude that during the Franco years ETA commanded considerable admiration (or at least tolerance)—even within non-Basque, Spanish and international circles—as the only counterweight to an oppressive dictatorship. The crowning achievement in that particular confrontation was undoubtedly the assassination of Luis Carrero Blanco, whose passing was lamented by practically no one.

The legitimacy (and support) of ETA's protagonism within Basque politics is further complicated and clouded by its being embedded (and with equal vigor) within two highly contrastive political systems—the one totalitarian (1959–1975), the other democratic (1977 on). At this juncture, perhaps both anomalously and ironically, ETA has existed for slightly longer within the latter context than in the former. It is therefore difficult to see ETA (as some do) as merely a response to totalitarianism, on the one hand, or as particularly amenable to democracy on the other. Rather, ETA is the incarnation of irredentist, radical Basque nationalism arrayed against its Spanish and French counterparts and willing to pay the price in human life that is necessary to secure (impose) its vision (version) of an independent Basque state.[9] In this perspective there really *are* no innocent victims of the conflict because the world is divided into good and evil, allies and enemies. The real enemies are Madrid and Paris, as well as Basque collaborators (traitors) willing to settle for too little or unwilling to join the struggle at all. In this Manichean drama it matters little (to ETA) whether the suppression of Basque nationhood emanates from an autocrat (Franco) or a duly elected democratic leader (González, Aznar).

---

8. The common means of assessing ETA's support are public opinion polls regarding the violence, together with the electoral tally for HB/EH/Batasuna. There are, however, problems inherent in both. Broad segments of the Basque public were (and are) leery of expressing political opinion (in one recent poll no less than 40 percent of the respondents admitted to being fearful of doing so outside of their intimate circles or even at all, Eusko Barometro 2001). Public opinion is also highly time sensitive and vulnerable to (temporary) fluctuations in response to current events. Furthermore, the very wording of the questions is often obfuscating. In the interest of easier tabulation and reducing ambiguity in interpretation, questions regarding complex matters and sentiments are often worded in simplistic, dichotomous fashion. If there is the gain of a certain amount of (forced) clarity, it is offset by respondent ambivalence when forced to answer in absolute terms regarding issues about which they might harbor relativistic feelings. The electoral results are likewise subject to fluctuations in response to recent and current events. It is also unclear whether every vote for HB was necessarily one for ETA. In fact, voting for HB had certain "protest" appeal for several groups, including greens, feminists and punks.

9. It might be noted in this regard that ETA shares the same determination and commitment characterizing the national liberation movements that gave rise to the majority of states warming seats at the United Nations. In short, most states were birthed in adversity and bathed in blood—Spain and France being no exceptions.

In several ways Spain's democratic leaders have been no shrewder than Franco in dealing with ETA (and Basque nationalism in general). While, as we shall see, a few abortive attempts have been made at political negotiation, Madrid's consistent approach to the "problem" of ETA has been to ignore its demands while seeking to exterminate it through both legal and extralegal measures. The latter include torturing detainees (denounced regularly by Amnesty International), harassing prisoners and their families (regarding ETA members, the right of Spanish citizens to be incarcerated in their home region is ignored), and using paramilitary assassination squads (in the 1980s).[10]

A less spectacular, but no less important, effect has been the Spanish State's reticence and foot dragging in the transfer of all powers accorded to Eusko Jaurlaritza by the Statute of Autonomy. Nearly a quarter of a century later, the process, conceived in part to defuse ETA's arguments and appeal, remains incomplete. This failure to act decisively and expeditiously obviously undermined the public relations value of the exercise, while serving as a constant irritation between Spanish and Basque nationalist moderates. Such discontent obviously plays into ETA's propaganda as prima facie evidence of the unreliability and duplicity of the Spanish State.

Finally, we look at the issue of ETA's violence itself. We have noted that the assassination of Carrero Blanco had immediate and profound political consequences. It is equally true, however, that in this regard it was an aberration. For all its gory impact upon its victims *qua* individuals, the effect of the violence upon the system is far more symbolic than instrumental. While ETA employs bellicose rhetoric and sees itself as being at war with the Spanish State, in fact it is incapable of waging it. Although Basque political violence constituted Western Europe's second deadliest conflict during the second half of the twentieth century, it still must be placed in perspective. Over the past four decades, ETA has killed about 800 people, or a mean of 20 deaths annually. The conflict in Ulster claimed roughly 3,200 victims over a quarter of a century, that is, an average of 128 deaths per year. Consequently, the *absolute* mortality rate in the Northern Irish conflict is more than six times greater than in the Basque one. Disparity in their *relative* rates is far greater when we consider the more telescoped time frame of the Ulster troubles and the size of the national populations of Spain and Ulster respectively. In a sense, then, it has been far easier to "normalize" (as in "accommodate") the violence within the Basque/Spanish political system.[11]

---

10. Reference is to GAL (Grupos Antiterroristas de Liberación), which from 1983 to 1987 sent death squads into Iparralde to exterminate alleged ETA operatives and their supporters. In all twenty-seven people were killed. Eventually, GAL was denounced from within and the ensuing investigation implicated several Spanish military and political officials. Minister of the Interior José Barrionuevo was tried and incarcerated, and Socialist President Felipe González was himself investigated. Tellingly, if no less ironically, Barrionuevo was subsequently pardoned and released by González's successor, José María Aznar, of the victorious right-wing Partido Popular. (See Woodworth 2001 for a detailed analysis of GAL.)

11. We might note that Spain experiences approximately 7,500 traffic fatalities and 350–400 homicides annually. It is therefore difficult to argue that, in some instrumental sense, ETA's killings per se constitute sufficient critical mass (violence) so as to force the "system" either to its knees or to the negotiating table.

D. Basque Nationalism in the Post-Franco Era

As noted, the present Spanish democratic political framework emerged during the latter half of the 1970s. From the Basque perspective, the process was punctuated by two critical referenda. In 1977, all Spanish citizens were asked to vote on a draft of a possible Spanish constitution. Believing that the document failed to meet, even minimally, Basque nationalist aspirations and demands, the PNV called upon the Basque electorate to abstain. As a result, the referendum "lost" in Bizkaia, Gipuzkoa, and Araba. The defeat was calculated by subtracting the abstentions from the total number of eligible voters and then adding the "no" votes (of all the ballots actually cast, the "yes" ones were in the majority).

The desire of at least some Spanish nationalists to retain a willing Basque Country within the Spanish fold (and the related aim of ending the violence) produced a new series of political deliberations that resulted in the present autonomic framework. The original notion of accommodating the historic claims of the Basque Country (as well as Catalunya and Galicia—both of which were accorded autonomic status under the Spanish Republic) was expanded to the creation of seventeen autonomous regions within Spain. The idea was actually a ploy by Spanish ultranationalists designed to dilute any new privileges of the three regions by according them to everyone (the operative expression was "coffee for all"). It failed[12] since the cultural and linguistic uniqueness of Basques, Catalans, and Galicians with respect to other Spaniards was acknowledged when they were accorded the special status (and corresponding privileges) of "historic territories."

In 1979, a referendum on a Basque Statute of Autonomy was held in Bizkaia, Gipuzkoa, and Araba, though it was opposed by ETA as not going far enough, and particularly for excluding Navarra. However, the PNV urged approval and the measure passed.

Two of the immediate legacies of the Statute, then, were to create a mandate for Eusko Jaurlaritza while at the same time producing a serious rift within the ranks of Basque nationalism. HB emerged, incarnating the idea that the PNV had sold out to Madrid in the knowledge that it would likely dominate Eusko Jaurlaritza. For radical Basque nationalists, Navarra was a particularly acerbic issue.[13] By the late 1970s, the radicals had formed their MLNV (Movement for Basque National Liberation) front and proposed what came to be known as the KAS Alternative—a series of demands that included the incorporation of Navarra into Euskadi (without consulting the Navarrese)

---

12. This was no small irony, since, in their desire to blunt concessions to the three key regions, Spanish nationalists sowed the seeds and erected the institutions (seventeen autonomic governments) that may result in future ethnonationalist or regionalist challenges to Spanish national unity.

13. The PNV, far from actually relinquishing the claim to Navarra, pursued a gradualist strategy devised to entice the Navarrese to eventually seek union with Euskadi. Indeed, the PNV fielded its (successful) candidate for the presidency in the first autonomic elections from members of its disproportionately small Navarrese wing, and subsequently secured appointments of Navarrese to key ministerial posts as well as to the head rectorship of the nascent Basque university system. Ironically, it would be Karlos Garaikoetxea, first president of Euskadi, who would provoke the subsequent schism in the ranks of the PNV that resulted in EA—a new, yet equally centrist, Basque nationalist party.

and the right of Basques to self-determination. General amnesty was also to be granted to political prisoners (the vast majority of whom were ETA operatives). Meanwhile, HB contested the Basque elections, filling any posts that it might win at the municipal and provincial levels, while refusing to occupy its seats in the Basque Parliament (to underscore that body's presumed illegitimacy).

By the early 1980s, then, Basque nationalism had shaken out into two coalitions. The dominant one (in terms of electoral strength) was the moderate centrists epitomized by the PNV (and later EA); their challengers consisted of the radical left, with HB on the political point. Reference is made, in fact, to two social movements rather than just political parties, strictly speaking. The PNV maintained *batzokiak,* or centers, throughout Euskadi that were as much social as political in their activities (typically they have bars, restaurants, meeting and classroom space, and even athletic facilities). The PNV has labor, youth, and women's groups, and typically holds an annual patriotic rally that doubles as an outdoor excursion attended by thousands of its adherents from throughout the Basque region.

For its part, the radical left has the MLNV, a broad coalition of labor, youth, and cultural groups, as well as HB and a strong link with ETA.

Consequently, throughout the quarter century of post-Franco Spanish democracy, Basque politics has been highly confrontational and largely gridlocked. Two Spanish nationalist political parties remain arrayed against two Basque nationalist social movements. The latter, in turn, contest the turf of Basque nationalism. In the wake of each autonomic election, a new ruling coalition must be cobbled together out of these disparate forces, a process that at times takes months to complete. It is the usual fate of those who end up within to be accused of selling out by those on the outside.

Mention should be made, however, that, despite the mutually antagonistic acerbic rhetoric and their clear political differences, a kind of truce obtains most of the time between the two Basque nationalist forces. Historically, the PNV is more likely to blame the Spanish State than to condemn ETA for the violence. With a few exceptions, ETA has pretty much shied away from targeting the PNV, particular for assassinations. It is also fair to say that, within the ranks of the PNV members hold a wide range of opinions and endorse a variety of actions regarding ETA. Some sympathize with it to the extent of providing shelter to ETA operatives on the run and then assisting them to flee the country. It is equally clear that the PNV and ETA dialogue periodically.

Finally, we note that there have been at least three initiatives since the late 1980s that prefigure the present political climate in Euskadi. In 1988, at the behest of then Basque President Ardanza, a serious attempt was made to bring together all parties to the conflict for negotiations. Called the Table of Ajuria Enea (the name of the Basque president's residence, akin to the White House), both Spanish political parties and the two Basque moderate ones responded (HB refused to participate). A condition for inclusion was that violence cease, which ETA rejected. However, in 1989, ETA declared a temporary ceasefire and entered into negotiations held in Algeria with Spanish government representatives.

While they failed, a precedent now existed both for suspension of the violence and for political negotiation regarding the Basque conflict.[14]

There would not be similar movement for almost a decade. In the interim, positions were hardened, particularly by the accession to Spanish national rule of the PP in 1996.[15]

In response, ETA increased its attacks and broadened its targets beyond the traditional "military" ones (the Spanish police and army) to include Spanish nationalist politicians (particularly members of the PP).

In the mid-1990s, street violence (*kale borroka*) performed by bands of roving (at times hooded) youths disrupted daily life to the degree of calling into question whether the Basque Country was still governable. The targets of these attacks were diverse, but there was concentration upon such symbols of capitalism as banks and ATM machines. Attacking buses, monuments, and other public property was also common. The degree of ETA's direct involvement in the *kale borroka* is unclear,[16] although it obviously reinforces the organization's view that the Basque Country has become ungovernable and will only become manageable again after serious negotiations regarding configuration of a new Basque political framework.

Another phenomenon emerged during the 1990s on the Basque political scene in the guise of various peace movements, some of which have thousands of supporters. The two most prominent are Gesto Por La Paz (Peace Gesture), which demonstrates periodically in favor of unconditional cessation of the violence. The other, Elkarri (Together), concurs in the call for peace, but only as a necessary precondition of negotiation among all parties to the Basque conflict.

In August 1998, a renewed attempt was made to bring the parties to the conflict together. When that initiative was rejected by the two Spanish nationalist parties, a number of organizations and individuals, including all the Basque nationalist parties, trade union representatives, leaders of the peace movements, and the MLVN, met in the Navarrese town of Lizarra (Estella). There they forged a common front committed to working toward bringing Spanish nationalism to the table to negotiate the terms of Basque political self-determination. In September, ETA announced a unilateral ceasefire.[17]

Faced for really the first time in the post-Franco era with a united Basque nationalist front, Spanish nationalism reacted in the most negative terms. The ruling directorate of HB was incarcerated on the charge of publicizing the demands of ETA regarding any political negotiation, and thereby collaborating openly with a criminal organization. Spain's

---

14. Cf. Robert Clark 1990.

15. During his first term in office President Aznar, lacking a clear majority, collaborated with both Catalan and Basque nationalists. When the PP gained an absolute majority in the 2000 elections, Aznar broke off the relationship.

16. It is questionable whether ETA is directly involved in, let alone organizes, this particular form of civil disobedience. It is simply too chaotic and indiscriminate, and hence risky, for an organization whose very survival rests upon its ability to elude sophisticated Basque, Spanish, and international police campaigns. Of greater relevance, however, is the extent to which *kale borroka* serves as a seedbed and training ground for future ETA operatives.

17. Ironically, President Aznar was informed of the move during a press conference in Bogotá. He was in Colombia to urge President Pastrana to negotiate with his country's FARC while offering his services as mediator. When asked by a reporter if ETA's gesture might lead to negotiations with *it*, Aznar's reply was "never."

Minister of the Interior, Jaime Mayor Oreja, pronounced ETA's ceasefire to be a trick designed to buy the beleaguered criminals some breathing space. He vowed to redouble his extermination efforts. When a degree of pressure began to build within Spanish public opinion favoring some kind of talks, the Aznar government agreed to meet with ETA's representatives in Switzerland in May 1999. The encounter lasted but a day—and shortly thereafter ETA's negotiators were arrested in France and deported to Spain.[18] Six months later, ETA rescinded its ceasefire. In doing so it reserved its harshest criticism for the PNV, which it accused of foot dragging and waffling regarding the "understanding" or "spirit" of Lizarra that committed all Basque nationalists to the project of self-determination.

The renewed killings quickly provoked a profound crisis within the Basque political system. On the one hand, after more than a year of peace, the vast majority of Basques were simply unwilling to accept reversion to a status quo ante. ETA and its supporters therefore became even more marginalized within Basque society than they had been as their popularity had waned during the 1990s.[19] On the other hand, the Spanish nationalists not only forged an "Antiterrorist Pact" that committed them to an uncompromising campaign against ETA, but also denounced both the PNV and the Basque government as its collaborators.[20] In short, today the line between Spanish and Basque nationalist is now drawn more sharply than at any time since the Franco years.

When EH (the reincarnation of HB) withdrew its parliamentary support of the ruling Basque nationalist coalition, new elections were scheduled for May 2001. Given the obvious broad-based rejection of the violence, the Spanish nationalist parties believed that they had a chance of winning over an absolute majority of the Basque electorate. For a while the idea was anything but farfetched. It seemed that Jaime Mayor Oreja might actually become the next *lehendakari* (president). As it turned out, the Basque electorate pulled back from that particular brink. While the combined vote for the PP and PSOE reached an all-time high, it did not constitute an absolute majority. The real loser was EH, its support falling drastically to a single-digit level. The voters' repudiation of the violence, as represented by the ultras on both sides, was palpable. In the aftermath of its defeat, EH disbanded and was then reconstituted as the Batasuna political party.

Since the May 2001 election, little movement has occurred on any front. ETA continues with its violent actions. The Spanish State, emboldened by Aznar's close relationship with President George Bush (they have exchanged heads-of-state visits) and the post-9/11 American-led international counterterrorism campaign,[21] continues committed to the

---

18. It was all a bit as if the British had arrested the leaders of Sinn Fein and Gerry Adams while professing a certain willingness (at least for public consumption) to negotiate an end to the Irish conflict.

19. Elsewhere we have discussed in great detail how ETA's violence has proven progressively counterproductive with respect to the party's own aims (Ibarra and Douglass, n.d.). Arguably, the violence has impeded rather than furthered ETA's own project—achieving serious negotiation regarding restructuring of the Basque political system.

20. In March 2002, Aznar refused to receive the leader of the PSOE because the latter was reputed to have simply spoken with Basque President Ibarretxe.

21. In March 2002, the United States froze the assets and bank accounts of twenty-one alleged supporters of ETA, a list presumably supplied by the Spanish State intelligence agencies.

abolition of ETA through police measures.[22] Despite its electoral reversal, Batasuna held the critical balance in the 2002 Basque Parliament and proceeded to block passage of most of Eusko Jaurlaritza's budget until late summer. At that time, and for reasons unrelated to the Basque parliamentary process, Batasuna came under attack in the Spanish Parliament, which initiated steps to delegalize it, alleging that it is an ETA front organization. In the interim, a Spanish judge has suspended Batasuna's rights to function as a political party. These moves further exacerbated tensions between Spanish and Basque nationalists, since the latter regard the hamstringing of Batasuna to be an ominous precedent and a frontal assault against the Basque nationalist movement as a whole.

On September 27, 2002, President Ibarretxe gave an address to the Basque Parliament in which he outlined a Political Proposal for Peaceful Coexistence (between Spain and the Basque Country). In it he proposed that all inhabitants of Euskadi[23] should negotiate the terms of a new social contract that would provide for a partnership of equals (Spaniards *and* Basques), inspired by mutual respect, while sharing a single state structure (Spain). The new formula would be subjected to a referendum of the electorate of Euskadi.

We now turn to the issue of whether such a referendum should be held to resolve the Basque question, and we consider its likely difficulties and possible consequences.

E. Prefiguring a Referendum and Its Possible Outcomes

Within the contemporary rhetoric of the various parties to the Basque conflict, we might discern three hypothetical perspectives regarding its possible resolution:

Scenario One: A Referendum held throughout Spain

Such a referendum would be largely perfunctory and inspired by the view that there is simply no Basque conflict in need of resolution. The degree to which a Basque political system is (and ought to be) configured at all was debated and determined by approbation of the Statute of Autonomy of 1979—end of the story. Any violence that might persist in Euskadi, the thinking goes, is a simple criminal (rather than political) matter to be dealt with by the authorities.

---

22. The wisdom of such an (exclusive) approach may be questioned. Perhaps a lesson is to be found in the recent declarations by Martin van Creveld, an internationally recognized military historian at Hebrew University (Jerusalem), who pronounced that the world's second most powerful army (that of Israel) faces utter demoralization and defeat because it has proven to be incapable of crushing a few hundred terrorists. The problem, according to Creveld, is that "…we have no targets to hit. Ninety-nine percent of everything we have is irrelevant." He believes that "utter defeat" awaits regular armies fighting nationally motivated insurgents (*Daily Telegraph*, March 1, 2002,18). For more than forty years, almost half of them under a dictatorship unconstrained by the scrutiny of and restraints inherent in the democratic process, the Spanish State has proven to be incapable of eliminating its never more than a few hundred violent insurgents.

23. Ibarretxe's proposal remains open to the possible future peaceful union with Euskadi of Navarra and Iparralde, should their electorates so desire.

This view, currently espoused by Spanish nationalists, contends that the Basque "problem" has already been resolved democratically through the approbation/institutionalization of Spanish democracy, in a national referendum on Spain's present constitution. Even accepting the qualified interpretation that it was rejected by the Basques, the argument becomes that within a democratic process the minority is expected to accept the decision of the majority. The subsequent approval of the Statute of Autonomy in 1979 further supports this viewpoint.

This prodemocratic interpretation fails, of course, to acknowledge that the democratic imperative always privileges the possibility of future change in any of its aspects—indeed, modification even of such foundational documents as the very constitutional charters of the system itself.

Logically, then, if even over their objections a future referendum on the Basque question were to be held, proponents of this viewpoint would likely insist that all Spanish voters be included. The argument would be that to exclude most of the Spanish electorate from the process would be tantamount to disenfranchising most Spaniards regarding a decision with profound implications for *their* foundational constitution. Were the referendum to be held at the Spanish national level, its outcome would obviously be a foregone conclusion. In this event, the result, instead of some sort of equitable and ethical one capable of putting to rest political tensions and their associated violence, would easily be interpreted as simply tyranny of the majority. The potential for enhanced (rather than reduced) discontent is clear, particularly if a majority of the electorate of, say, Euskadi approved greater Basque sovereignty.[24]

If we consider the possible consequences and implications of such a referendum, it seems obvious that they are unabashedly unfavorable. Its foreordained outcome would satisfy neither Spanish nor Basque nationalists. The former would have been forced into an exercise that they reject out of hand as demeaning, unnecessary, and incompatible with Spanish national unity. The latter would feel their efforts and aspirations had been terminated in a transparent political charade. In sum, the political legacy of such an exercise would undoubtedly be negative and would lack any redeeming grace for all of the parties.

Scenario Two: A Referendum held exclusively throughout the Basque Country, the language of which was configured exclusively by the Basque nationalist political parties

This alternative envisions political negotiation among the Basque nationalist parties (and particularly the two contending Basque sociopolitical fronts writ large) regarding the details of a possible new configuration of the Basque political system that would include greater sovereignty, up to and including the possibility of an independent Basque state. The results would be put in the form of a referendum limited in some fashion to the Basque electorate.

---

24. In our view such an outcome would be far more likely as a "protest" vote within this scenario than if the referendum were limited to the electorate of Euskadi.

The problems are legion. Such an exercise, even assuming that all Basque parties to the conflict could agree on language and scope (a huge assumption), would be opposed vehemently by Spanish nationalists and the Spanish State. It seems unlikely that the outcome would be recognized by either Spain or the European Union, let alone the United Nations.

Furthermore, under such a scenario, the potential for heightened tensions among the various Basque nationalist forces is enormous. The MLNV front has been on record since the early 1980s of favoring Basque self-determination to be ascertained through a referendum. However, there are immediate definitional issues. In the broad view "Basque" includes Navarra and Iparralde. The ultimate or radical (utopian?) view demands that those regions be included in the future Basque state. Obvious logistical problems, however, beset a referendum on that score, since, by all indications, it would likely receive no more than single-digit support in Iparralde, and possibly in Navarra as well. Thus, even granting the farfetched supposition that the French government and that of Navarra would consent to the referendum process, likelihood of its passage would thereby be greatly reduced.

Assuming that the referendum were limited to the Basque Autonomous Community, a related issue is who would be enfranchised. Would the Spanish civil guard—or, for that matter, Spanish government officials or schoolteachers posted in the area for, say, the previous year—be allowed to vote? What about the worker from Extremadura with two years residence in Bilbao? Conversely, would one need Basque genealogical credentials in addition to residential ones to qualify? In short, considerable bickering would undoubtedly occur over the very enfranchisement of the eligible electorate.

Possibly the greatest challenge of all would be crafting acceptable language. No real precedent or model exists at this time, and it is hard to imagine language that would be acceptable to all factions and interests within Basque nationalist ranks. Writing an appropriate text could well prove even more difficult that actually polling the electorate, however defined.

Again, if we consider the possible consequences and implications in terms of their positive and negative potentiality, the latter would seem to far outweigh the former. The foremost stumbling block is that for ETA to compromise its demands for the Basques' self-determination of their own political future would represent a historic shift. As self-styled possessors and protectors of the Truth, anything short of totalistic, black-and-white, all-or-? language would practically be tantamount to ETA's self-dissolution.

The foregoing question mark is meant to elicit a related issue. Would ETA accept a democratic rejection by the Basque electorate of a totalized referendum on Basque independence? It is at least doubtful. Similarly, were it to pass, but then (as it obviously would) be denounced and finally ignored by the Spanish State, one could envision a dramatic upsurge in ETA's violence. Not only would such an outcome likely enhance ETA's support within Basque society, its claim to represent the militant response of a frustrated Basque political will would also command greater credence. Similarly, the rhetoric of Spanish nationalism, which depicts all Basque nationalists as either perpetrators of violence or at least sympathizers with and collaborators in it, would be equally furthered. In sum, the present political polarization would simply be exacerbated—and probably with greater violent overtones.

There would also be the danger that the ultras within Spanish nationalism would argue that the very celebration of such a referendum constitutes prima facie evidence of the failure of the autonomic process. If the concessions made in the Statue of Autonomy failed to satisfy the demands for Basque sovereignty, what—short of total surrender and acquiescence in (unacceptable) full Basque independence—might? The logical argument might then become that the autonomic process in fatally flawed and must be actively reversed rather than further accommodated. One may envision a heightened campaign by Spanish nationalists to marginalize and trivialize, if not downright dismantle, current Basque autonomic political institutions. The grim possibility also exists that increased ETA violence might be met extralegally with some sort of renewed GAL response.

For all the foregoing negatives, the second scenario does hold out some positives, particularly for moderate Basque nationalists and the Basque government. One might argue that the latter's mandate would be strengthened regardless of the outcome, even if ignored by the Spanish State. Rejection of the referendum by the Basque electorate would solidify the PNV's historic support of the autonomic alternative and the Basque government's implementation of it. Regarding ETA and the MLNV, the argument that the present autonomic arrangement reflects the Basque popular political will would gain in plausibility and stature.

Similarly, if the referendum passed, the PNV's and Eusko Jaurlaritza's case for expanded power both within and outside of the autonomic framework would be greatly enhanced. The argument "there is no Basque political problem" loses credibility.

Scenario Three: A Referendum in Euskadi after all the parties agree to its language

This alternative assumes political negotiation among all parties to the conflict (Spanish and Basque nationalist political parties and social movements alike, including the respective governments) regarding modification of the existing political framework. The electorate of Euskadi would then be asked to adjudge the proposed new political order through a referendum. The alternatives might presumably be (1) to ratify the present Basque autonomic framework, (2) to modestly enhance the political power of the Basque government, but firmly within a Spanish national framework, or (3) to dramatically broaden Basque sovereignty, including the possibility of full Basque political independence outside the orbit of the Spanish national framework (yet most certainly within that of the European Union).

It seems fair to state that this third possibility is the one receiving the greatest attention at present—whether in the form of support from both Basque nationalist coalitions as well as the Basque government (President Ibarretxe has recently underscored the Basques' right to a referendum on self-determination as the only possible exit out of the current political impasse) and the Elkarri peace movement. Even the very stridency with which Spanish nationalists rejected the negotiated-referendum alternative to the status quo privileges this alternative over the other two.

In a sense this scenario best captures the spirit of Ajuria Enea and Lizarra, since both were attempts to realign the disparate forces across the broad continuum of Basque politics in the hope of breaking the impasse. While each summit had a somewhat different cast of players, and notably at the polar extremes (HB was absent at Ajuria Enea but present at Lizarra; the PP and PSOE were present at Ajuria Enea but absent at Lizarra), during its particular conjunctural moment each summit was designed to force concessions from the parties viewed by the others as the recalcitrant obstacles to resolving an otherwise intractable conflict (HB vis-à-vis Ajuria Enea and the PP/PSOE vis-à-vis Lizarra).

Once again the likely implications of such a referendum can be evaluated in both positive and negative terms. From ETA's standpoint, the favorable and unfavorable consequences previously discussed when considering the second scenario would still obtain, even in exacerbated form. Indeed, the involvement of Spanish nationalism and the Spanish State would lend greater legitimation to ETA's political protagonism by providing credence to the argument that its violence had produced (or provoked) the successful negotiation/referendum project. Conversely, should the referendum fail, ETA would have the credible claim that it is Spain (not ETA) that purports to hold ineluctable a Truth (the sanctity of Spanish national unity) that is, on ethical grounds, impervious to change through a flawed democratic process producing political error. In this regard, ETA shares with the ultrareactionary wing of Spanish nationalism the same possible propensity to only respect an electoral outcome that agrees with its self-proclaimed (and "self-evident," if not necessarily to others) political (ethical) Truth.

In short, the referendum, even one whose terms had been prefigured by all parties to the conflict, would still rest precariously upon the probable unwillingness of either ETA or the Spanish ultraright to accept a result unfavorable to its position. The potential is considerable for any outcome's further aggravating, rather than ameliorating, the violent confrontation between these two forces. It is therefore difficult to see how the referendum project can be expected, *as a simple matter of course,* to resolve the issue of the violence.

Of course, in the aftermath of the referendum there would presumably be a considerable new cost in the form of opprobrium for *both* ETA and its Spanish ultra foes. The impatience of the Basque and Spanish publics with the prospects of violence postreferendum (whatever its outcome) would likely become even more palpable. ETA and the ultras would thereby lose some credibility, and the loss would probably result in their being further marginalized within their respective Basque and Spanish nationalist circles.

Paradoxically, such mutual marginalization of the "radicals" might very well prove positive to (indeed even prefigurative of) an eventual "moderate" resolution of the Basque conflict, but such an outcome is by no means preordained.

From the standpoint of Basque nationalists as a whole, either outcome of any referendum is pregnant with both favorable and unfavorable consequences and implications that might be sketched as follows:

1. Unfavorable consequences in the event of defeat: Basque nationalism would have received a body blow, its claim to the support of a majority of the Basque electorate having been damaged severely and possibly irreparably. We need only recall that Québècois nationalism came within 1 percentage point of victory in a referendum that would have likely led to the disintegration of Canada, yet today in the aftermath of (slim) defeat is considerably diminished as a political force even within Quebec. The most charitable spin would suggest that Québècois nationalism is currently in some sort of rebuilding phase.

2. Favorable consequences in the event of defeat: One benefit would be that Basque nationalism would be relieved of the considerable burden of having to "walk the walk." While neither is simple, the nation-building process is arguably far easier than its state-building counterpart. In some respects, the former regards dreams translated into aspiration, while the latter addresses harsh realities and quotidian disappointments. In short, it is far easier to imagine an independent Euskadi than to make it.

   With respect to ETA, it might be speculated that in the wake of democratic political rejection the pressure upon it to cease the violence would increase. The Basque electorate would have, in effect, ratified the status quo, thereby giving a mandate to both the Spanish and the Basque governments to treat ETA's violence exclusively as a criminal matter.

3. Unfavorable consequences in the event of passage: As the converse to the argument in the foregoing point, creating and then situating within the global order an independent Basque state would pose a wide range of daunting new challenges to the Basque political establishment. It is by no means clear that the economy of an independent Basque Country would be able to deliver the same (or better) levels of employment and standard of living as those obtaining at present. Two huge questions marks would be the access of an independent Basque Country to the Spanish market (its traditional mainstay) and the future willingness of capital (international, Spanish, and even Basque) to invest in the fledgling political project.

   The issue of the violence and its resolution must also be confronted. While it is fanciful to think that Navarra and Iparralde would be included in the referendum, it is equally so to believe that ETA (or more accurately some of the factions within it) would relinquish its totalizing demand for the independence of all Basques—including those who oppose Basque independence—in return for a Basque state limited to Bizkaia, Gipuzkoa, and Araba. It is therefore likely that ETA would be emboldened by (while rejecting) the partial victory and would rededicate itself to pursuing a "Basque" future for Navarra and Iparralde as well through its violent protagonism. Under such a scenario, France would likely be drawn into the conflict.

Continued violent activism by ETA in the name of Basque independence would likely also create a "halo effect" that would undermine, or at least complicate, the nascent (diminished) State of Euskadi's attempts to gain full status and recognition within the global political order, while no doubt diminishing its access to international financing agencies and to private investment capital.

4. Favorable consequences in the event of passage: It might be argued that the ineluctable goal of any nationalist movement, irrespective of the costs, is sovereign statehood. Indeed, it is possible to overstate the historical differences *regarding the national question* (as distinct from the social one) between the two Basque nationalist coalitions. Reference is made to the fact that many adherents of the PNV and EA differ with HB and the MLNV more over tactics than the ultimate goal. For such "moderates" the argument is that you take what you can get and then build on it. In a word, regarding Basque independence, they are "gradualists" rather than "confrontationalists," yet both advocate Basque political irredentism. In sum, whether independence conferred limited (albeit greater) or full sovereignty to a part or all of Euskal Herria, it would appeal at some level to *all* Basque nationalists, whatever their individual reservations as to details. In this regard, the outcome would indeed be a historic collective victory for Basque nationalism writ large.

By contrast, the possible results of the referendum's outcome may be considered in the same quadripartite fashion from the perspective of Spanish nationalism:

1. Unfavorable consequences in the event of defeat: ETA would most certainly refuse to respect the outcome and would likely do all that it could to increase its pressure upon the system, probably with an evident sense of desperation of having entered the "all or nothing" or "nothing to lose" end-game phase of the conflict. Over at least the short term, there would likely be lethal consequences for Spanish nationalists.

   For moderate Spanish nationalists there could also be the unfavorable consequence that their moderate Basque nationalist counterparts might be undermined to the degree that they were no longer effective partners in defending the current autonomic framework. The moderates could come under assault from the emboldened ultras within the ranks of the Spanish nationalists regarding any accommodation of the Basque autonomic framework. In short, the argument obtained during the May 2001 election—that a majority of Basques were simply fed up with the Basque nationalist political project—could well be revisited and tested.

2. Favorable consequences in the event of defeat: This would be the obvious (collective) victory of Spanish nationalism writ large, the converse of the consequences of victory for Basque nationalism (scenario two, subsection 4, above).

3. Unfavorable consequences in the event of passage: One immediate development would be a likely split within the ranks of Spanish nationalists, with the ultras

remonstrating with the moderates for political miscalculation in agreeing to the referendum in the first place. Given the past history of, at times, differing postures of the PP and PSOE regarding Basque nationalism, if the referendum were passed the result might well be to exacerbate an already acerbic political rivalry, with both predictable and unpredictable implications for future Spanish national politics.

In the likely event that Navarra were not included in the approved referendum, the issue of its future would remain at least potentially unresolved. Consequently, passage of a limited referendum would not necessarily terminate the conflict between Basque and Spanish nationalism, and it would unlikely (as noted earlier) result in cessation of ETA's violence.

4. Favorable consequences in the event of passage: If defined at least broadly enough to include Navarra, an approved referendum would resolve the Basque question for Spain. While it might leave a sour legacy over the short term, the fait accompli would likely be accommodated relatively quickly, even by the ultras within Spanish nationalism. It would reverse the thrust of the argument currently made by Spanish nationalism writ large, that the Basques' quest for political sovereignty is anachronistic within the wider framework of a European Union whose agenda is to obliterate (rather than erect) state differences. From that perspective, it would likely strike the rest of the EU's states as petty and unacceptable for Spain to refuse to cooperate with the neighboring nascent Basque state. France might well prove the exception under such a scenario over wariness regarding Euskadi's (and ETA's) designs on Iparralde. However, that eventuality might be contained easily by holding a referendum in Iparralde that Basque nationalists would almost certainly lose, and that by a wide margin. Arguably, in the event of, say, an Euskadi that actually included Navarra *and* rejection of inclusion by a large majority of French Basques (particularly given that Iparralde is tiny in both territory and population), it is not inconceivable that ETA would declare a victory and disband. Indeed, such an outcome is not impossible even if Navarra were left out of the referendum, but with the possibility that one day it might choose to hold its own referendum on possible union with Euskadi.

F. The Ibarretxe Proposal

If the foregoing were merely hypothetical configurations of possible referenda, there is a real initiative under active consideration (as of this writing in April 2003). In September 2002 President Ibarretxe proposed that a referendum be voted upon by the electorate of Euskadi (but with the possibility of a similar exercise in Navarra and even Iparralde at some future date). His underlying premise was that the 1979 Statute of Autonomy is essentially flawed and anachronistic; consequently, the relationship between Spain and the Basque Country needs to be reconfigured. His proposal would therefore seek to clarify and establish the Basque citizenry's claim to separate nation status while providing the Basque government with the parameters of a mandate to negotiate a new arrangement in which both parties (Spaniards and Basques) enjoy equal sovereignty and mutual respect, leading eventually to a mutually acceptable new political order. All sectors—political and social—within Basque society would be parties to the negotiations that would determine the referendum's specific language. Great pains would be taken to respect the opinions and civil rights of every inhabitant of the Basque Country. In sum, the proposal is quite similar to the hypothetical scenario three, with the exception that it precludes the full independence of Euskadi and, eventually, Euskal Herria. In most respects it represents a return to the ancient foral regime (as interpreted and perceived by the Basque nationalists). Under the exercise, at the same time that the Basque electorate is asked to formulate and assert its Basque political identity it would be asked to affirm its Spanish one as well.

Advantages: In several fashions, while it obviously requires compromise by both Spanish and Basque nationalist ultras, the Ibarretxe proposal does proffer certain benefits to both sides. For Spanish nationalism, the proposal holds out the prospect of solving the Basque question while excluding the possibility of Basque independence. In short, it respects the integrity of the Spanish State (albeit in modified form). For Basque nationalists, the proposal offers the possibility of greater recognition, if not of full sovereignty, then of at least greater autonomy. It also envisions a symmetrical political relationship of mutually respectful coequals rather than the present asymmetrical one obtaining between a dominant Madrid and a subordinate Eusko Jaurlaritza. From the latter's viewpoint, it would further consolidate its legitimacy as Euskadi's formal political voice. Finally, given the present precarious and beleaguered position of ETA and a disenfranchised Batasuna, there may be a willingness on the part of both to accept the results of such a referendum—particularly if it triumphs. To do otherwise would be to run the risk of flouting the expressed will of a majority of the Basque electorate. Cessation of the violence would presumably be viewed as desirable by moderate Basque and Spanish nationalists alike.

Difficulties: Despite the obvious advantages, the Ibarretxe proposal has fared badly. The Spanish political parties, Aznar's government and ETA alike, have rejected it out of hand. Consequently, should such a referendum be held, it will likely be without the sanction of the Spanish institutions and would probably be declared illegal by them. It would also lack the support of radical Basque nationalism. Consequently, even if it were to pass, it would likely barely do so (55 percent or less), and would therefore constitute yet one more ineffectual, divisive chapter within the book of a gridlocked contemporary Basque political order. Even if such an unendorsed referendum were to pass by a significant majority vote (an unlikely outcome) of the Basque electorate, the victory would remain symbolic. The issues of the Basques' claim to political sovereignty and their right of self-determination would remain unclarified.

In sum, the mere prospect of President Ibarretxe's referendum has further polarized relations between the Basque Country and Madrid, on the one hand, and the two Basque nationalist movements on the other.

G. Final Reflections

We close this section with consideration of the overarching risks incurred by Basque and Spanish nationalism, respectively, if *any* referendum, however configured, is held.

For Basque nationalism passage is far from assured, and the exercise entails a degree of "betting the farm" on the turn of a single card. In the wake of defeat, Spain and the world would likely be less sympathetic to the argument that future referenda were in order. Furthermore, if the referendum passes, but the margin of victory is slim, Spanish nationalists would likely argue that it was inconclusive. Indeed, such an outcome might simply transfer the mantle of political frustration and opposition within Basque politics from the Basque to the Spanish nationalists. The latter might then feel perfectly justified to work against the agenda of a nascent Basque state from within. In short, a close outcome could simply further rigidify political conflict and gridlock within the Basque political system.

Spain's acerbic reaction to the Ibarretxe proposal invokes the specter of a possible counteroffensive. If Ibarretxe seeks, through the referendum process, to broaden his government's mandate by abandoning the Statue of Autonomy in favor of a renegotiated new political framework for the Spanish State, Spanish ultras equally question the viability of the Statute's evident outcome (an Eusko Jaurlaritza disposed to continually test the boundaries of its authority, a gridlocked Basque electorate, and continuation of ETA's violence). They may declare the existing Statute of Autonomy to be a failed project and seek to nullify it authoritatively by means of the state institutions that Spanish nationalism controls, or through a national referendum, that is, one held throughout Spain. Clearly, the referendum process is potentially a double-edged sword.

For Spain and Spanish nationalism, a localized (i.e., limited to Euskadi) referendum on the political future of the Basques is fraught with a related danger that is, in our opinion, so great as to pretty much rule out the possibility that Spain would acquiesce to any Basque referendum. Reference is to the likelihood that to do so for the Basques is to become vulnerable to the demands of other regions for similar treatment. Catalunya is the first that comes to mind. A referendum on Catalan independence would be of far greater territorial, demographic, and economic significance; its passage would truly signal the dismantling of Spain (particularly if Euskadi had already also seceded). Given that Catalan culture has been far more successful than its Basque counterpart in assimilating and accommodating migrants from other parts of Iberia, it is not at all clear that Spanish nationalists would defeat Catalan nationalists in such a referendum.

Is the situation, then, entirely hopeless? While it is difficult to be optimistic, a few developments might be noted that could incite movement toward political compromise. Currently, both Basque and Spanish nationalist ultras are in political trouble. The support within Basque society for ETA's violence has diminished notably, and the electoral defeat of EH in 2001 was so pronounced as to provoke its self-dissolution and reincarnation as Batasuna. Similarly, the reelection prospects of Aznar's PP party have plummeted over his slow response to the disastrous oil spill of the *Prestige* and his full endorsement (despite the opposition of the overwhelming majority of the Spanish public) to the war in Iraq.

Aznar has already announced that he will not run for reelection, and the PP candidates are behind the PSOE ones in the current polls. There is also movement in Catalunya within both socialist and Catalan nationalist circles to propose renegotiation of that region's status within a federal (rather than monarchical) Spain.

Finally, we must consider a certain "weariness" factor. After a century characterized more by mutual confrontation than accommodation, both Spanish and Basque nationalists are tired of the gridlock. Arguably, their respective constituencies feel that Basque as well as Spanish leaders are prone to "play politics" with the stalemate when it suits their purposes. A perceptible and growing cynicism regarding the political process, more than ETA's violence or the state's propaganda regarding it, might ultimately force the Basque and Spanish political establishments alike to consider genuine compromise.

H. Conclusion: Prognostication or Plaintive Postscript?

Rather than sorting through the edifice (or ruin) of the foregoing analysis in order to espouse one or some combination of the various discussed alternatives as the most likely scenario for Basques (and Spaniards) in the configuration of their political futures, we will instead submit the muddle in the Basque referendum model as a challenge to current political thinking that posits radical democratic resolution of particularist conflicts (like the Basque one) within the framework of a universalist ethic. Reference is to the work *Contingency, Hegemony, Democracy: Contemporary Dialogues on the Left* (Butler, Laclau, and Žižek 2000). Ernesto Laclau's treatment of political praxis (2000a and 2000b) is, to our minds, the book's main contribution. For Laclau, radical democracy supposes a state of indefinite tension between contending particularities and a legitimated universality. The latter is not assumed, rather it is configured out of the very terms of the political debate. Each of the subjects (always a particular Subject) contesting hegemony within a political structure seeks to demonstrate the "universal" nature and appeal of its particularist Subject position. Its capacity to convince, that is, to have its discourse understood and apprehended to be global and emancipatory, determines the extent to which it will be perceived as universalizing and legitimated by the other parties to the process. The "universal," then, is itself constituted of empty signifiers that must be capable of being shared by the other particular Subjects.

Ideally, the "universal" is not only greater than the sum of its constituent parts; it is also capable of being embraced by each of them. In principle, then, Laclau's radical democratic model should accommodate resolution, or at least amelioration, of the Spanish/Basque conflict while respecting the respective Subject positions of the two entities. It would certainly be open to the referendum process as possibly the most radical (purest) form of democratic expression, since it entails an entire electorate's deciding on matters affecting its voters' futures.

Nevertheless, it is discouraging to contemplate the weight of conventional thought in even such an innovative thinker as Laclau. While underscoring the importance of subsurface tension to the health of the radical democratic project, he notes:

> If the community…is to be a democratic one, everything turns around the possibility of keeping always open and ultimately undecided the moment of articulation between the particularity of the normative order and the universality of the ethical moment. Any kind of full absorption of the latter by the former can lead only either to totalitarian implication or to the implosion of the community though a proliferation of purely particularistic identities. (This is frequently the atomistic version of the totalitarian dream. The secret links between both is often produced by the defense of religion or ethnic fundamentalism in terms of the right to cultural diversity.) The only democratic society is one which permanently shows the contingency of its own foundations—in our terms, permanently keeps open the gap between the ethical moment and the normative order. (2000a:85–86)

We concur with most of the foregoing and regard it to be an elegant statement of what Laclau calls "democratic identity" (2000b:268). At the same time, we are bothered by the parenthetical material, a critique that would presumably make the entire Basque nationalist project an "atomistic version of the totalitarian dream." Aznar could not have said it better! Laclau, then, seemingly posits the extremely conservative view that the current globalized world order, in which the planet is politically parsed into existing states, is not only defensible but also desirable insofar as they practice democracy. In our view, this reifies the democratic ideality while glossing over its flaws, thereby leaving Basque politics speared upon the twin horns of ETA's tyranny of the minority and PP/PSOE's tyranny of the majority.

Furthermore, our time in the trenches, as it were, causes us to question whether *Contingency, Hegemony, Universality* configures an unbridgeable gap between political reality and ideality—at least to the degree of becoming inapplicable or inefficient in our Basque case. Nor is Judith Butler insensitive to this dilemma. She discusses the relationship between theory and practice, as well as the possible disjuncture between the practitioners of each. Her solution is to suggest that theory should not precede practice nor action follow from theory, rather they should ideally enter into a dynamic dialectic whereby each constantly reconfigures the other (2000: 263–64). We concur, in principle, but remain at least somewhat skeptical. When we refer to ourselves as being "in the trenches," reference is not to our ground zero protagonism in the Basque conflict (though we have each played a minor role in the peace movements), rather we view ourselves as middle level theorists, that is, two thinkers pondering the many quandaries, conundrums, anomalies, and ironies of a specific case in light of current political theorizing. Metaphorically, then, we are situated in the purgatory of doubt somewhere between the often hellish reality of Basque quotidian political life and the celestial realm of political philosophy. Both, in our view, regularly engage in overkill—that of the former being of the emotional (and physical) kind, that of the latter of the didactic variety.

We would assume that by normative order within the democratic system Laclau means their actual structural incarnations as well, as configured by the give-and-take of the democratic process. We are far less certain what he means by the "universal ethic" with which the normative order must remain in a perpetual state of tense indeterminacy if democracy is to survive at all. Laclau defines the universal ethic negatively by rejecting the notion (one he ascribes to Butler) that it is culturally defined and therefore specific (applicable) to only one cultural context (2000b:285). Similarly, he laments that socialist truth seems unattainably utopian "in a world in which dreams of a global human emancipation are rapidly fading away" (2000a:86). We therefore know, at least in part, what the universalist ethic capable of interacting with the normative order within democratic ideality is *not*, while what we remain unsure of is what it *is*. Until matters are further clarified on that score we would withhold judgment regarding it efficacious applicability (both practical and theoretical) to the Basque case. At the same time, pending further developments along these lines of theoretical inquiry, we remain unsure as to whether *Contingency, Hegemony, Universality* represents an intellectual breakthrough or simply one more sophisticated restaging in post-postmodern guise of the age-old debate between the absolutism of Parmenides and the relativism of Heraclitus.

Finally, we question whether the embedding of the radical democratic project within the "global" context is capable of serving as an alternative path to an egalitarian new world order, or whether it is the "playing out" of illusory freedom within the shackled framework of a "globalization" that is in reality a euphemism for a *Pax* (Pox?) *Americana*. If the cost of entry for Basques (and many others) into this new radicalized democratic utopia is the sacrifice of their ethnic persona and political aspirations, we suspect that at least some of them will refuse to pay it. One can then envision the kind of world portrayed in the film *Brazil* in which the "perfect" society includes endemic "normalized" violence—in our specific case of the ETA *or* GAL variety.

Works Cited

Butler, Judith. 2000. "Dynamic Conclusions" in Judith Butler, Ernesto Laclau, and Slavoj Žižek, *Contingency, Hegemony, Universality: Contemporary Dialogues on the Left*. London and New York: Verso. Pp. 263–80.

Butler, Judith, Ernesto Laclau, and Slavoj Žižek. 2000. *Contingency, Hegemony, Universality: Contemporary Dialogues on the Left*. London and New York: Verso.

Clark, Robert P. 1990. *Negotiating with ETA: Obstacles to Peace in the Basque Country, 1975–1988*. Reno: University of Nevada Press.

Douglass, William A., and Joseba Zulaika. 1990. "On the Interpretation of Terrorist Violence: ETA and the Basque Political System," *Comparative Studies in Society and History* 32(2):238–57.

Ibarra Güell, Pedro. 1987. *La evolución estratégica de ETA: De la 'Guerra revolucionaria' (1963) a la negociación (1987)*. Donostia: Kriselu.

Ibarra Güell, Pedro, and William A. Douglass. N.d. "El impacto de ETA sobre el sistema político vasco."

Laclau, Ernesto. 2000a. "Identity and Hegemony: The Role of Universality in the Constitution of Political Logics" in Judith Butler, Ernesto Laclau, and Slavoj Žižek, *Con-

tingency, Hegemony, Universality: Contemporary Dialogues on the Left. London and New York: Verso. Pp. 44–89.

———. 2000b. "Identity and Hegemony: The Role of Universality in the Constitution of Political Logics" in Judith Butler, Ernesto Laclau, and Slavoj Žižek, *Contingency, Hegemony, Universality: Contemporary Dialogues on the Left.* London and New York: Verso. Pp. 182–212.

Woodworth, Paddy. 2001. *Dirty War, Clean Hands: ETA, the GAL and Spanish Democracy.* Cork: Cork University Press.

Out of Their Minds?: On Political Madness in the Basque Country

Begoña Aretxaga

On March 9, 2001, the Basque separatist group ETA (Euskadi Ta Askatasuna—Basque Land and Freedom) killed Iñaki Totorika, a patrol officer in the Basque police force, with a bomb planted on the bottom of his patrol car. It was the first time that this organization targeted a regular officer of the *ertzaintza* (or Basque police), and the news caused another convulsion in the long list of events that had shaken the Basque Country since ETA broke a fourteen-month cease-fire in December 1999. A well-known political journalist characterized this killing as "a qualitative change in terrorism" in an article entitled "Terror a la Deriva" (Terror at a Loss), a title suggesting a violent intervention that had lost direction, a terror out of control and making no sense. The killing of Totorika, said Alberto Surio, the journalist, extended this criminal phenomenon to the social body of the *ertzaintza* and their families and friends. It seems, said the journalist, that analysts in the Basque police had thought about the possibility "of a major bloody action, an indiscriminate massacre [that] performed a kind of kamikaze craziness extending the panic everywhere."[1] The expression came, he wrote, from a high-ranking nationalist in the Basque government. The protagonist of this horror scene, imagined, anticipated, and feared by the high-ranking nationalist, was none other than "a mad ETA ready to burn all bridges, needing to show an image of invincibility." The background of this scenario, Surio wrote, is "a political context marked by a confrontation between institutional and radical nationalism." With this background, the scenario created with the death of the police officer points, said the journalist, to the Basque Nationalist Party (Partido Nacionalista Vasco) that is dominant in the Basque government—as a target of ETA. This last scene is the

---

1. Alberto Surio, "Terror a la Deriva," *Diario Vasco,* Oct. 3, 2001.

epitome of nationalist dystopia—a horror story that ends in self-destruction of the national self. But Iñaki Totorika, the Basque policeman, was not only important because he symbolized the violent opposition between nationalist projects, and signaled a profound rupture within Basque nationalism as a whole, but because his affiliations signaled also the complexities of Basque identity in the Basque Country today. For while Inaki Totorika was a member of the Partido Nacionalista Vasco—that is, a nationalist himself—he was also a member of a Spanish labor union (UGT). It is precisely this kind of ambiguity, in which Basqueness is not defined in a relation of exclusion to Spanishness, that ETA has tried to eliminate since the end of the cease-fire. I will come back to this ambiguity later, but first let me return to the theme of madness in the article I referred above.

During the second half of the 1990s, madness became a prominent trope in the discourse on Basque politics, signaling a fear of unpredictable nationalist or state violence. Here I will restrict my discussion to the figure of madness in relation to nationalist violence. Madness has become the domain of anguished paroxysm after the separatist group ETA called off its cease-fire in December 1999 and initiated an all-out campaign for national sovereignty (called "NOW"), which has reached a toll of about thirty assassinations so far, as well as a high number of arsonist attacks and widespread intimidation performed by radical nationalist youth. Since the break in the cease-fire, the violence of both ETA members and young radicals has targeted members of non-nationalist parties such as the socialist party and the right-wing Partido Popular, the party of the Spanish government, as well as journalists, intellectuals, and artists, who have voiced their disagreement with nationalist violence; it has also intimidated members of the moderate nationalist PNV (dominant in the Basque government). A nationalist town councilor described the situation in this way: "There is a kind of madness now in which everybody could be a victim." From the perspective of the ideological history of ETA, which has been leftist in character, the new campaign of violence does not make sense. Some of those killed had leftist histories and had served prison terms for their activities against Francoism. Others were representatives in small town councils or figures known for favoring a politics of dialogue with ETA rather than military confrontation. This was the case with Ernest Lluch, a professor and former health minister in the socialist government, who had strongly advocated negotiating with ETA as a solution to the ongoing nationalist violence. Negotiation has been a long-lasting demand on the part of radical nationalists, one strongly resisted by the Spanish government. In killing Lluch, ETA appeared to be eliminating a space of mediation necessary for a potential political negotiation. The killing didn't seem to make any sense. The Communiqué signed by all political forces condemned "la sinrazon de ETA" (the unreason of ETA).[2]

The violence unleashed by ETA after the cease-fire is increasingly foreclosing the space of the political as the space of the nation. Furthermore, it has had the seemingly paradoxical effect of reinforcing the anti-nationalist Spanish right-wing in the Basque

---

2. "Todas las Fuerzas Políticas Condenan la Sinrazón de ETA," *El País,* Nov. 22, 2000.

Country as well as debilitating the social fabric that constitutes Basque nationalism at the local level. In other words, rather than *strengthening,* the violence of ETA and of the young activists has the effect of *weakening* nationalist aspirations and the possible political avenues to achieve them. The harder the radical nationalists try to will into being an independent Basque Nation (which they portray as imminent) through discourse and violent action, the lower is the desire for national existence among the Basque population. So bewildering is the new strategy of Basque radicalism, and so much in the profit of the right-wing party in the Spanish government, that it would seem that ETA had been cleverly infiltrated by the Spanish state to provoke the destruction of Basque nationalism once and for all. But this, of course, is nonsensical conspiracy theory. For Juan Jose Ibarretxe, the president of the Basque government and a member of the Partido Nacionalista Vasco (Basque Nationalist Party), "ETA is out of reality."[3] At a loss for other explanations, the most common reaction of commentators is that radical nationalists have gone totally out of their minds. But what exactly is insane about it?

In this paper I would like to reflect on this figure of madness as the categorization of a violent politics that destabilizes epistemological and political certainties. What does it signify? What does it do? And ultimately what *does it say?* In asking this last question I want to suggest a connection between a form of political intervention that is deemed deranged and a kind of knowledge that the political subject of radical nationalism might not want to know. I follow here the lead of a large body of scholarship that, from Freud to Lacan and Nietzsche to Foucault and Derrida, has posed madness as a problem of knowledge: "Madness fascinates," says Foucault, "because it is knowledge...intimate knowledge, which is offered and at the same time evaded" (1988 [1965]: 21–22). Recently Johannes Fabian has made a related argument, namely, that the knowledge produced in the colonial encounter was not the product of rational epistemologies but the outcome of various states of insanity. My goal here is not to discuss the conditions of knowledge production, but rather, to ponder what kind of intimate knowledge a putative political madness might point to, and to wonder what "the strange paths" of this knowledge (Foucault 1988:25) might say about the complicated (dis)articulation of the nation-state form more generally. Let me first discuss, albeit briefly, the political background of this discourse on political madness in the Basque Country.

Background

The trope of madness became prominent during the 1990s at a moment when a Basque police force entered the scene of Basque politics and a moment when a new youth movement emerged as an aggressive nationalist subject. Let me backtrack a little: ETA was born in 1959 as a response to the military regime of Francisco Franco. ETA's ultimate goal was the unification of the French and Spanish Basque provinces into an independent nation-state. Until the death of General Franco in 1975, however, its actions had an essen-

---

3. "Comunicado del Presidente del Gobierno Vasco," *El País,* Nov. 28, 1999.

tially anti-fascist character. Most of ETA's targets during that period were members of the Francoist security forces. After Franco died, Spain undertook a period of democratic reform, called (not very originally) "La Reforma" (the Reform). The Constitution of the current democratic regime was a cornerstone of the Reforma and was endorsed by the Spanish people in a referendum held in 1977 but not approved in the Basque Country with a 70 percent combination of abstention and negative votes for not including "the right to self-determination" for the *nationalidades,* or ethnic regions within the Spanish state—that is Catalunya, the Basque Country, Galiza. What the Constitution envisioned instead was a process of increasing regional autonomy, and so during the following ten years—from 1975 to 1985—the Basque Country developed an array of state-like institutions: a government and parliament, judicial and educational apparatus, its own police force, and even its own revenue system—a unique structure in the whole of Spain. Although this set of administrative and political institutions is subordinated to the Spanish Constitution and legislation, they enjoy a considerable degree of autonomy that for all practical purposes produces state effects in the everyday lives of individuals living in what is officially called "the Autonomous Community of the Basque Country." In this scenario where the goal of an independent Basque Country could be pursued through the conventions of democratic politics—say, by growing popular demand—ETA's armed strategy was expected to stop. But it did not. Its rationale was that the regime had not really changed, and that despite the appearance of democracy there was still a dictatorial state. This rationale was aided by a succession of emergency legislation in the Basque Country, which permitted the infringement of civil and human rights of those accused of having some relationship with Basque terrorism. In spite of the hard blows suffered by radical nationalists during the democratic transition, ETA survived and even attracted the sympathy of a vibrant youth movement, making its appearance during the mid-1980s. By the mid-1990s, a time when ETA was extremely weak after its leadership had been arrested in toto, a new brand of radical nationalist youth become the stars of the Basque political theater. This new breed of nationalist youths became the subject of a new kind of urban insurgency, characterized by arson attacks on public buildings and services as well as police vehicles and rioting, a violence that for the first time systematically transgressed the moral boundaries of local communities by intimidating and attacking both neighbors and peers who opposed their politics, including other nationalists. This new form of violence was largely incomprehensible to the majority of the population, triggering a heightened anxiety about civil confrontation (and more importantly about the radicalization and widening spectrum of nationalist violence). Jabi, one of the leaders of this youth movement who has now disappeared, most likely into the ranks of ETA, explained its logic, which he called "la lógica del tensionamiento" (the logic of tensing): "After 1992, with the leadership of ETA in prison, the enemy says that's it, we have finished with them, and then the enemy springs a trap in the form of a debate about whether the armed struggle is good or bad for the political process, if we should take part in the institutional dynamic… and radical nationalists fell into this trap and it is then that Jarrai [the youth organization] and ETA itself says *that's it,* this is a false debate that only leads us to kill ourselves. And from then on the question for us is that if we are going to have an adequate peace at the end of the war, then what we have to do is to make sure that there *is* war and not to deactivate it. So we redirect that false debate about violence and we begin to put things in their place. This is when we enter into the strategy of *tensionamiento* (tensing), which means that in order for it to be distension (untensing) there needs first to be tension. That is to say we are not going to sign a peace at which we arrive as defeated, so if they want peace what we have to do is to tense the political climate so that then both parts can talk about distensing. The enemy itself takes you to that path." But who is the enemy? Jabi: "During the years of pseudo-democracy certain judicial people, certain journalists, politicians, etc. have positioned themselves in defense of the current political system, in defense of the state, and have shown total disrespect for Basque national aspirations; those people can only be catalogued as enemies."

In September 1998, after indeed a very tense few years, ETA called a cease-fire as part of a new political agreement with moderate nationalists (PNV and EA). The support for radical nationalist politics, which had been steadily diminishing in the last years, changed overnight with the end to violence and higher vote counts in the following elections, with the result that the radical nationalists became the second largest nationalist force, the third largest force after the socialist party in the Basque Country. Their support made possible a nationalist government in the Basque Country that could govern without the support of non-nationalist parties, the Socialist and Popular (which means conservative). This was the first time that such a configuration was actualized in the Basque Government. Overnight, radical nationalism had passed from a socially marginalized force to a central-stage political player, showing that there was substantial support for their leftist political program, that was conditioned on ending violence. Political possibility was in the air, and the cease-fire triggered within the political culture of the Basque Country a new sense of excitement and a general demand for political negotiations with ETA that would make their cease-fire permanent. The Spanish government stalled on the negotiations for a definite peace, using as an excuse that youth violence and intimidation (now labeled "low-intensity terrorism") had not disappeared. Frustrating popular expectations in the Basque Country, the Spanish government seemed to be doing everything possible to indeed deter the peace process.

After more than a year of lack of progress on a possible negotiation between ETA and the Spanish government, ETA called off the cease-fire on December 3, 1999. A goodly number of political organization and analysts blamed the Spanish government for the break of the cease-fire. But shortly thereafter, ETA published a communiqué in which it explained that the cease-fire never had as a goal the attainment of peace but rather wanted the building of a sovereign Basque State. ETA said that that was an opportunity to "change the old juridical-political framework that unfolded from the reform of the dictatorship in favor of a new juridical-political framework based on democracy for the Basque People." ETA contended that they halted the cease-fire because *el proceso* ("the Process") had been stalled by the PNV, their nationalist allies, who had "attempted to modify the very nature of the peace initiative, which was a process of national construction ('construcción del Pueblo [Vasco]') and which they tried to make into a mere process of peace ('un proceso de paz sin contenido')."[4] The time, ETA said, was ripe for the Basque people to act as a de facto sovereign nation by creating a Constituting Sovereign National Assembly elected by all Basque citizens in the provinces divided now between the French and Spanish states. This proposal seemed so far from the current horizon of the politically possible that an elected representative from within the radical nationalist coalition was prompted to say that "ETA was confusing desire with reality."[5]

If ETA confused desire with reality, it was determined to make the logic of desire prevail. After the cease-fire, ETA emerged radicalized in its actions that targeted local politicians, journalists who wrote against ETA, former state officials, and university professors, and finally in March 2000 also targeted the *ertzaintza,* the Basque police who had become —an official legitimate target because, as "a repressive body subject to Spain," it was incessantly repressing Basque society.[6] The common denominator connecting the victims was their association with what ETA called "the Spanish project" (el projecto de España). The logic of "tensing," which was associated with youth street violence during the late 1990s, had now come to find its full dramatic expression in the killings of ETA.

More so than before, ETA's violence was restructuring the semantics of social space around the mutually exclusive categories of Basque and Spanish. What seemed crazy was the ease with which one could be violently expelled from the field of Basqueness into the dangerous field of Spanishness, such that the sphere of Basqueness, strictly identified as a national space—the idealized Basque People, or Euskal Herria—was increasingly being reduced to a hard core of radical nationalists. It was thus the disjunction between a discourse of citizenship, national sovereignty, and institutional building and the violent reduction of those who are supposed to constitute the national community—the disjunction, that is, between a discourse of democracy and a ruthless authoritarian policing of identity, the disjunction, in sum, between an idealized national object and the disappearance of national or even nationalist community—it was these disjunctions that precipitated the worried conclusion that there was no rational explanation, not just in the rhetoric of the mass media but in the concerned commentary of friends and acquaintances. Radical nationalists, in short, were out of their minds.

The Local Semantics of Madness

Let me now come back to my initial question. What defines this state of insanity? At the local level, what is signaled by the figure of madness is a state of incomprehensibility, an impossibility of making sense, a state in fact of epistemological arrest: ETA's actions are

---

4. Declaración de Euskadi Ta Askatasuna (ETA) en la que anuncia el final de la tregua (ETA declaration in which it announced the end of the ceasefire), Nov. 1999. At <http://www.filosofia.org/his/h1999eta.htm>.

5. Milagros Rubio, *Diario Vasco,* Dec. 2, 1999.

6. *El País,* March 31, 2001.

undermining the very goal of national sovereignty it is pursuing. Madness is also associated with a breach in the moral order that bounds local (and political) community, a breach that constitutes a traumatic excess, a violent eruption within the familiar order, of that, which—in its inability to be apprehended—defamiliarizes it. The gasoline bombing of a bookstore that is a symbol of leftist resistance to Francoism, because its owner is a member of the socialist party; the intimidation of an elderly and well-known artist, Agustin Ibarrola, because he expresses his opinion against nationalist violence; the harassment of neighbors who openly disagree with radical nationalists—all of these are examples of this traumatic breach of the moral community that is felt as a state of madness. More than anything, madness figures a fracture in reality, articulated not just in action but also in a discourse that takes the form of a delirium in which radical nationalists figure as the people-nation occupied by foreign enemies. (In the communiqué issued after breaking the cease-fire, ETA asserted its "commitment to defend Euskal Herria—the Basque people-nation—from the oppression, occupation, and attacks by Spain and France.")[7]

I would argue that to pose the question of violence in the Basque Country as a question of madness vis-à-vis democratic (shall we say State) reason is already to perform a particular kind of operation by which this violence is severed from the realm of the political. To oppose violence to the reason of a state of law is to entrench nationalist violence in the space of unreason as well as to open a space of pure confrontation where the possibility of dialogue between these positions is eliminated. Patxo, a high-ranking journalist for the newspaper *El País* who has written widely against nationalist violence and who is now under police protection because of death threats (like some 700 other people) issued by ETA, put it to me very clearly: "To kill a man is to kill a man," he said. "You cannot talk with ETA because they don't listen to reason. The only thing to do is to apply the law!" This is, of course, the position of the Spanish government, which counteracts violence with growing repressive legislation. Yet in the Basque Country the law has an ambiguous character, inscribed as it has been in a long history of police abuse. A politics of violent confrontation feeds into the logic of occupation of radical nationalism, reproducing a spiral of endless violence.

Yet if this critique of the figure of madness as sustaining the violence of state reason allows us to see a configuration of the political as an increasingly polarized and foreclosed space, it does not bring us any closer to the reality animating the seemingly incomprehensible and traumatic violence of ETA and radical youth—the paradox that this form of *willing* the nation into being appears to be destroying it.

---

7. ETA and radical youth have indeed taken the position of sovereignty, as defined by Giorgio Agamben, that is a position of absolute force, of the law as absolute force from which only them are excluded. In two recently issued communiqués, one in January, the other in March of this year, ETA announces that anybody in the Basque police, from officer to those in command are now targets of its violence as well as political forces that position themselves against nationalist violence.

Madness as Secret Knowledge

I want to take seriously this figure of madness, not as a figure organizing a discourse of political exclusion, but instead as a domain of knowledge, one characterized in the words of Lacan by "a fault, a point of rupture in the structure of the external world that finds itself patched over by fantasy" (1993, 45). Part of the knowledge of this political madness signal refers to the violence of the civil war and the thirty-six years of dictatorship, buried but not dead, after the death of Franco and over which silence the birth of the democratic regime was pacted. Mario Onaindia, a member of ETA in the early 1970s and condemned to life in prison by the Francoist regime, thinks of ETA as the only "leftover of Francoism,"[8] while Felipe Gonzalez, former president of the Spanish government, wrote in an article of ETA as a "phantom of the former regime that we have not overcome."[9] If the silence of the civil war and the dictatorship organized the reality of the democracy as a fissureless state of law, what organizes the reality of the current nationalist violence as a madness? By *reality* I do not mean an external reality, but rather what Freud called "psychic reality" and what French psychoanalysts Nicolas Abraham and Maria Torok have defined as "what is rejected, masked, denied precisely as *reality;* it is that which *is* all the more so since it must not be known; in short Reality is defined as a secret." What I intend to do in the rest of the paper is to discuss the Reality, thus understood, that organizes the dynamic of radical nationalist violence. To do so I will focus on what Abraham and Torok would call a phantomatic word, a word that is strange to the vocabulary of the subject, yet one that organizes a stage within which the Reality of the subject is revealed as it is simultaneously disguised. Lacan puts it in similar fashion: "Beginning with an utterance, a game is instituted" (1993, 51). In the Basque nationalist madness, the word, the utterance that institutes the game and organizes the scenario of madness, is the term *cipayo,* which is used by radical nationalists to address the *ertzaintza,* or Basque police.

Let me briefly say that during the 1990s the *ertzaintza* proved itself as a police force that could violently repress demonstrations, gather intelligence, and conduct anti-terrorist operations. In acting against radical nationalists, the *ertzaintza* challenged the latter's ideology that nationalist violence was the result of a conflict between Spain and the Basque Nation, situating that violence squarely within a Basque field. In performing as state (Basque state), the *ertzaintza* had introduced an unbearable ambiguity at the core of the nation imagined by radical nationalists. Moreover this ambiguity was compounded by the fact that this (Basque) "state" was enforcing Spanish law and thus it could be seen as Spanish as well as Basque. It was at this point that the word *cipayo* appeared on the scene. As a metaphor, *cipayo* had the mission, to echo Jim Fernandez, of covering up this ambiguity, best articulated as the problematic character of Basque identity (riddled as it is with unrecognized difference). It was to do so by rigidly redrawing the boundaries of ethnic

---

8. Emilio Alfaro, "Doblemente Condenados," *El País,* Feb. 4, 2001.

9. See Felipe Gonzalez, "Chile, Argentina y las Comisiones de la Verdad," *El País,* April 22, 2001.

identity so that difference was strictly positioned outside the boundaries of national identity and not within it.

Cipayo: The Intolerable Ambiguity of National Being

I first encountered the term *cipayo* in 1993 as part of some graffiti that read "*cipayos asesinos.*" I remember my puzzlement at this word, about which I had no previous knowledge. A friend explained that *cipayos* was the term used by radical nationalists to insult the *ertzaintza. Cipayos,* she said, was the name used some hundred and fifty years ago for the soldiers of Indian origin serving in the British colonial army. The graffiti then began to make sense to me. Radical nationalists in Basque Country were accusing the *ertzaintza* of betrayal of their own people and culture. I was still unaware of the motivations triggering the election of such an obscure word, much less of the train of its complex associations. But after I saw its accusatory presence for the first time, it was suddenly all around me. I realized that radical nationalists habitually referred to the *ertzaintza* as *cipayos* in their everyday speech. Equally interesting was the talk that followed my inquiries about the *ertzaintza.* Friends and acquaintances from different sides of the political spectrum were preoccupied with what they thought to be a growing animosity between radical nationalists supporting the violence of ETA and people supporting the established autonomous institutions. The fabric of social life having been so tightened in the Basque Country now appeared to them to be rupturing, and my interlocutors feared what they called a Balkanization of the Basque Country.

The metaphor/insult *cipayo* appears both as a manifestation of an anxiety about the rupturing of identity and as an attempt to repair it. By attributing a treacherous identity to the Basque police, radical nationalists suggest that the Basque police is not truly Basque. By extension neither are truly Basque those who support the police, particularly those in the Basque Government, which is directly responsible for the actions of the *ertzaintza.* What *cipayo* conceals, though, is the existence of different forms of being Basque that do not coincide with a nationalist project—an alterity of being that lies at the core of Basque identity and that translates into divergent political projects. The term *cipayo* negates that alterity and symptomatizes a profound anxiety about it. What *cipayo* asserts by exclusion, then, is a unity of identity projected into a utopian national community.

Nationalist Ambivalence: The Colony We Never Were

There are two dimensions to the metaphor *cipayo* that I would like to explore further. One is the image associated with the signifier *cipayo,* the other is its predication of betrayal. Here I move to what Jane Gallop has called "a metonymic reading:" "whereas a metaphoric interpretation consists in supplying another signifier which the signifier in the text stands for [e.g. *cipayo* represents *ertzaintza,* in our case] a metonymic interpretation supplies a whole context of associations" (1985:129). Let's then look more carefully into this context. Radical nationalists could, of course, call the Basque police simply traitors, assassins, or *txakurras* (dogs), terms with a long history of use in debasing the Spanish police, for example.[10] Instead of direct accusations or readily available insults that could have equally legitimized violence against the *ertzaintza,* radical nationalists chose the new and obscure term *cipayo.*

What the metaphor *cipayo* does that the other words do not is frame the political conflict in the Basque Country in colonial terms. By associating the *ertzantza* with the figure of *cipayo,* radical nationalists are not only calling them betrayers, they are also positing a relation of analogy between the Basque Country and a colonial context. In so doing they are stating that the relation between the Basque Country and Spain is a colonial one. By virtue of its inherent domination, this colonial relation can only be one of polarized opposition between colonizers and colonized that admits no middle ground. It is as if radical nationalists had reinvented the Battle of Algiers. In the discourse constructed by these associations, the Basque Country remains colonized as long as it stays part of the Spanish state, regardless of how autonomous its "autonomous" institutions might be. Within this logic, the Basque Government and Basque Parliament are not truly Basque as long as they remain part of Spain nor as long as they do not encompass *all* the Basque provinces in France and Spain. It is precisely to reinforce this scenario that a new significant word, *partition,* made its debut in radical nationalist political discourse. ETA issued a communiqué in February 2000 to affirm that "[T]he institutions of the *partition* not only are useless [*muertas*] but they have become a total obstacle to overcome the conflict [between Euskal-Herria and Spain] and as a consequence they constitute the conflict itself."[11] The *ertzaintza* are *cipayos* and not merely betrayers, because they act in the interest of a colonizer state and a state of partition when they suppress the resistance of radical nationalists now figuring as the homogeneous totality of Basque citizens. In this fantasy scenario of a colonial context, violence is legitimized by the identification of "Basque" with "the colonized" who must use any means to get rid of the colonizer, thus legitimizing violence against the Basque police who by virtue of their subordination to the Spanish state are not Basque anymore.

The associative chain described above has led to a political and social situation of increasing polarization, hostility, and violence within the Basque Country from the late 1990s to the present day when those who disagree with the colonial scenario staged by the metaphor *cipayo* are being violently excluded from the sphere of Basque identity. Txema Montero, a former representative in the European Parliament for Herri Batasuna (the radical nationalist party) in 1988, and now outside this organization as a result of his disagreement with the violent politics of ETA, expressed it this way in an interview when he said that "ETA seeks an ideological war between two communities, something that did not exist except in the war of 1936." This colonial scenario emerges at a moment when the meaning of Basqueness is not taken for granted but instead is subject to debate

---

10. See in this respect Zulaika (1988).
11. *El País,* May 11, 2000. The communiqué was issued by ETA at the end of February.

and contestation, a moment of rearticulation of what it means to be Basque in an increasingly globalized world. What the metaphor of *cipayo* conceals is the anxiety and uncertainty that such rearticulation produces. But it could be also that what is really feared and resisted is the dissolution of a fantasmatic unity of national identity bound to occur with the disappearance of an outside enemy. Let me elaborate.

The colonial scenario evoked by the metaphor *cipayo* is also linked by metonymic contiguity to the scenario of an independent nation. This is a scenario where the imaginary unity produced in the anti-colonial struggle might give rise to internal division, as well as struggles of power and violence. (It is telling that the image chosen to accuse the *ertzaintza* was taken from the British/Indian context). One could argue that the actual political reality of the Basque Country, with its autonomous institutions, political parties, and force relations, constitutes a preview of an independent nation. Radical nationalists' violent resistance to this scenario of nationhood by predicating a colonial situation would suggest that a resistance to achieving an independent nation coexists with a desire to form it. Thus if *cipayo* attempts to dispel political ambiguity, it also manifests profound ambivalence toward the national-state form. This would explain why the growing indiscriminate violence of radical nationalists threatens to destroy the very nation it purports to construct. During the last few years this violence has not only considerably damaged the fabric of social relations, it has also played in favor of anti-nationalist parties that have notably risen in recent elections.[12] Let me explore the play of ambiguity and ambivalence a bit further by returning to the treacherous identity that *cipayo* predicates.

National Intimacy

I have said that *cipayo* attempts to dispel the ambiguity of a Basque "state" of being that is simultaneously Spanish. It does so by effecting a move that divests the *ertzaintza* of Basque identity through the accusation of betrayal, and placing this police body and those who support it firmly on the Spanish side of the Basque/Spanish boundary. Once this is done the *ertzaintza* becomes a legitimate target of nationalist violence and the boundaries of national identity are clearly reestablished. And yet, the notion of betrayal that *cipayo* conveys suggest a bond, a (national) intimacy that cannot quite be shaken off. Unlike the invader, or the stranger, the traitor retains a trace of self. The betrayal itself ties betrayer and betrayed together. It makes the betrayer part of the betrayed—a wounded part, to be sure, but still a part that cannot be extricated until the betrayal itself has disappeared or been forgotten. The *cipayo* contains the traumatic residue of an imaginary unity that has not been given up, while it signals the fact that it no longer exists. It is thus an ambivalent object, a threat, and an object of identification. This ambivalence complicates

---

12. The well-known politician and former mayor of Barcelona explicitly affirmed that (Basque) terrorism had benefited the right-wing Partido Popular currently running the government, helping it achieve an absolute majority in the last parliamentary elections. The Partido Popular government is virulently anti-nationalist and has systematically refused to negotiate a cease-fire with ETA. It would seem that radical nationalists are doing everything possible *not* to achieve their goals.

the relation between radical nationalists and the Basque police with an excess of affect that is absent in the relation with the Spanish police. This excess manifests itself in practices of disclosure such as the public uncovering of individual *ertzainas* in towns and villages, their public humiliation and punishment, ritualized attacks, and now assassinations. Such practices of ritualized attacks are de facto policing practices aimed at enforcing the boundaries of ethnic identity by punishing those who are thought to threaten them. In the last year these policing practices have extended to other Basques who openly condemn nationalist violence. These practices suggest a movement in which the trauma of difference within national identity is repeatedly played out without resolution. For radical nationalists the *cipayo* becomes, then, both a threat and a necessity, a despised object that challenges the fantasized unity of the national community and one that by virtue of evoking the Basque state is an object of desire; a despised object that stands in their way of unity and the one that by suggesting a colonial scenario legitimizes nationalist violence.[13]

This ambiguity and ambivalence of a figure that represents at once national betrayal and nationalist identification can be tracked in the metonymic traces contained in the signifier *cipayo,* as it shifts etymologically from a representation of the colonial British army in India *(sipahi)*—to a representation of anti-colonial forces emerging with the mutiny of *sipahies* against the British in 1857—to a representation of the police *(sipai)* in the postcolonial nation.[14] This etymological history points to the ambiguity of the *sipai* as a threat not only to national liberation but to colonial rule as well. This ambiguity is concealed yet present in the use of the Basque *cipayo,* which acts simultaneously as a metonymy of the Basque nation and a metonymy of the hegemony of the Spanish state. Such ambiguity and its concomitant ambivalence manifests itself both in the distrust periodically expressed by the Spanish government in relation to the *ertzaintza,* and in the suspicion voiced by radical nationalists that the *ertzaintza* is infiltrated by the secret services of Spain.[15]

To recapitulate, then, a kind of madness can be seen in the violence of Basque radical nationalists. But this madness is not defined by their belief that they embody the nation-people, or that the moment is ripe to achieve national independence now. That is the fantasy that hides a reality unspeakable and rather shameful, organized around the knowledge that an actual nation-state would necessarily entail the loss of an idealized unified nation as a utopic object of desire. The possibility of such loss engenders a deep ambivalence toward the actual possibility of a nation-state. In fact, never was the Basque Country more in on a fast track to national sovereignty than during the cease-fire, when a coalition of nationalist forces began to orchestrate institutional forms for self-govern-

---

13. Many examples can be found of the ambiguity associated with the Basque police. The latest appeared in the form of a communiqué published by all major newspapers on May 24, 2000. In the communiqué radical nationalist youth accuse the *ertzaintza* of being *cipayos* for arresting a group of youths charged with arsonist activities. The communiqué accuses the *ertzaintza* of acting against the Basque people and being "a servant of Spanish parties," ending by threatening the *ertzaintza* if they stand in the way of national sovereignty (*El País,* May 24, 2000; *Gara,* May 24, 2000).

14. See Metcalf (1964) and Mukherjee (1984) for more extensive etymology of the word *sipahi,* and for a history of the rebellion of 1857 in India.

15. See for example *El Mundo,* Jan. 15, 1997; and *Egin,* Jan. 15, 1998, April 20, 1997, and April 22, 1997.

ment, with wide popular support. The breakdown of the cease-fire and the radicalization of ETA's violence has destroyed those initiatives for self-government and triggered a great deal of hostility and distrust toward a project of national sovereignty. Thus while radical nationalists strive madly indeed to obtain their object of desire—a Basque nation-state—they do everything possible to ensure that it will not happen. Yet I would like to suggest that this political madness unfolding in the Basque Country might be an expression of something intrinsically mad, or maddening, in the nation-state form itself. I'd like to suggest that something is profoundly at odds in this hegemonic form of the modern polity that engenders a constant tension between the logic of nationhood as a utopian, fraternal community sustained by imaginary acts of identification and the practice of statehood as a force of law sustained by multiple relations of power. For radical nationalists throughout the Basque Country, the state effects produced by a variety of institutions and political processes are reified into a subject that is still experienced as a forceful enemy, yet one that also constitutes an object of identification. This identification is best manifested in the sanctioning form of ETA's violence that acts as a sovereign power. And thus we have this ongoing state of paralysis characterized by increasing violence on the part of ETA, young radicals, and the different manifestations of Statehood, which seems geared to perpetuate itself ad infinitum. Why? Because while the nation is an object of desire, radical nationalists can maintain a unified sense of national self as colonized people and can continue to figure as main characters in a story that, to quote Samuel Weber, "is split into a present that never comes full circle and a future that is always oncoming but never fully here" (S. Weber, 16). It is precisely this state of expectation that the electoral poster produced by radical nationalists for the oncoming elections to the Basque government illustrates.

The nation is represented here not as a political community but literally as a body of imaginary identification, a body that in the form of the fetus is anticipated but not quite born yet. Notice that the state/father is absent from this picture—a patent force nowhere to be seen.

Works Cited

Foucault, Michel. 1988 [1965] *Madness and Civilization: A History of Insanity in the Age of Reason.* New York: Random House.

Gallop, Jane. 1985. *Reading Lacan.* Ithaca: Cornell University Press.

Lacan, Jacques. 1993. *The Psychoses.* Book III of *The Seminar of Jacques Lacan 1955–1956.* New York: W.W. Norton and Co.

Metcalf, Thomas. 1964. *Aftermath of Revolt: India, 1857–1870.* Princeton: Princeton.

Mukherjee, Rudrangshu. 1984. *Awadh in Revolt, 1857–1858: A Study of Popular Resistance.* Delhi: Oxford University Press.

Zulaika, Joseba. 1988. *Basque Violence: Metaphor and Sacrament.* Reno: University of Nevada Press.

Self-Fulfilling Prophecy and Unresolved Mourning: Basque Political Violence in the Twenty-First Century

ALFONSO PÉREZ-AGOTE

To Begoña Aretxaga, good scholar and nice friend

Five Questions About Present-Day Basque Nationalism

In this paper I try to provide an answer to five questions.

The first is: During the Francoist period, why was there such a strong process of radicalization in Basque nationalism? Political violence emerged within Basque nationalism, which was not the case with Catalan nationalism, though it too had been subjected to the political pressure of Francoism. My answer is as follows: Because of the production of a traumatized consciousness, owing to the repression of a culture and a language anchored in the affective ties of a generation. This is not an exhaustive answer, given that I have already published many pages on this question. In reality, I formulate and respond to this question so as to be able to formulate my second question, which constitutes the central concern of this paper and to which its title refers.

The second question is this: Why, then, once its causes had disappeared with the establishment of democracy in Spain, does this political violence continue to subsist? My answer is: Because of a prophecy, a false prophecy, which by determining the behavior of the actors becomes a true prophecy for the very actors who had formulated it. The prophecy was this: *Nothing has changed with democracy;* and the actors continue to act as if nothing has changed; the consequences of their behavior are then, for them, the proof that indeed nothing has changed.

The third question: Does Basque nationalism as a whole sustain this prophecy? The present Spanish government, that of the Popular Party, would immediately give an affirmative reply. My reply is going to be in the negative, but it will be a nuanced negative. Because while it is true that there is a tendency toward fusion within Basque nationalism, we also find a tendency toward fission, rupture. And there are also at present two models of social reproduction of nationalism.

The fourth question concerns the nature of these two models. But before anticipating my response, it is worth pausing for a moment to consider what the model of reproduction of Basque nationalism was during the Francoist period. Without entering into the argument over the nature of the Francoist regime (authoritarian regime? dictatorship? fascism?), what is certain in any case is that it produced a situation in which there was exhaustive control[1] of the public space, of the public mechanisms of the reproduction of consciousness (the educational system, political and other associations, means of mass communication...)—all of this to uphold a monolithic, official truth. Oppositional forms of consciousness and their reproduction had to withdraw into the private sphere or were forced underground. Basque nationalism thus became a subculture that was half private and half clandestine, something that some sociologists have termed a *subculture of opposition* or even a *religious subculture of opposition*.[2]

But let us return to the nature of the two present-day models. The model of reproduction of moderate nationalism is one that principally functions in the public sphere,[3] using all the public means of reproduction of consciousness: the educational system, means of mass communication, party political apparatuses, and so forth—that is to say, all the means that democracy has made it possible to use in freedom. On the contrary, the model of reproduction of radical nationalism, because of its prophecy, continues to be (at least in part) the model of reproduction that the Francoist regime produced as an unintended consequence of its political repression. This model also includes the use of public means, though it can take refuge in determinate social places that are not easily accessible to political control when this nationalism finds itself harassed by the various public powers (judicial, police, and even legislative).

Finally, the fifth question refers to the vision, to the definition of the situation, to the prophecy sustained by the model of reproduction of radical nationalism. That extremely negative vision of the situation, upheld since the death of Franco, leads me to think in terms of the category of mourning, with the distinctly sociological dimension that Freud incorporated into that notion: the period of time in which society, through affectively con-

---

1. With the passage of time this control was to become less rigorous, this change becoming noticeable above all at the end of the 1960s and the start of the 1970s.

2. Hank Johnston: "Towards an Explanation of Church Opposition to Authoritarian Regimes: Religio-Oppositional Subcultures in Poland and Catalonia," *Journal for the Scientific Study of Religion* 28 (1989), 493–508; *Tales of Nationalism, Catalonia, 1939–1979* (New Brunswick, N.J., Rutgers University Press, 1991; "Religio-nationalist Subcultures and Soviet Nationalisms: Comparisons and Conceptual Refinements" (1991, duplicated); "Nuevos movimientos sociales y viejos nacionalismos regionales en Espana y la Union Sovietica," in *Los nuevos movimientos sociales de la ideología a la identidad*, eds. Enrique Larana and Joseph Gusfield (Madrid: CIS, 1994), 369–91.

3. Which logically does not mean that it *doesn't* function in the private sphere.

noted social relations, aids a person who has lost a *loved one* (a child, a mother, a husband), a loss that his *libido* refuses to accept, to reestablish his *reality principle,* and to become gradually reincorporated into his *normal everyday life.* So then, in my opinion, the acceptance of the need for political violence in the contemporary Basque Country and the violent behavior in itself constitute the expression of poorly resolved, or unresolved, mourning.

Schematic View of the Model of Reproduction During Francoism

Basque nationalism emerged at the end of the nineteenth century as a response to the processes of industrialization, urban expansion, and immigration that occurred in that period. In the Civil War of 1936–1939, nationalism, in spite of its conservative and Catholic-clerical ideology, aligned itself with the Republicans and the left, against the Catholic right led by Franco.

At the end of the war, the price to be paid for this alignment was the severe persecution, by the Francoist regime, of the Basque language and culture and of the nationalist ideology. We can recall that the street and the school[4] were the areas where the Basque language was subjected to the greatest political repression, as an extended prolongation of the spirit of the wartime and postwar legislation, which attempted to erase Euskara from the public space.[5]

The members of the Nationalist Party who had not fled into exile were reduced to public silence. This party cultivated the belief that the western democracies would manage to overthrow the Francoist regime, but in the early 1950s the blockade of Spain decreed by the United Nations was lifted and relations between the United States and Spain began. This coincided with the entry into the public, political arena of the first generation of those born after the Civil War within the nationalist families. This generation was no longer able to harbor that belief in the western democracies. This also coincided with a strong growth of Basque industry and with the arrival of large groups of immigrants from other parts of Spain.

Within nationalism, within the nationalist families, a generational radicalization took place. This first generation of the postwar period maintained ambivalent relations with their parents. Ambivalent because, on the one hand, they were positive, affective relations with a generation frustrated by the war and humiliated by the regime; but, on the other,

---

4. Speaking in *Euskara* at school was systematically punished.

5. Such as the Order of 18-5-1938 (Official Bulletin of 21-5-1938), which stated: "The morbid exacerbation of some provinces with a regionalist sentiment must be indicated as the origin of registered anomalies, which brought to certain registers a good number of names that are not only expressed in a language different from the official Castilian, but also carry a meaning contrary to the Unity of the Fatherland. Such occurs in the Vascongadas, for example, with the names Iñaki, Kepa, Koldobica, and others that betray an undisputable separatist meaning.... In virtue of this, I set out Article 1: ...in any case, since it concerns Spaniards, the names must be registered in Castilian." Or the Order of 16-5-1940 (Official Bulletin of 30-5-1940), which forbade "the use when denominating trade marks, commercial names, the signs of establishments and any other form of industrial property, of any other language than Castilian," Luis Núñez, *Opresión y defensa en Euskera,* (San Sebastián: Txertoa, 1977), 14–17.

relations of confrontation, given the passive posture of their predecessors in regard, above all, to the Basque language and culture.[6] The most visible and radical part of this first generation was that which founded ETA in the mid 1950s.[7] From in-depth interviews carried out[8] since the late 1980s with historical militants, I have been able to conclude the following:

The experience of fear and frustration suffered by their parents; the ambivalence of those parents in the transmission of symbols and the language; the cultural and political passivity of the older nationalists—these are the factors that produced the generational radicalization. All these aspects modulated the image that these members of the first nationalist generation had of the language, culture, and symbols, as well as the means it was necessary to put into practice to conserve these elements of the Basque cultural and political universe, with the goal of liberating their parents from their humiliation and frustration and achieving their *redemption*. This was, above all at the beginning, a radicalization of the form *and* the means. The youths favored action and, in the end, violence as a means. At first, they did not employ a revolutionary political language: Rather, the ideological content of their first pamphlets is a very primary or defensive nationalism, one that emerges directly from the foundational discourse, united in the final term to a legitimation of a religious type.

In the 1950s and, above all, in the 1960s and 1970s, Basque society was crisscrossed by a dense network of intersubjective and associative relationships, in spite of its high level of industrialization. Even today, it is a society with a high *social capital*.[9] What is happening, as I showed in (1987), is that at present this capital is not constitutive of a subculture of opposition, as it was during the Francoist dictatorship, owing above all to its political control of the public sphere. To constitute a subculture of opposition meant, on the one hand, that the network constituted an interrelationship, a totality, and, on the other, that while it lacked an explicit or intentional finality, it at least constituted a structure of plausibility and maintenance of a collective identity. I have studied the following aspects of this subculture of opposition:

1. The composition and functioning of the *cuadrillas,* or the groups of friends, as well as the political overdetermination—or an absence of this—of friendship, and the issues and subjects that formed the content of intersubjective communication.

---

6. Such inactivity was understandable if one bears in mind the severity of the regime and the experience of the war, contrasted with the hope that they professed.

7. We should recall that violence is a means that has been present in the Basque social and cultural panorama since, at least, the War of the Convention (1808–1814). It is a means that is culturally available in the sense that from that period onward, for one or another reason, within one or another social sector, the youths (primarily) have been called upon to employ it.

8. See two of my works: *La reproducción del nacionalismo: El caso vasco* (Madrid: Centro de Investigaciones Sociologicas—Siglo XXI, 1984) and *El nacionalismo vasco a la salida del franquismo* (Madrid, CIS—Siglo XXI, 1987).

9. R. D. Putnam, *Bowling Alone: The Collapse and Revival in American Community* (New York: Simon & Schuster, 2000).

2. The daily collective ritual of the *poteo*: a repetitive and ritualized visit to a round of bars situated in a few streets in each neighborhood or town. During the Francoist period this was the only ritual in each neighborhood or town in which there was an interrelationship between the groups of friends (age groups) of different ages, from the youngest to the oldest. The changes that have occurred in this ritual explain, or at least express (as we shall see), the changes in the model of reproduction.
3. The dance, sporting, cultural, gastronomic, mountaineering, and other associations, within which a genuine activity of political socialization was concealed.
4. The family and its forms of transmission. And of osmosis, since transmission occurred even though the family wanted, for pragmatic reasons, to hide its culture, its ideology, even its knowledge of the Basque language.
5. The hidden side of the Catholic church. Its institutional dimension facilitated and provided cover for a great part of the associative and, in general, intersubjective activity. This is why I have spoken of a religious subculture of opposition.

This entire ensemble of elements functioned increasingly as a whole. This ensemble of elements constituted a vehicle for the regime, and increased the opposition to it. And all this social life had no public form of expression, which increased its internal pressure. The only public expression of this consciousness occurred with the emergence of a transgressive political violence, carried out by an organization that was also clandestine. This organization, ETA, created at the end of the 1950s, managed to form itself into the expression of this whole subculture of opposition and even into the moral guarantor of its own activities.[10] In (1984 and 1987) I spoke of this violence as a language expressive of the public silence imposed on the whole of this framework. Within the latter, affective adhesion to the violence grew day by day, and this became the most important subject[11] of intersubjective communication.

All this intersubjective framework, all this collective life without public expression, was really a clandestine collective. In the intimate space of the family, within the *cuadrillas,* in the back rooms of the associations or the parishes—through all these channels the critical and nationalist forms of consciousness were transmitted, and through them also came an increase in both affective support for the violence and affective negation of the state apparatuses. The confrontation between these two violences, that of ETA and that of the state, in a society that was demographically small and socially very dense, made it possible for politics and the violence to form a part of everyday life and of personal biographies. Two processes, that of confrontation between the two violences and that of mutual reinforce-

---

10. In response to the question why he justified violent action, a sympathizer told me in the 1980s: "ETA has said so and that's sufficient."

11. It is necessary to bear in mind that the *cuadrillas,* or age groups, to which I have referred are not groups at the highest level of friendly intimacy. Within them, each member has a special relationship with another or other members, which constitutes a more private and intimate relationship. Therefore, when the *cuadrilla* is together, the subjects of communication are not the most intimate, but rather those of a more general interest.

ment between the violence of ETA and its affective social support, produced a rapid increase in the internal pressure of the social network that had been reduced to silence.

This situation broke in 1970 with the Burgos Trial. Starting in that year, all this collective life exploded, came out into the daylight, occupied the street during the moments of social conflict. From then onward, there was a relationship of reinforcement among collective life, occupation of the street, and ETA's violence. And these three interlaced elements confronted the state and its forces of order. This dynamic found its culmination in the big popular mobilizations of the early post-Francoist period, thus making the political rationalization of Basque society very difficult during the period of the Spanish political transition. As a result of these processes a social conglomerate emerged, a sort of social movement whose social denomination in its day was the *izquierda abertzale*,[12] the patriotic left.

The Post-Francoist Period: Toward a Double Model of Reproduction

Following the death of Franco in 1975, the progressive establishment of the so-called State of the Autonomous Communities put certain new elements to work that directly affected the model of reproduction of Basque nationalism.

A first new element was the possibility of forming political parties, and the first consequence of this element was the progressive rupture of the relative unanimity that had been found among the forces of opposition to Francoism; within this rupture, the unanimity of Basque nationalism was also broken. The second consequence of this element (which implied the possibility of political expression in the public sphere by means of the parties) was a rapid decrease of the internal pressure of intersubjective collective life. And this decrease in the internal pressure produced, in turn, a gradual change in the attitudes of the population toward ETA's violence.

With the appearance of the parties a series of new political discourses emerged, many of which denied the need for violence as a means of obtaining political ends; others favored political control over military violence, while some did not modify their vision at all, considering the need for violence to be fully in force.[13] Within nationalism, what was beginning to be called moderate nationalism denied the need for violence, considering that its consequences were negative. Radical nationalism, by contrast, upheld the idea of violence as a suitable means.[14] Nonetheless, it can be said that within nationalism a certain *continuum* of attitudes could be observed, since all the persons within the nationalism movement maintained their affective adhesion. Even those who denied its *political rationality* accepted it affectively. The mechanism that I have termed *the reason/feeling split* made pos-

---

12. Jose Manuel Mata, *El nacionalismo vasco radical: Discurso, organización y expresiones* (Bilbao: Servicio Editorial Universidad del País Vasco, 1993).

13. Of course, in general, the range was broader. I avoid giving the names of parties since their positions varied over time and this would not add anything to the scheme of functioning that I am attempting to show.

14. Naturally, this separation is more complex and suffers from the vicissitudes of time, but what I am trying to provide is an interpretative scheme.

sible a certain continuity of attitudes.[15] The imbrication of the violence in personal life,[16] and the lived experience of the violence through the dense intersubjective network, continued to hold weight. But, in any case, it must be emphasized that the superimposition of different political discourses concerning the violence progressively imposed the need (during the time of elections, for example, but not only then) of choosing between them, and, therefore, of opting to be either in favor or against. Civil society started to become permeable to political discourse. But the process did not stop there; rather it moved toward a rupture in the *continuum* of attitudes.

A second new and fundamental element was the constitution of a new autonomous political power, which meant a progressive liberalization of the culture, the language, the political symbols, and so forth. A very important consequence of this autonomous power was a certain interiorization of the so-called Basque political conflict.[17] The coming into operation of the autonomous political institutions, together with the existence of juridical, administrative, and economic means for cultural and linguistic recovery, brought about a strengthening of this internal dimension of the conflict, concerning what should be done and with what means.

Table 1—Change in the image of the members of ETA among the general population

Image	1978	1989
Patriots	3%	5%
Idealists	35%	18%
Manipulated	33%	11%
Madmen	11%	16%
Criminals	7%	16%
Uncertain/No reply	1%	34%
Total	100%	100%

Source: F. J. Llera, *Los Vascos y la política. El proceso político vasco: Elecciones, partidos, opinión publica y legitimación en el País Vasco* (Bilbao, Servicio Editorial de la Universidad del País Vasco, 1994), 103.

---

15. I most clearly saw this mechanism at work in the course of a long, in-depth interview. The interviewee had been a member of ETA (military violence); later he had been a member of Politico-Military ETA (political control over the violence, which always implies the progressive abandonment of violence); and finally, at the time of the interview, he was a member of Euskadiko Ezkerra (which implied a clear break with the violence). To my question about what he felt when ETA killed a Spanish policeman, his first answer was a rational response, in terms of the important negative consequences that violence brought with it. I asked him time and again about his feelings, and he avoided answering me. After a long time and with his guard down, he did so: "Those actions produce very negative consequences...I know...but when I am alone, I feel glad."

16. Almost all the nationalists whom I interviewed in the 1970s and 1980s had had direct or very close experience with ETA's violence and the violence of the state.

17. Or, more precisely, a strong increase in the internal dimension, since the external dimension, *conflict with Madrid, with the state,* continued to exist. This external dimension even flared up again in the most recent positions of the Spanish parties in the latest general elections of 2001.

From Franco's death up until the present time many changes have taken place that I cannot detail here in full. But I do want to talk about some that imply a strong change in the model of reproduction of nationalism. In the first place, the continuing decline of social acceptance of ETA's violence must be outlined, which can be appreciated in Table 1.[18] But, besides, the penetration of the political discourse and, probably, the fact of the progressive lack of *anti-Basque signification* of the victims has led to a rupture in the *continuum* of attitudes toward the violence, in the sense that a progressive confrontation takes place between two poles that are becoming increasingly irreconcilable: the pole of those who accept violence and that of those who are against it.[19] This means that a deep crisis exists in the mechanism that I have called the *reason/feeling split*. And the progressive disappearance of this mechanism results in two very important consequences. The first is that it introduces an increasingly strong tension within nationalism, and the second is that radical Basque nationalism is progressively losing its capacity for mass mobilization, owing to its loss of positive affective projection, which constitutes an important factor of social mobilization.

From the foregoing analysis, a lack of unanimity within nationalism can be deduced. As I have proposed in another work,[20] Basque nationalism is immersed in two types of tendency: fusion and fission. The first arises from the fact that this is a political nationalism, which means that a certain community of aims is present. But, in addition, the collective memory of Francoism and the social proximity that can imply a certain affective sympathy must be reckoned with; I have already said that this happens with increasing infrequency. This relative community might also arise, at determinate moments, from issues such as the fight for *Euskara* and for the transfer of Basque prisoners to jails closer to their families, or from the agreements between (moderate and radical) nationalist trade unions.

The tendencies toward the fission of nationalism arise, principally, from the political attitudes and positions in relation to the violence: in the first place, the military violence of ETA, about which I have talked; and in the second place, from the firm rejection by moderate nationalism of a new form of violence that has emerged in recent years, the so-called *kale borroka,* or street struggle. This is an urban struggle, but of a new type: urban youth violence, quotidian and not derived from mass mobilization. The *kale borroka,* understood in the new sense I have just mentioned, is a social issue that has arisen in recent years. A certain street violence has always proceeded from the world of radical youth. But this was the final result of a mass action or, at least, of a mass rally. It was a violent ritualization of the end of the rally and, in this sense, it was both a foreseeable action

---

18. Interpretation of this table is not easy, above all due to the fact that the high number of those who do not reply, in the second column, might be related to the social control that is exercised over the response.

19. This does not mean to say that there are no disputes within the pole that does not accept violence. Disputes exist, precisely because of the lack of agreement over the course to follow to put an end to it.

20. Alfonso Pérez-Agote et al., *Institucionalización política y reencantamiento de la socialidad: Las transformaciones en el mundo nacionalista* (Vitoria: Gobierno Vasco, 1999).

and, in principle, unplanned. However, at present another series of events is unfolding: the arrival in a neighborhood or town of a group of youths who, with their faces covered, carry out acts of force, such as the burning of bank cash dispensers, buses, stores, and the like. This is not a spontaneous mass action, but one that is planned, organized, and directed.

In every situation of social tension, an increase implies greater fusion at each of the poles. In this case the elements that imply a tendency to nationalist fission produce a certain integration at the poles that are forming. On the one hand, it implies a certain capacity of coexistence and of political agreement between the moderate nationalist currents and nonnationalist political forces.[21]

On the other hand, the other pole of nationalism—radical nationalism—is integrating itself, becoming more isolated and smaller. For these reasons, a densification is taking place, a fusion of the radical nationalist world. This is the structure of its maintenance, the social-plausibility structure of the prophecy.

The Radical Social World and Its Prophecy

The rupture of the mechanism of the *reason/feeling split* weakens, partly at least, the plausibility of broad mass mobilizations in response to radical slogans. The radical political organizations must undergo a functional change to adapt themselves to the situation: from the attempt to mobilize masses of sympathizers to the formation and instruction of nuclei that are more specialized and more highly motivated by a central doctrine. Social isolation has resulted in the central discourse becoming progressively more self-centered and free of fissures, as corresponds to a feeling of isolation and a lack of dialogic confrontation with others.

To understand how this dynamic of progressive, but not total, social isolation of the radical world has come about, it is necessary to consider the transformations that have occurred in what constituted the dense social texture of the Francoist period, and very specifically the transformations in the world of leisure.

In previous works, I have analyzed how there has been a pronounced decline in the Basque Country of the density of the intersubjective and associative framework, in such a way that the progressive process of privatization of life has acquired a very fast rhythm, in spite of the fact that determinate social phenomena continue to constitute a brake on this process. This refers especially to the periodical recourse taken by the political actors to moments of social indifferentiation, which adopt the form of demonstrations organized from a supposedly nonpartisan position.

We can observe this decline of social density, in relation to the intersubjective world, through a general panorama of a district of Bilbao with a strong tradition of both asso-

---

21. Up until now, moderate nationalism has been able to form a pact with the United Left and the Spanish Socialist Workers Party, with which it has managed to form government coalitions. This has not so far been possible with the Popular Party.

ciation and social and political mobilization. This outline was sketched for me by a *general informer* from that district:

> In the 1960s, the end of Francoism and the start of the democratic transition, there was an associative effervescence, which constituted a vehicle for the strong political mobilizations that took place.

> From the 1980s onward, there was a great increase in the sports associations and those of social volunteers, but the political projection of those that already existed dropped sharply.

> There was a loss of capacity to mobilize the youth by both the Church and the political parties.

Let us see what occurs in relation to the other fundamental support of the intersubjective framework. I am now referring to the *poteo,* that everyday ritual that was territorially delimited and pursued on a daily basis, by means of which *cuadrillas* of friends, under Francoism, kept together and maintained a form of diffuse social cohesion among themselves. This was a ritual that was very important in the 1960s and 1970s. This world of the *cuadrilla* and the ritual of its maintenance was, without any doubt, the plausibility structure of the broad social mobilizations whose start can be dated to the first years of the 1970s and whose zenith was reached in the first years of the post-Francoist period. The ritual was carried out in a central area of each neighborhood or each town and the fundamental, although not the only, communicative subject was the political situation and the violence. The *cuadrilla* is an interpeer group governed by relations of friendship. The particular form that it adopted during the 1960s and 1970s was that of a broad group, involving homogeneous ages, communication in general, and political communication in particular. Since the *cuadrilla* was a group with a homogeneous age, the global dimension (by town or neighborhood) of the ritual was intergenerational, owing to the spatial coincidence of the different *cuadrillas,* each following its own preestablished route, in a single central area of each neighborhood or town.

During the Transition there appears to have been a certain abrupt transformation of this world, as it became divided by political affinities as a result of the rupture of the unanimity of opposition to Francoism. At present, one can talk of a very pronounced decline of this social world of the *cuadrillas* and their collective ritual. So much so that the private world of the social actors is becoming increasingly important and is taking over the time they dedicated to the intersubjective world, which had such great public-political projection. We can establish a series of characteristic transformations:

1. The survival of the ritual and of the old meaning of the *cuadrillas* is found, above all, among the older generations. In the other age groups it has not disappeared but a greater decrease can be noted.
2. The activity of this world has moved toward the weekends. And, for financial reasons, it is more intense at the beginning of the month than at the end. With regard

to the timetables involved, this is becoming shorter. And it is becoming increasingly normal to go straight home after work.

3. The cuadrillas that persist in the ritual are in general ideologically homogeneous. Those of the youth are generally smaller, with a more intimate character and ideologically more plural; the exception to this youth pluralism is found in the cuadrillas of radical nationalist youths.

4. The bars in general are not politically denoted. However, besides those that are social centers for political organizations, there are others with a marked political signification, but there are few of these and they generally belong to the nationalist radical milieu.

5. The communicative subject has generally ceased to be political, and general issues and sports have acquired more importance. It is only "permissible" to talk about politics in the political social centers and in the bars that are politically denoted. By age groups, only the older and the younger generations can find time in everyday life for the morning and evening poteo. Those who have family responsibilities cannot nowadays exercise this ritual.

In any case, the strength and quotidian importance of this form of relationship has declined and it no longer occupies the central place in the social life of each neighborhood and town. The central place is progressively passing over to the private space of each family. If to this we add the progressive importance of excursions during "long weekends" and holidays, and the increase of sporting activities on weekends, we can understand the growing level of privatization of social life.

But, by contrast, new forms of relationship, of sociality, particularly on weekends, are being sketched out among the younger generations above all. In general, in each neighborhood of the city and in each town we find one or several zones of social relationship. These are areas with a high density of bars, which are taken over by the youths, with the other generations finding themselves displaced. In each nucleus there is at least one such area, generally referred to as the "zone." Besides, there are supralocal zones, that is to say, areas that are taken over on weekends (and during the summer festivals) by the youth population from the locality and from other neighborhoods and nearby towns.

We can now compare the two prototypical forms of ritual occupation of the space and time of leisure: the circuit of the *poteo*, which was more characteristic under Francoism, and the zone. The formal differences would be as follows:

1. In the circuit, there is a preestablished succession of short stops at different bars, with a timetable established in an approximate form. In the zone, new stops are made and more time is spent during each.

2. In the circuit, at each stopping place, everything occurs inside the establishment, while in the zone what happens outside is as important as inside. This new usage interacts with the new timetables, which are later, giving rise to conflicts between the hostelry guild and the youths of the "zone" on one side, and the residents of the neighborhood and the town council on the other.

3. From talking, and at times singing, during the *poteo*, there is now talking against background music.
4. The days and timetables have also changed. Now the youths go out basically on Fridays and Saturdays and they do so late at night, remaining in the zone until the early hours of the morning.
5. The collective ritual of the *poteo* was carried out in a central area; the intragenerational relations of each *cuadrilla* coincided with those between *cuadrillas*. In each neighborhood or town there is not one area but several areas, each of which corresponds to a certain age group.
6. "The zone" is a generational space of the youth, where access by members of other generations, by people of other ages, is made socially difficult. Those who are visitors to a zone can change and go to another and in any case usually attend the zones that I have termed supralocal.
7. The subject of communication has changed from politics to not speaking in general about politics.
8. There is a loss of functionality in terms of plausibility structure, of the maintenance of a unanimous, symbolic universe. Besides, in the zone it is principally a question of private relations.
9. New forms of behavior emerge. One of these consists of acquiring, prior to the friendly reunion, alcohol and refreshments at a supermarket, with the aim of consuming the mixture in the street and thus saving money.

We can therefore observe how in social life in general there is a process of privatization, in the sense that new types of social practices and activities are produced that have no political projection, that have nothing to do with a subculture of opposition. We have moved from a period of collective, intergenerational ritual, whose subject of communication was politics, and from an associative world with hidden functions of political socialization, to another in which there is a recovery of the explicit functions of the associations and an explosion in different age groups of leisure practices with a loss of political meaning.

If we now consider the spatial projection of these practices, we can also observe how there is a relevant exception to the previous patterns that also has a spatial projection. These are areas where a social activity is condensed that continues to be intergenerational and that has a direct political projection; its basic communicative subject is politics in general and the political violence in particular. This occurs in the social centers of the radical nationalist organizations and in certain bars that are socially denoted as radical nationalist. In some neighborhoods and towns there is even a street, or a part of a street, or a large street corner in which these establishments are situated, forming what is socially denoted as a zone. But this zone is intergenerational and monochrome from the point of view of political ideology. The interior of radical nationalism constitutes a social world, densely interconnected within and strongly disconnected from the exterior.

The internal connection occurs through age groups, interpeer groups, that are ideologically homogeneous; and, besides, there are social places in which there is intergenerational coexistence and communication. This social world is therefore a network of social control of political ideas and activities. Rather than an organizational control, this is control through generational *and* intergenerational social relations, with a certain hierarchy of age in the latter. With the progressive isolation and the progressive inability to convene great mass mobilizations, this world is becoming increasingly dense, coherent, monolithic, and self-referential, without the ability to contrast opinions. There is thus an increase in its capacity as a network to recruit adepts[22] and to indoctrinate them.[23] And, on the other hand, there is also an increase in its capacity to serve as logistical plausibility for the actions (*kale barroka*) of the youth movement (social centers of radical nationalism and politically denoted bars).

During the political transition, a great part of the social framework of Basque radical nationalism made a very hard-line definition of Basque political life, affirming that nothing was changing. In reality, this was a prophecy that has been self-fulfilling[24] in the exclusive sense that we will now discuss. Basque radical nationalists' definition was that nothing had changed and, therefore, they continued to act as before, some of them practicing violence and others legitimizing it. The consequence of their acts was that the state repressed the violence, persecuting and, as far as possible, imprisoning its authors. The prisoners were common prisoners for the part of society that had accepted the democratic transition. But those who had not accepted that transition continued, and continue, to consider them political prisoners. The intergenerational and closed social world of radical Basque nationalism constitutes a plausibility structure for maintaining these definitions and these attitudes in relation to the violence. A family that has prisoners, common or political (depending on who is speaking about them), among its members is a medium in which these definitions are reproduced. The intergenerational world, concentrated in specific spaces in each neighborhood or town, probably constitutes the intersubjective confirmation of these definitions and attitudes. The school medium might be a medium in which reinforcements are to be found for that vision, but in my view it is not the cause of the appearance of those attitudes and opinions.

Even today we can find in the social world of extreme radical nationalism a definition of the situation in terms that we will now summarize:[25]

1. An oppressive colonial situation by the center, by the state, over the Basque Country persists.
2. The Basque Country today is still in need of a political solution: in general, political independence and, in a more strategic sense, political negotiation with ETA.

---

22. Its capacity to recruit youths is greater in comparison with other political organizations, given the greater politico-religious pluralism that is found in the interpeer youth groups that are not radical. Its power of recruitment and support in relation to social conflicts in general is also greater.

23. Concerning the present concern of Jarrai (radical youth organization) for the educational world and for indoctrination within this world, see *El Correo,* April 1, 1998.

24. Robert K. Merton, *Teoría y estructura sociales* (México: Fondo de Cultura Económica, 1980).

25. Definition of the situation made in a *group discussion* held with qualified members of radical nationalism between forty and fifty years of age.

3. The present-day political institutionalization has done no more than inhibit popular political participation. The political parties bear a particular responsibility for this. The Political Transition has not resolved the problems of the Basque Country.
4. There continues to be a reason for the existence of ETA's violence: the situation of domination of the Basque Country. And, besides, a constant reminder is needed that the situation has not changed.[26]
5. The economic crisis makes evident the capitalist domination suffered by the Basque Country. It is another reason for the violence, above all that of the youth.
6. The street violence of the youth (*kale borroka*) is a direct consequence of the political and economic situation of the Basque Country.

The social world we have described constitutes the plausibility structure of this prophecy and is also its self-fulfillment. In Merton we can observe how a prophecy that fulfils itself is a process by which a false definition of reality becomes a true one through its mere enunciation; so long as it is believed, it induces patterns of behavior that modify reality in such a way that this comes to adapt itself to the first definition, which, now, ceases to be false. In this way Merton believed that he was showing us the most perverse side[27] of social reality. However, we can see here how a false definition manages to obtain a structure of social plausibility, a social medium in which to reproduce itself, in such a way that the actors can continue to believe that it is true. The perversity of social reality is such that it can be pure convention, without any confrontation with *objective reality*. Could one say that the further the definition is from reality, the more closed and lacking in exterior confrontation the plausibility structure must be?[28]

Unresolved Mourning

Mourning: For Freud "intense mourning, reaction to the loss of a loved one, forms part of the same painful state of mind (as melancholy), a loss of interest in the exterior world—insofar as it does not recall the deceased person, the loss of the ability to choose a new amorous object—which would be the equivalent of replacing the one disappeared, and the separation from all activity unconnected with the memory of the loved one."[29] Shortly afterward, Freud wondered about the nature of the labor, the work, the function performed by this period of time in which the individual introduces himself into that situation. "We can describe it (the labor) in the following way: examination of reality has shown that the loved object no longer exists and demands that the libido surrenders all

---

26. Note the paradox: It is necessary to remind people that nothing has changed.

27. Although we should recall that he also enunciated the possibility of prophecies that destroy themselves: definitions that by the mere fact of being enunciated become false definitions of reality.

28. But this reflection should not lead us onto philosophical paths; what we must do is pursue it in sociological terms.

29. S. Freud, "Mourning and Melancholy," in *Obras Completas,* tomo 6 (Madrid: Biblioteca Nueva, 1972), 2092.

of its ties to it. A very natural opposition to this demand arises, since we know that man does not easily relinquish any of the belongings of his libido... The normal thing would be for respect for reality to emerge victorious, but its mandate cannot be carried out immediately and is only achieved in a gradual way...”[30] In a later essay, Freud counterposed the notions of pain, anguish, and mourning: “Pain, then, is the true reaction to the loss of the object, and anguish the true reaction to the danger that such a loss implies and, given a greater displacement, a reaction to the danger of the loss of the object itself.”[31] That is to say that one of the differences existing between pain (internal, psychic pain, since external or physical pain is narcissistic, as the object is the part of our own body that hurts us) and anguish consists of the fact that pain is a reaction to the loss of the object, while anguish might be an anticipation of that loss, since the individual can feel the danger of losing the object (besides, anguish could be a perception of the danger represented by the loss of the object). Freud notes that the breast-feeding child jointly suffers pain and anguish when he finds a strange person instead of his mother. “It seems as if the elements, which will later have to separate, flow together in him. He still cannot differentiate the temporary absence from definitive loss. When he cannot see the maternal figure next to himself, he acts as if he was no longer going to see her, and needs repeated experiences of consolation to come to learn that such disappearances of the mother are followed by a new appearance. The mother helps him to mature this knowledge, which is so important for him, by playing at covering her face in front of him and uncovering it to his great joy.”[32] Further on he distinguishes, with respect to pain, the “other affective reaction to the loss of the object: mourning... Mourning arises under the influence of an examination of reality, which definitively imposes separation from the object, given that the object no longer exists.”[33]

Mourning, viewed in these terms by Freud, has an immediate social translation. Each social group has established a social mechanism for helping a person to resolve mourning. This gives rise to a situation of social exceptionality, in which those closest to the person, or persons, who have a closer relationship in affective terms to the one who has disappeared, form a bubble of exceptionality for him, or for them. This is a question of accompanying them in the transition to a new situation in which the reality principle begins to assert itself. This is a relatively short period since all the actors have interrupted their everyday life and must return to it: to their home, to their work, to their school.

Mourning as a mechanism that the social milieu employs to enable a person to recover the supremacy of their reality principle, varies in space and with time, as the social anthropologists have shown us. Nowadays, we can observe a weakening of certain family and social structures, and with this a weakening of the socially structured

---

30. Ibid.

31. S. Freud, “Inhibition, Symptom and Anguish,” in *Obras Completas*, op. cit., 2882.

32. Ibid., 2881.

33. Ibid.

mechanism of mourning. We can understand how the passage from a rural family to an urban nuclear family and from the latter to more destructured situations (Gehlen) of organization of sexual relations and even of procreation, has also been able to weaken mechanisms such as the anchorage of mourning in relationships of family and neighborhood. Frequently, the state and its forms of support—what we call social security—has been the inhibitor of these mechanisms, and in other cases, perhaps, the state has had to act where these have not functioned for other reasons. Nonetheless, we can also see how, in a progressive way, initiatives emerge from society that functionally replace other weakened structures and the social mechanisms of aid that depended on them. We are frequently witnessing this, in the birth of what we term *self-help* and *hetero-help* associations. We can also test this in the case of mourning. As an example, we can cite the founding, facing the inefficacy of the existing mechanisms of mourning, of a *self-help* association by mothers who had lost a child. We can observe how the different mechanisms of the neighborly and family milieu had failed in their case: *people from outside think that what we are doing is not positive, because it is a case of resolving your problem and that of the others. The milieu sets a time, and once that has passed, they say: "you have to get out; enjoy yourself, forget it...." In general we don't know how to talk about death. And we need to talk a lot, bring everything out into the open. The people around us want everything to return swiftly to normality, for us to lead the same life as before. It costs them an effort to realize that our lives are never going to be the same again.* Other, more distant social resources had also failed: *...the women's association of [a district of Bilbao] set up a group for women suffering from mourning and thus we started to work with [a psychologist, in individual therapy]. [But] we saw that this group was more specific, with its concrete needs. We came to hear of the existence of these self-help groups in other areas, but in the Basque Country there weren't any. There is individual care, but not group therapy, where they understand you: Because when something like that happens to you, you need to talk a lot and you need to be listened to.* The resolution of mourning comes with acceptance of the disappearance of the loved one and the recovery of a normal life: *You have to learn to live with that pain. In the end, you have to reach the point of leaving your child in peace. There are two phases in mourning: You move from incredulity to acceptance, you gradually learn to live, but you miss [the child] and you have to accept the fact that he is not coming back.*[34] The question that arises over the functionality of this association is whether what is really being created is an association for resolving mourning and reintegrating the person into normal life, or whether it is more a case of creating a plausibility structure for not resolving the mourning, with the person in question remaining in a state of rapture. This tension can also be perceived in the statements chosen here. For the time being we cannot know the answer, since it depends on pragmatic results. It remains to be seen whether the mothers who enroll in that association progressively rid themselves of their mourning and rejoin normal life or, on the contrary, they collectively maintain the rapture of each of them regarding the loved one who has now disappeared.

---

34. Taken from *El Correo*, March 9, 2002.

Exile as unresolved mourning: In another earlier work[35] I interpreted "political exile" in terms of mourning. I employed the term in a sense that I called metaphorical but, in any case, this was a strong sense. An exile is someone who involuntarily abandons the place where he lives to go to another. The place he abandons is a space, but it is more than this. It is the space in which he has developed his biography and in which he finds the majority of his affective relationships. What he abandons is his territory, a space that is affectively connoted. From that concrete situation we deduce a series of characteristics whose value is more analytical than descriptive.

1st Characteristic: Exile as Involuntary Emigration

In exile for economic reasons there is a certain dose of willfulness, alongside the involuntariness that is signified by a lack of access to the socially necessary means of subsistence. In the final term, in emigration for political reasons there is a smaller dose of willfulness, in the sense that, in the first place, the emigrant does not see systemic conditions that make his emigration necessary; what he sees is a large dose of willfulness on the part of those who hold power and therefore, in general, he feels himself to be in danger and obliged to emigrate. It must also be said that in general the exile, being an emigrant for political reasons, more clearly sees the culpability of persons than does the emigrant for economic reasons.

2nd Characteristic: The "Mourning" of Exile and the Lack of Meaning

"*In mente,* our parents never departed from there." With these words, an "unconscious exile" defined with perfect clarity the fact that for his parents, who were the ones who in fact went into exile, the territory of arrival held no meaning. His parents were deprived of the possibility of living in the place where (for economic reasons) they were able, and wanted, to live. And that is why emotional meaning remained in the territory from which they departed, and did not arrive where they arrived. Exile was therefore a perpetual mourning, in a metaphorical sense.

In exile, the loss of the object, the territory where one lived, implies a series of objective problems and difficulties that the individual must face in order to live, in order to reorganize his life. It also represents an important loss in subjective terms since when the exile departs, he leaves behind his whole "world." The territory condenses emotionally all the biography, the history, the life, and the affective relations of the individual, which remain behind when the individual leaves it. In emigration of an economic type, all this is also

---

35. Alfonso Pérez-Agote, *Mantener la identidad: Los vascos del Carabelas* (Bilbao: Servicio Editorial Universdiad del País Vasco, 1997). For this work I carried out in Buenos Aires a *discussion group* of Basques exiled because of the Civil War, as a *contrast group* in relation to the social group I was analyzing, the *Basques of Carabelas.* In reality, these were adults whose families had gone into exile with them when they were children. The interviewees defined themselves as "unconscious exiles" in the sense that it was their parents who had been obliged to emigrate for political reasons. They are aged around fifty years; they are married and have children. A large part of their everyday life is spent in the Basque center of Buenos Aires called Laurak Bat.

true, yet the individual has made the decision to go to another territory to do something, to behave in a pragmatic and strategic way, to adapt. In emigration for political reasons, adaptation might come, but in principle the individual encounters difficulties because his desire is to return, which he cannot do; nor can he project his affectivity onto the new territory, to which he arrived. In reality, his emotive object, his territory of origin, has not disappeared, though he has been deprived of it. His sentiment oscillates between the hope of being able to return and the anguish of being unable to do so. Clearly, in exile there is a gradual emergence of a pragmatic spirit, necessary to be able to survive with one's family. Even so, the object in question never disappears and its existence far away is perceived, which generates a deep nostalgia that prevents affective projection onto the new territory. Pain is produced insofar as there has been a depriving of a loved object, and anguish is produced because although the object has not been lost, the danger exists of not seeing it again or, in this case, of not living there again.

In any case, the new territory holds no meaning for the exile, emotively speaking. The emigrant for economic reasons usually encounters this, given his decision to behave practically, in his projection of the original territory onto the present one: Bearing in mind that the territory is the condensation of emotiveness, the territory of arrival holds meaning insofar as it gives him the means to be able to support his family, which could remain in the territory of origin, or else he himself is able to return there when the time arrives. Even so, he has been deprived of his territory, but he can visit it and he nurtures the hope of return.[36]

The more emotive, rather than pragmatic, attitude of their parents meant that the Basque unconscious exiles were inserted from the beginning into a milieu of Basque exiles. For this reason, this generation of those who arrived as children inherited from this family and social milieu a sense of a territory of origin as well as a deficit of meaning of the land of arrival; as we will see, they never came to feel themselves Argentinian. But generations pass, each one playing a different role in the process of reproduction of the collective identity, and changing the very nature of it. The children of these unconscious exiles inherited a certain problem of identity, but they were born in Argentina and, besides feeling Basque, they feel Argentinian. A growing exogamy (although slowed down by the dense Basque social milieu) of the new generations leads them, in spite of everything, to be members of the Basque collective in Argentina.

The clear identity facet in this lack of identification with the territory is that our interviewees have never felt Argentinian and, nonetheless, all their family, or the most important part, is in Argentina and all their life unfolds in Argentina. This gives rise to interesting consequences, as we shall see, in the world of these exiles: a dramatic identity, a syndrome of impossible return, and a deep ambivalence in the transmission of their world to their descendants.

---

36. Let us suppose that in other cultures the idea can be found of emigrating with no intention of returning. In our culture this would not appear as normal, but in any case this question exceeds our aims here.

3rd Characteristic: Social Plausibility of the Meaning of Euskadi

For the interviewees, meaning continued to be held by the Basque territory, to which they could not accede and to which, for reasons that we shall see, they cannot now, in practical terms, return to live. The maintenance of the meaning of something so distant makes it necessary to construct and maintain a plausibility structure: That continuous sense of privation must be upheld socially in a different territory whose solicitations have nothing to do with the lost territory.

In Argentina, land of immigration, we find many *collectives* with more or less established collective identities. Some of them have centers where the associates from the same geographic origin maintain their old collective identity. The unconscious exiles interviewed used the Basque center in Buenos Aires, Laurak Bat, to maintain their identification with the lost territory. One of them expressed this very clearly:

"We have lived in Argentina in Basque centers. That is what you must understand.… Everything that surrounds us is Argentinian, apart from the few hours we spend in the Basque center. This is our home. Here is where we meet and here we are really Basques and we think…Take note! We always think as Basques. But here is where we realize ourselves."

4th Characteristic: Problematic Identity and the Syndrome of Impossible Return

Basque identity centered on the home region of Euskadi, was experienced dramatically by the interviewees, the children of Basque exiles. On the one hand, they were persons who were well situated socially and professionally, that is to say, persons with a well-established reality principle. But this pragmatic behavior contrasted with their emotive-territorial dimension, which made them think and feel daily that their true place in the world was in Euskadi. In their everyday life they reproduced this meaning in that closed world of the Basque center. But not only was there this split between their pragmatic professional world centered on Argentina and their emotive world. The split was greater still because even their emotive world was split on the inside: their origin, their territory, their childhood, their political affect lay in Euskadi, while their children, their friends, their closest affects were at the moment in Argentina. This multiple split was lived as a drama: They themselves termed it as such. Their deepest wish was to return, but they knew they could not do so since it would mean leaving their livelihood and, above all, their closest and most familiar relationships and affects: They desired an impossible return.

5th Characteristic: The Problematic Transmission of a Problematic Identity

The generation of the children of the interviewees had been born in Argentina. They had received from their parents the idea of being Basques, and they had been introduced by their parents into the Basque social milieu, the plausibility structure that in this case was the "Laurak Bat" Basque association of Buenos Aires. They had received an identity whose center was problematic, but, as their own parents recognized, the Argentinean character of their identity had become very strong within them.

Their parents perceived that they were making the collective identity of their children problematic. Family osmosis and the pretensions of the father or of both parents, together with the social milieu in which they spent part of their everyday leisure time, led them to the adoption of a Basque identity; their birth, their daily life, and a great part of their affectivity led them toward an Argentinian identity that, in itself, was incompatible with Basque identity, by way of belonging to the Basque collective of Argentina. Their belonging to the Basque collective of Argentina was even fomented by their parents. But did the children fail to perceive that their parents considered Basque identity and Argentinian identity to be incompatible, because this is how it was for them? Their parents preached love for Argentina but they presented a certain demand that they all be Basques, which in the code of their parents was not clearly compatible.

6th Characteristic: Basque Political Identity

The lack of meaning and, above all, the lack of *political* meaning that Argentina had for the interviewees, the children of exiles, had as the other side of the coin the conservation of a Basque political identity, with reference to Euskadi. Exile is separation from one's own territory, for which reason the political destiny of that territory is what interests the exile, and more so because the exile owes his situation to political reasons and depends (or at least depended at the origin of his situation, on the political conditions of the territory he abandoned. And in that sense, the interviewees (the children of exiles) considered the Basque government to be "their" government and believed that it should take an interest in their problems.

The political vision of these unconscious exiles (the interviewees) was not linked to the concrete, everyday practice of the politics of Euskadi, and hence their vision of politics was utopian in the strictly etymological sense of the term, that is to say, it was not conditioned by the concrete situation, by the place, with what this implies in terms of limitation. They lacked a sense of what was feasible; theirs was a pure nationalism based on the consideration that for them nothing had changed politically since the end of the Civil War. They knew that the political situation *had* changed following the death of Franco; that therefore for political reasons they could return to Euskadi, and for affective reasons they wanted to do so; but other affects and reasons held them in Argentina. They said that they would appreciate a gesture from the Basque government, one facilitating their return, although they knew they would be unable to accept it.[37]

The Meaning of Today's Violence: Another Case of Unresolved Mourning

Following the death of Franco, an absolutely peaceful process of transition to democracy took place in Spain in general and in Euskadi in particular. This implied, of course, that none of the significant political and social sectors managed to obtain the totality of their

---

37. In fact, they requested this of the president of the Basque government on the first visit he made to Buenos Aires.

aims. Obviously the maximalist positions were those that felt the greatest frustration. From the most radical positions of Basque nationalism the transition was interpreted in terms of the nonexistence of a *rupture* with the previous political regime. Blood had not been shed in the process; the so-called new system had taken no reprisals against the armed forces and the state security forces, which had been the support of the hard-line policies of the previous regime; in Euskadi, advantage had not been taken of the situation to obtain political independence. This vision in terms of the absence of rupture produced frustration, to varying degrees, depending on the degree of radicality of the political positions. Among the radicals who had recognized that armed struggle was not necessary, and even among those who favored political control over military violence, which de facto meant the progressive disappearance of the latter, frustration was produced, which can be summed up in that slogan on flyers that were posted on all the streets and in all the towns of the Basque Country: *Berrogei urte ta gero hau (forty years for this)*. But, little by little, the frustration of these sectors was to become a passion for party politics. Nonetheless, in certain social and political sectors a greater frustration was produced, such that they continued thinking that the violence still was because in a deep sense nothing had changed. The progressive split in the social conglomerate called the *izquierda abertzale* (the patriotic left) developed from disagreement not so much over the ends as over the means to achieve them. Whether or not ETA's violence was pertinent became a fundamental line of division. For a long time, however, the memory of Francoism, the collective and biographical memory of the harshness of that regime and the meaning that ETA's violence had while it lasted, produced the continuum of attitudes to which I have referred. Whoever was not in agreement for political reasons had, nonetheless, sympathy, a feeling of affective adhesion, in relation to the violent actions of ETA. This ambiguity implied by the continuum of attitudes was maintained by a mechanism denominated the "reason/sentiment split." And it is now time to recall that the progressive loss of efficacy undergone by this mechanism has led to the present situation of a sharp rupture of the continuum of attitudes toward the violence.

The social sector that has continued to accept ETA's violence has been catalyzed by a political organization that at different times has been denominated *Herri Batasuna, Euskal Herritarrok,* and *Batasuna.* In my opinion, the political vote for this organization is the best sociological indicator of the magnitude of this social sector, given that opinion surveys cannot be reliable on this point, above all if we bear in mind the great social (as well as political) control existing on the expression of opinions concerning violence; more so since the collapse of the reason/sentiment split. And, besides, it must be borne in mind that this vote is also the indicator that is used socially (by the social actors) to establish the magnitude of adhesion to the violence. This social sector is what we have denominated radical Basque nationalism and is that which has undergone the process of progressive isolation and progressive self-reference in its discourse that I have talked of.

This social sector continues in a situation of mourning, given that it has not resolved this. It has not accepted the disappearance of the object, it (still?) does not permit the reality principle to work, nor does it permit a return to normal everyday life. The question that immediately arises is whether that object, whose disappearance is not accepted, is a loved object. And, going still further, there is the question of what that object really is.

A first manner of responding to these questions is as follows. The object is a political regime, defined by the actors themselves in terms of *dictatorship,* of a *situation of colonial oppression.* The object is not loved in itself, but instead because it produces a situation of legitimacy for the violence. It means that, at least up to a certain point, the violence has become an end; it is no longer only a means. The violence would be the loved object.

This mechanism of unresolved mourning does not, obviously, attempt to explain the total complexity of the social phenomenon of acceptance of the violence, but it does enable us to see how any social institution can maintain itself even after the motives that led to its emergence have disappeared. Marx, in *Das Kapital,* distinguished between the model that explained the maintenance and the reproduction of the capitalist form of production, and that other model that explains the historical appearance of the elements that intervene in this model. In sum, it is a question of distinguishing between the model of birth, or the foundational model, and the model of reproduction and change.

That world, increasingly isolated, denser, and increasingly self-referential, constitutes a plausibility structure for the maintenance of mourning, for the nonresolution of mourning. That is why radical nationalist Basques are only able to talk among themselves, and that is why they cannot enter into a normalized (political) life.

Part III

POST 9/11

How to Live with Catastrophes?

SLAVOJ ŽIŽEK

The repulsive anti-intellectualist relatives whom one cannot always avoid during holidays, often attack me with common provocations like "What could you as a philosopher tell me about the cup of coffee I am just tasting?" However, once, when a thrifty relative of mine brought my son a *Kinder Surprise* egg and then asked me with a patronizing ironic smile, "So, what would be your philosophical comment on this egg?," he got the surprise of his lifetime—a detailed long answer.

Kinder Surprise, one of the most popular chocolate products on sale all around Central Europe, are empty eggshells made of chocolate and wrapped up in lively-colored paper; after one unwraps the egg and cracks the chocolate shell open, one finds in it a small plastic toy (or small parts from which a toy can be assembled). A child who buys this chocolate egg often nervously unwraps it and just breaks the chocolate, not bothering to eat it, worrying only about the toy in the center—is such a chocolate-lover not a perfect case of Lacan's motto "I love you, but, inexplicably, I love something in you more than yourself, and, therefore, I destroy you"? And, effectively, is this toy not *l'objet petit a* at its purest, the small object filling in the central void of our desire, the hidden treasure, *agalma,* in the center of the thing we desire?

This material ("real") void in the center, of course, stands for the structural ("formal") gap on account of which no product is "really *that,*" no product lives up to the expectation it creates. In other words, the small plastic toy is not simply different than chocolate (the product we bought); while materially different, it fills in the gap in the chocolate itself, that is, it is on the same surface as the chocolate. As we know already from Marx, commodity is a mysterious entity full of theological caprices, a particular object satisfying a particular need, but at the same time the promise of "something more," of an unfathomable enjoyment whose true location is fantasy—and all publicity addresses this fantasmatic space ("If you drink X, it will not be just a drink, but also…"). And the plastic toy is the result of a risky strategy to directly materialize, render visible, this mysterious excess: "If you eat our chocolate, you will not just eat a chocolate, but also…have a (totally useless) plastic toy." The *Kinder* egg thus provides the formula for all the products that promise "more" ("buy a DVD player and get 5 DVDs for free," or, in an even more direct form, more of the same—"buy this toothpaste and get one third more for free"), not to mention the standard trick with the Coke bottle ("look on the inside of the metal cap and you may find that you are the winner of one of the prizes, from another free Coke to a brand-new car"): The function of this "more" is to fill in the lack of a "less," to compensate for the fact that, by definition, a piece of merchandise never delivers on its (fantasmatic) promise. In other words, the ultimate "true" merchandise would be the one that would need no supplement, the one that would simply fully deliver what it promises—"you get what you paid for, neither less nor more."[1]

This reference to the void in the middle of a dessert, the void enveloped by a dessert, has a long history.[2] In Elizabethan England, with the rise of modern subjectivity, the difference emerged between the "substantial" food (meat) eaten in the great banquet hall and the sweet desserts eaten in the separate small room while the tables were cleared ("voided") in the banquet hall—so the small room in which these desserts were consummated was called "void." Consequently, the desserts themselves were referred to as "voids," and, furthermore, in their form, they imitated the shape of the void—sugar cakes in the shape of, usually, an animal, empty in its inside. The emphasis was on the contrast between the "substantial" meal in the large banquet hall and the insubstantial, ornamental, dessert in the "void": The "void" was a "like-meat," a fake, a pure appearance—say, a sugar peacock that looked like the peacock without being one (the key part of the ritual of consuming it was to violently crack the surface to reveal the void inside). This was the early modern version of today's decaffeinated coffee or artificial sweeteners, the first example of the food deprived of its substance, so that, eating it, one was in a way "eating nothing." And the further key feature is that this "void" was the space of deploying the "private" subjectivity as opposed to the "public" space of the banquet hall: The "void" was consumed in a place where one withdrew after the public ceremony of the official meal; in this separate place, one was allowed to drop the official masks and give over oneself to the relaxed exchange of rumors, impressions, opinions, and confessions, in their full range from the trivial to the most intimate. The opposition between the substantial "real thing" and the trifling ornamental appearance that enveloped only the void thus overlapped with the opposition between substance and subject—no wonder that, in the same period, the "void" also functioned as an allusion to the subject itself, the void beneath the deceptive appearance of social masks. This, perhaps, is the first, culinary, version of Hegel's famous

---

1. No wonder, then, that these eggs are now prohibited in the United States and have to be smuggled in from Canada (and sold at triple the price): Behind the official pretext (they solicit you to buy another object, not the one publicized), it is easy to discern the deeper reason—these eggs display too openly the inherent structure of a commodity.

2. See Chapter 4 ("Consuming the Void") in Patricia Fumerton, *Cultural Aesthetics* (Chicago: University of Chicago Press, 1991).

motto according to which one should conceive the Absolute "not only as Substance, but also as Subject": You should eat not only meat and bread, but also good desserts...

Should we not link this use of "void" to the fact that, at exactly the same historic moment, at the dawn of modernity, "zero" as a number was invented—a fact, as Brian Rotman pointed out, linked to the expansion of the commodity exchange, of the production of commodities into the hegemonic form of production, so that the link between void and commodity has been present from the beginning.[3] In his classic analysis of the Greek vase in "Das Ding," to which Lacan also refers in his *Ethics of Psychoanalysis,* Heidegger also emphasizes how the vase as an emblematic Thing is formed around a central void, that is, serves as the container of a void[4]—one is thus tempted to read together the Greek vase and the *Kinder* chocolate egg as designating the two moments of the Thing in the history of the West, the sacred Thing at its dawn, and the ridiculous merchandise at its end: *Kinder* egg is our vase today.... Perhaps, then, the ultimate image condensing the entire "history of the West" would be that of the ancient Greeks' offering to the gods in the vase: a *Kinder* egg plastic toy. One should effectively follow here the procedure, practiced by Adorno and Horkheimer in their *Dialectics of Enlightenment,* of condensing the entire development of Western civilization into one simple line—from prehistorical magic manipulation to technological manipulation, or from the Greek vase to *Kinder* egg. Along these lines, the thing to bear in mind is that the ancient Greek dawn of philosophy occurred at the same time (and place) as the first rise of commodity production and exchange—one of the stories about Thales, the first philosopher, is that, to prove his versatility in "real life," he got rich on the market, and then returned to his philosophy... The double meaning of the term "speculation" (both metaphysical and financial) is thus operative from the very beginning. So, perhaps, one should risk the hypothesis that, historically, the Greek vase to which Heidegger refers *already was a commodity,* and that it was this fact that accounted for the void in its center, which gives to this void its true resonance—it is as a commodity that a thing is not only itself, but points "beyond itself" to another dimension inscribed in the thing itself as the central void. Following Beistegui's indications about the secret hegemony of the notion of *oikos* as closed "house" economy in Heidegger, that is, about Heidegger's ignorance of the market conditions, of how the market always/already displaces the closed *oikos,*[5] one could thus say that the vase as *das Ding* is the ultimate proof of this fact.

No wonder, then, that there is a homology between the *Kinder* egg, today's "void," and the abundance of commodities that offer us "X without X," deprived of its substance (coffee without caffeine, sweetener without sugar, beer without alcohol, and so on): In both cases, we seem to get the surface form deprived of its core. However, more fundamentally, as the reference to the Elizabethan "void" indicates, is not there a clear structural

---

3. See Brian Rotman, *Signifying Nothing* (London: MacMillan, 1987).

4. See Martin Heidegger, "Das Ding," in *Vortraege und Aufsetze* (Pfullingen: Neske, 1954).

5. See Miguel de Beistegui, *Heidegger and the Political* (London: Routledge, 1998).

homology between this structure of the commodity and the structure of the bourgeois subject? Do subjects—precisely insofar as they are the subjects of universal human rights—also not function as these *Kinder* chocolate eggs? In France, it is still possible to buy a dessert with the racist name *la tête du negre* (the nigger's head): a ball-like chocolate cake empty inside ("like the stupid nigger's head")—the *Kinder* egg fills in this void. The lesson of it is that we *all* have "nigger's heads," with a hole in the center—would the humanist-universalist reply to the *tête du negre,* his attempt to deny that we all have "nigger's heads," not be precisely something like a *Kinder* egg? As humanist ideologists would have put it: We may be indefinitely different, as some of us are black, others white, some tall, others small, some women, others men, some rich, others poor, and on and on—yet, deep inside us, there is the same moral equivalent of the plastic toy, the same *je ne sais quoi,* an elusive X that somehow accounts for the dignity shared by all humans, or, to quote Francis Fukuyama:

> What the demand for equality of recognition implies is that when we strip all of a person's contingent and accidental characteristics away, there remains some essential human quality underneath that is worthy of a certain minimal level of respect—call it Factor X. Skin, color, looks, social class and wealth, gender, cultural background, and even one's natural talents are all accidents of birth relegated to the class of nonessential characteristics.... But in the political realm we are required to respect people equally on the basis of their possession of Factor X.[6]

In contrast to transcendental philosophers who emphasize that this Factor X is a sort of "symbolic fiction" with no counterpart in the reality of an individual, Fukuyama heroically locates it in our "human nature," in our unique genetic inheritance. And, effectively, is genome not the ultimate figure of the plastic toy hidden deep within our human chocolate skin? So it can be a white chocolate, a standard milk chocolate, a dark one, with or without nuts or raisins—inside it, there is always the same plastic toy (in contrast to the *Kinder* eggs that are the same on the outside, while each has a different toy hidden inside). And, to cut a long story short, what Fukuyama is afraid of is that, if we mess too much with the production of the chocolate egg, we might generate an egg without the plastic toy inside—how? Fukuyama is quite right to emphasize that it is crucial that we experience our "natural" properties as a matter of contingency and luck: If my neighbor is more beautiful or intelligent than me, it is because he was lucky to be born like that, and even his parents could not have planned it that way. The philosophical paradox is that if we take away this element of lucky chance, if our "natural" properties become controlled and regulated by biogenetic and other scientific manipulations, we lose the Factor X.

Of course, the hidden plastic toy can also be given a specific ideological twist—say, the idea that, after one gets rid of the chocolate in all its ethnic variations, one always encounters an American (even if the toy is in all probability made in China). This mys-

---

6. Francis Fukuyama, *Our Posthuman Future* (London: Profile Books, 2002), 149–50.

terious X, the inner treasure of our being, can also reveal itself as an alien intruder, an excremental monstrosity even. The anal association is here fully justified: The *immediate* appearance of the Inner is formless shit.[7] The small child who gives his shit as a present is in a way giving the immediate equivalent of his Factor X. Freud's well-known identification of excrement as the primordial form of gift, of an innermost object that the small child gives to his or her parents, is thus not as naive as it may appear. The often overlooked point is that this piece of myself offered to the Other radically oscillates between the Sublime and—not the Ridiculous, but, precisely—the excremental. This is the reason why, for Lacan, one of the features that distinguishes man from animals is that, with humans, the disposal of shit becomes a problem: not because it has a bad smell, but because it came out from our innermost being. We are ashamed of shit because, in it, we expose/externalize our innermost intimacy. Animals do not have a problem with it because they do not have an "interior," like humans. One should refer here to Otto Weininger, who designated volcanic lava as "the shit of the earth."[8] It comes from *inside* the body, and this inside is evil, criminal: "The Inner of the body is very criminal."[9] Here we encounter the same speculative ambiguity as with penis, organ of urination *and* procreativity: When our innermost is directly externalized, the result is disgusting. This externalized shit is precisely the equivalent of the alien monster that colonizes the human body, penetrating it and dominating it from within, and that, at the climactic moment of a science-fiction horror movie, breaks out of the body through the mouth or directly through the chest. Perhaps even more exemplary than Ridley Scott's *Alien* is here Jack Sholder's *Hidden,* in which the worm-like alien creature forced out of the body at the film's end directly evokes anal associations (a gigantic piece of shit, since the alien compels humans penetrated by It to eat voraciously and belch in an embarrassingly disgusting way).[10]

The Factor X guarantees not only the underlying identity of different subjects, but also the continuing identity of the same subject. Twenty years ago, *National Geographic* published the famous photo of a young Afghani woman with fierce bright yellow eyes; in 2001, the very woman was identified in Afghanistan—and although her face was changed, worn out from difficult life and heavy work, her intense eyes were instantly recognizable as the factor of continuity. However, two decades ago, the German Leftist weekly journal *Stern* made a rather cruel experiment that in a way empirically undermined this thesis: It paid a couple of destitute homeless men and women to allow themselves to be thoroughly washed, shaved, and then delivered to the top designers and hairdressers; in one of its

---

7. See Dominique Laporte, *History of Shit* (Cambridge: MIT Press, 2000), 11. Martin Heidegger, "Hoelderlin's Hymne 'Der Ister,'" *Gesamtausgabe 53* (Frankfurt: Klostermann, 1984), 94.

8. Otto Weininger, *Ueber die letzten Dinge* (Munich: Matthes und Seitz Verlag), 1997, 187.

9. Ibid., 188.

10. There is, of course, also the opposite way to exploit the example of *Kinder* eggs: Why not focus on the fact that the chocolate cover is always the same, while the toy in the middle is always different (which is why the name of the product is "Kinder Surprise")—is this not how it is with human beings? We may look similar, but inside, there is a mystery of our psyche; each of us hides an inner wealth of abyssal proportions. Also, one could cite the fact that the plastic toy is composed of small parts—in the same way we are supposed to form our ego.

issues, the journal then published two parallel large photos of each person, in his or her destitute homeless habit, dirty and with unshaved or unmade-up faces, and dressed to the hilt by a top designer. The result was effectively uncanny: Although it was clear that we were dealing with the same person, the effect of the different dress and so on was to shake this belief of ours that beneath the different appearance was one and the same person. It was not only the appearance that was different: The deeply disturbing effect of this change of appearances was that we, the spectators, somehow perceived a different (better?) personality beneath the appearances... *Stern* was bombarded by readers' letters accusing the journal of violating the homeless persons' dignity, of humiliating them, submitting them to a cruel joke—though what was undermined by this experiment was precisely the belief in Factor X, in the kernel of identity that accounts for our dignity and persists through the change of appearances. In short, this experiment in a way empirically demonstrated that we all have a "nigger's head," that the core of our subjectivity is a void filled in by appearances.

To return to the scene of a small kid violently tearing apart and discarding the chocolate ball to get at the plastic toy—is he not the emblem of so-called "totalitarianism," which also wants to get rid of the "inessential" historical contingent coating in order to liberate the "essence" of humankind? Is not the ultimate "totalitarian" vision that of a New Man arising out of the debris of the violent annihilation of the old, corrupted humanity? Paradoxically, then, liberalism and "totalitarianism" share the belief in Factor X, the plastic toy in the midst of the human chocolate coating. The problematic point of this Factor X that makes us equal in spite of our differences is clear: Beneath the deep humanist insight that, "deep inside ourselves, we are all equal, the same vulnerable humans" lies the cynical statement "why bother to fight against surface differences when, deeply, we already *are* equal?" –This is rather like the proverbial millionaire who poignantly discovers that she shares the same passions, fears, and loves as a destitute beggar.

Does, however, the ontology of subjectivity as lack, the pathetic assertion that "we all have nigger's heads," really provide the final answer? Is Lacan's basic materialist position not that *the lack itself has to be sustained by a minimum of material leftover,* by a contingent "indivisible remainder" that has no positive ontological consistency, but is just a void embodied? Does the subject not need an irreducible "pathological" supplement? This is what the formula of fantasy ($\$ - a$, the divided subject coupled with the object-cause of desire) points toward. Such a convoluted structure (an object emerging as the outcome of the very operation of cleansing the field of all objects) is clearly discernible in what is the most elementary rhetorical gesture of transcendental philosophy, that of identifying the essential dimension ("Factor X") by way of erasing all contingent content. Perhaps the most seductive strategy with regard to this Factor X resides in one of the favored intellectuals' exercises throughout the twentieth century, namely the urge to "catastrophize" the situation: Whatever the actual situation, it *had* to be denounced as "catastrophic," and the better it appeared, the more it solicited this exercise—in this way, irrespective of our "merely ontic" differences, we all participate in the same ontological catastrophe. Heidegger denounced the present age as that of the highest "danger," the epoch of accomplished nihilism; Adorno and Horkheimer saw in it the culmination of the "dialectic of enlightenment" in the "administered world"; up to Giorgio Agamben, who defines the twentieth-century concentration camps as the "truth" of the entire Western political project. Recall the figure of Horkheimer in the West Germany of the 1950s: While denouncing the "eclipse of reason" in the modern Western society of consumption, he *at the same time* defended this same society as the lone island of freedom in the sea of totalitarianisms and corrupt dictatorships all around the globe. It was as if Winston Churchill's old ironic quip about democracy being the worst possible political regime, though all other regimes were worse than it, was here repeated in a serious form: Western "administered society" is barbarism in the guise of civilization, the highest point of alienation, the disintegration of the autonomous individual, and so forth—however, all other sociopolitical regimes are worse yet, so that, comparatively, one nonetheless has to support it. One is thus tempted to propose a radical reading of this syndrome: What if the thing the unfortunate intellectuals cannot bear is the fact that they lead a life that is basically happy, safe, and comfortable, so that, to justify their higher calling, they *have* to construct a scenario of radical catastrophe? And, effectively, Adorno and Horkheimer are here strangely close to Heidegger:

> The most violent "catastrophes" in nature and in the cosmos are nothing in the order of Unheimlichkeit in comparison with that Unheimlichkeit which man is in himself, and which, insofar as man is placed in the midst of beings as such and stands for beings, consists in forgetting being, so that for him das Heimische becomes empty erring, which he fills up with his dealings. The Unheimlichkeit of the Unheimischkeit lies in that man, in his very essence, is a katastrophe—a reversal that turns him away from the genuine essence. Man is the only catastrophe in the midst of beings.[11]

The first thing that cannot but strike a philosopher's eye here is the implicit reference to the Kantian Sublime: In the same way that, for Kant, the most violent outbursts in nature are nothing compared to the power of the moral Law, for Heidegger the most violent catastrophes in nature and social life are nothing compared to the catastrophe that is man itself—or, as Heidegger would have put it in his other main rhetorical figure, the essence of catastrophe has nothing to do with ontic catastrophes, since the essence of catastrophe is the catastrophe of the essence itself, its withdrawal, its forgetting by man. (Does this include the holocaust? Is it possible to claim, in a nonobscene way, that the holocaust is nothing compared to the catastrophe of the forgetting of being?) The (ambiguous) difference is that while, for Kant, natural violence renders palpable in a negative way the sublime dimension of the moral Law, for Heidegger the other term of the comparison is the catastrophe that is man himself. The further ambiguous point is that Kant sees a positive aspect of the experience of the catastrophic natural outbursts: In witnessing them, we experience in a negative way the incomparably sublime grandeur of the moral Law,

---

11. Heidegger, "Hoelderlin's Hymne 'Der Ister'," 94.

while in Heidegger it is not clear that we need the threat (or fact) of an actual ontic catastrophe to experience in a negative way the true catastrophe that pertains to human essence as such. (Is this difference linked to the fact that, in the experience of the Kantian Sublime, the subject assumes the role of the observer perceiving the excessive natural violence from a safe distance, not being directly threatened by it, while this distance is lacking in Heidegger?)

It is easy to make fun of Heidegger here—though there is a "rational kernel" in his formulations. While Adorno and Horkheimer would dismiss these formulations with scathing laughter, are they themselves not caught in the same predicament? When they delineate the contours of the emerging late-capitalist "administered world/*verwaltete Welt*," they are presenting it as coinciding with barbarism, as the point at which civilization itself returns to barbarism, as a kind of negative *telos* of the whole progress of Enlightenment, as the Nietzschean kingdom of the Last Men: "One has one's little pleasure for the day and one's little pleasure for the night: but one has a regard for health. 'We have invented happiness,' say the last men, and they blink."[12] However, at the same time, they nonetheless warn against the more direct "ontic" catastrophes (different forms of terror, and so forth). The liberal-democratic society of Last Men is thus literally the worst possible, the only problem being that all other societies are the worst, so that the choice appears as the one between Bad and Worse. The ambiguity is here irreducible: On the one hand, the "administered world" is the final catastrophic outcome of the Enlightenment; on the other hand, the "normal" run of our societies is continually threatened by catastrophes, from war and terror to ecological outbreaks, so that while one should fight these "ontic" catastrophes, one should simultaneously bear in mind that the ultimate catastrophe is the very "normal" run of the "administered world" in the absence of any "ontic" catastrophe.[13] The *aporia* is here genuine: The solution of this ambiguity through some kind of pseudo-Hegelian "infinite judgment" asserting the ultimate coincidence between the subjects of the late capitalist consumerist society and the victims of the holocaust ("Last Men are Muslims") clearly does not work. The problem is that there is no pathetic identification possible with the Muslims (the living dead of the concentration camps)—one cannot say, "We are all Muslims" in the same way ten years ago we often heard the phrase "We all live in Sarajevo," for things went too far in Auschwitz. (And, in the opposite direction, it would

---

12. Friedrich Nietzsche, *Thus Spake Zarathustra*, quoted from *The Portable Nietzsche* (New York: Viking, 1968), 130.

13. Interestingly enough, the same goes for Heidegger's critique of psychoanalysis: What cannot but attract our attention are the two levels at which it operates. On the one hand, there is the easy philosophical game of transcendental dismissal (which can even be accompanied by a patronizing admission of its use for the medical purposes): "Although psychoanalysis can be of clinical use, it remains an ontic science grounded in the physicalist and biologist naïve presuppositions characteristic of the end of nineteenth century." On the other hand, there are concrete rebuttals, concrete attempts to demonstrate its insufficiency—say, how Freud, by focusing all too fast on the unconscious causal chain, misses the point of the phenomenon he is interpreting, and so on. How are these two procedures related? Is the second one just an unnecessary surplus or a necessary supplement, an implicit admission that the direct philosophical rejection is not sufficient? Do we not find reproduced here, at a different level, the ambiguity of the notion of catastrophe, at the same time an ontological fact that always/already occurred *and* an ontic threat?

also be ridiculous to assert one's solidarity with 9/11 by claiming "We are all New Yorkers!"—millions in the Third World would cry, "Yes!"...)

How, then, are we to deal with actual ethical catastrophes? When, two decades ago, Helmut Kohl, seeking to designate the predicament of those Germans born too late to be involved in the holocaust, used the phrase "the mercy of the late birth/*die Gnade des spaeten Geburt*," many commentators rejected this formulation as a sign of moral ambiguity and opportunism, signaling that today's younger Germans can dismiss the holocaust as simply outside the scope of their responsibility. However, Kohl's formulation does touch a paradoxical nerve of morality baptized by Bernard Williams "moral luck."[14] Williams evokes the case of a painter ironically called "Gauguin" (not the original) who left his wife and children and moved to Tahiti to fully develop there his artistic genius—was he morally justified in doing this or not? Williams's answer is that we can only answer this question *in retrospect*, after we learn the final outcome of his risky decision: Did he develop into a painting genius or not? As Jean-Pierre Dupuy pointed out,[15] we encounter the same dilemma apropos of the urgency to do something about today's threat of different ecological catastrophes: Either we take this threat seriously and decide today to do things that, if the catastrophe will not occur, may appear ridiculous, or we do nothing and lose everything in the case of the catastrophe, the worst case being the choice of a middle ground, of taking a limited amount of measures—in this case, we will fail, whatever occurs (that is to say, the problem is that there *is* no middle ground with regard to the ecological catastrophe: either it will or it will not occur). Such a predicament would horrify a radical Kantian: It renders the moral value of an act dependent on thoroughly "pathological" conditions, that is, on its utterly contingent outcome—in short, when I make a difficult decision that involves an ethical deadlock, I can only say, "If I'm lucky, my present act *will at some point have been* ethical!" However, is not such a "pathological" support of our ethical stance an a priori necessity—not only in the common sense that, if we (most of us, at least) are to retain our ethical composure, we should have the luck of not being exposed to excessive pressures of temptations (a large majority of us would commit the worst betrayal when tortured in a horrifyingly cruel way). When, in our daily lives, we retain our ethical pride and dignity, we act under the protection of the *fiction* that we would remain faithful to the ethical stance also under harsh conditions; the point here is not that we should mistrust ourselves and doubt our ethical stance, but rather that we should adopt the attitude of the philosopher Alonzo in Mozart's *Cosi Fan Tutte,* who advises the two deceived lovers: "Trust women, but do not expose them to too many temptations!"

It is easy to discern how our sense of dignity relies on the disavowal of the "pathological" facts of which we are well aware, but nonetheless we suspend their symbolic efficiency. Imagine a dignified leader: If he is photographed in an "undignified" situation (crying, throwing up, hugging the wrong woman), this can ruin his career, although such

---

14. See Bernard Williams, *Moral Luck* (Cambridge: Cambridge University Press, 1981).
15. See Jean-Pierre Dupuy, *Pour un catastrophisme eclaire* (Paris: Editions du Seuil, 2002), 124–26.

situations are parts of the daily life of all of us. At a slightly different level, recall the high art of the skilled politicians who know how to make themselves absent when a humiliating decision is to be made; in this way, they are able to leave intact the unconscious belief of their followers in their omnipotence, sustaining the illusion that, if they were not accidentally prevented from being there, they would have been able to save the day. Or, at a more personal level, imagine a young couple on their first date, the boy trying to impress the girl, and then they encounter a strong bullying male who harasses the girl and humiliates the boy who is afraid to oppose the intruder; such an accident can ruin the entire relationship—the boy will avoid ever seeing the girl again, since she will always remind him of his humiliation.

However, beyond the Brechtian fact that "morality is for those who are lucky enough to be able to afford it," there is a more radical gray zone best exemplified by the figure of *Musulmanen* ("Muslims") from the Nazi concentration camps: They are the "zero-level" of humanity, a kind of "living dead" who even cease to react to the basic animal stimuli, who do not defend themselves when attacked, who gradually even lose their thirst and hunger, eating and drinking more out of blind habit than on account of some elementary animal need. For this reason, they are the point of the Real without symbolic Truth, that is, there is no way to "symbolize" their predicament, to organize it into a meaningful life-narrative. However, it is easy to perceive the danger of these descriptions: They inadvertently reproduce and thus attest the very "dehumanization" imposed on them by the Nazis. Which is why one should insist more than ever on their humanity, without forgetting that they were in a way dehumanized, deprived of the essential features of humanity: The line that separates the "normal" human dignity and engagement from the Muslim's "inhuman" indifference is inherent in "humanity," which means that there is a kind of inhuman traumatic kernel or gap in the very midst of "humanity" itself—to put it in Lacanian terms, the Muslims are "human" in an ex-timate way. What this means is that, as Agamben was right to emphasize, the "normal" rules of ethics are suspended here: We cannot simply deplore their fate, regretting that they are deprived of the basic human dignity, since *to be "decent," to retain "dignity," in front of a Muslim is in itself an act of utter indecency.* One cannot simply ignore the Muslim: Any ethical stance that does not confront the horrifying paradox of the Muslim is by definition unethical, an obscene travesty of ethics—and once we effectively confront the Muslim, notions like "dignity" are somehow deprived of their substance. In other words, "Muslim" is not simply the "lowest" in the hierarchy of ethical types ("they not only have no dignity, they even lost their animal vitality and egotism"), but the zero-level that renders the whole hierarchy meaningless. Not to take into account this paradox is to participate in the same cynicism that the Nazis themselves practiced when they first brutally reduced the Jews to the subhuman level and then presented this image as the proof of their subhumanity—they extrapolated to the extreme the standard procedure of humiliation, in which I, say, take the belt from the trousers of a dignified person, thus forcing him to hold his trousers by his hands, and then mock him as undignified... In this precise sense, our moral dignity is ultimately always a fake: It depends on our being lucky to avoid the fate of the Muslim. This fact, perhaps, also accounts for the "irrational" feeling of guilt that haunted the survivors of the Nazi camps: What the survivors were compelled to confront at its purest was not the utter contingency of survival, but, more radically, the utter contingency of our retaining our moral dignity—the most precious kernel of our personality, according to Kant.

This, perhaps, is also the principal lesson of the twentieth century concerning ethics: One should abandon all ethical arrogance and humbly accept the luck to be able to act ethically. Or, to put it in theological terms: Far from being opposed, autonomy and grace are intertwined, that is, we are blessed by grace when we are able to act autonomously as ethical agents. And we have to rely on the same mixture of grace and courage when facing the *prospect* of a catastrophe. In his "Two Sources of Morality and Religion," Henri Bergson describes the strange sensations he experienced on August 4, 1914, when war was declared between France and Germany: "In spite of my turmoil, and although a war, even a victorious one, appeared to me as a catastrophe, I experienced what William James spoke about, a feeling of admiration for the facility of the passage from the abstract to the concrete: Who would have thought that such a formidable event can emerge in reality with so little fuss?"[16] Crucial here is the modality of the break between before and after: Before its outbreak, the war appeared to Bergson "*simultaneously probable and impossible*: a complex and contradictory notion which persisted to the end;"[17] after its outbreak, it all of a sudden become real *and* possible, and the paradox resides in this retroactive appearance of probability:

> I never pretended that one can insert reality into the past and thus work backwards in time. However, one can without any doubt insert there the possible, or, rather, at every moment, the possible insert itself there. Insofar as inpredictable and new reality creates itself, its image reflects itself behind itself in the indefinite past: this new reality finds itself all the time having been possible; but it is only at the precise moment of its actual emergence that it begins to always have been, and this is why I say that its possibility, which does not precede its reality, will have preceded it once this reality emerges.[18]

The encounter of the real as impossible is thus always missed: It is experienced either as impossible but not real (the prospect of a forthcoming catastrophe that, however probable we know it is, we do not believe will effectively occur and thus dismiss as impossible) or as real but no longer impossible (once the catastrophe occurs, it is "renormalized," perceived as part of the normal run of things, as always/already having been possible). And, as Jean-Pierre Dupuy makes it clear, the gap that makes these paradoxes possible is the one between knowledge and belief: We *know* the catastrophe is possible, probable even, yet we do not *believe* it will really happen.[19]

---

16. Henri Bergson, *Oeuvres* (Paris: PUF, 1991), 1110–11.

17. Ibid.

18. Ibid., 1340.

19. Dupuy, *Pour un catastrophisme éclairé*, 142–43.

What such experiences show is the limitation of the ordinary "historical" notion of time: At each moment of time, multiple possibilities are waiting to be realized; once one of them actualizes itself, others are cancelled. The supreme case of such an agent of the historical time is the Leibnizean God who created the best possible world: Before creation, he had in his mind the entire panoply of possible worlds, and his decision consisted in choosing the best one among these options. Here, the possibility precedes choice: The choice is a choice among possibilities. What is unthinkable within this horizon of linear historical evolution is the notion of a choice/act that retroactively opens up its own possibility: the idea that the emergence of a radically New retroactively changes the past—of course, not the actual past (we are not in science fiction), but the past possibilities, or, to put it in more formal terms, the value of the modal propositions about the past—exactly what happens in the case described by Bergson.[20] Dupuy's point is that, if we are to properly confront the threat of a (cosmic or environmental) catastrophe, we need to break out of this "historical" notion of temporality: We have to introduce a new notion of time. Dupuy calls this time the "time of a project," of a closed circuit between the past and the future: The future is causally produced by our acts in the past, while the way we act is determined by our anticipation of the future and our reaction to this anticipation. This circuit, of course, generates a host of the well-known paradoxes of self-realizing prophecy: If we expect X to occur and act accordingly, X will effectively occur. More interesting are the negative versions: If we expect/predict X (a catastrophe) and act against it, to prevent it, the outcome will be the same whether the catastrophe effectively occurs or does not occur. If it occurs, our preventive acts will be dismissed as irrelevant ("you cannot fight destiny"); if it does not occur, *it will be the same,* that is, since the catastrophe (in which we did not believe, despite our knowledge) was perceived as impossible, our preventive acts will be again dismissed as irrelevant (recall the aftermath of the Millennium Bug!). Is, then, this second option the only choice to follow as a rational strategy? One paints the prospect of a catastrophe and then one acts to prevent it, with the hope that the very success of our preventive acts will render ridiculous and irrelevant the prospect that prompted us to act—one should heroically assume the role of excessive panic-monger in order to save humanity… However, the circle is not totally closed: Back in the 1970s, Bernard Brodie pointed the way out of this deadlock of the closed circle apropos the strategy of MAD (Mutually Assured Destruction) in the Cold War:

> It is a strange paradox of our time that one of the crucial factors which make the nuclear dissuasion effectively function, and function so well, is the underlying fear that, in a really

---

20. There is, of course, also an ideological way of projecting or inserting possibilities into the past. The attitude of many a libertarian Leftist about the disintegration of Yugoslavia is: "The full sovereignty of the ex-Yugoslav republics may be a legitimate goal in itself, but what is worth the price—hundreds of thousands dead, destruction…?" What is false here is that the actual choice in the late 1980s was silently reformulated, as if it was: "Either disintegration of Yugoslavia into separate states—*or* the continuation of the old Tito's Yugoslavia." With the advent to power of Milosevic, the old Yugoslavia was over, so the only *third* way with regard to the alternative "Sovereign republics or Serboslavia" was, in a true political *act,* to thoroughly reinvent a new Yugoslav project; and for this there was neither the ability nor the inclination in any part of Yugoslavia.

serious crisis, it can fail. In such circumstances, one does not play with fate. If we were absolutely certain that the nuclear dissuasion is one hundred per cent efficient in its role of protecting us against a nuclear assault, then its dissuasive value against a conventional war would have dropped to close to zero.[21]

The paradox is here a very precise one: The MAD strategy works not because it is perfect, but on account of its very imperfection. That is to say, a perfect strategy (if one side nukes the other, the other will automatically respond, and both sides will thus be destroyed) has a fatal flaw: What if the attacking side counts on the fact that, even after its first strike, the opponent continues to act as a rational agent? His choice is now: With his country mostly destroyed, he can either strike back, thus causing total catastrophe, the end of humanity, or *not strike back,* thus enabling the survival of humanity and thereby at least the possibility of a later revival of his own country? A rational agent would chose the second option. What makes the strategy efficient is the very fact that we cannot ever be sure that it will work perfectly: What if a situation spirals out of control for a variety of easily imaginable reasons (from the "irrational" aggressivity of the one party to simple technological failures or miscommunications)? It is because of this permanent threat that both sides do not even want to come close to the prospect of MAD, *so they avoid even conventional war:* If the strategy were perfect, it would, contrarily, endorse the attitude "Let's fight a full conventional war, since we both know that no side will risk the fateful step toward a nuclear strike!" So the actual constellation of MAD is not "If we follow the MAD strategy, the nuclear catastrophe will not take place," but instead "If we follow the MAD strategy, the nuclear catastrophe will not take place, *except for some unforeseeable incident.*" And the same goes today for the prospect of an ecological catastrophe: If we do nothing, it will occur, and if we do all we can do, it will not occur, *except for some unforeseeable accident.* This "unforeseeable factor *e*" is precisely the remainder of the Real that disturbs the perfect self-closure of the "time of the project"—if we write this time as a circle, it is a cut that prevents the full closure of the circle (exactly the way Lacan writes *l'objet petit a*). What confirms this paradoxical status of *e* is that, in it, possibility and impossibility, positive and negative, coincide: *It renders the strategy of prevention effective precisely insofar as it hinders its full efficiency.*

It is thus crucial not to perceive this "catastrophist strategy" in the old terms of linear historical causality: It does not work because today we are faced with multiple possibilities for the future, and, within this multitude, we choose the option to act so as to prevent catastrophe. Since the catastrophe cannot be "domesticated" as just another possibility, the only option is *to posit it as real*: "[O]ne has to inscribe the catastrophe into the future in a much more radical way. One has to render it *unavoidable.*"[22]

What one should introduce here is the notion of minimal "alienation" constitutive of the symbolic order and of the social field as such: Although I *know* very well that the

---

21. Bernard Brodie, *War and Politics* (New York: Macmillan, 1973), 430–31, quoted in Dupuy, *Pour un catastrophisme eclaire,* 208–209.

22. Dupuy, *Pour un catastrophisme eclaire,* 164.

future fate of both me and the society in which I live causally depends on the present activity of millions of individuals like me, I nonetheless *believe* in destiny, that is, I believe that the future is run by an anonymous power independent of the will and acts of any individual. "Alienation" consists in the minimal "objectivization" on account of which I abstract from my active role and perceive historical process as an "objective" process that follows its path independently of my plans. (At a different level, the same goes for the individual agent on the market: While fully aware that the price of a product on the market depends [also] on his acts, his selling and buying, he nonetheless holds the price of a product there for fixed, perceiving it as a given quantity to which he then reacts.) The point, of course, is that these two levels intersect: In the present, I do not act blindly, but I *do* react to the prospect of what the future will be.

This paradox designates the symbolic order as the order of virtuality: Although it is an order that has no existence "in itself," independent of individuals who relate to it, that is, as Hegel put it apropos of the social substance, although it is actual only in the acts of the individuals, it is nonetheless their *substance,* the objective In-itself of their social existence. This is how one should understand the Hegelian "In- and For-Itself": While it is In-itself, existing independently of the subject, it is "posited" as independent by the subject, that is, it exists independently of the subject only insofar as the subject acknowledges it as such, only insofar as the subject relates to it as independent. For this reason, far from signaling a simple "alienation," the reign of the dead specters over living subjects, this "autonomization" is coexistent with ethics: People sacrifice their lives for this virtuality. Dupuy is therefore right to emphasize that one should reject here the simplistic Marxist "critique" that aims at "sublating" this alienation, transforming society into a self-transparent body within which individuals directly realize their collective projects, without the detour of "destiny" (the position attributed to the Lukacs of *History and Class Consciousness*): A minimum of "alienation" is the very condition of the symbolic order as such.

Onc should thus invert the existentialist commonplace according to which, when we are engaged in a present historical process, we perceive it as full of possibilities and ourselves as agents free to choose among them, while, for a retroactive view, the same process appears as fully determined and necessary, with no opening for alternatives: It is, on the contrary, the engaged agents who perceive themselves as caught in a Destiny, merely reacting to it, while, retroactively, from the standpoint of later observation, we can discern alternatives in the past, possibilities of the events taking a different path. (And is the paradox of Predestination—the fact that the theology of predestination legitimized the frantic activity of capitalism—not the ultimate confirmation of this paradox?) This is how Dupuy proposes to confront the catastrophe: We should first perceive it as our fate, as unavoidable, and then, projecting ourselves into it, adopting its standpoint, we should retroactively insert into its past (the past of the future) various counterfactual possibilities ("If we were to do this and that, the catastrophe we are in now would not have occurred!") upon which we then act today. And is not a supreme case of the reversal of positive into negative destiny the shift from the classical historical materialism into the attitude of Adorno's and Horkheimer's "dialectic of Enlightenment"? While the traditional Marxism enjoined us to engage ourselves and act in order to bring about the necessity (of Communism), Adorno and Horkheimer projected themselves into the final catastrophic outcome perceived as fixed (the advent of the "administered society" of total manipulation and end of subjectivity) to solicit us to act against this outcome in our present.

Such a strategy is the very opposite of the American attitude in the "war on terrorism," that of avoiding the threat by preventively striking at *potential* enemies. In Steven Spielberg's film *Minority Report,* criminals are arrested even before they commit their crime, since three humans who, through monstrous scientific experiments, acquired the capacity to foresee the future can exactly predict their acts—is this a parallel with the new "Cheney doctrine," devised by the U.S. Vice President, which proclaims the policy of attacking a state or enemy force even before this state develops the means to pose a threat to the United States, that is, already at the point when it *might* develop into such a threat?[23] And, to pursue the homology even further, was Germany's Gerhard Schroeder's disagreement with the American plans to preventively attack Iraq not precisely a kind of real-life "minority report," signaling his disagreement with the way others saw the future? The state in which we live now, in the "war on terror," is the state of the endlessly suspended terrorist threat in which the Catastrophe (the new terrorist attack) is taken for granted and forever anticipated, yet endlessly postponed. Whatever will actually happen, even if it proves to be a much more horrible attack than that of 9/11, will not yet be "that." And it is crucial here that we accomplish the "transcendental" turn: The true catastrophe *already is* this life under the shadow of the permanent threat of catastrophe.

Terry Eagleton recently drew attention to the two opposed modes of tragedy: the big, spectacular catastrophic Event; the abrupt eruption from some other world; and the dreary persistence of a hopeless condition—the blighted existence that goes on indefinitely, life as one long emergency.[24] This is the difference between the big First World catastrophes like 9/11 and the dreary permanent catastrophe of, say, Palestinians in the West Bank. The first mode of tragedy, the figure against the "normal" background, is characteristic of the First World, while in much of the Third World catastrophe designates the all-present background itself.

And this is how the 9/11 catastrophe effectively functioned: as a catastrophic figure that made us in the West aware *both* of the blissful background of our happiness *and* of the necessity to defend it against the foreigners' onslaught...in short, it functioned exactly according to Chesterton's principle of Conditional Joy—to the question "Why this

---

23. The difference between the Cold War enemy and today's terrorist, cited to justify America's right to preemptive strikes, is the alleged "irrationality" of the terrorist: While Communists were cold, rational calculators who cared for their own survival, fundamentalist terrorists are irrational fanatics ready to blow up the entire world. Here, more than ever, one should insist that (as Hegel would have put it) such a figure of the "irrational" enemy is a "reflexive determination" of America's own self-adopted position as the sole hegemonic world power.

24. See Terry Eagleton, *Sweet Violence* (Oxford: Blackwell, 2003).

catastrophe? Why couldn't we be happy all the time?," the answer is "And why should we be happy in the time without catastrophes?" September 11 served as a proof that we are happy and that others *envy* us this happiness. Along these lines, one should thus risk the thesis that, far from wrenching the United States from its ideological sleep, 9/11 was used as a sedative enabling the hegemonic ideology to "renormalize" itself: The period after the Vietnam War was one long, sustained trauma for the hegemonic ideology—it had to defend itself against critical doubts, the gnawing worm was continuously at work and couldn't be simply suppressed, every return to innocence was immediately experienced as a fake...until September 11, when America became a victim and thus was allowed to reassert the innocence of its mission. In short, far from awakening us, 9/11 served to put us to sleep again, to continue our dream after the nightmare of the last decades.

The ultimate irony here is that, to restore the innocence of American patriotism, the conservative U.S. establishment mobilized the key ingredient of the Politically Correct ideology that it officially despises: the logic of victimization. Relying on the idea that authority is conferred (only on) those who speak from the position of the *victim*, it relied on this implicit reasoning: "We are now all victims, and it is this fact that legitimizes us to speak (and act) from the position of authority." So when, today, we hear the slogan that the liberal dream of the 1990s is over, that, with the attacks on the World Trade Center, we were violently thrown back into the real world, that the easy intellectual games are over, we should remember that such a call to confront the harsh reality is ideology at its purest. Today's cry "America, awake!" is a distant echo of Hitler's "Deutschland, erwache!," which, as Adorno wrote long ago, meant its exact opposite.

The Second Cold War and Postmodern Terror

CHRIS HABLES GRAY

We live in complicated times. The premise of analysis is that patterns and processes reoccur in natural systems, including human culture. Understanding these should help us survive longer. Labels, such as the ones in the title of this chapter ("second Cold War," "postmodern terror"), are tools that access the power of stories and the nuances of metaphor… but they don't guarantee usefulness. They have to be used.

That is the plan here: to think through the premise that we are currently living through a second cold war in the context of an international system that can accurately be labeled "postmodern terror." The story starts with one of the most violent of political forms, the nation-state, and its primary popular (if not ideological) justification: nationalism.

Twenty-First Century Nationalism

States are above all cultural artifacts. Another way of looking at this is to see states as information produced by and through practices of signification—from the writing of foundational documents (constitutions) to the discourses of smart bombs and the global spread of Coca-Cola. Sovereign identity, then, is composed of bits rather than atoms (Everard 2000: 7).

Yes, states, *and* nations, are imagined communities, but they are more than bits. Bits need atoms for transmission but, even more, bodies are crucial. You need citizens, or at least consumers, to have a state, but perhaps nations are not the same, even if they both depend on a type of national identity.

The emotional system we call nationalism, or human loyalty to (indeed identification with) a greater whole, is part of a larger identity-formation system than just nations or nation-states. It is also what vitalizes the "Nation of Islam," the dream Caliphate, whether it is over traditional Muslim lands, any place that has ever been Muslim, or all the world; the Taliban proudly proclaimed that they fought not for Afghanistan, but for all of Islam.

Nationalism is the Kingdom of Christ brought on by Armageddon. It is whatever temporal forms the fundamentalist Hindus believe in, even though it is all Maya. It is one Communist world. Basically, it is making everyone fit into a system of "us" and "them," sometimes on a limited scale (ranging from organized crime to ethnic cleansing), sometimes taking in the whole globe (Believers of the world, unite!).

And isn't it global capitalism as well? The belief in the right to be rich, or at least shoppers, above all else, the malling of America and the Disneyfication of the world? McWorld is another form of identity, like nationalism: all buyers created equal to their own capitalization. Still, even while most nation-states are becoming regions (Europe) or just growing weaker, national identity systems are proliferating. Nationalism is still one of the key "contested" engines of identity, even as it changes from a primary focus on the nation-state to nationalism without a state (Euskadi), or cultural identity (especially in exile), or a commodity ("Kiss me, I'm Irish" buttons).

It is a paradox of postmodernity that even as technologies (the Internet, telecommunications, jet travel) that knit the world together multiply there has been a resurgence of nationalism and a proliferation of nations, some aspiring to statehood and others not. Manuel Castells (1997) has gone so far as to argue that the new technologies of "The Information Age" actually produce "nations without states," and he uses Catalans and the Basques as his main examples. Some label this "postnationalism" since it replaces identification with a nation-state (Gabilondo 2002). But there is really no agreement about what makes a "real" nationalism, nor has there ever been. As Mark Juergensmeyer (2001: 227) remarks, "The uncertainty about what constitutes a valid basis for national identity is a political form of postmodernism."

But where has the power of nation-states gone? Not to the nations, despite the desperate scrambling of Serbians, Chechens, Kurds, and Pashtuns as well as the increased autonomy of the Catalans, Basques, Welsh, and Scots. It has gone in large part to corporations, of course. The Global Market is growing incredibly fast. Jessica Mathews of the Council of Foreign Relations says, "[T]echnology is the driving force, shifting financial clout from states to the market with its offer of unprecedented speed in transactions." She concludes that "More and more frequently today, governments have only the appearance of free choice when they set economic rules. Markets are setting de facto rules enforced by their own power" (1997: 57).

Contemporary informatics make the postmodern system logistically workable just as modern technologies made the modern nation-state possible. These states, together with modern science, the machine age, modern war, and European Imperialism, all developed simultaneously in a messy, bloody conversation. This is all the more sobering when we realize that today we are in the midst of a similar conversation, or more likely a further elaboration of the "modern" one, as technoscience and politics make another staggering transition, this time under the sign/trope of the cyborg instead of the soulful automaton of Thomas Hobbes.

The age of the hegemony of the nation-state is ending. For Hobbes, the world was meant to be a community of Leviathans, autonomous nation-states with clear borders and stable sovereigns—a world of kings. Today, few see a world map as clear. A proliferation of political forms overlap and even contradict each other. While postmodern states struggle against devolution from below and empire from above, their bodies are drained of sovereignty by multinational corporations on one side and the nongovernmental organizations and international subcultures that are sustained by worldwide mass telecommunications on the other.

A young knowledge worker in Barcelona may be a Basque, a Spaniard, an English-speaker, an IBM bureaucrat, a feminist, a physicist, a mother, a European, a bisexual, a rock and roller, and many other intermittent and ongoing allegiances all at the same time. Identity is now clearly a matter of discourse choices made (or accepted) by individuals, within the limits of their personal histories. Choice looms everywhere. This is true globally. A Nigerian has his tribal, religious, economic, familial, political, and consuming allegiances as well as his national Nigerian identity. True, people have always had complex subjectivities, but they are more complex now than ever, and while nation-state identity used to be particularly strong and waxing, it is now dispersed and waning, although still potent.

The larger political system is similarly a discourse system, and one that can be modified by how it is defined. After all, as the Basques say, *"Izena duen guzia omen da"* (That which has a name exists). So one of the key struggles today that will determine the possible futures of nationalisms and terrorisms is the struggle over what we're going to call the post-9/11 world. Some have claimed it is a "new normal" (a term coined in Oklahoma City after the bombing there), but it seems more like the old Cold War.

The Second Cold War

The New Normal of the twenty-first century is the normal of the second half of the twentieth century: Cold War. At the most it marks a new stage of what really should be called the Second Cold War.[1] It is a war just as the Cold War was a war and it is even, in many ways, a continuation of that conflict. We still have two ostensibly different worldviews colliding around the world, always below the threshold of total war. The vast range of the conflict, from the "shock and awe" blitzkrieg that overran Iraq to the suicide bombers of New York City and Israel to the hacking of websites and the freezing of bank accounts, is just like the bricolage of the old Cold War, which was a mosaic that includ-

---

1. After I reached this conclusion I read in Yosef Bodansky's book *Bin Laden* that Prof. Mark Juergensmeyer of the University of Hawaii had already described the growing US–Bin Laden conflict as "a new Cold War between the religious Third World and the secular West" (quoted in Bodansky 1999: xvii). I frame it a bit differently, since the US invasion of Iraq, for example, wasn't actually aimed at the religious Third World so much as the unsubdued Third World, which includes unreconstructed (into the global market) national socialist regimes as well as rebellious fundamentalists. It can't be ignored that the more aggressive parts of US policy are driven by Christian fundamentalism in alliance with both Orthodox Jewish and Zionist fundamentalist currents (in Israel and the US).

ed set battles over Korea, poisoned cigars for Fidel Castro, the jungles of Vietnam, and gigantic nuclear arsenals. The centrality of information, the intense *"media-ation"* of conflict, the explosion of technological options, are all the same. This new Cold War is a postmodern war (Gray 1997), just as the first was.

And the official issue of this worldwide struggle is basically the same: defining justice.[2] One could say "rights" or even "freedom" but justice seems to fit best, and it is a word that has been used often by all sides. As the First Cold War pitted against each other two opposed visions of justice (or at least they strongly claimed to be different), so does the Second Cold War. Cold War I faced off communism (of several forms) against capitalism (really, various mixed economies dominated by corporate interests); Cold War II has fundamentalism versus the same capitalism (also known as secularism). The First World, led by the US and incorporating the Second World (Russia, China, and most of their former allies), is now facing a foe that is made up from parts of the former communist system (especially the older Palestinian groups and the socialist national regimes in Iraq, Syria, Algeria, and Libya) plus a new wave of fundamentalism that is not limited to Moslems; just as communism had many different, often competing flavors, so does fundamentalism.

Hindu and Christian fundamentalists hate Islamist extremists, as Chinese communists hated Soviets, but all sides of both groups share a totalitarian worldview that is as closed intellectually as it is culturally. And, different as they are, the fundamentalists often find common cause. For example, Hamas and other Islamist extremists share with some fundamentalist (extreme orthodox or even hyper-Zionist) Jews an aversion to peace in Israel, a view that is also held by some North American Christian fundamentalists who see Armageddon in the Middle East as a necessary precondition for the Rapture. So fundamentalist Jews set up settlements on captured Palestinian land with Christian fundamentalist backing while Moslem fundamentalists use the settlements as the pretext for more suicide bombings in Israel itself. More moderate believers find themselves either supporting "their" fundamentalists or allied with the secular-capitalist coalition, just as Social Democrats and other leftists found themselves strange, reluctant bedfellows, either with Communist totalitarianism or with the semicapitalist system they were trying to reform.

One can think of the First Cold War as a struggle between those who claimed to prioritize economic justice and those who above all professed to value political justice (often called freedom or democracy). In actuality both systems produced super-rich elites and middle classes, both savaged the environment, both relegated the rest of the world to bit players in their Cold War drama, and both did great violence to their own principles with their desire to frame the whole world around their conflicts. The West often chose right-wing dictatorships and immoral wars abroad while curtailing liberties at home as a

---

2. Not that this is the real issue. But in terms of official reasons for the conflict, justice seems to be a theme that continually reappears in many different guises. It is interesting that many activists opposed to capitalism and fundamentalism consider themselves in a "global justice movement." "Peace and Justice" is a longstanding radical slogan going back at least to the early 1970s when I first heard it.

strategy for saving democracy. The communists, for all their claims of economic justice, not only ended up with an elite new class much more closed and limited than the West's upper classes, but in the long run also failed to economically produce enough for their systems to even survive, let alone establish economic justice.

Both systems claimed that their primary "justice" would lead to the other. At least the "capitalist" system generated great wealth that trickled down to a high percentage of the middle and working classes in the First World, even though it left millions brutally poor in the West's own heartlands and produced more millions of starving, dying people in the Third World.[3] The communists, far from proving that their version of economic justice would lead to political justice, actually set up totalitarian and imperialistic regimes that were more like fascism than anything else.

Notice how similar the two Cold Wars are militarily. There was/is worldwide terrorism supported secretly by states; there is/was an ongoing spy-vs.-spy dance; there were/are outbreaks of large-scale battles, uprisings galore, and many other conflicts that were/are subsumed under the larger struggle. Technology keeps changing the rules, offering glimmers of hope for easy victories and bloodless conflicts while in reality constantly raising both the stakes and civilian casualties. And the feeling is the same. Where once we feared every day that some accident or demagogue would plunge us into nuclear war, now we fear that some terrorist will plunge our mundane life into terror. And nuclear or biological war haunts us still, just as smaller acts of terror punctuated the First Cold War.

The similarities between the First Cold War and the Second weren't clear until recently because the Second Cold War developed slowly within the First. But now we can see that, just as with Cold War I, Cold War II is hardly cold—rather, it is very diffuse, and it pretends to explain almost all world conflicts when in actuality it once again disguises the four (by my count) major overlapping fault lines in human culture, which are:

1. The gap between humans and the nature that sustains us
2. The chasm between the rich and the poor
3. The divide between the "true believers" who will kill rather than doubt themselves and who will die rather than learn tolerance—and the rest of us
4. Those who can get justice (economic and political) and those who cannot

The different justices that the two sides are emphasizing in the Second Cold War initially seem somewhat different than those in the First. The "Infinite Justice" that the United States called for with its (now rejected) name for its response to the September 11, 2001, attacks is very much about revenge. "Whether we bring our enemies to justice or

---

3. Most North Americans and Europeans don't realize to what extent Third World countries are disrupted by the world economy. Old economic relationships are destroyed as traditional cultures undergo forced modernization. Industrialization often becomes militarization, and massive international debts are accumulated to finance the process and the continued control by military and civilian kleptocracies.

bring justice to our enemies, justice will be done," President George W. Bush proclaimed in his September 20, 2001, speech. But behind this avenging angel idea we hear many protestations that it is the "freedom" of the West that the fundamentalists most fear. Meanwhile, Osama bin Laden and others call for "God's justice" but on a closer examination they spend more time decrying both the systematic underdevelopment of the Third World (even the parts awash in oil) and the economic and cultural domination of the First World over the rest.

Of course, both views have some truth to them, as many of us who think and live outside the Cold War systems have long argued. Economically the First World exploits the rest of the world, and nature, in ways that threaten the very future of human survival while at the same time mining every authentic human emotion and action for potential profit in a quite soul-less consumerist frenzy. And the fundamentalists are not interested in freedom any more than the communists were. In some ways they are even worse, since they combine a proud, virulent misogyny with barely concealed sectarian, ethnic, and racist hatreds galore.

It is not a pretty picture, and thanks to ever-improving military technology it is one that directly threatens everything and everyone. It is postmodern war, the system we've lived with since 1945.

Other Models

Obviously, this Cold War analogy is not the only interesting way of describing what is going on. Two other theories seem particularly relevant in the light of my claim that we are in the midst of a Second Cold War: Samuel Huntington's "Clash of Civilizations" (1993) idea and Benjamin Barber's "Jihad vs. McWorld" (1995).

The "Clash of Civilizations" theory is, not to put too fine a point on it, racist, simplistic, and wrong. It is actually almost an embarrassment to read. In many ways it is an intervention into the conflict more than an analysis of it. I'm all for interventions by academics, as one might guess, but this one of Huntington's is particularly crude and unhelpful. Maybe it isn't as bad as "strategic hamlets," one of his contributions to the Vietnam War, but it is pretty bad nonetheless. He posits that future (and current) conflicts will be between nine great civilizations: Western (including Israel), Confucian, Japanese, Islamic, Hindu, Slavic, Orthodox (Russian, Greek, and so on), Latin American, and African. His descriptions of all these are simplistic and, in particular, the West as he portrays it is unrecognizable. Apparently, it monopolizes most virtue and certainly the majority of democratic values. All the other cultures are pretty much defined as inferior inversions or pale imitations of the Western model. In actuality, as we see with the Second Cold War, the real conflicts that concern us cut across these civilizations more than between them, as Bin Laden hates the Saudi government more then anything else, for example. For fundamentalists, as for a communist, interestingly enough, the greatest enemy is the one who claims to be of your faith but doesn't follow your line exactly. Communists, once they are in power, have always persecuted Trotskyites, anarchists, and social democrats with much more venom than capitalists. The first enemy of Islamist fundamentalists are moderate Moslems.[4]

By contrast with Huntington, Benjamin Barber's *Jihad vs. McWorld* is a much more interesting way of framing things. Barber argues that the major conflict in the world today is between those who want a holy war or crusade for purity (Jihad) and those who think everything in the world should be for sale (McWorld). He knew he was risking misunderstanding by using the term *Jihad,* which in his framework is pretty much fundamentalism as I define it. He said of Jihad: "In its mildest form, it betokens religious struggle on behalf of faith... I use the term in its militant construction to suggest dogmatic and violent particularism of a kind known to Christians no less than Muslims, to Germans and Hindus as well as Arabs" (9).

His definition of McWorld comes close to what I'd rather call capitalism. He says, "McWorld forges global markets rooted in consumption and profit, leaving to an untrustworthy, if not altogether fictitious invisible hand issues of public interest and common good" (6–7). He goes on to debunk the myth that free markets lead to freedom and that consumerism is the same as citizenship. So far, well and good, and he gets better.

The most valuable part of his analysis stresses how the two forces feed each other in their interactions:

> Jihad not only revolts against but abets McWorld, while McWorld not only imperils but recreates and reinforces Jihad. They produce their contraries and need one another (5).

This, he argues, is not surprising because both forces share a disdain, perhaps even a hatred, for democracy. Basically, he concludes, the real struggle today is Jihad *and* McWorld vs. democracy (295).

He might have done better to keep to the terms of his subtitle, "globalism and tribalism." They are more complex categories then Jihad and McWorld, with many positive characteristics even as they contain McWorld and Jihad within them, but they too are binary. Binaries, even dynamic dialectical ones, aren't complicated enough to explain reality. They always have the danger that our rich, complex world will be dichotomized into "us" and "them," which indeed is the stunted logic of war.

The officials are right about one thing at least: It could be a long, long war. Cold War I went from the late 1940s (it too had multiple beginnings) to 1989, although some communist regimes still linger today at least in form, and the whole thing could be revitalized if Chinese communism undergoes another Maoist phase, which, while not likely, is not impossible. Cold War II started in the late 1960s but its roots go back further, at

---

4. As far back as 1975, the Egyptian Islamist ideologue Wail Uthman wrote in his book *The Party of God in Struggle with the Party of Satan* that, indeed, that was the fundamental conflict in the world. But, for him, the leaders of the Party of Satan were people like President Sadat of Egypt and other Muslims. "The party of Satan is that group of people who pretend to believe in Islam but in reality are Islam's first enemies," he declared (quoted in Bodansky 1999: 5).

least to 1948 and the establishment of Israel, but probably back at least to World War I and the betrayal of the Arabs by the British and French.[5]

But the existence of Cold War II didn't become clear until September 11. Why has the war come out into the open now? Here Samuel Huntington is helpful. He wrote in *Foreign Affairs* in 1997 that the United States needs an enemy. He even quotes Rabbit Angstrom, the main character from a number of John Updike novels, who whines, "Without the cold war, what's the point of being an American?" (29). At least Rabbit Angstrom can be glad that the Cold War has returned. And Huntington must be gratified as well. At the end of his article he argues for keeping US resources uncommitted until some future "security threat and moral challenge" requires "Americans once again to commit major resources to the defense of national interests" (49). September 11 was the perfect trigger for the new mobilization Huntington called for in 1997.

As far as the "other" side is concerned, it seems they've been trying for years to do something like this. A whole string of attacks has been launched at the United States over the last decade by the network that destroyed the World Trade Center. They finally got the world's attention.

Unintended Consequences

For most of us who study contemporary war, September 11 was no surprise, and it wasn't even the worst thing we have predicted. Because, horrible as it was, it could have been so much worse. On one level, September 11 should be taken as a terrible warning about what might happen if this Cold War runs on and on like the first one. The continued development and proliferation of weapons of mass destruction in the context of the current international system means that we can expect even more terrible acts of terror in the near future. These assaults could come from independent groups, from government proxies, or from states themselves.

There are many labels, as discussed above, that can be used for contemporary war, but whatever you call it, this is it. It is asymmetrical, in that a tiny group can severely hurt the greatest superpower in history. It is aimed at civilians, as most war is these days. It is experienced in real time by the world, thanks to global media. And civilian casualties are maximized because of high technology. Still, as with all war, it is out of control.

Edward Tenner has called the unintended consequences of technologies "revenge effects." He points out in his book *Why Things Bite Back* that the revenge of unintended consequences is so common that we must analyze each new technology with it in mind. It is not as if many of these consequences aren't predictable, but rather that they are unintended. Political decisions have unintended consequences as well. These have become so common in the nether world of espionage and covert wars that a special word has been coined for it: *blowback* (Johnson 2000).

---

5. Yosef Bodansky goes even further back, citing Napoleon's invasion of Egypt (1789) and including the Crimean War and the Russian conquest of Central Asia as key points in the decline of the core Islamic nations—the "Hub of Islam," as he calls it—that culminated in the fall of the Ottoman Empire (1999: xii).

Osama bin Laden, the Taliban, and Saddam Hussein are all examples of blowback. Once they were our allies, if not our creatures. Osama bin Laden, for example, was fostered through Pakistan's Inter-Services Intelligence Agency (ISI), which funneled the weapons, training, and funds the CIA wanted him to have in his war against the Soviet infidels. This is the same source that suckled the ferocious Taliban, the nightmarish theocratic fanatics who ruled Afghanistan. They, and the other Islamists too, were popular with the CIA because of their enthusiasm for killing Russians and because their virulent form of Islam was seen as a great "infectious agent" to introduce into the Moslem republics of the Soviet Empire. Militants from bin Laden's group of volunteer "Arab Afghans" returned to their homes in Algeria to massacre moderate Moslems and assassinate Berber poets, to Egypt to slaughter tourists, and to Saudi Arabia where they blew up the Khobar Towers (killing nineteen US soldiers) and bombed Riyadh in 1996 and 2003. They have also killed Hindus in India, Jews in Israel, Russians in Moscow, Africans of all religions in various countries, and, as we know too well from 9/11, Americans (and citizens of sixty other countries) in New York and Washington, D.C. Joseba Gabilondo has described this self-absorbed dynamic perfectly, in reference to the illegal counterterrorist murder squad the Spanish government set up in the 1980s: "This is the narcissistic moment when the state drowns in the reflection of its own violence" (2002: 65).

Zbigniew Brzezinskii, one of the architects of arming the Islamists, defended it by asking, "What was more important in the world view of history? The Taliban or the fall of the Soviet Empire! A few stirred-up Muslims or the liberation of Central Europe and the end of the Cold War?" (quoted in Rashid 2000: 130). Of course, the verdict of history is not yet in.

Lessons

> Hegel remarks somewhere that all facts and personages of great importance occur, as it were, twice. He forgot to add: the first time as tragedy, the second as farce.
>
> —Karl Marx, *The Eighteenth Brumaire*

The wit of the remark conceals the fact that it is profoundly wrong. History actually doesn't repeat itself at all, and if it did it would never be as farce. Our tragedies only deepen through time because at every turn of the spiral the technology of war becomes more powerful (and the destruction so much worse) and the hunger for justice more palpable (and therefore more painful). But certain *patterns* in history do repeat, which is why I have put forward this idea of the Second Cold War.

What can we understand about our current situation through this Cold War analogy? For the only good it does is what it helps us comprehend so that we can predict, or even shape, what happens next. Analogy is not repetition, by the way. The Second Cold War won't be any more like the First then the First World War was like the Second, but there were real similarities, and a real relationship, between the two World Wars and we should look for similar links between the Cold Wars.

In the First Cold War there was a disturbing tendency for the two sides to converge; communists longed to become consumers and capitalists strove for a security state. All other conflicts and dilemmas in the world were crammed onto the Procrustean bed of the Cold War and trimmed to fit it, whether they did or not. This failed to lead to many solutions of world problems, as we can see with the Palestinian–Israeli conflict, though it must have been satisfying to the elites of both sides with their simple binary thinking.

The idea of a Second Cold War is also an analogy to the two World Wars. It argues, therefore, for a close, causal link between Cold War I and Cold War II. Perhaps the lesson to be drawn from World War II, and how easily it turned into the Cold War with nuclear overkill always lurking just ahead, is that hard choices have to be made about allies as they do about enemies. In World War II the United States and the United Kingdom both decided to support the Soviets so that they could bleed the Germans, thus sparing American and Commonwealth casualties. But at what cost? A nightmare for the people who lived in the Soviet Empire, occupation throughout Eastern Europe, and the first Cold War with its nuclear terror. Short-term solutions lead often to long-term problems. At this point in world history it will only take one catastrophic war based on short-term miscalculations to destroy civilization. We need a long-term solution, which means a fundamental reordering of international relations.

The World Wars were most of all about the organization of the international system. The victors chose that system and then turned on each other. The Cold Wars are equally about the political organization of the world. In this case, the allies who have switched sides are the Russians and the Chinese. But that doesn't mean that this struggle is easily won, for the old rules of force don't apply. In postmodern war God is not necessarily on the side of the big battalions.

So what is new beyond the First Cold War? How is postmodern war changing? Manuel Castells claims that power relations are profoundly shifting because of the centrality of information in all aspects of society. In his book *The Power of Identity* (1997: 359) he argues that

> The new power lies in the codes of information and in the images of representation around which societies organize their institutions, and people build their lives, and decide their behavior. The sites of this power are people's minds.

What this means concretely, he goes on, is that "projects aimed at cultural codes must be symbol mobilizers" (361). He describes two main agencies for doing this: prophets and networks. Prophets can be inspirational and nonviolent, such as the Catalan leader Jordi Pujol or the American civil rights leader Martin Luther King, Jr., or they can be revolutionaries like Subcommandante Marcos of the Zapatistas, or lone fanatics such as the Unibomber, or someone like bin Laden.

But, important as they are, prophets are expendable. It is networks that are the prime agency for change now, Castells concludes. They are harder to recognize than the centralized movements of the past, but are no less powerful for that. And since they aren't grounded on traditional forms of power, they are difficult to pinpoint, let alone conquer or defeat. But this is not just the problem of this new Cold War, even broadly defined; it as about fundamentalism in all its forms. The forces that seek to commodify all life become their own network, one that is even harder to clearly see than the network that links fundamentalists from vastly different creeds.

We are starting to understand that the world isn't binary and it isn't a simple Newtonian system of cause = effect. It is a complex, living world, where small events can have gigantic consequences (the butterfly effect), where certain events forever change everything (singularities, bifurcations), where events and energies are drawn together around seemingly inconsequential entities (strange attractors), and where beautiful new systems can emerge out of chaos and dysfunction (emergence). It is a world that cannot have perfect information (Godel, Church-Turing), where not only do actions change reality but where observation—what we pay attention to—changes reality (Heisenberg).

This is why realpolitick doesn't work, because it is based on illusions of simple rationality, of simple cause and effect, of a disjunction between beliefs and consequences, and, fatally, on very simplistic notions of power. We cannot be so simple-minded any more, for the stakes are too great. And a good place to start thinking complexly is with our understanding of technology.

The atomic bomb did not cause postmodern war. Atomic and nuclear weapons are merely among its symptoms. The fire bombings of Tokyo, after all, killed more people then died at Hiroshima or Nagasaki. It is not any particular technology that makes war too horrible to be called "politics by other means" anymore, it is technology as a whole. And it isn't just weapons of mass destruction, although they are the greatest direct threat. We can see that very weak or small groups can use the complex technologies of everyday life to wreak incredible havoc. Without jet planes and skyscrapers, both of which are totally dependent on computerization on every level from construction to utilization, then September 11 would have been impossible. And the broadcasting of the attacks and their aftermath around the world instantaneously and continuously, equally dependent on technology, magnified their impact a million-fold. The Vietnamese and the Afghans won against the superpowers because they used appropriate technologies for victory, not the most sophisticated technologies available. And, of course, they spent freely of their lives to liberate their homelands and to serve their implacable ideologies.

One other major difference between the First Cold War and the Second needs to be emphasized. Victory won't come through the economic collapse of the weaker states this time. The economic troubles in the Third World are the fuel of this fire. The economic success of nations such as Afghanistan and the Sudan would be more of a setback to the hopes of bin Laden and the Taliban than any economic, or perhaps even military, blow could be. But this must be balanced by an understanding that, in the long run, unrestrained corporate capitalism, with its incredible inequalities and the hyperexploitation of humans and nature, would be everyone's loss. We need a new world system that goes beyond postmodern war and the McWorld it nourishes and the Cold Wars it spawns.

Unfortunately, the only way out seems first to go deeper into the horror of September 11 and try to understand what it can teach us. So, what lessons can we draw from this tremendous act of murder?

Amoral political realism will come back to haunt not just its practitioners, but innocents as well.

Technology not only will not solve everything, it is a problem in itself. Old forms of understanding, of power for example, are rendered irrelevant by new technologies and by the technologization of society itself.

When you kill civilians with bombs—with technology, in other words—you can't expect the victims to accept this as inevitable collateral damage. Is it morally different to kill civilians with strategic bombing aimed at residential neighborhoods (World War II), "free-fire zones" including villages (Vietnam), or "killing boxes" full of civilians (Gulf War) as opposed to suicide planes? In a war with Afghanistan or Iraq, New York City is a legitimate target for their military. And the high-tech "legitimate" methods of killing civilians work much better than the most successful "terrorist" attacks. So why is one moral and the other not? Just because they seem psychologically different?

There is no such thing as bloodless war, as some people have hoped. Crashing airliners is a favorite scenario in Information War theory. Does it seem bloodless?

The political realities of post-9/11 will mean that in the Western industrial countries, and especially for "nations without states," terrorism will be much harder to justify while state "counter" terrorism will be more common. Joseba Gabilondo (2002: 62), agreeing with Joseba Zulaika, concludes, "After bin Laden no Western terrorist group can resort to violence as a means to achieve political revolution or utopia (from the workers' revolution to national sovereignty)." Increased governmental repression and declining popular support will both be important factors. But for religiously motivated terrorists 9/11 is encouragement, if anything, and it is religious-oriented terrorism that is on the increase.[6] Besides that, 9/11 has already justified increased state repression and state terrorism along with nationalism in established nation-states such as the United States and Israel. The inevitable use of weapons of mass destruction in the near future could well provoke even more religious and state terrorism and xenophobia by and in established nation-states.

Revenge leads to revenge. Any response that is quick and easy and without sacrifice will be useless, if not actually counterproductive. Horrors such as 9/11 have their origins in the real world and in complex situations. There are no easy solutions.

----

6. Mark Juergensmeyer (2001: 6) reports that the US State Department listed thirty religious terrorist groups in 1998 (roughly half the list), none in 1980. A glance at the world situation seems to indicate that more than half of the main non-state terrorist centers are fundamentally religiously motivated.

In the long run war is our greatest enemy. The longer it takes us to confront that truth, the more likely it is that war will win out. But peace is not just the absence of war. Real peace is justice and tolerance; and national identities that fail to foster these, or at least allow for them, are a threat to everyone, considering the reality of weapons of mass destruction. All other kinds of peace are merely pauses before the next spasm of killing, the next terror, which is what war has become.

On Terror

> Terrorism discourse must be disenchanted…
>
> —Joseba Zulaika and William Douglass (1997: 239)

Terror is fear, great fear. All the dictionaries say so. For example, from the *Barnhart Dictionary of Etymology* (1988: 1127–28). we learn that in 1375 "terroure" meant "Great Fear," from the old French and earlier the Latin "Terror": "Great Fear, Dread." From the Sanskrit "trasat": "he trembles." The *Oxford English Dictionary* makes it clear that many of the earlier uses of the word were to describe the terror of damnation or of death by nature; and war was a part of nature, as "terrror breathing warre" by Drayton in 1598 (OED: 3268) makes clear.

In 1795 "terrorism" came to mean "government by intimidation," thanks to the French Revolution with its busy guillotine. Since then the word has been used often to describe violence by states or groups by those who oppose them (OED: 3268). The very act of labeling terrorists has become one of intimidation, aimed at provoking fear and disillusionment, while it opens the terrorist to be the possibility of being countered with sudden violence—terror.

Joseba Zulaika and William Douglass have done the best job of explaining how deadly the term "terrorism" can be. They participated in, and studied, the culture of the Basques, and so they inevitably heard much about "terrorism," met many so-called "terrorists" from all sides, and even felt "terror" on occasion. They were troubled by the "referential invalidity" and "rhetorical circularity" of the uses of "terrorism"; the term seemed useless and dangerous. They noted that

> It is the reality-making power of the discourse itself that most concerns—its capacity to blend the media's sensational stories, old mythical stereotypes, and a burning sense of moral wrath. (ix)

Which leads inevitably to counterterrorism—terrorism that is to counter earlier acts labeled terrorism—because it is "seemingly the only prudent course of action" (ibid., ix).

In 1997 in *Terror and Taboo* Zulaika and Douglass pointed out that terrorism was "becoming a functional reality of American politics." It had "been 'naturalized' into a constant risk that is omnipresent." Their conclusion is chilling: "Now that it has become a prime *raison d'état,* its perpetuation seems guaranteed" (1997: 238). *Terror is a political per-petual-motion machine, a form of violent discourse that isn't supposed to be won.*

The official, as opposed to working, definition of terrorism has been a matter of some debate. In the United States alone there are dozens of "official" definitions, from the CIA, DoD (Department of Defense), FBI, State Department, and many smaller units. *The Terrorism Reader* begins with nine different definitions from various institutions and individuals. The definitions are mutually contradictory and deeply unsatisfying. Almost all of them could apply to any war (Whittaker 2001: 3). As Zulaika and Douglass wryly observe, we are indeed "dealing as much with who has the power to *label* as much as *level* their adversaries" (1997: 81, original emphasis).

Implicitly agreeing with this logic, a *Los Angeles Times* article cynically argues, "Political manuals [are] more useful than [a] dictionary in defining 'terrorism'" (2002). It ends with three different definitions: by the FBI, the Israeli government, and the US State Department. The FBI definition (unlawful use of force) and the Israeli ("killing and making attempts…on citizens") so clearly apply to many of their own actions that one almost suspects governmental irony. The State Department, on the other hand, avoids this problem by simply restricting its definition of terrorism to "sub national groups or clandestine agents."

Terrorism is, however, certainly not restricted to nonstate actors. The term was first used to describe the actions of the French government during the Great Revolution, and the idea, of defeating your enemy psychologically through killings, rapes, and mutilations, is as old as war itself. Terror plays a major role in contemporary war since many of the powerful weapons used are horrific in their normal use, which often relies on their shock as much as anything. Rather than a war *on* terror it really might make sense to talk more about a war *of* terror or even *for* terror. The two sides need each other. As Joseba Gabilondo (2002: 61) points out, "…bin Laden has become the condition of possibility that holds the global capitalist system together." The two discourses feed each other as Barber (see below) and Gabilondo (2002: 73) detail in their arguments.

Back in 1982 Edward Herman made a distinction between "retail" and "wholesale" terror. As he rightly pointed out, most terror was (and is) perpetuated by nation-states and on a scale of difference that Herman characterized as wholesale, as opposed to the retail terror of nonstate actors. There are two problems with this distinction, though. First, many of us would condemn *all* terror, from the beating of a child to the bombing of a city. Second, with the increasing technical complexity of our society it is now possible for a handful of terrorists to kill thousands. Weapons of mass destruction make this even clearer. Still, Herman's main point remains: The system of terror includes nation-states, not just networks and other nonstate actors and individuals, and many of them have the resources to do the most terrible of things. The West is particularly hypocritical about terrorism, as the whole "blowback problem" has made painfully clear. Herman and Gerry O'Sullivan do a fine deconstruction of what they call "The Western Model and Semantics of Terrorism" of the 1980s (1989: 37–51).

Perhaps a central paradox of this Second Cold War is that the gap is closing between the different types of terrorism, thanks to information technology (IT) and the techno sciences it fosters. A network such as Al Qaeda could not threaten the United States if it lacked the sophisticated technologies it appropriates for communication, targeting, and destruction. The Al Qaeda revolution in military affairs is that radically decentralized nonstate actors can kill thousands with major international effects, thanks to the existence of global communications, commercial airliners, and skyscrapers.

So what is postmodern terror? The answer is simple and horrible: *postmodern terror is war and postmodern war is terror.* Today, all war is terrorism. Startling as this seems, in retrospect it was inevitable. War has always been very much about terror, often mainly about terror. Now, with war politically limited and extraordinarily dangerous because of powerful military technologies, terror has come to the fore completely.

Zulaika and Douglass could not have been more prescient when they said:

> The concept of "war" itself is no longer the same when deprived of the goal of military victory: the traditional meaning of war is being replaced by terrorism (defined as "surrogate war") and deterrence (defined as "mutual balance of terror"). (1997: 82, original emphasis)

War has always evoked terror; now war *is* terror. They are indistinguishable. This seems to have happened almost gradually. War has seldom been noble, but the slaughter usually followed certain rules and was confined to combatants. Sometimes prisoners were even taken and the wounded succored. Sometimes when cities were sacked only a few women were raped and none even sold into slavery. But as weapons were developed that could kill at great and indiscriminate distances, terror became all. The terror of the front lines was moved to the shelled cities (Atlanta, Paris) and then to the bombed ones (Shanghai, Guernica, Barcelona).

In World Wars I and II the military worked hard at developing "strategic" (that is, "terror") bombing. It was no accident that even though the Italians (in Libya before the World War I) and the Germans (Zeppelin raids on London in World War I, rockets in World War II) were pioneers in indiscriminate aerial attacks on civilians, it was the Allies who perfected it. In his brilliant history of US strategic bombing *The Rise of American Air Power: The Creation of Armageddon,* Michael Sherry argues that the political fanaticism of the Axis powers was matched by the technological fanaticism of the Allies. For the Germans, Italians, and Japanese, nationalistic/racist politics justified both the exterminations (of Gypsies, Jews, Slavs, Chinese, Koreans) and the war on civilians. For the Allies, the existence of the technologies of strategic bombing and nuclear weapons justified the extermination of cities. Sherry explains that it was the product

> ...of two distinct but related phenomena: one—the will to destroy—ancient and recurrent, the other—the technical means of destruction—modern. Their convergence resulted in the evil of American bombing. But it was a sin of a peculiarly modern kind because it seemed so inadvertent, seemed to involve so little choice. Illusions about modern technology had made aerial holocaust seem unthinkable before it occurred and simply imperative once it

began. It was the product of a slow accretion of large fears, thoughtless assumptions, and at best discrete decisions. (1987: 137)

Strategic bombing led to atomic bombs and then hydrogen weapons, the primary systems and symptoms (but certainly not the cause) of postmodern war. These incredible weapons and other new technologies led to the very structure of the international system under the First Cold War: a balance of terror. The current crisis of this Second Cold War was caused by the collapse of that balance. The United States is hegemonic, and the "enemy" is an idea even more than a network.

But terror didn't just determine nuclear strategy in the First Cold War, it was integral to low-intensity conflict. The details should prove instructive since the central conflict of the Second Cold War lies squarely within the low-intensity definitions.

Because nuclear weapons were thought too horrible to use, all postmodern wars have to be "managed." Crisis management is what this approach is called, but often it can look more like the harshest of coercions: torture.

Daniel Ellsberg recalls that it was his wife who, after looking through the Pentagon Papers, pointed out "in horror" that the US Vietnam War strategy was described by its architects in "the language of torturers." He gives numerous examples ("'water-drip' technique," "fast/full squeeze," "the 'hot-cold' treatment," "ratchet," "one more turn of the screw") used by such luminaries as William P. Bundy, Robert S. McNamara, John T. McNaughton, and Richard Helms (Ellsberg 1972: 304–305).

The other side certainly thought the same way, and they had a fine pedigree for the idea that terror was justified. Trotsky wrote an essay called "On Terror" when he was commander of the Red Army. In it, he noted approvingly (if not accurately) that even when you terrorize and kill the innocent your enemy's will grows weaker. While Trotsky had long been out of favor, during the Vietnam War communist theory and practice certainly followed his reasoning.

Of course this language of torturers is the language of terrorists as well: the language of pure coercive violence. The long-drawn-out blockade and bombing of Iraq seem remarkably similar to many Vietnam War operations, even to the extent that they were both ineffectual and murderous to women, children, and the elderly, hundreds of thousands of whom died in both countries.

Apparently, the Iraqis are supposed to forget this and the many betrayals of democracy in Iraq by the US, which go back to the imposition of European colonialism after World War I, and become a good little client state. It is all part of a strategic plan, and "the plan is for the US to rule the world" (Armstrong 2002: 76).

A series of official reports by Secretaries of Defense Cheney (1992, 1993) and Donald Rumsfeld (2002) and by key staff (Paul Wolfowitz and Colin Powell) lay out the current US grand strategy. It is for the United States to be the "biggest bully on the block," in Powell's phrase (Armstrong 2002: 78). It involves developing new technologies (nuclear "bunker busters" and other computerized weapons), new doctrines such as preemptive war and dominance of outer space (under the pretense of ballistic missile defense). It is a policy of terror conducted by nuclear, conventional, and special forces.

One of the leading theorists, Colin Gray (no relation to the present author), has put it quite clearly in the leading theoretical journal of the US military, *Parameters*: "For example, special forces can be unleashed to operate as 'terrorists in uniform.' Unconventional warfare of all kinds, including terrorism (and guerrilla operations), is a politically neutral technique" (2002: 6). He goes on to complain, "The US armed forces have handfuls (no more) of people amongst their substantial special operations forces who truly can think 'outside the box' and who can reason and, if need be, behave like 'terrorists in uniform'" (2002: 11).

Could this really be what is behind the US conquest of Iraq? An occupied base in the Middle East, an object lesson, all that oil, revenge for Daddy? Is it a coincidence that Saddam's Iraq was the Republic of Terror par excellence? Fear is its very definition. "Since 1991, the tyrant has remained in power not because he is loved (never the case in Iraq), nor because he exerts genuine authority...but out of fear of what lies in store in the future," explains Kanan Mariya in *Republic of Fear* (1998: xxxi).

Perhaps our terror of war has been turned into a denunciation of "terrorism" and our fear displaced onto the "other," for surely we are never terrorists. But the fear is ours, all of ours, now—whatever the side. Not just that of the soldiers. And yes, soldiers fear. Terror is with them always. This is why there is coercive discipline. Even with it—and the aid of camaraderie, nationalism, drugs, rage, and ideology—many soldiers desert and, eventually, most burn out. Killing and dying are two of the most frightening things humans do. Studies of US troops after World War II revealed that in the case of an Army division fighting in France in 1944, at a heavy time of combat, 65 percent of the troops admitted that fear severely affected them. In a division fighting in the Pacific almost all the soldiers reported such symptoms of fear as "violent pounding of the heart" (84 percent), shaking or trembling (over 60 percent), vomiting (over 25 percent), and diarrhea (21 percent). Before recounting these statistics, Gwynne Dyer reminds us that "Fear is not just a state of mind; it is a physical thing" (1985: 141–42). Fear can also lead to desperate acts.

In comments made about the Kosovo bombing Prime Minister Tony Blair remarked that "War is never civilised but war can be necessary to uphold civilisation" (quoted in Rasmussen 2000: 1). But can terror be necessary to uphold civilization? If so, what is this civilization?

The Bush doctrine is really "Terror Firma," in Grenville Byford's view, and it "is destined to be morally unsatisfying" to the extent that it will lead to "disappointments" (41–42). Or much worse. Bob Dylan sang: "Terror is my constant emotion. I deal in terror. I buy it, sell it, and make a profit" (quoted in Zulaika and Douglass 1997: 117). A future where this is true of most of us would be the victory of terror.

And since the problem of terror is the problem of war and peace itself, perhaps understanding this will clarify the situation. To end terror is to end war, which means fundamentally transforming the international system.

Works Cited

Armstrong, David. 2002. "Dick Cheney's Song of America: Drafting a Plan for Global Dominance," *Harper's Magazine,* Oct., 76–83.

Barber, Benjamin R. 1995. *Jihad vs. McWorld: How Globalism and Tribalism are Reshaping the World,* New York: Ballantine.

Barnhart, Robert K. (ed.). 1988. *The Barnhart Dictionary of Etymology,* New York: H. W. Wilson Co.

Bodansky, Yosef. 1999. *Bin Laden: The Man Who Declared War on America,* Forum/Random House.

Byford, Grenville. 2002. "The Wrong War," *Foreign Affairs,* July/Aug., 81(4): 34–43.

Castells, Manuel. 1997. The Power of Identity, vol. 2 of *The Information Age: Economy, Society and Culture,* Oxford: Blackwell.

Cheney, Dick. 1992. *Defense Planning Guidance for the 1994–1999 Fiscal Years,* Washington, D.C.: Dept. of Defense.

______. 1993. *Defense Strategy for the 1990s,* Washington, D.C.: Dept. of Defense.

Dyer, Gwynne. 1985. *War,* New York: Crown Publications.

Ellsberg, Daniel. 1972. *Papers on the War,* New York: Simon and Schuster.

Everard, Jerry. 2000. *Virtual States: The Internet and the Boundaries of the Nation-State,* London and New York: Routledge.

Gabilondo, Joseba. 2002. "Postnationalism, Fundamentalism, and the Global Real: Historicizing Terror/ism and the New North American/Global Ideology," *Journal of Spanish Cultural Studies,* 3(1): 57–86.

Gray, Chris Hables. 1997. *Postmodern War: The New Politics of Conflict,* New York and London: Guilford/Routledge.

Gray, Colin S. 2002. "Thinking Asymmetrically in Times of Terror," *Parameters,* spring, 5–14.

Herman, Edward. 1982. *The Real Terror Network,* Boston: South End Press.

Herman, Edward, and Gerry O'Sullivan. 1989. *The "Terrorism" Industry: The Experts and Institutions that Shape Our View of Terror,* New York: Pantheon.

Huntington, Samuel. 1993. "The Clash of Civilizations," *Foreign Affairs,* summer, 72(3): 22–49.

______. 1997. "The Erosion of American National Interests," *Foreign Affairs,* Sept./Oct., 76(5): 28–49.

Johnson, Chalmers. 2000. *Blowback: The Costs and Consequences of American Empire,* New York: Metropolitan Books.

Juergensmeyer, Mark. 2001. *Terror in the Mind of God: The Global Rise of Religious Violence,* Berkeley: University of California Press.

Los Angeles Times staff. 2002. "Political Manuals More Useful than Dictionary in Defining 'Terrorism'," *Great Falls Tribune,* July 6, 2A.

Mariya, Kanan. 1998. *Republic of Fear: The Politics of Modern Iraq.* Updated Edition, Berkeley: University of California Press.

Mathews, Jessica T. 1997. "Power Shift," *Foreign Affairs,* Jan./Feb., 76(1)50–66.

Oxford University Press editors. 1971. *The Compact Edition of the Oxford English Dictionary,* Oxford: Oxford University Press.

Rashid, Ahmed. 2000. *Taliban: Militant Islam, Oil and Fundamentalism in Central Asia,* New Haven: Yale University Press.

Rasmussen, Mikkel Vedby. 2000. "War Is Never Civilised"; "Civilisation, Civil Society and the Kosovo War," Copenhagen: DUPI Working Papers.

Rumsfeld, Donald. 2002. *Defense Planning Guidance for the 2004–2009 Fiscal Years,* Washington, D.C.: Dept. of Defense.

Sherry, Michael. 1987. *The Rise of American Air Power: The Creation of Armageddon,* New Haven: Yale University Press.

Whittaker, David J. (ed.). 2001. *The Terrorism Reader,* New York: Routledge.

Zulaika, Joseba, and William A. Douglass. 1997. *Terror and Taboo: The Follies, Fables, and Faces of Terrorism,* New York: Routledge.

Performing Populism: A Queer Theory of Globalization, Terror, and Spectacle (on *Lord of the Rings* and 9/11/2001)

JOSEBA GABILONDO

Alternative Pagan Histories and Global Populism

Lately, popular culture and global politics seem intent on writing "alternative histories" to that of modernity and modernization in such an unprecedented way that even the postmodern break from modernity becomes secondary or irrelevant.[1] If we look at some of the more central cultural texts involved in creating a global hegemonic ideology—that is, Hollywood blockbusters—we can analyze in detail this writing of alternative histories to modernity/modernization. Many movie blockbusters in the 1990s turned their eyes away from both future and science fiction, and back to the past as in *Forrest Gump* (1994), *Titanic* (1997), and *Saving Private Ryan* (1998). Yet, more recent blockbusters have also taken a turn for "alternative" histories as in *Lord of the Rings* (2001, 2002) and *Harry Potter* (2001). If we include films such as *Gladiator* (2000), we see that there is a new taste for alternative *pagan* history: Romans, wizards, and hobbits. Considering that the other two topgrossing films of 2001 were *Shrek* and *Monsters Inc.*, we could, in a sense, extend the above definition of "pagan" to ogres and monsters as well. Even in the case of *The Matrix* or the new *Star Wars* installment (both 1999), their persistent penchant for the future is very much hybridized with messianic and divinatory practices that spice up these films with the

---

1. I would like to thank Jo Labanyi for her invitation and comments and Giorgina Tampico for her commentaries on Baroque culture. This article was given originally under the title of "Performing the Gaze: A Queer Theory of Globalization and Terrorism (from *Lord of the Rings* to *Torrente* and Back to Hegel)" at the King Juan Carlos I of Spain Center at New York University.

same pagan flavor.[2] In short, one could conclude that Hollywood is writing alternative histories of pagan worlds and, given the box office return (the most immediate index of popular interest), we can conclude that *Lord of the Rings* is the crucial text in which this writing of alternative history can be examined.

Yet if we consider the double meaning of *pagan* as "nonbeliever in our religion" and also "as inhabitant of the borders of the empire," that is, of the *pagus*,[3] then we realize that another type of "pagans," Muslim fundamentalists, have also taken up as their task to write an alternative history, from the border of the new North American/global empire, by resorting to new reformulations of Islam that emphasize its difference with both the West and traditional Islam. As Ahmed Rashid explains for the case of the Taliban, their ignorance of their own traditional Islamic history created a vacuum that only a return to their fundamentalist origin could fill in: "As such the younger Taliban barely knew their own country or history, but from their *madrassas* [religious schools] they learnt about the ideal Islamic society created by the Prophet Mohammed 1,400 years ago and this is what they wanted to emulate" (23). The result of this ignorance of Muslim history and values was not a reconsideration of Islamic history but rather the fashioning of a new antimodernist history, that is, an alternative history of the *pagus:* "the Taliban are vehemently opposed to modernism and have no desire to understand or adopt modern ideas of progress or economic development… The Taliban and their supporters present the Muslim world and the West with a new style of Islamic extremism, which rejects all accommodation with Muslim moderation and the West" (93).

Thus, the comparison of these alternative and pagan representations, Western and Muslim, shed light on a new phenomenon that most critics so far have not discussed: the fact that Western discourses such as Hollywood films also attempt to fashion a new history and tradition that is alternative to modernity/modernization. *Both Western and Islamic discourses have in common their desire to be an alternative to the global expansion of modernity/modernization.* Therefore, the opposition is not between the West and fundamentalist Islam, but rather between modernity/modernization and any alternative tradition, including the Western one. In more general terms, the opposition is between globalization and any ideology

---

2. In the case of the *Star Wars* film, *Star Wars: Episode I—The Phantom Menace* (1999), one could make a more historical reading: The audiences were not driven to the film theaters to see the film itself, but rather to reenact the *Star Wars* euphoria of the late 1970s and early 1980s. Therefore, this film was truly historical in a metafilmic sense. In the case of *The Matrix*, on the other hand, its messianic subtext resounds with overtones of Christian religion, which in its inception was a pagan alternative to the Roman empire. In this sense this film is also pagan.

3. The Oxford English Dictionary explains its etymology in the following sense: **Pagan,** n. and a. [ad. L. pāgān-us, orig. 'villager, rustic; civilian, non-militant,' opposed to mīlēs 'soldier, one of the army,' in Christian L. (Tertullian, Augustine) 'heathen' as opposed to Christian or Jewish. The Christians called themselves mīlitēs 'enrolled soldiers' of Christ, members of his militant church, and applied to non-Christians the term applied by soldiers to all who were 'not enrolled in the army'… The explanation of L. *pāgānus* in the sense 'non-Christian, heathen,' as arising out of that of 'villager, rustic' (supposedly indicating the fact that the ancient idolatry lingered on in the rural villages and hamlets after Christianity had been generally accepted in the towns and cities of the Roman Empire). **Pāgus,** i (old *gen.* PAGEIEI, which prob. is an error for PAGEI, Inscr. Orell. 3793), m. [root pak-, pag-, to make fast or firm, whence pango, pax, pagina; Gr. pêgnumi, pagos, etc.; prop., a place with fixed boundaries; hence], *a district, canton, province* (opp. to the city), *the country* (cf. vicus): paganalia. It is important also to remember that the word 'peasant' comes from pagus.

that articulates itself as globally alternative by vindicating its different, local nature—hence the fundamentalist turn of all these discourses. In this context, *fundamentalism* simply means any historical narrative that cannot be co-opted or absorbed by globalization: *Both Hollywood and extreme Muslim ideology are fundamentalist* (Said 310). As Richard Krooth and Minoo Moallem explain:

> Indeed, under the impact of worldwide economic recession and political crisis, the revival of religious fundamentalism has not been confined to Muslim countries. The return of religion and ethnicity characterizes many countries. From the Eastern European countries to the former Soviet Union, from the United States to South America, a religious or nationalist language can be observed infusing social movements with ideas and ideals. (106)

The other element that these alternative accounts of globalization have in common is their spectacularity. Many critics have commented on the fact that the attack on the Twin Towers of the World Trade Center on 9/11/2001 was already anticipated by Hollywood, thus suggesting that there is a circular logic that encompasses both terrorism and Western representations. Yet what most critics have not emphasized is the fact that these new forms of fundamentalism, Western and Muslim, in their refashioned representation as alternative to modernization, structure their respective societies according to a logic of *spectacle*. The West experiences violence, terrorism, and war as film or televised events, that is, as *spectacular* events. The fall of the Berlin Wall, the Rodney King beatings, the O. J. Simpson trial, the CNN coverage of the two Gulf Wars, or the failed coup d'état in the Russian Parliament, are some of the highlights of this spectacular logic. Yet this spectacular order of the public space and violence finds its symmetrical match in the visual regulation of public spaces effected by fundamentalist Muslim regimes, such as the Taliban regime in Afghanistan, whereby non-Muslim sculptures are destroyed and the appearance of men (beards) and women (veil and shoes) is fully regulated so that no aspect of the public life escapes this visual order. In this context, the events of both 9/11 and the two Gulf Wars stand for the ultimate spectacles that then regulate and reorganize the visualization of the public spaces and spheres in both fields, the Western and the Muslim.

My emphasis on this double writing of alternative history as pagan and spectacular, both from the center of Empire—Hollywood—and from the *pagus* or border of the empire—Iran, the Taliban, Al Qaeda—wants to highlight the fact that there is *one and the same logic operating in this global writing of alternative history as both pagan and spectacular—and, thus, ultimately fundamentalist*. There can be many alternative histories (probably as many as civilizations can clash, following Samuel Huntington's formulation) but the logic is the same. The underlying structural unity of such different discourses as Hollywood or Al Qaeda's must be repeatedly emphasized at this moment in history when we find ourselves caught in the middle of a global war triggered by both terrorism and imperialist terror. Only by emphasizing the unity of this logic can we challenge it and go beyond the formation of a new global ideology centered on this new spectacular and alternative history of violence.

On a first approach it seems clear that these alternative and spectacular histories are articulating new global populist discourses; they represent the reemergence of populist politics. As poverty and disenfranchisement continue to grow throughout the world, and capital is being further accumulated by a new global elite on both sides of the split between the West and the Muslim world (as well as in other areas such as China and Russia), these populist discourses serve to articulate new ideologies that respond to the same "pagan and spectacular logic" but yet organize themselves as oppositional discourses both to globalization and to the other populist hegemonies—hence Huntington's recourse to the metaphor of "civilizational clash." This double opposition (against both globalization and other populisms) defines these fundamentalist, populist discourses. The new element is the number of populisms coexisting simultaneously.

It remains to be seen why these new populisms take this specific shape and, by doing so, become highly effective in interpolating large masses of people, beyond the nation-state and its nationalist discourse. Against totalizing discourses such as "the society of the spectacle" (Debord), "the clash of civilizations" (Huntington), or "the biopolitization of sovereignty" (Agamben; Hardt and Negri), this article attempts to explain the specific interlocking between specularity, paganism, and populism by resorting to similar previous moments in history, such as Baroque culture in Europe in the seventeenth century, or to similar historical practices carried out by minorities, such as queer culture's use of camp and gender performance. Only a very specific and historical analysis of these new forms of alternative historical writing and spectacular can help us overcome the historical pessimism that the aforementioned totalizing discourses create. After the cheerful neoliberalist celebration of a Hegelian universalization of capitalism attempted by Francis Fukuyama, Samuel Huntington's conclusion to his theory of the clash of civilizations seems the epitome of the type of political and historical analysis against which we have to write. He concludes his work with the following warning: "On a worldwide basis Civilization seems in many respects to be yielding to barbarism, generating the image of an unprecedented phenomenon, a global Dark Ages, possibly descending on humanity" (321). These words seem torn directly from the film *Lord of the Rings,* hence the importance of rehistoricizing these teleological narratives.

Needless to say, the risk of any scholar specialized in Western culture, such as myself, is to Orientalize Muslim culture and fundamentalism. I also believe that it is necessary to engage in a multicultural analysis to avoid further legitimation of Western ideologies by default. Thus, fully aware of this risk of Orientalization, I believe it is also important to localize and deuniversalize the West so that a new multicultural and post-Orientalist analysis emerges.

Pagan History

At first sight it appears as if these new fundamentalist ideologies had no sense of history. Their indiscriminate and even disrespectful ability to cannibalize or disregard any past historical element, subject, or narrative, points simply to the fact that they establish a distinction that is not historical—rewriting or following the existing historical narratives of their respective traditions—but rather is presentist. These new histories respond to the divide between the present globalized ideological elements that constitute fundamentalist ideology and any earlier historical element that echoes or amplifies this presentist ideology, regardless of any historical continuity. Western fundamentalism tends to mix earlier different pagan representations to invoke imperialist elements that exceed any present nationalist framework and convey a nonnationalist, imperialist past, whereas Muslim fundamentalism tends to purify its own history of any non-Muslim "impurity"—including many aspects of traditional Muslim culture—to recentralize marginal elements of Muslim history. Yet both strategies respond to the same presentist logic of articulating an alternative—pagan history—and thus it is important to understand the specific ways in which this presentist history is articulated in each case.

At first, one could theorize this presentist history simply as a posthistorical return to myth. Lévi-Strauss had stated in 1956 that myth is totalizing and represents a form of political ideology:

> [W]hat gives the myth an operational value is that the specific pattern described is timeless; it explains the present and past as well as the future. This can be made clear through a comparison between myth and what appears to have largely replaced it in modern societies, namely, politics [*idéologie politique*]. When the historian refers to the French Revolution, it is always as a sequence of past happenings, a non-reversible series of events the remoter consequences of which may still be felt at present. (209).

By reflecting the way the French Revolution as historical event is turned into a foundational moment, and thus into an ahistorical event, Lévi-Strauss concludes: "It is that double structure, altogether historical and ahistorical, which explains how myth...can also be an absolute entity" (210). In 1957, Barthes concluded in his *Mythologies* for contemporary French bourgeois culture that "myth has the task of giving an historical intention a natural justification, and making contingency appear eternal... And just as bourgeois ideology is defined by the abandonment of the name 'bourgeois,' myth is constituted by the loss of the historical quality of things: in it, things lose the memory that they once were made... The function of myth is to empty reality" (142–43). Here Barthes conflates ideology with myth and concludes along similar lines to those of Lévi-Strauss. The latter defends the proposition that myth is no different from science, history, or political ideology; only the material is different (147). Thus we can theorize that the present return to pagan history is precisely a new moment in myth–making: the myth of the global, or the ideology of globalization. Yet this does not explain the specific choice of pagan and spectacular elements. A more detailed analysis is necessary to determine this new fundamentalist articulation whereby any sense of history we had is conflated as a presentist effect.

A cursory look at films such as *Lord of the Rings* or *Harry Potter* shows their voracious appetite for mythological motives, plots, and illustrations, which also permeates other media such as video games—as the filmic renditions of the video games *Mortal Combat* or

Tomb Raiders make clear. The pagan emerges with a synergy that just a few years earlier would have been unthinkable. The indiscriminate and completely disrespectful ability to cannibalize any pagan tradition points simply to the fact that the distinction made by these films or video games is not national and historical but rather presentist and imperialist. It responds to the divide between the present globalized culture of the First World and any other earlier traditions, including some Western premodern cultures. Consequently, traditions that technically could not be thought of as pagan become such under this new, powerful category. In this light, it is no surprise that the Middle Ages are also turned into pagan: They precede Western modernity and thus they also constitute an alternative history. Thus, to categorize this indiscriminate cannibalization of history we might be tempted to opt for a general discourse of otherness at first, or for a more specific reconsideration of Orientalism, although this new alternative pagan history is neither. Any past, whether it be or look pagan, is appropriated as such, as the "other" of contemporary times, and thus as "other history."

In this respect, the various journalistic commentaries on *Lord of the Rings* are a privileged index to understand the logic of this film. First, many reviews made reference to the filmic continuity between *Star Wars* (1977) and *Lord of the Rings* (2001) as if they constituted the two highlights of a single filmic historical logic and history spanning almost twenty-five years. As Elvis Mitchel states, referring to the director of *Lord of the Rings*, "[R]ather than emphasize the similarities to George Lucas's mythology, Mr. Jackson gallops straight through them, trimming away as many of the complications as possible. 'Fellowship' may still feel like 'Star Wars' and just about every other otherworldly battle epic of the last 30 years—a whopping composite of Christian allegory, Norse mythology and a boys' book of adventure." As Mitchel clearly emphasizes, this is a logic that has been hegemonic in Hollywood for the last three decades and at the same time relies on a "compositing" of different Western religions and mythologies. Yet Mitchel also does not explain the logic of this nonhistorical compositing.

Furthermore, other critics have established the genealogy that links *Lord of the Rings* to the other most successful film of 2001, *Harry Potter*. Stephen Kinzer quotes the director of the Kalamazoo-based Medieval Institute, Paul E. Szarmach, as stating that "[W]e're putting ourselves back into the Arthurian story. That accounts for the popularity of Tolkien and Rowling." Polly Shulman also suggests that "'The Lord of the Rings' casts such a shadow over the genre it created that 'Harry Potter' could hardly exist without it." After making references to the importance of *Beowulf* and Wagner, and revising the Manichean and dual nature of most of these filmic myths, Marina Warner concludes: "the century that has just ended and the one that has just begun have not experienced the rise of Christian or Islamic fundamentalism so much as the revival of Zoroastrianism." Thus, Christianity, Arthurian myths, or even Zoroastrianism can be invoked to explain the mythical elements that conform this new alternative historical imagination—yet such invocations ultimately fail to explain the underlying pagan logic.

J. Hoberman is the only critic who, by paying more attention to the iconographic origin of the filmic elements of *Lord of the Rings*, emphasizes the fact that the film's mythological heterogeneity is brought together under a Pre-Raphaelite iconographic order:

> Although the Elvish settlement of Rivendell resembles an Alpine ski lodge for garden gnomes, and the more rustic Elves of Mirkwood would appear to dwell in a kind of tree house expansion of the Enchanted Tiki Room, the movie only rarely achieves a sense of kitsch grandeur—as in the image of colossal statues in the river mist. More often, it's a cluttered attic of cloying pre-Raphaelite visual notions.

In short, the visual order that regulates the heterogeneous nonmodern elements is precisely a Victorian iconographic logic. Once this Victorian visual order is isolated, then the pagan nature of *Harry Potter* also comes forth more clearly. Regardless of the mythological origin of the monsters or different magical elements present in the film, *Harry Potter* is also regulated by a Victorian iconography of collegial life marked by the Neogothic architecture of that era. In short both it and *Lord of the Rings* respond to the same logic of a Victorian sameness and a nonmodern difference. In turn, this logic explains most of the historical blockbusters of the last thirty years, including *Titanic*.

In perspective one can see that *Star Wars* and most science fiction films of the 1980s and early 1990s, because of their utopian content, are based on the ideology and iconography of the Western, that is the "Victorian," era of North American expansion in the Western frontier, even if the Jedis in *Star Wars* are Japanese in origin or Princess Leia is Arthurian. Thus, over the last thirty years, the mythology of Hollywood film has shifted from the myth of the Western frontier to the Victorian era of British imperialism. Therefore, we can see that both *Lord of the Rings* and *Harry Potter* are ultimately a return to the British era of imperialism. Yet, this mythic logic of British imperialist sameness and nonmodern difference still remains to be examined. After all, these films do not simply resort to a representational nostalgia or melancholia for British imperialism and its subject. Or to put it another way, the hero of *Lord of the Rings* is a hobbit, Frodo Baggins, not a human, while the hero of *Harry Potter* is a wizard, not an upper-middle-class boy. Furthermore, these films' stories are not about conquest and expansion but rather about restitution or restoration. In both cases, an earlier order is restored whereby imperial harmony is brought back to Middle Earth (*Lord of the Rings*) or to Hogwarts School (*Harry Potter*).

Following Lévi-Strauss, if we approach these stories of pagan heroes and restoration as myths, then we can infer that, once the different permutations are compared, the films portray a return to an imperialist origin in which the colonial and imperialist subjects are restored to a premodern or preimperialist indifferentiation. If the Western frontier narrative of *Star Wars* and most science fiction films is about refashioning the nationalist and foundational moment of modern North American history, these new pagan histories are about dissolving the foundation of British nationalism into its imperialist inception; furthermore these new myths dissolve its imperialist subject into the colonial subject and its premodern time. That is, in *Lord of the Rings,* characters fashioned according to a Pre-Raphaelite logic of whiteness portray the hobbits and the rest of the heroes that follow them in their quest of restoration. Yet, the story and the film racialize this whiteness through its mixing with nonwhiteness by means of size alteration, uncivilized body parts, and extra hair. Conversely, both the evil character of the film and its followers are also racialized as "darker" characters, as their nonwhite anatomy shows. In short, the division between the white imperialist subject and the nonwhite colonial subject is blurred to the point that, although the hero, a hobbit, remains white, nevertheless he draws most of his differentiating and defining characteristics from not being white and vice versa. A hobbit ultimately is a "white pygmy," the landscapes of New Zealand shown in the film constitute a nonimperialist location for British imperialism, and so on. In short, *Lord of the Rings* represents a myth about a return to imperialist times, rather than nationalist ones, in which, nevertheless, the imperialist subject is as colonial as the colonial subject (properly speaking), and thus is free of guilt or imperialist violence. The pagan, in its double identity as Western *and* nonmodern, represents this restorative moment of indifferentiation that nevertheless no longer is signified as nationalist but as imperialist.

Furthermore, gender is crucial to these narratives of restoration and imperialist indifferentiation. As several critics have noted (Warner), *Lord of the Rings* is a very masculinist film, despite the fact that actually the scriptwriters, one of whom is a woman (Frances Walsh), made an effort to incorporate stronger female characters, as in the case of Arwen (played by Liv Tyler) and Galadriel (Cate Blanchett). At the same time, the importance of the landscape and earth (the Orks are spontaneously generated from the earth) as space of exploration, penetration, and boundary-marking clearly suggests its female characterization. That is, even if historically this film is a myth of imperialist indifferentiation, the indifferentiation can only be carried out by clearly stating the masculinity of the heroes so as to clearly differentiate them in the present. In turn, this present distinction between hero and landscape, good and evil (both male), justifies the myth of imperialist indifferentiation and restoration.

Lévi-Strauss already explained the way in which a double structure of basic differences permits mythic logic to elaborate new ideas or conclusions—in this case an imperialist restoration. Before we proceed to understand what this mythic thinking of imperialist indifferentiation and gender differentiation means as a double set of differences that ultimately signifies a nonnationalist and imperialist restoration, it is important to explore whether other forms of fundamentalism, such as those that can be found in the Islamic, also structure their ideology along similar lines.

Krooth and Moallem explain that Iran's Islamic revolution, to give one example of fundamentalism, has its origins in the crisis of modernity and the nation-state, which a new generation of youth has rearticulated as a return to their sources—that is, Islamic religion. In this case too, the return to Islamic origins is made in a selective way, by choosing only certain elements of historical Islam:

Coming from middle and lower middle classes, this group of young people had a religious orientation grounded in popular culture, and tried to make sense of their own culture and the society in which they had been raised. Along with identification based on regional similarities, Islam became a source of communalization. And this revivalism emerged within a single ideology focused on a meaningful selection of scriptural sources, popular Islam, and individualism. (1995: 113)

Moallem furthermore explains that different versions competed for hegemony: "Using the example of contemporary Iran, two different versions characterize Islamic revivalism. One formulated by Ali Sharayati emphasizes the building and construction of a local identity as a way to de-alienate and politicize the masses; the other calls for the construction of an identity, which is in polar opposition to the West and for a pure Islam.… After the Iranian revolution of 1979, this fundamentalist-dominated ethnicity became state ideology" (1995: 113). In this case, it would seem as if Islamic fundamentalism would constitute a return to a differentiated origin, by which the Western is excluded from the Islamic political project. Yet, the effect is precisely the opposite—one of imperialist indifferentiation. That is, Islamic fundamentalism attempts to return to a point in history when Islam was in its phase of expansion and thus all peoples were possible subjects of Islamic conquest (including the Christians, as in the case of medieval Spain), hence the importance of the rhetoric of jihad.

Unlike in the case of Iran, in the other most important case of Islamic fundamentalism, Afghanistan, another historical event helped to emphasize this idea of return to an imperialist, undifferentiated moment of Islamic expansion: the end of the Cold War and the Soviet Union's unsuccessful retreat from Afghanistan. As Rashid explains:

> Most of these radicals speculated that if the Afghan jihad had defeated one superpower, the Soviet Union, could they not also defeat the other superpower, the US and their own regimes? The logic of this argument was based on the simple premise that the Afghan jihad alone had brought the Soviet state to its knees. The multiple internal reasons which led to the collapse of the Soviet system, of which the jihad was only one, were conveniently ignored. So while the USA saw the collapse of the Soviet state as the failure of the communist system, many Muslims saw it [as] deeply evocative of the Muslim sweep across the world in the seventh and eighth centuries. A new Islamic Ummah, they argued, could be forged by the sacrifices and blood of a new generation of martyrs and more such victories. (130–31, my emphasis)

Here, then, the pagan is the Islamic rebel living on the edge of an empire that can challenge and redefine paganism, precisely because is not subject to the empire. Thus, here too the pagan refers to a moment of imperialist indifferentiation.

However, a return to an imperialist original moment of fullness is compensated for by a presentist differentiation in Islamic fundamentalism: the reorganization of social spaces through gender. As Rashid argues, the youth of the Taliban, lacking knowledge of their nation's history and tradition and provoked by their upbringing in madrassas in

refugee camps, prompted a new redefinition of the Taliban though gender redifferentia-
tion:

> Moreover, they had willingly gathered under the all-male brotherhood that the Taliban lead-
> ers were set on creating, because they knew of nothing else. Many in fact were orphans
> who had grown up without women—mothers, sisters or cousins. Others were madrassa stu-
> dents or had lived in the strict confines of segregated refugee camp life, where the normal
> comings and goings of female relatives were curtailed… [After their victory] they felt threat-
> ened by that half of the human race which they had never known and it was much easier
> to lock that half away, especially if it was ordained by the mullahs who invoked primitive
> Islamic injunctions, which had no basis in Islamic law. The subjugation of women became
> the mission of the true believer and a fundamental marker that differentiated the Taliban
> from the former Mujaheddin. (32–33)

Here, too, imperialist indifference is built upon a gender differentiation—hence the
highly symbolic and ideological status that the veil has taken in fundamentalist interpretations of Islam. There are feminists who defend the veil, averring that it can be an
empowering social tool for women (Afary 94–95). However, the main reason for the
implementation of the veil is precisely the necessity of a gender differentiation that, then,
can justify imperialist indifferentiation.

Martin E. Marty concludes that the four most important characteristics of any form
of fundamentalism are literalism (unmediated reading of the written sources),
Manichaeanism, zealotry, and patriarchalism. The above analysis of both Western and
Islamic ideologies would explain the connection between these four characteristics, in the
sense that literalism allows for the creation of a Manichean effect, which, in turn, articulates a sense of historical and imperialist indifferentiation through zealotry, and a clear
subject differentiation in the present through patriarchalism.

In view of this double analysis of Hollywood and radical Islam, we can conclude that
we are developing a fundamentalist taste for the pagan as the referent for an alternative
history to modernity and its aftermath—that is, globalization. This requires new fundamentalist differentiations in gender ideology, which can, in turn, ground an ideology of
imperialist indifferentiation that the pagan myth brings forth. This is the reason that alternative, pagan history feeds on any nonmodern tradition as the mythic marker and signifier of an "other history," an alternative history, or a history otherwise—that is, of myth.

These new alternative histories are simply another way to narrate globalization,
another chapter in an alternative and pagan history that predates modernity. In short,
they convey the message that globalization is different everywhere. Any globalized place
is ultimately different, that is, it is not affected by globalization, since it remains fundamentally different, mythically different—always capable of articulating itself as imperialist
rather than colonial. This type of fundamentalist ideology gives us the reassurance that
we have always been pagan, we have always been alternative, and thus any form of globalization will not change our histories. Moreover, and given the fantasies of imperialist
indifferentiation, pagan history conveys the message that any alternative to globalization

always begins at the location of fundamentalism: "since we have always been alternative, any form of historical otherness is not such but a variation of our sameness. Since we are all pagan there are no other pagans but us. We are the real other of globalization, and the only global alternative to globalization. In other words, these alternative and pagan histories allow us to experience two contradictory messages as simultaneously natural and compatible: we are globalization and we also are its others.

The Pagan Myth as the Performance of Allegorical Camp

As stated above, these pagan, historical discourses show very little regard for historical coherence. My above analysis shows that it is a result of their populist character and thus it is a consequence of their ideological character: Historical accuracy is sacrificed to ideological coherence. Yet one could also posit that this new presentist cannibalization of history might respond to a new historical and geopolitical logic that does not simply explain fundamentalist ideologies, and also to a cultural logic of globalization that would affect as well other areas of culture, including historiography itself.

As Hayden White states, even historiography would not be exempted from a mythic effect such as the one I have analyzed in the above fundamentalist myths of imperialist restoration. Citing Northon Frye, White states:

> Historians, no less than poets, can be said to gain an "explanatory affect"—over and above whatever formal explanations they may offer of specific historical events—by building into their narrative patterns of meaning similar to those more explicitly provided by the literary art of the cultures to which they belong... [I]t follows that there are at least two levels of interpretation in every historical work: one in which the historian constitutes a story out of the chronicle of events and another in which, by a more fundamental narrative technique, he progressively identifies the kind of story he is telling—comedy, tragedy, romance, epic, or satire, as the case might be. It would be on the second level of interpretation that the mythic consciousness would operate most clearly. (59)

Thus, it is worth analyzing the kind of narrative technique to which the restorative and imperialist ideologies of fundamentalism resort. In this way we can determine whether the mythical structure I have isolated above responds to a more general historical constant that also affects other areas of culture, including academic historiography. Following classical rhetoric, White identifies four fundamental types of narrative or emplotments in which history is conveyed (comedy, tragedy, romance, and satire), which he makes correspond to the four basic tropes of rhetorics (metaphor, metonymy, synecdoche, and irony) (73). Yet those four types of narratives in which history is emplotted or told, rely on the fact that the referents used by the historian—the raw historical data—refer to the same historical moment or sequence. In short, one can talk about the French Revolution by depicting it as a comedy, tragedy, romance, or satire, but the raw historical data pertaining to the revolution belong to the same period (including or excluding the preceding and following events).

Yet what the historical narratives I have analyzed above show is precisely a disregard or lack of respect for the historical continuity of the historical data emplotted. White does not contemplate this possibility—it would be a historiographical anomaly—precisely because it corresponds to a narrative logic that precedes the nineteenth century, the era when historiography became consolidated as both discourse and discipline. This historiographical anomaly, this discourse that is not respectful of the coevalness of the raw historical data, is precisely allegory.

Allegory is the narrative device or structure that was outlawed after the Romantic revolution and, consequently, was relegated to the margins of modern culture. Since the Middle Ages, however, allegory has been one of the most important devices to organize historical narrative, as in the medieval chronicles whose genealogy of kings and queens was organized according to a mixture of both biblical and classical references, proving the divine genealogy of their royal lineage. In short, any medieval chronicle presents references to Noah or Hercules next to other barbarian kings who destroyed the Roman Empire, or to Christian kings and royal houses that developed in the aftermath. Although this hypothesis would have to be tested in different areas of culture that deploy historical narratives, it seems that by looking at contemporary fundamentalist discourses we can conclude that allegory is making a comeback. Allegory, a narrative structure that traditional historiography and its metahistorical critics, such as White, could not foresee, has become a hegemonic discourse in many areas in the world. Therefore it is worth analyzing this new allegorical rendition of fundamentalist history in order to understand its cultural and social consequences.

If the above analysis is correct, the first important difference we must note between modern historiography and these new fundamentalist discourses is the latter's breakdown of historical referentiality. Traditional historiography, regardless of the narrative and mythic structure adopted, always preserves the difference between narrative and historical period so that all data belong to the same moment. Referentiality is constituted as historical precisely because the two historical moments—that of the events, and that of their telling—are different and all the events belong to the same historical moment. In sum, modern historical imagination is referential. Furthermore, referentiality is the foundational myth of all modern historiography. Yet allegory breaks away precisely with this basic historiographical myth: It does away with historical referentiality. Allegory tends to fuse in a single narrative elements from different historical moments in order to underscore precisely the irrepresentability of history. In allegory, history takes place as the temporal discontinuity or break created by the fusion of different historical elements. Allegory does not create historical referentiality, rather it creates historical disruption as a way to access history. The founding myth of allegorical history is not referentiality but disruption—hence the importance of ruins in allegory. When analyzing Baroque theater, for example, Walter Benjamin lays out the consequences of the allegorical contemplation of history:

> [I]n allegory the observer is confronted with the facies hippocratica of history as petrified, primordial landscape... And although such a thing lacks all "symbolic" freedom of expres-

sion, all classical proportion, all humanity—nevertheless, this is the form in which man's sub-jection to nature is most obvious…This is the heart of the allegorical way of seeing, of the baroque, secular explanation of history as the Passion of the world; its importance resides solely in the stations of its decline. (1990: 166)

Furthermore, allegory also shifts the emphasis from narrative to performance. History no longer is told but is performed; it is brought forth in front of an audience. History becomes "the Passion of the world," as Benjamin puts it.

The only other modern thinker who has understood the mythical and performative nature of history is precisely the most sagacious critic of modern history: Fredric Niet-zsche. As he states in his *Use and Abuse of History*, history must be dramatic rather than narrative, that is, it has to be performative rather than referential:

Might not an illusion lurk in the highest interpretation of the word "objectivity"?… [T]his would be a myth, and a bad one at that. One forgets that this moment is actually the pow-erful and spontaneous moment of creation in the artist, of "composition" in its highest form, of which the result will be an artistically, but not a historically, true picture. To think objec-tively, in this sense, of history is the work of the dramatist… (37)

Furthermore, Nietzsche proposes that rather than discovering unknown facts and then generalizing from them, thus foregrounding the effect of referentiality, history must tell us what we already know. History has to turn events we already know into an alter-native history: "in inventing ingenious variations on a probably commonplace theme, in raising the popular melody to a universal symbol and showing what a world of depth, power and beauty exists in it" (39). Nietzsche is already propounding an allegorical and performative history, which seems to return with the rise of the restorative and imperial-ist histories that we have detected in contemporary fundamentalist ideology.

Yet to understand the allegorical and performative nature of these alternative, fun-damentalist histories, so that we can then examine both contemporary historiography and other areas of global culture, it is important first to turn to an area, queer culture, where this form of historical performance is already practiced as a way of telling the his-tory of the queer self as "alternative self." At least since Oscar Wilde, the historical refash-ioning of oneself has been a common practice in queer culture. From clothes to cultural references, queer subjects effect a performative and allegorical fashioning of the self by having recourse to camp. Camp, in turn, is a performative and allegorical historiography of the self.

Against more traditional definitions of camp (Babuscio, Bergman, Ross, Meyer), I would maintain that camp is nothing else but the strategic and archaeological rescuing of past hegemonic cultural objects for the purpose of rewriting a new genealogy, an alter-native history, between the lost worlds from which the objects are rescued and the pres-ent moment. By resorting to camp, the queer subject proclaims himself or herself as the knowing subject of an alternative cultural genealogy, an alternative history, of which he or she attempts to erect himself or herself as the new hegemonic subject. This claim usually remains at the margins of hegemonic culture, that is, remains at the *pagus,* but can also reach the mainstream when its queer origin is obliterated or suppressed. Perhaps the most noticeable form of camp is drag performance whereby gender and historical identity are performed by resorting to allegory.

Judith Butler reflects the gender effects of camp in drag performance. She does not analyze other performative aspects of drag such as its camp, historical dimension. However, she clearly states the structure of gender performance in drag, which then can also be expanded to camp's historical performance. For Butler gender is a performance in which

> ...acts, gestures, and desire produce the effect of an internal core or substance, but produce this on the surface of the body, through the play of signifying absences that suggest, but never reveal, the organizing principle of identity as a cause. Such acts, gestures, enactments, generally construed, are performative in the sense that the essence or identity that they otherwise purport to express are fabrications manufactured and sustained through corporeal signs and other discursive means. That the gendered body is performative suggests that it has no ontological status apart from the various acts which constitute reality... I would suggest as well that drag fully subverts the distinction between inner and outer psychic space and effectively mocks both the expressive model of gender and the notion of a true gender identity. (137)

When an older artist or character is performed through drag, the performance also incorporates a historical component; drag becomes also camp.[4] The effect of a historical referentiality is subverted by camp so that historical depth appears as an effect of the surface; history becomes the effect of the performance of the different historical elements incorporated in the appearance of the camp performer. In sum, historical originality and referential depth are performed and subverted by camp.

From this analysis of camp, we can now conclude that the new alternative, fundamentalist histories I have isolated above follow the same logic of rescuing discarded or forgotten discursive elements through a very vigorous archaeological activity of digging out objects, rather than full-fleshed histories or narratives, with the result that the outcome is allegorical history.

Departing from camp, I will propose a different definition of this new fundamentalist tendency to write alternative, pagan histories. Such histories are performative practices, and at their core lies the act of rescuing lost or forgotten pagan objects. That is, the rescued objects do not matter per se, for what matters is the *performance* of rescuing them. Ultimately the objects only stand in for a lost history or tradition, and thus the performative action of rescuing them is the one that makes meaningful the bridge between lost history and rescued object—hence performance's allegorical and antireferential nature. The subject of the historical performance and his or her performance are historically "true and

---

4. Camp also happens outside drag when a new fashion is acted out by resorting to a historical imagination of dressing whereby different historical fashions are recombined, as in the case of Oscar Wilde and his sartorial camp.

meaningful," not the objects or data themselves. Furthermore, the lack of referential coherence is not a mistake or error; the historical "distortion and fabricatedness" of which all fundamentalisms are accused is not such but, rather, the opposite: It is a statement about the mythic and fabricated nature of any historical discourse, whereby the only historical truth left is that of the performer and his or her historical performance. This is the reason why fundamentalism feels so real to its followers and yet so fabricated to outsiders.

A film such as *Gladiator,* as an example of rescuing lost history and myths, was one of the most complex historical narratives to come out of Hollywood in recent years. Yet, at the end, little is taught in it about Roman history. The Coliseum, the Roman arena, was ultimately rescued as a site of spectacle and gore, a site comparable to one of the most watched shows on contemporary North American television: professional "wrestling." Only as long as the Coliseum is historically performed as a site from which to rethink our spectacular present is the filmic object *Gladiator* valid as history.

At the same time, the defeat of the Soviet troops at the hands of the Afghani army was perhaps one of the most important examples of this new historical performance of Muslim fundamentalism. The combination of Muslim soldiers who resist the Soviet troops in a newly fashioned jihad, next to the collapse of the Soviet Union, becomes an allegorical rendition of history by which the return to Islamic origins, the imperialist moment of Muslim expansion in the world, is rewritten, performed, and celebrated. In turn, this action brings about a rehashing and rewriting of the original Muslim expansion of the seventh and eight centuries. Although these two sets of events cannot be reduced to one single order of analysis, and although their historical causality is "flawed," they are performative and allegorical in the sense that different historical events (a local Soviet defeat in Afghanistan and the decline of the Soviet Union as a result of economic and social changes) are combined to create a single fundamentalist Islamic history.

The above analysis of camp as historical performance can also allow us to reread one of the most influential histories of recent times: Samuel Huntington's *Clash of Civilizations and the Remaking of World Order*. One can analyze, in this text, the return of allegory and the breaking down of historiographical referentiality. On the one hand, Huntington explains the resurgence of civilizational formations as a result of modernization:

> In the early phases of change, Westernization thus promotes modernization. In the later phases, modernization promotes de-Westernization and the resurgence of indigenous culture in two ways. At the societal level, modernization enhances the economic, military, and political power of the society as a whole and encourages the people of that society to have confidence in their culture and to become culturally assertive. At the individual level, modernization generates feelings of alienation and anomie as traditional bonds and social relations are broken and leads to crises of identity to which religion provides an answer. (76)

As a result he concludes "[M]odernization, instead, strengthens those cultures and reduces the relative power of the West. In fundamental ways, the world is becoming more modern and less Western" (78). Yet he does not analyze this individualist return to religion, which lies at the origin of the fundamentalist turn taken by most societies around the world, as a new phenomenon—that is, he does not historicize. Instead, Huntington resorts to allegory and salutes this return to religion as a throwback to tribalism and barbarism. To do so, he first emphasizes the civilizational nature of world history: "The world will be ordered on the basis of civilizations or not at all" (156). Then he turns this civilizational history into an allegory of tribalism and barbarism: "Civilizations are the ultimate human tribes, and the clash of civilizations is tribal conflict on [a] global scale" (207). In this way, Huntington renounces historical referentiality and instead turns each "civilization" into an ahistorical entity, so that it appears to be present from the beginning of time and, thus, is ultimately ahistorical: History become tribal or barbarian. In effect, Huntington is also resorting to an allegorical rhetoric of pagan, alternative history.

Yet, in the case of Huntington we can also see the other element that creates this allegorical performance of a tribal history: the inclusion and indifferentiation of the postcolonial subject into a myth of Western imperialist indifferentiation. In other words, his attempt to pull different postcolonial developments into a single history of Western imperialist restoration also resorts to incorporating the postcolonial subject in a moment of imperialist indifferentiation: We are all clashing tribes and barbarians, although the only barbarian that is not originally barbarian but imperialist is the West itself. This moment of imperialist indifferentiation creates the allegorical effect of telling global history as a fundamentalist and ahistorical narrative of the West.

In Huntington's allegorical rendition, only the decay and rise of empires dictates history, so that, once again, ruins are the true index of historicity, as in any allegory. His allegorical history of globalization as a fundamentalist history of Western imperialist restoration and indifferentiation, whereby any global tribe is likely to rise to power or sink in oblivion, ends with the allegorical contemplation of the ruins of the West, which is also hailed as the true beginning of new dark ages of barbarism.

Other historical accounts will have to be analyzed in this light to ascertain the impact of allegory and performance in historiography. However, the unparalleled success of Huntington's work shows that historiography is not exempt from the mythical effect of performance and allegory, which is ultimately triggered by the Western inclusion and indifferentiation of the postcolonial subject.

Thus, I would like to posit that global history has become a performative and allegorical endeavor whereby we look for alternative historical objects, fragments, and references that might allow us to confirm the present as the only and definitive historical form of our times: the time in which we perform history in order to become the subjects of globalization.

Performance and Spectacularity

At the same time it is important to emphasize that the performative and allegorical nature of this new fundamentalist history is not simply reduced to the text or discourse itself; it also affects the people involved in performing these histories—that is, the people who do not contemplate history from a referential distance from which they can identify with historical subjects and events. The people become performers of these historical events and discourses and thus they themselves become the fundamental subjects of their performed histories. In this sense, performative history is populist precisely because it incorporates people in an allegorical history of indifferentiation whereby all people become the fundamental subject of politics—the fundamental political subject of globalization.

Yet it is important to analyze one other aspect of this performative and allegorical history: its spectacular reorganization and structuration by the media and other state institutions. Here "spectacular" refers to the fact that history is organized as a *spectacle*.

An important change has happened in Hollywood in recent years. Because of the masses' capacity to purchase cultural objects (books, tabloid newspapers, action figures, CDs, DVDs) and thus make those objects popular and marketable, Hollywood has progressively shifted to producing films that deal with cultural objects or characters already made popular, so that then it Hollywood can resell their popular, cultural capital through tie-ins—merchandise connected to the film. The example of comic superheroes turned into film characters is the clearest example, although music artists or tabloid celebrities function the same way. Moreover, the interface between the Internet and Hollywood has also amplified the power of users through "fandom" websites. Thus, Hollywood is creating spectacles based on a popular culture that already exists.

In this sense, *Lord of the Rings* is once again a very good starting point to think how the public is becoming performative. Neither British nor North American nationalist cultures ever considered the book *Lord of the Rings* as a canonical book—for example Edmund Wilson, one of the most respected critics of the time of its publication and a neighbor of Tolkien's in Oxford, despised his work (Allen-Mills). No academic list, school curriculum, or cultural institution connected with the state ever considered *Lord of the Rings* important as cultural text. Yet Tolkien's work became one of the most-sold books of the twentieth century (Allen-Mills). The popularity of the book grew out of unregulated, popular practices of reading and promotion, which traditionally are referred to as "cult." Tolkien's work gathered a very large following to the point that it became a cultural phenomenon that Hollywood could no longer ignore. Thus, Hollywood had no choice but to embrace the project of turning *Lord of the Rings* into a filmic spectacle. In short, Tolkien's work is performative also in the sense that it has been read and turned into a cult work by a popular readership independent of any state institution. In this sense, *Lord of the Rings* as both book and cultural phenomenon is popular. Furthermore, considering the different cult practices (from websites to informal academic associations) generated by the book, we can conclude that *Lord of the Rings* is not simply a text but also a cultural, popular event in which the book is performed in different ways by different readers.

Yet the cult of *Lord of the Rings* is performative but not spectacular. Until Hollywood decided to turn the book into a film, the populist performance of the book had not become a global spectacle; yet with the film, the performance of the book has also become spectacular. The transition from popular performance to Hollywood high-tech spectacle is worth studying in detail. *Lord of the Rings* is also the first film in which Hollywood has used its popularity to promote it in a new and innovative way. The film's production company, instead of fighting the different websites and chat-rooms dedicated to the *Lord of the Rings* on the basis of copyright infringement, as many have done in the past, used those websites and fan clubs to distribute a variety of advertisement kits and promotional items so that the fans themselves worked as an amplifying machine of Hollywood's already powerful advertisement machine (Powers). The reliance on fandom and cult in order to identify the cultural texts that are popular creates a new form of filmic culture: The film becomes the crowning, global spectacle of a popular performance of history, which begins with the reading public and fans.[5]

More generally, as Hollywood has relied increasingly on popular performance of cultural objects, the performative inclination of its fans has forced Hollywood to shift from filmic representation to spectacle. According to a new trend, which is at the center of the entertainment industry, video games have become a more important source of revenue than filmmaking for both Hollywood and the computer industry. This shift from image to game shows the new tension between the fan's performative inclination and Hollywood's transformation of performance into spectacle. Although I began this article by referencing films, video games, from their newly gained central position in Hollywood, are setting a trend for a more performative and spectacular interaction within visual culture. Redmon Wash had already hinted at this trend in 1999 when he wrote this headline: "Nintendo's 'Zelda' Video Game Outdraws Top Hollywood Holiday Releases; $150 Million 'Box Office' in Six Weeks." But in 2002, and in a very film-industry style, Wash announced that "World Discovers Key Player in Entertainment Industry Is a Plumber; Nintendo Video Game Character Mario Surpasses Hollywood's Harrison Ford in Global Revenues." The same agency explained in the introductory paragraph that "[S]ince his first appearance in the 1981 arcade game Donkey Kong(R), his heroic antics have made him one of the largest leading men in the world. With his charming voice and unforgettable mustache, he has helped push the video game industry past the film industry with projections eclipsing $10 billion in revenues by the end of 2002." One might argue that video games, at least in general, are intended for children. However, and as most studies on global culture over the last twenty years point out, children lead culture and set new trends (Stokes and Maltby; Gans, Andrew Ross, Medved), just as the youth did till the late 1960s, and the thirty- and forty-somethings till the late 1950s when the Brat Pack and Sinatra were the cultural standard.

Video games are the new visual realm where popular performativity and industry-regulated spectacularity meet. The player enters the world of the software game and thus becomes connected to the informational world in ways that films do not permit, due in part to their need for complete darkness in the theater and for the traditional teleological narrative of an hour and a half. That is, interactive performativity connects the player

---

5. Music swapping online is the other area in which this phenomenon can be seen more clearly.

not only to the game but also to the world—the electronic world—whereby the game also becomes a global spectacle. The fact that even cell phones and computers carry video games, which can be played virtually anywhere, points to the ever-expanding capability of the medium and its ability to bridge performance and spectacle. As Walter Benjamin understood all too well long before the birth of computers ("Work of Art"), this expansive ability is the ultimate sign of a new medium's power. It represents a medium's ability to expand further, and by doing so to incorporate and cannibalize the previous hegemonic media—motion picture film. This cannibalization in turn forces the assimilated medium to develop a protective aura of status, class, and conservatism. The latest DVD medium, which offers the viewer several ways to interact with "film" (extra sequences, explanation of effects, back story, director's comments, and so on), is simply another sign of the power of interactivity by which even film is being adapted to a more video-game-like structure.

Yet video games also respond to the logic of fundamentalist history. They show even a more voracious appetite than films for performative and allegorical representations of the pagan. As shown by the filmic renditions of the most popular video games [I think this word is superfluous show]—*Don Mario, Mortal Combat,* and *Tomb Raiders*—references to mythic, Orientalist, and colonial representations abound. In video games too, the allegorical recourse to the pagan responds to the logic of imperialist indifferentiation and restoration I have isolated above. The fact that, therefore, performativity and spectacularity further increase in the new and most central media of Hollywood, video games, points to the importance of the masses' participation in the populist performance of history as well as to Hollywood's tendency to reorganize populist performance as spectacle.

On the Muslim side, too, the origin of fundamentalism must be found in new organizations of young masses that mobilize and resort to religious culture to perform an identity that neither traditional clerical culture nor the state and its institutions provide. As Krooth and Moallem discuss for the case of Iran, "As opposed to some Orientalist views that portray fundamentalism as an outcome of the antagonism between the traditional clergy and a modernist secular elite, the growth of fundamentalism is in direct relationship with the rebellion of the masses of young men and women who look to such fundamentalism as a source of identity, self-worth and social action" (116). This performative culture includes the circulation of sermons on cassette tapes and the new deployment of old customs (among which the veil or a long beard stand out as different ways to perform publicly an inner Muslim identity that seems to be old-fashioned); yet they are public performances of a fundamentalistic self.[6] However, and just as in camp, this deployment is more complex than a simple throwback to a long-overcome, traditional practice. Afary cites Leila Ahmed who, in her study on women's uses of the veil, or *hijab,* shows

---

6. Tattoos are the in-corporation, the attempt to en-body in ourselves, the new spectacular and fragmentary logic of special effects *qua* pagan discourse. To get "tribal tattoos" is another way to visualize our desire to be pagan and to turn our own bodies into pagan stages of spectacularity.

that the veil is part of a populist performance and that "there is a direct correlation between the hijab [veil] and the educational level of the female students. The lower the class of the parents, the more chances of the student adopting the veil... The new hijab, therefore...marks a 'broad demographic change—a change that has democratized mainstream culture'" (94–95). Thus on a first moment, these new public performative practices of young masses across the Muslim world have the same effect of acting out, through the allegorization of old Islamic elements, a new historical identity that represents a moment of imperial indifferentiation and restoration.

It is important to emphasize that, in the Muslim world, there is also a reorganization of popular performance into spectacles regulated from above. Different state governments such as the Iranian or the Afghani, under the rule of the Taliban, resorted to the banning of Western media and, instead, fostered spectacles such as public executions and demonstrations. If this is so, it is important to understand the reorganization of popular performance into spectacles regulated by nonpopulist institutions such as Hollywood media or Islamic fundamentalist states.

Spectacular Allegories of the Global

Wars and organized violence are becoming spectacular; the two most exemplary cases are the events of 9/11/2001 and the Gulf Wars (1991 and 2003). These events rallied large numbers of people around the world, precisely because of their spectacular nature. In this context, "performance" and "spectacle" are part of the same visual continuum, but they respond to different strategies and subjects. Spectacular wars are not staged from below, by the masses, as in the case of populist performances. Violence, be it either imperialist terror or terrorism, responds to the interests of large capitalist companies and governmental elites, as in the case of the industrial complex built around the Pentagon in the United States or the elites of Iraq, Afghanistan, Pakistan, and Saudi Arabia. Thus, it remains to be seen how these global spectacles of war staged by military complexes and governmental elites will interact with the masses' tendency to articulate a fundamentalist ideology through historical performance. To do so, it is important to revisit the relationship between war and history.

Georg Lukács points out that history, as both mass experience and discourse (literature and historiography), began precisely after the Napoleonic wars, when the French Revolution mobilized mass armies (as opposed to mercenary armies), which for the first time exposed the masses to the experience of historical change. The Napoleonic wars placed the masses in history. Those wars took the masses irreversibly out of the agricultural conception of cyclic time and into a new perception of history as ever-changing time:

> It was the French Revolution, the revolutionary wars and the rise and fall of Napoleon, which for the first time made history a mass experience, and moreover on a European scale. During the decades between 1789 and 1814 each nation of Europe underwent more upheavals than they had previously experienced in centuries... In its defensive struggle against the coalition of absolute monarchies, the French Republic was compelled to create

mass armies. The qualitative difference between mercenary and mass armies is precisely a question of their relations with the mass populations... (23, my emphasis)

More specifically, Lukács links directly the masses' war experience with the birth of nationalism in the form of patriotism toward the motherland: "In France it was only as a result of the Revolution and Napoleonic rule that a feeling of nationhood became the experience and property of the peasantry, the lower strata of the pretty bourgeoisie and so on. For the first time, they experienced France as their own country, as their self-created motherland" (25). Lukács concludes that this mass experience of nationalism through war mobilized the new popular feeling of historicity. Ultimately for Lukács, history is the masses' geopolitical experience of change resulting from nationalist wars.

At the end of the twentieth century, after the Cold War disintegrated, the larger armies around the world began to organize themselves professionally as in pre-Napoleonic times, and their technological ability to target military objectives without involving the masses continued to increase—with the exception of ethnic cleansing. Thus, contemporary wars are no longer a geopolitical movement that involves the masses in a nationalist ideology of history. They are becoming more and more spectacular in the sense that the media's ability to represent them directly—and in real time, as in both Gulf Wars—is increasing proportionally to the masses' ability to become involved only as spectators. Therefore, the new wars are spectacular in the sense that they are staged as spectacles for the masses. Furthermore the recent development of sophisticated media networks in the Middle East have created two separate and symmetrical spectacular renditions of war—those of the cable network CNN and of the Arabic network Aljazira. The Gulf Wars and the destruction of the Twin Towers in New York on 9/11 have been among the most organized and watched spectacles since the dawn of mankind. n world history. Yet their spectacular nature had the effect of changing the meaning of history, since now the masses shift from the position of history's subjects—modern nationalist and imperialist wars—to that of spectators of history—global wars. New wars and terrorism do not involve directly the masses except as spectators, and thus history no longer is narrative and teleological, but spectacular.

The visual and staged continuity between performance and spectacle, populism and elite politics, fundamentalism and war, is a direct consequence of the allegorical nature of both. Neither performance nor spectacle presents a referential and narrative system of nationalist identification. Each performance or war is in itself an allegory: The repetitive images of bombs flying at night over Baghdad or the filmic rendition of a mythic story already known by a large part of the audience (*Lord of the Rings*) shows that narrative, although necessary, is secondary to allegory. The effect of allegory is not narrative but instead performative and spectacular. That is why fundamentalism is permeable to war and violence. Thus it is important to understand the allegorical continuity that grounds the coexistence of performance and spectacle, to understand the relationship between fundamentalist populism and institutional terror.

Each war or violent event (the Rodney King case, the coup d'état of the Russian Parliament, 9/11), once it is broadcast, also becomes an allegory of history. Yet the allegorical perception of time changes now from nationalist teleology to the staging of imperialist ruin and decay. In this new allegorical understanding of history, the present is the only time from which the past and future, as ruin of the present, can be understood. History becomes a presentist discourse and can only be perceived as change through the allegorical tropes of ruin and decay. Once again Walter Benjamin notes this connection with critical insight: "The allegorical physiognomy of the nature-history…is present in reality in the form of the ruin. In the ruin history has merged into the setting. And in this guise history does not assume the form of the process of an eternal life so much as that of irresistible decay… Allegories are, in their realm of thoughts, what ruins are in the realm of things" (1990: 177–78). Thus each war or violent event is also an allegory of history, so that we are actually returning to an all-encompassing presentist history in which historical change is no longer articulated as a nationalist teleology but rather as an imperialist allegory and ruin. Therefore, to understand the connection between populist performance and violent spectacle, one must understand the repercussions of staging history as allegorical ruin.

At least since the Frankfurt School and Guy Debord, most critics have emphasized the visual and spectacular nature of contemporary society and culture. In their accounts, spectacularity is made to stand for an explanation of late capitalist society *tout court*. However, to my knowledge, no critic has yet explained what makes late capitalism so spectacular. In this sense, my recourse to the distinction between performance and spectacle, as well as to their common allegorical nature, can lead us to a better understanding of contemporary culture and history as elements central to late capitalism and globalization.

At this point, every massive spectacle—from Hollywood film to terrorist attacks—is ultimately an allegorical staging of globalization. Some reviewers of *Lord of the Rings,* such as Claudia Puig, captured very well its spectacular, allegorical nature by stressing the film's connections with video games and the events of 9/11: "The battle scenes are presented more like video games than fierce clashes… Ultimately, this morality play will resonate powerfully in these post-Sept. 11 days." If Benjamin referred to "the passion of the World" as the ultimate sense of allegory, now war, terrorism, and spectacular film have become "the passion of globalization." In just the same way a community of believers gathered to celebrate the Christian mass is supposed to follow a strict ritual so that they become a component of a larger spectacle (the manifestation of God on earth), so too do contemporary video games and films as well as terrorist acts constitute rituals. The viewer becomes one more special effect in a new worldwide liturgy celebrating the epiphany of globalization. Thus we could conclude that there was a turning point somewhere around the late 1990s in which globalization became a spectacular reality in the global masses' minds—it became history—and as such, became an imagined reality. In a twist that Benedict Anderson did not foresee, we can conclude that in the 1990s *the globalized world became an imagined community through war and spectacle,* that is, finally globalization became hegemonic.

If this new allegorical history is spectacular, in the above global sense, then the new reality of terror and video games, terrorists and high-tech armies, is no longer centered on an individual subject—the bourgeois individual and the nation-state as the field of its own representation and legitimation—but around a new mass subject—the spectators of the technological theater of globalization. In the violent spectacle of globalization, the mass spectator is made to gaze at, is forced to watch, not a teleological, narrative history, but instead the appearance of pagan elements from a forgotten past on this new global and technological stage that constructs its viewers not as nationalist individuals but rather as massified, global subjects.

In this new global and spectacular logic, the gaze is no longer a biological activity that departs from the viewer's eye and works through visual and narrative identification (primary and secondary identification, according to Baudry) so that referentiality is saved. The gaze, the viewing of the global spectacle, is not a mimetic process of individual dis/identification. Rather, the viewer is incorporated into the visual apparatus—the special-effects film, the video game, the terrorist scenario—whereby he or she is repositioned as just one more element of the allegory of globalization. Rather, like those TV comedies that have prerecorded laughs built into the soundtrack and thus laugh for us, special-effects films, wars, and terrorist acts stage a spectacle for us and, by doing so, incorporate us into that spectacle as just another part of a larger global allegory. Here there is no individual dis/identification; there is only massive incorporation. That is why filmic special effects are put together according to a preestablished sequence; they have to escalate in size and intensity and must climax in the last important sequence of the film. Films such as *Lord of the Rings* or *Harry Potter* are closer to Calderón de la Barca and Shakespeare than to Orson Welles and Godard, closer to the religious theater of the Spanish Golden Age than to the psychological and individual narratives of modernist film. We are today paradoxically closer to the Baroque than to Modernism.

It also important to observe the way in which advertisements and TV commercials incorporate the size of the special effects as part of a film's allure. The *Los Angeles Times* reviewer of *Lord of the Rings,* Kenneth Turan, presented the film in the following way:

> With an endeavor like "The Lord of the Rings" trilogy, it's the numbers that catch your eye first—and how could they not? An unprecedented three feature films shot simultaneously in 274 days…spread over 15 months at a cost of nearly $300 million are enough to get anyone's attention. Not to mention 26,000 extras and a special foam latexing oven for baking prosthetic devices—including 1,600 pairs of feet and ears—that ran 24 hours a day, seven days a week, including Christmas and New Year's Day.

The special-effects movie is an allegory in which globalization and its history are turned into a spectacle; in this sense, the continuity between war, terrorism, and film is clear. The fact that the attack on the Twin Towers on 9/11 was foretold by films such as

Independence Day (1996) is not a coincidence or some uncanny foresight on the part of the producers. Instead, it is proof that the same spectacular logic regulates all these areas of culture and politics.

Thus it is important to emphasize that two different dynamics—a populist fundamentalist, which performs the local, and a technological-elitist, which spectacularizes the global—are coming together under a new history that is allegorical and visual in nature. To understand why the two logics interact, it is important to return to Louis Althusser and his theorization of the Ideological State Apparatuses, or ISA. The fact that Hollywood, war, and terrorism interpellate different individuals as a global mass of both subjects and spectators points to the fact that late capitalism is constructing its poststate ideological apparatuses. I have suggested elsewhere that they be denominated "ideological global apparatuses," or IGA (2002: 83). Unlike the ISA, which interpellate individuals as national subjects, the IGA interpellate individuals as global, mass subjects through allegory. The fact that the main representational form of interpellation is spectacular allegory points to the fact that the subject is constituted by a double act of interpellation. On the one hand, the individual is assimilated into a global spectacle as spectatorial mass; in this sense the individual becomes a global subject. On the other hand, because of the violent and destructive nature of these spectacles, the individual is also interpellated as the subject that is incorporated into the global spectacle of destruction and thus views his own destruction in globalization—in this sense the subject also perceives his own limits and his inability to transcend globalization. This is the allegory of paganism: The individual becomes simultaneously the subject of globalization and its other. This is why the IGA are successful in their interpellation.

Yet at the same time, this interpellation creates a contradiction that needs to be examined to understand the limits of globalization and thus the possibility for global politics.

Populism and the Limits of Globalization

The spectacular form in which the performative and fundamentalist practices of the masses are interpellated and articulated by the ideological global apparatuses through allegory points to one of the limits and chief contradictions of globalization: populism. On the one hand, Francis Fukuyama is correct in asserting the triumph of capitalism throughout the world, a claim that resounds with Marxist overtones. As many critics have pointed out, even fundamentalist Muslim attempts to organize an alternative economy end up in a full embrace of capitalism (Krooth and Moallem 104). At the same time, fundamentalism shows that this generalization of capitalism does not respond to a consolidation of global political structures. Globalization is not the consecration of neoliberal state democracy, as Fukuyama would have it. Rather, the opposite, fundamentalism, represents a populist response to the crisis of the nation-state and to the lack of new political structures that can substitute for the state. The fact that fundamentalism is organized as both performative and populist points to the radical crisis that late capitalism brings about in globalization.

The fact that only the spectacular logic of wars and terrorism can interpellate different individuals as masses on a global scale shows that, in the last instance, late capitalism can only legitimize itself as crisis: hence its resorting to historical allegory to represent ruin and decadence. The allegorical and spectacular nature of globalization through violence lets us see its historical limits and, thus, a glimpse of its demise—rather than of its consolidation. The only way in which this interpellation by the ideological global apparatuses is ideologically successful comes through spectacular war and terrorism, which, in turn, further legitimizes the fundamentalist ideologies of the populist movements that perform them. The global interpellation of individuals as masses is creating new populist identities that, since they are fundamentalist and performative, further resist globalization.

In short, and against Fukuyama, it is important to reclaim the end of history as also the end of globalization: the ruination of globalization. Furthermore, it is clear that this crisis is not simply political but biopolitical, that is, it affects the way the subject is constituted in globalization. If Michael Hardt and Antonio Negri understand globalization as a universal and teleological biopolitization of the masses, populism points to the opposite historical reality: Populism both diversifies and makes impossible the complete biopolitization of its subjects.

Along the same lines, Agamben rescues the figure of the "sacred man" to explore the alleged increasing biopolitization of the masses, which for him is the most threatening and worrisome fact of globalization. It is important to emphasize, this time against Agamben, that the "sacred man" cannot be thought of in individual terms or as a single group. The sacred man today gives rise to multiple forms of barbarism and paganism, that is, to the popular subject as collective. The sacred man is the tribe, the horde. Biopolitization gives rise to forms of collective politics that global capital can only but exacerbate. The sacred man is both individual and tribal, citizen and fundamentalist, present and historical. It only points to a new form of politics that the modern idea of the city and its institutions—the sacred man—cannot explain.

As a first step to think about a new form of global politics, it is important to emphasize that the entire rhetorical and technological spectacularization effected by the ideological global apparatuses of both Western and Islamic fundamentalist institutions does not respond to opposite logics: They are part of the same globalizing discourse that needs of differences internal to capitalism. In this sense, Hollywood, imperialist terror, and fundamentalist terrorism cannot be denounced on moral grounds either as a necessary enterprise for world peace or as a tragic but ultimately evil activity. Terror/ism must be denounced as the main and hegemonic form in which globalization is spectacularized and ideologically legitimized. Rather than zooming in on terror/ism, we must turn our gaze toward the global capitalist system that creates terror/ism as its byproduct, in just the same way that industrialism created national wars in which masses or workers were sacrificed. *Terrorism, just like imperialist terror, is a form of structural violence that is inherent to both spectacular globalization and late capitalism.* Yet war and terrorism only lead to further fundamentalism, which exceeds any form of biopolitical control or interpellation. They create internal contradictions that they cannot solve: again, populism.

As a second step, we must look at other forms of politics, of radical democracy, that cannot be framed and allegorized through spectacular violence and terror. We are becoming new subjects, populist subjects, who are performative but not spectacular. Therefore any politics will have to depart from this new performative populism that both is fundamentalist and exceeds any biopolitical control and interpellation.

Works Cited

Agamben, Giorgio. 1998. *Homo Sacer: Sovereign Power and Bare Life*. Stanford, Calif.: Stanford University Press.

Allen-Mills, Tony. 2001. "Hobbits Take Revenge on America," in the *Sunday Times*, July 1, Lexis-Nexis. University of Nevada, Reno Getchell Library, April 10, 2003. www.library.unr.edu/subjects/databases.html.

Althusser, Louis. N.d. "Ideology and Ideological State Apparatuses," in *Lenin and Philosophy and Other Essays by Louis Althusser*. Trans. Ben Brewster. New York: Monthly Review Press, 127–86.

Babuscio, Jack. 1984. "Camp and the Gay Sensibility," in *Gays and Film*. Ed. Richard Dyer. New York: Zoetrope, 40–57.

Barthes, Roland. 1972. *Mythologies*. New York: Hill and Wang.

Baudry, Jean Louis. 1986. "Ideological Effects of the Basic Cinematographic Apparatus" in *Narrative, Apparatus, Ideology*. Ed. Philip Rosen. New York: Columbia University Press, 286–98.

———. 1986. "The Apparatus: Metapsychological Approaches to the Impression of Reality in the Cinema," in *Narrative, Apparatus, Ideology*. Ed. Philip Rosen. New York: Columbia University Press, 299–318.

Benjamin, Walter. 1968. "The Work of Art in the Age of Mechanical Reproduction," in *Illuminations*. New York: Schocken, 217–51.

———. 1990. *The Origin of German Tragic Drama*. Trans. John Osborne. London: Verso.

Bergman, David, ed. 1993. "Introduction," in *Camp Grounds: Style and Homosexuality*. Amherst: University of Massachusetts Press, 3–16.

Butler, Judith. 1990. *Gender Trouble: Feminism and the Subversion of Identity*. New York: Routledge.

Debord, Guy. 1983. *Society of Spectacle*. Detroit: Black & Red.

Fukuyama, Francis. 1992. *The End of History and the Last Man*. New York: Maxwell Macmillan International.

Gabilondo, Joseba. 2002. "Postnationalism, Fundamentalism, and the Global Real: Historicizing Terror/ism and the New North American/Global Ideology," *Journal of Spanish Cultural Studies* 3(1): 57–86.

Gans, Herbert J. 1999. *Popular Culture and High Culture: An Analysis and Evaluation of Taste.* New York: Basic Books.

Hardt, Michael, and Antonio Negri. 2000. *Empire.* Cambridge, Mass.: Harvard University Press.

Hoberman, J. 2001. "Plastic Fantastic," in the *Village Voice,* Dec. 19–25. April 10, 2003. www.villagevoice.com/issues/0151/hoberman.php.

Huntington, Samuel. 1997. *The Clash of Civilizations and the Remaking of World Order.* New York: Touchstone.

Jameson, Fredric. *Postmodernism or, the Cultural Logic of Late Capitalism.* Durham, S.C.: Duke University Press.

Kinzer, Stephen. 2001. "An Improbable Sequel: Harry Potter and the Ivory Tower," in the *New York Times.* May 12. Sec. B-13. Lexis-Nexis. University of Nevada, Reno Getchell Library, April 10, 2003. www.library.unr.edu/subjects/databases.html.

Krooth, Richard, and Minoo Moallem. 1995. *The Middle-East: A Geopolitical Study of the Region in the New Global Era.* Jefferson, N.C.: McFarland and Co..

Laclau, Ernesto, and Chantal Mouffe. 1985. *Hegemony and Socialist Strategy: Towards a Radical Democratic Politics.* London: Verso.

Lévi-Strauss, Claude. 1963. *Structural Anthropology.* New York, Basic Books.

Lukács, Georg. 1983. *The Historical Novel.* Lincoln: University of Nebraska Press.

Maravall, José Antonio. 1986. *Culture of the Baroque: Analysis of a Historical Structure.* Minneapolis: University of Minnesota Press.

Marty, Martin E. 1995. "Comparing Fundamentalism," in *Contention* 4(2): 36.

Medved, Michael. 1992. *Hollywood vs. America: Popular Culture and the War on Traditional Values.* New York: HarperCollins.

Meyer, Moe. 1994. "Introduction: Reclaiming the Discourse of Camp," in *The Politics and Poetics of Camp.* Ed. Moe Meyer. New York: Routledge, 1–22.

Mitchel, Elvis. 2001. "Hit the Road, Middle-Earth Gang," in the *New York Times,* Dec. 19. Sec. E-1. Lexis-Nexis. University of Nevada, Reno Getchell Library. April 10, 2003. www.library.unr.edu/subjects/databases.html.

Nietzsche, Fredric. 1957. *The Use and Abuse of History.* New York: Liberal Arts Press.

Powers, Ann. 2000. "Fans Go Interactive, and Popular Culture Feels the Tremors," in the *New York Times,* Sept. 20. Sec. H-25. Lexis-Nexis. University of Nevada, Reno Getchell Library. April 10, 2003. www.library.unr.edu/subjects/databases.html.

Puig, Claudia. 2001. "Middle-earth Leaps to Life in Enchanting, Violent Film," in *USA Today,* Dec. 19. April 10, 2003. www.usatoday.com/life/movies/rings/2001-19-19-rings-review.htm//more.

Rashid, Ahmed. 2001. *Taliban: Militant Islam, Oil and Fundamentalism in Central Asia.* New Have: Yale University Press.

Ross, Andrew. 1989. "Uses of Camp," in *No Respect: Intellectuals and Popular Culture.* New York: Routledge, 135–70.

Ross, Karen, with Peter Playdon Aldershot. 2001. *Black Marks: Minority Ethnic Audiences and Media.* Burlington, Vt.: Ashgate.

Said, Edward. 1993. *Culture and Imperialism.* New York: Knopf.

Stokes, Melvyn, and Richard Maltby, eds. 2000. *Identifying Hollywood's Audiences.* Berkeley: University of California Press.

Turan, Kenneth. 2001. "Fulfilling a Grand Quest: The First Installment of 'The Lord of the Rings' Trilogy Triumphs with Skill and Passion," in the *Los Angeles Times,* Dec19. April 10, 2003. http://events.calendarlive.com/top/1,1419,L-LATimes-Movies-X!ArticleDetail-48515,00.html.

Warner, Marina. 2001. "Fantasy's Power and Peril," in the *New York Times,* Dec. 16. Sec. 4–5. May 12, 2001. Sec. B-13. Lexis-Nexis. University of Nevada, Reno Getchell Library. April 10, 2003. www.library.unr.edu/subjects/databases.html.

Wash, Redmond. 1999. "Nintendo's 'Zelda' Video Game Outdraws Top Hollywood Holiday Releases; $150 Million 'Box Office' in Six Weeks." Jan. 7. Lexis-Nexis. University of Nevada, Reno Getchell Library. Oct. 1, 2002. www.library.unr.edu/subjects/databases.html.

———. 2002. "World Discovers Key Player in Entertainment Industry Is a Plumber; Nintendo Video Game Character Mario Surpasses Hollywood's Harrison Ford in Global Revenues." Aug. 26. Lexis-Nexis. University of Nevada, Reno Getchell Library. Oct. 1, 2002. www.library.unr.edu/subjects/databases.html.

White, Hayden. 1978. *Tropics of Discourse: Essays in Cultural Criticism.* Baltimore: Johns Hopkins University Press.

Index of Concepts

A

acceptance of the need for political violence in the contemporary Basque Country constitute the expression of poorly resolved mourning, 179

affective ties to the state coexist with ethnonational consciousness, 23

affirmative is lacking in the notion of definite limit and therefore results in caverns of indeterminacy, paradox, and subalternity, 118

Ajuria Enea, 153

"Alienation" consists of "objectivization" where I perceive historical process as an "objective" process that follows its path independently of my plans, 214

allegorical and performative history, return with rise of restorative and imperialist histories detected in contemporary fundamentalist ideology, 249

allegorical staging of globalization, every massive spectacle from Hollywood film to terrorist attacks is ultimately an, 258

Allegory tends to fuse in single narrative elements from different historical moments in order to underscore precisely irrepresentability of history, 248

alternative histories of pagan worlds, Hollywood is writing, 238

American attitude in the "war on terrorism," that of avoiding the threat by preventively striking at potential enemies, 215

Americanist projects of Aranda, 95

antagonism

    discursive forms through equivalence annul all positivity of object and give a real existence to negativity as such, 119

    does not allow for something to be what it is insofar as this something depends for its existence on an external reality, 120

antagonistic situation, presence of 'Other' prevents me from being totally myself, 120

anti-institutional discourse, attempts by some dominant groups to constantly re-create the internal frontiers through an increasingly, 113

Anti-Semitism

    "more than understandable," and it was "salutary" and "useful to the Jewish character," Herzl wrote in diaries that, 67

    persistence of the Jewish question which had always been entangled with persistence of anti-Jewish sentiment, 57

"Antiterrorist Pact" committed Spanish nationalists to uncompromising campaign against ETA and denounced PNV and Basque government as its collaborators, 148

Aragonese-Catalan kingdom, urging the nineteenth century restoration of, 99

Arendt argues that human rights cannot depend upon national law if these rights truly derive from the fundamental status of human beings as humans, 38

articulating form, apart from its contents, produces structuring effects that primarily manifest themselves at level of modes of representation, 104

attempt at building communitarian spaces out of a plurality of collective wills can never adopt the form of a contract, 105

authority attempting to establish an objective order of social relationships is subverted by antagonisms that lack a definitive ground, 11

Autonomism contained degrees of freedom that the absolute despotism of the Old Regime reduced appreciably, 102

autonomy or independence movement may be based on regionalism rather than an ethnic homeland, 17

B

Basque hegemony hinges on using type of hegemonic formation based upon partial concentrations of power required for articulating progressive social order, 132

Basque nationalism, influence upon: defeat in Carlist wars, ethnicist concern for survival of Basque language, moral concern over survival of Basque church, demonstration effect of nineteenth-century European nationalist movements, 140

Basque Nationalist Party (PNV), 139

Basque nationalists are those who advocate Basque political sovereignty ranging from present autonomic configuration to outright political independence of Basques, 138

Basque political conflict, certain interiorization of the so-called, 183

Basque/Spanish political system, far easier to "normalize" (as in "accommodate") ETA violence within the, 144

Basque Statute of Autonomy (1979) won in Bizkaia, Gipuzkoa, and Araba, 145

Basque Togetherness (EA) Party, 139

Batasuna (Oneness) Party, 139

Belfast Agreement of spring 1998, 32

Blairism has reformed just enough to destabilize everything and make a reconsolidation of the once-sacred earth of British sovereignty impossible, 47

Britain (like Spain) is a multinational state, which is undergoing conflict between its center and its constituent parts, 42

Britain's major failing has been its inability to create a modern state, 46

British crisis of sovereignty with: (1) final fracturing of the Empire, (2) end of Protestant hegemony, (3) entry into single European Union (4) devolution of power, (5) impact of global technology, (6) Britain is multiethnic, 33

Burgos trial, 182

butterfly effect, complex living world where small events can have gigantic consequences, 227

C

Camp, is a performative and allegorical historiography of the self, 249

Catalan alternative posits Catalonia as part of the federal project of the Crown of Aragon extending it to all of Spain, 95

cease-fire, ETA communiqué explained that never had as a goal the attainment of peace but rather wanted the building of a sovereign Basque State, 167

census democracy, certain level of wealth that, in some cases, required ownership of urban or rural lands or a specific level of income, 101

centuries of clan and subclan warfare attest that highland Scotland and Ireland were aggregates of localized ethnocracies throughout most of their histories, 19

challenge that ethnonationalism poses to the survival of the multihomeland state, dismemberment of former Soviet Union, Federal Republic of Yugoslavia, and recognition of East Timor are only most recent manifestations of, 15

Chesterton's principle of Conditional Joy, aware both of blissful background of our happiness and necessity to defend it against foreigners' onslaught, 215

cipayo

    as a manifestation of an anxiety about rupturing of identity and as an attempt to repair it, 171

    contains the traumatic residue of an imaginary unity that has not been given up, 173

    representation of the colonial British army in India (*sipahi*), 174

circuit of the *poteo*: preestablished succession of short stops at different bars with a timetable, everything occurs inside establishment, talking during the *poteo* carried out in a central area, 187–188

clandestine collective, all collective life without public expression was really a, 181

"Clash of Civilizations" theory, 222

Cold War's based upon fault lines in human culture of: gaps between humans and nature, chasm between rich and poor, divide between "true believers" and others, and those who get justice and those who can't, 221

concept of communicative rationality expresses the prospect of a society that is or could become transparent to itself, 87

concept of political legitimacy that makes ethnicity the ultimate standard for judging legitimacy, 16

conflict between so-called free world and communism in Cold War was between forces of globalizing capitalism based in nation-state and those of ethnic nationalism, 84

"constitutional patriotism" for the European community that would place constitutional ideals and laws above questions of ethnic allegiance or national origin, 39

"constituent power," politics that would go beyond limits of both nation and forms of political and cultural representation bound up with idea of hegemony, 80 "constitutive alienation" of the subaltern national identity, 127

context of a closed system, incompatibilities between the principle of democratic equivalence and that of plurality arise only in the, 134

core of stateless nationalist movements, identity claims are at the, 116

cosmopolitanism no longer appeared to be an arduous, painful, and delicate conquest but rather the very condition of modernity, 74

Council of the Isles, 52–53

counterterrorism, terrorism that is to counter earlier acts labeled terrorism because it is "seemingly the only prudent course of action," 229

creating a field of discontinuity or exclusion, a definiteness of sense essential for naming and imaging, 122

creation of a centralized homogenous nation, a historical strategy in reaction to violence inflicted from without, 29

cryptic conceptual sustenance, Basque traditional mythology confronts the observer with a most, 117

cuadrilla: interpeer group governed by relations of friendship while form during 1960s & 1970s was of broad group involving homogeneous ages and communication, 186

cultural semantics can lead to an expansive process or alternatively to a reductive process of "empty" signifiers, 121

D

danger of aprioristic essentialism takes forms of historicism, statism, classism, and nationalism, 134

defining justice, official issue of this worldwide struggle is basically, 220

"democratic culture" is nothing more than reconstruction on a "political" scale of traditional or metropolitan cohesion on which freedom of smallest or most homogeneous communities is founded, 72

democracies constituted through exclusions of people that return to haunt them, stateless nationalisms in Europe and elswhere provide instances of, 10

Democracy is best equipped to satisfy national self-determination demands without recourse to secession, although the most vulnerable to demands, 28

"democratic deficit," 133

"democratic identity," turns around possibility of keeping open and undecided moment of articulation between normative order and universality of ethnical moment, 160

democratic multinational state is the most vulnerable to national self-determination demands, 28

democratic society permanently shows the contingency of its foundations, the gap between the ethical moment and the normative order, 11, 128

democratic state would tend to dissolve into as many states as there were nations within it, British scholar Ernest Barker assertion that a, 23

democratic subject, subject of demand conceived as differential particularity, 106–107 deterritorialization of national sovereignty, attribution of sovereignty to peoples rather than land, 35

discourses of decline have themselves played a constitutive role in making of postwar English identity and implicitly the fragmentation of Britishness, 43

disjunction between an idealized national object and the disappearance of national or even nationalist community, 168

disposal of shit becomes a problem, because it came out from our innermost being, 205

divorce "community of will" of language, group experience, and psychology or "national character" from form of territoriality defined explicitly as "national," 86

dominant denial of subalternity is defined as no-saying, the identity of what is denied per se is secondary to its role as oppositional identity against the dominant order, 129

dynamic of popular culture is hybridity more than subalternity, 89

E

"eclipse of reason" in the modern Western society of consumption but same society as lone island of freedom in sea of totalitarianisms, 207

effect of allegory is not narrative but instead performative and spectacular, 257

elimination of violent antagonism increases both parties' freedom, democratic

equivalence should ensure that one party's gain also benefits other, since, 135

Elkarri (Together), concurs in the call for peace, but only as a necessary precondition of negotiation among all parties to the Basque conflict, 147

emergence, where beautiful new systems can emerge out of chaos and dysfunction, 227

emotional system we call nationalism, part of a larger identity-formation system than just nations or nation-states, 217

empathize with those engaged in violence and place the blame for the violence on others, a large percentage, 24

ETA (*Euzkadi ta Askatasuna* or "Basque Homeland and Liberty")
assasination of Luis Carrero Blanco, 141–142
Burgos Trial, 141
divisions of, 142
formation of, 141
inability to understand that "Hegemony is a political type of relation of politics but not a determinable location within a topography of the social," 130
incarnation of irredentist, radical Basque nationalism, 143
seeks an ideological war between two communities that did not exist except in war of 1936, 172

ethnonational aspirations are more obsessed by dream of freedom from domination by outsiders than by freedom to conduct relations with states, 25

ethnocracies prior to the twentieth century were certainly far more apt to be authoritarian than democratic, 22

ethnocracy, an ethnically homogeneous political unit, 16

ethnonational minorities manifest substantially less affection toward the state than do members of the dominant group, 23

ethnos, the ancient Greek word for a nation sense of a group characterized by common descent, 16

Euskal Herria, Hegoalde and *Iparralde*, 138

Eusko Jaurlaritza, autonomous government complete with a president, parliament, and several ministries, 139

exclusion itself becomes a particular form of affirmation, 124

exclusive unitary sovereignty over the same territory of Northern Ireland, official constitutions of both the Irish Republic and Britain claimed, 31

exile: involuntary emigration, loss of the object, social plausibility of meaning of Euskadi, problematic identity and syndrome of impossible return, problematic transmission of a problematic identity, Basque political identity, 193–196

F

fantasy is an attempt to fill out this lack of the Other, not of the subject, 127

Field Day as contributing to "solution of the present crisis by producing analyses of the established opinions, myths and stereotypes which had become both a symptom and a cause of the current situation," 50

figure of madness, a point of rupture in the structure of the external world that finds itself patched over by fantasy, 170

First Cold War, as struggle between those who claimed to prioritize economic justice and those who professed to value political justice, 220

folk visual form of such an "empty" placeholder is universality of the container/content dialectics of traditional mythologies, 123

foundation status of their own, in this hegemonic struggle both Spain and the Basque Country claim to have a, 132

four factors that constitute nationalism: community of blood, development of communication network, "mercantilism," syndrome of rejection, 75

freedom, "negative" of the unconditional in an entirely conditioned universe, 129

frontal opposition, becomes simply an internal contradiction, another difference, and that it may even serve as a necessary underpinning of the entire system, 130

fundamental types of narrative or emplotments in which history is conveyed (comedy, tragedy, romance, and satire) corresponding to four basic tropes of rhetorics (metaphor, metonymy, synecdoche, and irony), 247

fundamentalism

    any historical narrative that cannot be co-opted or absorbed by globalization, 239

    direct relationship with rebellion of masses of young men and women as source of identity, self-worth and social action, 255

    four characteristics of literalism, Manichaeanism, zealotry, and patriarchalism, 246

generalization of capitalism represents response to crisis of nation-state and lack of
new political structures, 260

organized as both performative and populist points to radical crisis that late capitalism brings about in globalization, 260

fundamentalist Islamic history, local Soviet defeat in Afghanistan and the decline of the
Soviet Union are combined to create a single, 251

fundamentalist tendency to write alternative pagan histories as performative practices
and performance of rescuing lost or forgotten pagan objects, 250

G

gemeinschaft, an association resting on a sense of kinship, real or imagined, gemeinschaft
groupings include the family, band, tribe, and nation, 16

gender performance in drag: acts, gestures, and desire produce effect of internal core on
surface of body that suggest organizing principle of identity as a cause, 250

generational radicalization: experience of fear and frustration suffered by their parents,
ambivalence in transmission of symbols and language, cultural and political passivity
of older nationalists are factors that produced, 180

Gerald of Cambrensis visited Ireland in the entourage of English Prince John and composed an influential History and Topography of Ireland, 30

gesellschaft, an association of individuals resting on the conviction that their personal self-
interest can be best promoted through membership in the group, 16

Gesto Por La Paz (Peace Gesture), which demonstrates periodically in favor of unconditional cessation of the violence, 147

global expansion of modernity/modernization, both Western and Islamic discourses have
in common their desire to be an alternative to the, 238

globalization becomes the new hegemonic discourse of late capitalism, some analysts have
referred to new nationalist formations as "postnationalist" as, 11

Godel, or Church-Turing principle, world that cannot have perfect information, 227

Good Friday Agreement, 9, 37, 48, 51, 53

governmental resistance accounts for the poor record of self-determination, 19

governments have been far more inclined to grant demands for autonomy in the cultural than in the political realm, specifics of autonomy is that, 26

governments of multinational states refuse to countenance demands for decentralization
at the peril of increasing separatist sentiment, 25

H

heart of nationalism understood as a 'daily plebiscite' is the will of men and not natural
events, 72

hegemonic agenda is positivization of negative as a dominant cultural strategy, 128

hegemonic articulations are needed to unify certain political spaces, because there is no
longer a transcendent order that, 134

hegemonic force, by not acknowledging relationship of dependence or by pledging allegiance to different hegemonic force or by defining hegemony of one's own, might be far more damaging, 125
hegemonic practices, articulatory logics of society's incomplete and open character, 128
hegemonic relations: unevenness of power, dichotomy universality/particularity is superseded, production of tendentially empty signifiers, generalization of relations of representation as condition of constitution of social order, 115–116
syntactic relations founded upon morphological categories which precede them, 117
hegemony
    "confrontation with antagonistic articulatory practices," 128
    founded on an outmoded distinction that links subalternity to premodern and hegemony to modern forms of culture, 89
    process by which a particular demand comes to represent an equivalential chain incommensurable with it, 108
    unstable relation between the ethical and the normative, 128
Hegoalde: Basque regions of Bizkaia, Gipuzkoa, and Araba constitute *Euskadi* plus Navarra, 138
Heisenberg principle, not only do actions but observation changes reality, 227
history, masses' geopolitical experience of change resulting from nationalist wars, 257

I

Ibarretxe Proposal, 156–157
idea of Britishness, 44
"identity" politics
    cultural logic of late capitalism" 83
    politics of the subaltern must be in some measure, 80
"ideological global apparatuses," Hollywood, war, and terrorism interpellate different individuals as global mass of subjects and spectators, 260
immigration policy, a former preserve of the central government is becoming increasingly viewed by homeland peoples as falling within notion of autonomy, 27
imperialist indifferentiation, attempt to pull different postcolonial developments into single history of Western imperialist restoration resorts to incorporating postcolonial subject in a moment of, 252
In countries where Palestinians granted equal legal rights they face unofficial discrimination with political campaigns by extremists calling for expulsion, 65
In those countries that refused to grant Palestinians equal rights they been languishing in refugee camps for fifty-four years with no rights and constant police harassment and militarized campaigns to massacre them, 65
internal frontier, no emergence of popular subjectivity without creation of an, 107
Iran's Islamic revolution, return to Islamic origins in a selective way, by choosing only certain elements of historical Islam, 244

Ireland's history as a clash of civilizations: English, Gaelic, Anglo-Irish, and Scottish-Presbyterian, 49
Islamic revivalism, 245
    building and construction of a local identity as a way to de-alienate and politicize the masses
    construction of identity which is in polar opposition to West and for pure Islam...
Israelis to become Arabs, against the idea of, 66
issue of ideological fantasy, cultural ideology of stateless nations as well as entire third world regions being nourished by oppositional negative, 126

J

Jewish Haskala emerged within European history of self-rejection as assimilationist project seeking to transform Jewish culture, 59
Jihad vs. McWorld, 223–224
justification of all government lay in voluntary submission of community ruled, 21

K

Kafr Qasim, the 1956 massacre of, 64
kale borroka (street struggle) firm rejection by moderate nationalism of new form of violence that has emerged in recent years the, 184
Kantian Sublime, subject assumes role of observer perceiving excessive natural violence from a safe distance, 208
KAS Alternative: a series of demands that included the incorporation of Navarra into Euskadi, 145
Kinder Surprise, 201–206

L

language of torturers, US Vietnam War strategy was described by its architects in, 232
late capitalism can only legitimize itself as crisis, hence its resorting to historical allegory to represent ruin and decadence, 261
liberalism facilitated restoration of rights and boundaries of the Crown of Aragon, 98
Lizarra, 153
logic of equivalence; assumption by particularity of function of universal representation
and logic of difference that separates links of equivalential claims are three hegemonic operations, 123
logics of difference, social logics operating according to this institutionalized differential model I will call, 106
loyalty to nation is intuitive rather than rational and based on sense of consanguinity, 17
loyalty to state is sociopolitical and is based in large part on rational self-interest, 17

M

MAD strategy works not because it is perfect but on account of its imperfection, 213
madness
> categorization of a violent politics that destabilizes epistemological and political certainties, 165
> has become domain of anguished paroxysm after ETA called off its cease-fire in December 1999 and initiated an all-out campaign for national sovereignty, 164
magic realism as entailing coexistence in a given social formation of temporalities and value systems corresponding to different modes of production, 89
majority of the involved group do not favor secession, which a separatist movement is active, 23
Markets are setting de facto rules enforced by their own power, 218
masses in history, Napoleonic wars placed the, 256
meaningful autonomy, most members of national minority are prepared to settle for, 26
members of ethnonational groups overwhelmingly reject the use of violence carried out in name of national group, in all cases for which there are attitudinal data, 24
migration of signifiers can be described if populism is conceived as a formal principle of articulation, 112
model of reproduction of moderate nationalism, one that principally functions in the public sphere by using all the public means of reproduction of consciousness, 178
moderate nationalism, denied the need for violence and considered that its consequences were negative, 182
movement not populist because politics or ideology presents actual contents identifiable as populistic but because shows logic of articulation of those contents, 104
multitude
> depends on a recognition of sociocultural difference and incommensurability, 91
> many-faced hydra-headed hybrid collective subject conjured up by globalization and cultural deterritorialization, 80
> resists is "interchangeability" from general commodification of labor and nature and affirms forms of cultural and psychic difference, 82
multitude's ultimate demand, demand for global citizenship founded on general right to control one's movement is, 81

N

nation
> a group of people sharing a myth of common ancestry, 16
> represented as a body of imaginary identification of a body that in the form of the fetus is anticipated but not quite born, 175
"nations without states," new technologies of "The Information Age" actually produce, 218
national or ethnic identities ["communities of will"] are determinate products of

impact of capitalist combined and uneven development on different populations, 85

national self-determination

become an accepted "principle" of international law, 20

democratic only in that it assumes a collective right inherent in every national group to choose its political attachments, 23

first appeared publicly in the First International's Proclamation on the Polish Question (1865), 18

resent rule by aliens, world of action, inseparable from popular sovereignty, 21–22

this deeply rooted aversion to domination by others when group is nation, 19

nationalism, identity with and loyalty to one's nation in pristine sense of that word, 17

necessity of separating the notion of nation (identity) from that of state (sovereignty) and from that of land (territory), 37

negation, basic oppositional structure that tends to forget the relational nature of that very identity as, 129

negative provides in culture concept of limit, whether material, psychological or logical, as well as liberation from labyrinthine consequences of affirmative, 118

New Normal of twenty-first century, normal of second half of twentieth century or Cold War is, 219

"nodal points," opposite result of Negation eliminating discourse is that it will not allow for partial fixations or, 129

no future for the Left if unable to create an expansive universal discourse, constructed out of proliferation of particularisms of the last few decades, 131

Norman Yoke, 19

Nordic Council, way in which these five nation-states and three autonomous regions succeeded in sorting out territorial conflicts, 36, 51

Northern Ireland remains dominated by two segregated and hostile communities, 48

not a "no" in the unconscious, but rather that a recognition of the unconscious is expressed in a negative formula, 119

notions of what constitutes an acceptable level of autonomy therefore differ (1) between palace and homeland view, (2) among individuals and (3) over time, 27

number do favor major alterations in the political system that would result in greater autonomy, regardless of their attitude toward secession, 24

O

"organic crises," institutional system becomes less and less able to differentially absorb social demands and this leads to internal chasm within society and construction of two antagonistic chains of equivalences, 113

organized community, regime becomes progressively institutionalized so that the differential logic starts prevailing again and equivalential popular identity governs less and less actual workings of politics, 113

OTG represents imaginative space beyond sectarianism of Troubles, 54

P

Palestinian resistance demands de-Europeanization of the Jew, 70

paradox of Predestination, the fact that the theology of predestination legitimized the frantic activity of capitalism, 214

Parekh report, equated Britishness with racism, 45

participation of indigenous groups in armed struggle in Guatemala was directed in part against their proletarianization and acculturation/transculturation, 83

particular kind of distortion that the equivalential logics introduces into the construction of "the people" and "power" as antagonistic poles, 108

particularistic claims, in the end appeal to universal principles, 123

Partido Popular (PP), 139

Patriotism, devotion to one's state and its institutions, 17

permanence of Basque autonomy "is due in large measure to this coincidence between autonomy and moderation," 101

persistence of anti-Semitism within Zionism accounts for much of the persistence of the Palestinian Question, 68

political democracy needs a "democratic culture" at its base, a series of tacit conventions on which to be founded, 72

political practices do not express the nature of social agents but, instead constitute those agents, 103

political proposal for peaceful coexistence, 149

"politics of despair" of subaltern may be driven by a resistance or skepticism about not only the official nation-state but also what constitutes civil society, 88

popular sovereignty, national self-determination is most frequent and emotional objectification of, 21

popular subject, subjectivity will result from the equivalential aggregation of a plurality of democratic demands, 107

populism

an ontological and not an ontic category, 104

diversifies and makes impossible the complete biopolitization of its subjects, 261

does not define the actual politics of these organizations but rather is a way of articulating their themes, 111

social situation in which demands tend to reaggregate themselves on the negative basis that they all remain unsatisfied, 106

populist discourse tends to privilege paradigmatic pole or relations of substitution between elements aggregated around only two syntagmatic positions, 109

postnational teleology operates in concept of hybridity/hybridization since it designates a dialectical process of "overcoming" of antinomies that are rooted in immediate cultural and historical past, 90 possibility of forming political parties led to rupture of relative unanimity that had been found among forces of opposition to Francoism and rapid decrease of internal pressure of intersubjective collective life, 182

poteo, that everyday ritual that was territorially delimited and pursued on a daily basis, 186

practices of ritualized attacks, de facto policing practices aimed at enforcing boundaries of ethnic identity by punishing those who are thought to threaten them, 174

precondition for democracy, universal is incommensurable with particular yet it cannot exist with particular, 123

prior to the twentieth century ostensible control over an extensive land area was more fictional than real, 18

process of rearticulation: keeping in operation central signifiers of popular radicalism while inscribing within a different chain of equivalences many of democratic demands, 110

prospect of catastrophe, rely on same mixture of grace and courage when facing, 211

psychological predisposition or predilection to perceive nation in references to the people, 21

R

radical and plural democracy project, struggle for maximum autonomization of spheres on basis of generalization of equivalential-egalitarian logic, 133

radical Basque nationalism, progressively losing its capacity for mass mobilization owing to its loss of positive affective projection, 184

radical democracy
    cannot be framed and allegorized through spectacular violence and terror, 262
    commitment of thinkers to, 115
    supposes a state of indefinite tension between contending particularities and a legitimated universality, 159

radical in multicultural demands, redefine identity of both nation and international order to universalize their singularity, 90

radical nationalism
    constitutes a social world, densely interconnected within and strongly disconnected from the exterior, 188
    substantial support for leftist political program conditioned on ending violence, 167
    upheld the idea of violence as a suitable means, 182

rationale for ethnocracy was furnished by democratic doctrine, 27–28

reality, as a secret whose fantasy defines existence, 170

referendum and possible political outcomes for the Basques, 149–156

republic has reinvented itself as Celtic Tiger, a service-based economy that has established itself as software, computer, and network center of Europe, 48 requests of this type in which demands are punctual or individually satisfied do not construct any chasm or frontier within the social, 106

revenge of unintended consequences, 224–225

revindication of Aragonese tradition during eighteenth century is *Representación* presented by four capitals of Crown of Aragon (Barcelona, Zaragoza, Valencia and Palma de Mallorca) in 1760, 97

ritual, as a mechanism for bringing about a transition between two indeterminate states to a cybernetic system in which information is quantified in negative terms, 121

S

"sacred man," 261

separating notion of nation from notion of state in order to think about sovereignty in apluralist way, 51

separation, takes place when subject realizes how the big Other is in itself inconsistent, purely virtual, 'barred,' deprived of Thing, 127

separatists draw from all social strata and age groups, but disproportionate comes from under thirty-five with above average education and income, 24

Scottish civic nationalism is based on a view of history where constitutions, popular sovereignty, and democratic machinery are normal course of modernity, 47

Scotland had all trappings of cultural nationalism but none of its political aspirations, 46

singularities, where certain events forever change everything, 227

Social Contract, individual must be extirpated from his community of origin in order to be integrated into a new society of laws, 73

social division, as long as we are going to have politics then we are going to have, 114

social world of extreme radical nationalism: oppressive colonial situation, need of a political solution, political institutionalization inhibit popular participation, situation of domination, economic crisis, 189–190

Spain divided into four categories of uniform (Crown of Castille), incorporated (Crown of Aragon), autonomous provinces (Basque) and colonial, 93

Spanish Socialist Workers' Party (PSOE), 139

specificity of populism requires starting analysis from units smaller than group, 104

spectators of technological theater of globalization, terrorists and high-tech armies are centered, 259

spectacularity, new forms of fundamentalism structure their respective societies according to logic of, 239

Stalinists' trials in which Party leaders needed accused's confession of guilt in order to avoid unbearable anxiety of having to admit that big Other does not exist, 127

state based on national identity that is firmly participatory and that does not tramp on minority rights, is it possible to create, 10

statelessness continues to be ultimate political subalternity for historical nations that failed to achieve statehood, 125 strange attractors, where events and energies are drawn together around seemingly inconsequential entities, 227

strategy efficient is fact that we can not ever be sure that it will work perfectly, 213

strategy of *tensionamiento*, in order for it to be distension (untensing) there needs first to be tension, 167

subaltern studies can only situate itself theoretically at juncture where we give up neither Marx nor "difference," 88

subalternity is not only a question of social groups dominated by other social groups, but of subalternity in global order, 79

supplant nation-states of Europe with a European union of regions, 51

survival of Aragonese civil rights beyond the crisis of 1707 was more vigorous and of longer duration than in other parts of the Crown, 96

survival of British nationalism beyond peace process in Ulster is an open question, 51

symbol mobilizers, projects aimed at cultural codes must be, 226

"symbolic condition" of autonomy, 100

"symbolic fiction," Factor X with no counterpart in reality of an individual, 204

T

Table of Ajuria Enea, 146

tendencies toward fission of nationalism, 184

tendentially empty signifiers, construction of a popular subjectivity is only possible on basis of discursively producing, 108

territoriality to designate relation between personal identity and space, 83

terror is a political perpetual-motion machine as form of violent discourse that isn't supposed to be won, 230

terrorism

    denounced as main and hegemonic form in which globalization is spectacularized and ideologically legitimized, 261

    form of structural violence that is inherent to both spectacular globalization and late capitalism, 261

    idea of defeating your enemy psychologically through killings, rapes, and mutilations, 230

Thatcherism, last desperate exercise in "denial" fantasy, 33

"time of a project," future is causally produced by our acts in past while way we act is determined by our anticipation of future and our reaction to this anticipation, 212

Tolkien's work is performative in that it has been read and turned into cult work by popular readership independent of any state institution, 253

Torres Villegas, map of, 93–94

traditional meaning of war, being replaced by terrorism and deterrence, 231

"transitional demand," a demand for a reform that if met would produce a chain of progressively more radical demands, 81 tribal no, cannot be spoken or imagined but only acted out, 121, 125

two groups remain that still embrace British identity: (1) unionists in Northern Ireland and (2) numbers of the black and Asian population living in England, 44

V

veil is part of populist performance and is a direct correlation between *hijab* [veil] and educational level of females with lower class more likely adopting veil, 256

Victorian iconographic logic, visual order that regulates the heterogeneous nonmodern elements is precisely a, 243

victory won't come through economic collapse of weaker states but economic success of nations would be more of a setback but unrestrained corporate capitalism would be everyone's loss, 227–228

video games

new visual realm where popular performativity and industry-regulated spectacularity meet, 254

respond to logic of fundamentalist history showing even more voracious appetite than films for performative and allegorical representations of pagan, 255

virtuality, paradox designates symbolic order as order of, 214

vote is not an adequate index to separatist sentiment, where separatist parties are allowed to contest elections, 24

W

Warsaw ghetto, Jews must learn even how the German army fought in the, 67

will of men, at the heart of nationalism understood as a 'daily plebiscite' is, 72

Wilson's representation of Belfast evokes traumatic and numbing effects of Northern Irish troubles as well as efforts of handful of individuals to rise above them, 49

Z

Zionism

adopted German enlightenment thought to assess Jewishness and Judaism and sought their transformation into European enlightenment, 60

as last settler colony, 69

objective was to ensure Israel's Europeanness and its non-Asianness, 63

only those Jews who answered its transformative call escaped fate that befell Jews who insisted on their diasporic/Jewish condition, 60

Zionist colonial settlement transformed Palestine's terrain by erecting new towns and cities on the ruins and traces of Palestinian lives, 62

zone: new stops, important what happens outside, talking against background music, youths go out Fridays and Saturdays, youth generational space, not speaking about politics, acquiring alcohol and refreshments at supermarket, 187–188

Index of People

A

Abraham, Nicolas, 170
Abu El-Haj, Nadia, 60
Adorno, Theodor, 58, 203, 207, 208, 215, 216
Afary, Janet, 256
Agamben, Georgio, 38–40, 207, 210, 261
Aguirre, Jose Antonio, 141
Aizpurúa, Fusi, 102
Albisu, Arrinda, 117
Albright, Madeleine, 63
Alibhai-Brown, Yasmin, 43
Amor de Soria, Juan, 95, 96
Anderson, Benedict, 38, 72, 258
Anderson, James, 52
Arafat, Yasir, 57
Ardanza, José Antonio, Basque President, 146
Aretxaga, Begoña, 126
Arendt, Hannah, 38, 58
*Aristotle, 73
Armstrong, David, 232
Arnold, Mathew, 31
Arrequi, Joseba, 101
Arrieta, Jon, 94, 100, 102
Ascherson, Neal, 51
Aznar, José María, 139, 143, 144, 147, 148, 157–160

B

Balaguer, Victor, 95
Barber, Benjamin, 222, 223
Barker, Ernest, 23
Baroja, Julio Caro, 74
Barrionuevo, José, 144
Barthes, Roland, 241
Bastinter, J. A., 72
Bateson, G., 122
Baudry, Jean, Louis, 259
Bauer, Otto, 85–87
Begin, Menachem. 64
Beistegui, Miguel de, 203
Ben Gurion, David, 64, 66, 68
Benjamin, Walter, 248, 249, 255, 258
Bennie, Lynne, 25
Bergson, Henri, 211, 212
Berlin, Isaiah, 72
Bertrán i Soler, Tom, 99
Beverley, John, 7, 125, 134
Bhabha, Homi, 89
Bismark, Otto von, 37
Bizet, Georges, 66
Blair, Tony, 32, 35, 36, 47, 233
Blanchett, Cate, 244
Bodansky, Yosef, 219, 223, 224
Bragg, Billy, 43
Brand, Jack, 25
Brenan, Gerald, 138
Brenes, Paul, 60
Brodie, Bernard, 212
Brown, Michelle, 31
Brzezinskii, Zbigniew, 225
Burke, Edmund, 31
Burke, Kenneth, 121, 125

Bush, President of the United States George
    W., 148, 222
Butcher, Frank, 41
Buthelezi, Mangosuthu Gatsha, 57
Butler, Judith, 115, 116, 122, 123, 128, 131,
    160, 250
Byford, Grenville, 233

C
Cambrensis, Joseph, 30, 31
Canclini, Nestor Garcia, 89
Carrasco, Francisco, 96–97
Carrero Blanco, Luis, 141, 143
Castells, Manuel, 218
Chakrabarty, Dipesh, 87, 88, 90
Cheney, Richard, 232
Churchill, Winston, 207
*Cleisthenes, 73
Cohen, Saul, 62
Colley, Linda, 36, 44, 54
Collins, Michael, 36
Condorcet, marquis de Marie-Jean-Antoine
    Caritat, 74
Connor, Walker, 7, 18, 19, 23
*Crespi de Valldaura, 102
Creveld, Martin van, 149

D
Davies, Norman, 42, 44
Dayan, Moshe, 61
Deane, Seamus, 50
Derrida, Jacques, 38
Deutsch, K., 72
Deutscher, Isaac, 58
Dillon, Mylas, 30
Disraeli, Benjamin, 110
Douglas, Neville, 48
Douglass, William A., 8, 134, 142, 148,
    229–231, 233
Dupuy, Jean-Pierre, 209, 212, 214
Durkheim, Emile, 72
Dworkin, Dennis, 7, 32
Dyer, Gwynne, 233

Dylan, Bob, 233

E
Eagleton, Terry, 215
Echeverría, Tomás, 102
Elorza, Antonio, 94
Ellsberg, Daniel, 232
Enaguila, Juan Antonio, 97
Erikson, E., H., 118, 121

F
Fabian, Johannes, 165
Fanon, Frantz, 90
Fernandez, Jim, 170
Fisher, R., 119
Fontecha Salazar, Pedro, 102
Foster, Roy, 49
Foucault, Michel, 124, 165
Franco, Francisco, 23, 127, 130, 131, 133,
    138–148, 165, 166, 170 178, 179, 182,
    184, 187, 196
Franco de Villalba, Didaco, 96
Freud, Sigmund, 58, 119, 190, 191, 205
Fukuyama, Francis, 204, 260, 261
Fusco, Coco, 83

G
Gabilondo, Joseba, 8, 218, 225, 228, 230
*Gadafy [Gaddafi], 34
Gallop, Jane, 171
Galtieri, Leopoldo Fortunato, 34
Geach, P. T., 118
Gierke, Otto, 20
Goenaga, A., 122
González, Felipe, 139, 144, 170
Gramsci, Antonio, 79–81, 88, 110, 113,
    124, 128, 129
Gray, Chris Hables, 8, 220
Gray, Colin, 233
Güell, Pedro Ibarra, 7, 144, 148
Guha, Ranajit, 80
Gunther, Richard, 24

H
Habermas, Jurgen, 38, 39, 87
Hall, Stuart, 45
Hamilton, Douglas, 52
Hardt, Michael, 79–86, 88, 89, 91, 261
Hegel, Georg Wilhelm Fredrich, 88, 104, 116, 122, 202, 214, 215, 225
Heidegger, Martin, 203, 205–208
Heisenberg, Werner, 227
Herman, Edward, 230
Herrero de Miñón, M., 94
Herzl, Theodor, 57, 59, 61, 64–67, 69
Hewitt, John, 33
Hitler, Adolf, 37, 216
Hoberman, J., 243
Hobbes, Thomas, 114, 218
Hobsbawm, Eric, J., 74
Horkheimer, Max, 58, 203, 207, 208, 215
Hume, John, 32, 36
Huntington, Samuel, 222–224, 239, 240, 251, 252
Hussein, Sadam, 34, 225

I
Ibarretxe, Basque President Juan Jose, 148, 149, 152, 156–158, 165
Ibarrola, Agustin, 169

J
Jabotinsky, Vladimir, 66
James, William, 211
Jameson, Fredric, 83, 89
Jáuregui, Ramón, 102
Johnson, Phillip, 45
Jordan de Asso, Ignacio, 97
Juergensmeyer, Mark, 218, 228

K
Kant, Emmanuel, 38, 74, 207, 211
Kautsky, Karl, 82, 85, 86
Kavanagh, Patrick, 29
Kearney, Richard, 7, 10, 42, 44, 50–52, 54
Kiberd, Declan, 50

King, Jr., Martin Luther, 226
Kinzer, Stephen, 242
Kliot, Nurit, 62
Kohl, Helmut, 209
Krooth, Richard, 239, 244, 245, 255

L
Lacan, Jacques, 125, 127, 165, 170, 201, 203, 205, 206, 213
Laclau, Ernesto, 7, 10, 103, 115–117, 119, 120, 122–124, 126–131 133, 135, 159–161
Laden, Osama bin, 222, 225, 226, 228, 230
Lafon, R., 118
Lanuza, Juan de, 98
Lenin, Vladimir, 85
Leon, Abram, 58
Lévi-Strauss, C., 241–244
Lluch, Ernest, 7, 164
Lukács, Georg, 256–257
*Luke, 73
Lurgen, Chuckie, 49
Luther, Martin, 119
Lyon, F. S. , 49

M
Machiavelli, Niccolo, 80
Mandela, Nelson, 57
Manuel, Miguel de, 97
Manzanas, Melitión, 141
Mariátegui, José Carlos, 83
Mariya, Kanan, 233
Marr, Andrew, 43
Marty, Martin, 246
Marx, Karl, 18, 58, 102, 104, 114
Massad, Joseph, 7, 10
*Mathew, 73
Mathews, Jessica, 218
Mayor Oreja, Jaime, 148
McCana, Proinsias, 30
Meabe, Tomas, 102
Menchú, Rigoberta, 83

Mendelssohn, Felix, 66
Merton, Robert K.,190
Mignolo, Walter, 79
Mitchel, Elvis, 242
Mitchell, James, 25
Moallem, Minoo, 10, 239, 244, 245, 255
Mouffe, Chantal, 115, 119, 120, 128, 129, 133
Montague, John, 33
Montero, Txema, 172
Mulhern, Francis, 47–48

N
Nairn, Tom, 32, 42, 46, 47, 51–54
Negri, Antonio, 79–86, 88, 89, 91, 261
Netanyahu, Benjamin, 63
Nietzsche, Fredric, 249
Nordau, Max, 68
Núñez, L. C., 125

O
O'Connor, Joseph, 31
O'Hegarty, P. S., 49
O'Sullivan, Gerry, 230
Onaindia, Mario, 170
Otazu, Alfonso de, 100–101

P
Palafox, General José de, 96–98
Parekh, Bhikhu, 45
Parsons, Talcott, 72
Partridge, Simon, 52
*Pastrana, President of Columbia, 147
Paxman, Jeremy, 43
Paul, Saint, 73
Peiró Arroyo, Antonio, 96–98
Pérez, Antonio, 98
Pérez-Agote, Alfonso, 8, 184, 193
Portillo, Txema, 100
Powell, Colin, 232
Prieto, Indalecio, 101
Puig, Claudia, 258
Pujol, Jordi, 226

R
Rada, Juan Pablo, 94, 95
Rappaport, R. A., 121
Rashid, Ahmed, 238, 245
Raul, F, 99
Rawls, J., 72
Renan, Ernest, 74
Ribot y Fontseré, Antonio, 99
Ricoeur, Paul, 38
Rotman, Brian, 203
Rousseau, Jean Jacques, 32, 74, 100, 104, 114
Rubert de Ventós, X., 7, 134
Rubinstein, Arthur 66
Rumsfeld, Donald, 232
Ryle, G., 118

S
Sartre, Jean Paul, 58
Sas, Antonio, 97
Schwartz, Pedro, 95
Schroeder, Gerhard, 215
Schuchardt, H.,118
Scott, Ridley, 205
Segev, Tom, 60, 62
Selzer, Michael, 59, 66
Shahad, Goldie, 24
Sharayati, Ali, 245
Sharif, Regina, 60
Sharon, Ariel, 64
Sherry, Michael, 231
Shirlow, Peter, 48
Sholder, Jack, 205
Shulman, Polly, 242
Sisón, Josef, 96
Sota, Ramón de la, 101
Spielberg, Steve, 215
Straw, Jack, 45, 46
Szarmach, Paul E., 242

T
Tenner, Edward, 224
Tocquevile, Alexis de, 102
Tolkien, J. R. R., 242, 253

Torok, Maria, 170
Torres Villegas, Francisco, 93, 94
Totorika, Iñaki, 163, 164
Trimble, David, 32, 52
Trotsky, Leon, 232
Tullius, Marcus, 73
Turan, Kenneth, 259
Turner, T. S., 121
Tyler, Liv, 244

U
Ugarte, Francisco, 94
Ury, W., 119
Uthman, Wail, 223

V
Valera, Eamon de 48
Varela, Juan, 100
Vattimo, Gianni, 38
Virno, Paolo, 82
Voltaire, Francois M., 38

W
Walker, Graham, 53

Wallace, George, 110
Walsh, Frances, 244
Walzer, M., 72
Warner, Marina, 242
Wash, Redmon, 254
Weber, Eugen, 18
Weber, Max, 72, 73
Weber, Samuel, 175
Weininger, Otto, 205
Weizmann, Chaim, 61
White, Hayden, 247, 248
White, Michael, 53
Wilde, Oscar, 249
Williams, Bernard, 209
Wilson, Robert McLiam, 49
Wilson, Woodrow, 18
Wolfowitz, Paul, 232
Wolton, D., 72

Z
Žižek, Slavoj, 10, 84, 85, 90, 115, 120, 123,
    126–128
Zulaika, Joseba, 7, 228–231, 233

Index of Places

A

Afghanistan, 205, 217, 225, 227, 228, 239, 245, 251, 256

Albania, 22

Algeria, 69, 71, 146, 220, 225

Angola, 69

Argentina, 84, 113, 170, 194–196

Armenia, 17

Austro-Hungarian Empire, 85

B

Bangladesh, 19

Basque Country [see also Euskadi], 9, 10, 38, 42, 99–102, 119, 131, 132, 138, 139, 141, 145, 147, 149, 150, 154, 156, 157, 163–167, 169, 171–175, 179, 185, 189, 190, 192, 197

Belgium, 19, 26, 27, 28, 51

Biafra, 19

Bosnia, 38

Britain [Scotland and England] , 19, 29, 30, 31, 34, 36, 37, 41, 42, 46

British Isles [Ireland and Britain], 10

C

Canada, 9, 17, 25–28, 154

Catalonia, 10, 42, 51, 94–96, 98, 99, 131, 134, 178

Chechnya, 10, 38

China, 113, 204, 220, 240

Corsica, 17

Cuba, 71

Cyprus, 38

E

East Timor, 15

England, 19, 31, 34, 38, 43–46, 50, 52, 202

Eritrea, 17

Estonia, 17

Euskadi [see also Basque Country] 17, 94, 100, 138, 139, 141, 145, 146, 149, 150, 152, 154–158, 168, 195–197

F

Falklands Islands, 33

Fiji, 17

France, 18, 19, 33, 38, 44, 46, 59, 75, 86, 109, 110, 113, 139, 143, 148, 154, 156, 169, 172, 204, 211, 233, 257

G

Georgia [Republic of], 17

Germany, 22, 38, 59, 66, 207, 211, 215

Gibraltar, 33, 51

Guatemala, 83

H

Hong Kong, 33

I

India, 33, 174, 225

Iran, 239, 244, 245, 255

Iraq, 63, 84, 158, 215, 219, 220, 228, 232, 233, 256

Ireland, 19, 29–34, 36, 42, 44, 48–53

Irish Free State (Ireland), 31

Israel, 38, 57, 60–70, 75, 149, 219, 220, 222, 224, 225, 228
Italy, 26, 38, 82, 112

J
Japan, 22

K
Kashmir, 9, 10, 17

L
Latvia, 17
Lebanon, 65
Libya, 220, 231
Lithuania, 17

M
Mozambique, 69

N
Nagaland, 17
Netherlands, 19
New Zealand, 244
Nigeria, 16
Northern Ireland, 10, 22, 32–34, 36–38, 42, 48, 49, 51–53, 140

P
Palestine, 10, 38, 61–63, 65–68
Pakistan, 33, 75, 225, 256
Poland, 108
Portugal, 15, 22, 69

Q
Quebec [Québèc, Québec], 10, 17, 25, 26, 154

R
Rhodesia, 69
Romania, 16
Russia, 240

S
Saudi Arabia, 225, 256
Scotland, 19, 25, 32–34, 38, 42–44, 46, 47, 52
South Africa, 68, 69, 90
Soviet Union, 15, 17, 20, 85, 239, 245, 251
Spain, 9, 10, 15, 19, 23, 24, 26, 28, 41, 42, 75, 86, 93–95, 98–101, 130–133, 138–145, 147–151, 153, 156, 158, 159, 166, 168–170, 172, 174, 177, 179, 196, 245
Sri Lanka, 72
Sudan, 227
Switzerland, 15, 25, 26, 28, 148

T
Tibet, 17, 72
Turkey, 16

U
United Kingdom [England, Scotland and Northern Ireland], 16, 28, 31, 34, 42, 46, 226
United States of America, 46, 48, 63, 70, 91, 125, 141, 148, 179, 202, 215, 216, 224, 226, 228, 230–232, 239, 256

V
Vietnam, 71, 220

Y
Yugoslavia, 15, 20, 85, 212

List of Contributors

Ernest Lluch (1937-2000) received his Ph.D. in Economics from the University of Barcelona and was *élève titulaire* at the University of the Sorbonne, Rector of the International University Menéndez y Pelayo (1989-1995), Spanish Minister of Health (1982-1986), Fellow of The Institute for Advanced Study at Princeton (1989-1990), member of the editorial board of the journal *History of Economics Ideas*, and co-founder of the Asociación Ibérica de Historia del Pensamiento Económico (the Iberian Association of the History of Economic Thought). He was the co-director of the collection *Clàssics del Pensament Econòmic Català* and the collection *Clásicos del Pensamiento Económico Aragonés*, to which he also contributed several works. He was a member of editorial board of the nine-volume *Economía y Economistas Españoles* (Barcelona: Círculo de Lectores-Galaxia Gutenberg, 1999-2003), which also included several of his own essays. Among the scores of books published by Professor Lluch, some titles include *El pensament econòmic a Catalunya (1760-1840)* (Barcelona: Edicions 62, 1973), *La vía valenciana* (Valencia: Editorial Tres i Quatre, 1975), (with Lluis Argemí) *Agronomía y fisiocracia en España (1760-1820)* (Valencia: Institución Alfonso El Magnánimo, 1985), *Escritos de Juan López de Peñalver* (Madrid: Instituto de Cooperación Iberoamericana, 1992), *La Catalunya vençuda del segle XVIII* (Barcelona: Edicions 62, 1996), *Las Españas vencidas del siglo XVIII. Claroscuros de la Ilustración* (Barcelona: Crítica, 1999), *Memorial del contador Luis Ortiz a Felipe II* (Dusseldorf: Verlag Wirtschaft, 2000) and *Aragonesismo austracista (1734-1742) del conde Juan Amor de Soria* (Zaragoza: Institución Fernando el Católico (CSIC); Diputación de Zaragoza, 2000). He helped create important centers of research in Valencia, Barcelona, Zaragoza and the Basque Country, and took an active role in advocating a climate of dialogue to resolve the Basque conflict. In November of 2000, at the climax of his intellectual life, he was assassinated by ETA.

Dennis Dworkin teaches British and Irish history and cultural theory at the University of Nevada, Reno. He is the coeditor (with Leslie Roman) of *Views Beyond the Border Country: Raymond Williams and Cultural Politics* (New York and London: Routledge, 1993) and the author of *Cultural Marxism in Postwar Britain: History, the New Left and the Origins of Cultural Studies* (Durham: Duke University Press, 1997). He is currently working on a book on recent historiographical debates on social class to be published by Pearson Longman.

John Beverley is Professor and Chair of the Department of Hispanic Languages and Literatures, University of Pittsburgh. His fields of interest include the Hispanic Baroque, cultural studies, postcolonial theory, and literature, film and politics. He was a founding member of the Latin American Subaltern Studies Group. His books include *Del Lazarillo al sandinismo* (Minneapolis: The Prisma Institute, 1987), *Literature and Politics in the Central American Revolutions* (Austin: University of Texas Press, 1990), *Against Literature* (Minneapolis: University of Minnesota Press, 1993), *Subalternity and Representation* (Durham: Duke University Press, 1999), *Una modernidad obsolete. Estudios sobre el barroco* (Los Teques, Estado Miranda: Fondo Editorial ALEM, 1997), *Testimonio: On the Politics of Truth* (Minneapolis and London: University of Minnesota Press, 2004), and many edited or co-edited collections, among them: *La voz del otro. Testimonio, subalternidad y verdad narrative* (Lima, Peru and Pittsburgh: Latinoamericana Editores, 1993), (with Jose Oviedo and Michael Aronna) *The Postmodernism Debate in Latin America* (Duke: Duke University Press, 1995) and most recently, *From Cuba* (Duke: Duke University Press, 2002). He is co-editor, with Sara Castro Klaren, of the University of Pittsburgh Press book series "Illuminations: Cultural Formations of the Americas."

Philosopher and politician, Bachelor in Law and Doctor in Philosophy, **Xavier Rubert de Ventós** has been visiting professor in several North American universities and is professor of Aesthetics at the University of Barcelona in the School of Architecture. In 1976 he participated in the foundation of the College of Philosophy at the University of Barcelona. In his work he has developed a criticism on the modern world and among his many books are *El arte ensimismado* (Barcelona: Ariel, 1963), the winner of the Ciutat de Barcelona prize, *Teoría de la sensibilidad* (Barcelona: Península, 1968), the winner of the Lletra d'Or prize, *Moral y nueva cultura* (Madrid: Alianza, 1971), *La estética y sus herejías* (Barcelona: Anagrama, 1974), the winner of the Anagrama prize, *De la modernidad* (Barcelona: Península, 1980), *Conocimiento, memoria, invención* (Barcelona: Muchnik, 1982), *Ensayos sobre el desorden* (Barcelona: Kairós, 1986), *Europa* (Barcelona: Salvat, 1987), *El laberinto de la hispanidad* (Barcelona: Planeta, 1987), the winner of the Espejo de España prize, *El cortesano y su fantasma* (Barcelona: Destino, 1991), the winner of the Josep Pla prize, *Nacionalismos* (Madrid: Espasa-Calpe, 1994), *Manies i afrodismes* (Barcelona: Edicions 62, 1995), *Catalunya. De la identitat a la independència* (Barcelona: Empúries, 1999), *Dios, entre otros inconvenientes* (Barcelona: Anagrama, 2000) and *Filosofia d'estar per casa* (Barcelona: Ara Llibres, 2004). He was a member of the Spanish Parliament for the PSOE (1982-1986) and the European Parliament (1987-1994). In English, he is the author of *Self-Defeated Man* (New York: Harper Colophon, 1975), *Heresies of Modern Art* (New York: Columbia University Press, 1980) and *The Hispanic Labyrinth: Tradition and Modernity in the Colonization of the Americas* (New Brunswick: Transaction, 1991), as well as several articles on philosophy and culture.

Slavoj Žižek, a philosopher and psychoanalyst, is Senior Researcher in the Department of Philosophy, University of Ljubljana, and at Birkbeck College, University of London. His most recent publications include *Iraq: The Borrowed Kettle* (London: Verso 2004), *The Puppet and the Dwarf: The Perverse Core of Christianity* (Cambridge, Mass.: MIT Press, 2003), and *Organs Without Bodies: Deleuze and Consequences* (London: Routledge 2003).

Walker Connor is currently Distinguished Visiting Professor of Political Science at Middlebury College. He has held resident appointments at, inter alia, Harvard, Dartmouth, the Woodrow Wilson International Center for Scholars, Oxford, Cambridge, the London School of Economics, Bellagio, Warsaw, Singapore, and Budapest. He has published over sixty articles and five books dealing with the comparative study of nationalism. He is currently working on a monograph concerned with the wellsprings of national identity.

Ernesto Laclau is Professor of Politics at the University of Essex and also Professor in the Department of Comparative Literature, SUNY at Buffalo. His publications include (with Chantal Mouffe) *Hegemony and Socialist Strategy: Towards a Radical Democratic Politics* (London: Verso, 1985), *New Reflections on the Revolution of our Time* (London: Verso, 1990), (as editor and contributor) *The Making of Political Identities* (London: Verso, 1994) and *Emancipation(s)* (London: Verso, 1996).

Richard Kearney holds the Charles B. Seelig Chair of Philosophy at Boston College and has served as a Visiting Professor at University College Dublin, the University of Paris (Sorbonne) and the University of Nice. He is the author of over twenty books on European philosophy and literature (including two novels and a volume of poetry) and has edited or co-edited fourteen more. He was formerly a member of the Arts Council of Ireland, the Higher Education Authority of Ireland and chairman of the Irish School of Film at University College Dublin. As a public intellectual in Ireland, he was involved in drafting a number of proposals for a Northern Irish peace agreement (in 1983, 1993 and 1995 respectively) and in speechwriting for the Irish President, Mary Robinson. He has presented five series on culture, thought and literature for Irish and/or British television and broadcast extensively on the European media. His most recent work in philosophy comprises a trilogy entitled *Philosophy at the Limit*. The three volumes are *On Stories* (New York: Routledge, 2002), *The God Who May Be* (Bloomington: Indiana University Press, 2001) and *Strangers, Gods and Monsters* (New York: Routledge, 2003).

Joseba Gabilondo has a licentiate in Basque philology from the University of the Basque Country and a Ph.D. in comparative literature from the University of California, San Diego. He has taught at several universities: Duke University, Bryn Mawr University, SUNY Stony Brook and University of Florida. He is currently an Assistant Professor at the Center for Basque Studies, University of Nevada, Reno. He has published several articles on Hollywood cinema and blockbusters in the context of global culture, Spanish nationalism, postnationalism, masculinity, and queer theory. He has also edited a monographic issue for the *Arizona Journal of Hispanic Cultural Studies* on the issue of the Hispanic Atlantic. He has just finished an essay collection on contemporary Spanish-, American- and French-Basque literature entitled *Nazioaren hondarrak* (Remnants of the Nation). He is currently finishing two book manuscripts, entitled *Before Babel: A Cultural History of Basque Literatures* (a cultural and postnational history of Basque literatures from the Renaissance to the 21st century) and *The Barbarian Divide: Neoliberalism and Multiculturalism at the New European Border (Intellectuals, Migrants and Terrorists in Spain)*.

Joseph Massad teaches modern Arab Politics and Intellectual History at Columbia University. He is the author of *Colonial Effects: The Making of National Identity* (New York: Columbia University Press, 2001), and *Desiring Arabs* (forthcoming, from Harvard University Press). He is also currently finishing a book of essays on Zionism and the Palestinians.

Joseba Zulaika is the Director of the Center for Basque Studies at the University of Nevada, Reno. He is the author of over a dozen books, including *Basque Violence: Metaphor and Sacrament* (Reno: University of Nevada Press 1988), *Crónica de una seducción. El Museo Guggenheim Bilbao* (Madrid: Nerea 1997), *Del cromañón al carnaval* (Donostia: Erein, 1996), (with William Douglass) *Terror and Taboo: The Follies, Fables and Faces of Terrorism* (New York: Routledge 1996), and *Enemigos, no hay enemigo* (Donostia: Erein, 1999).

Begoña Aretxaga (1960-2002) taught at the universities of Princeton, Harvard, Chicago and Texas-Austin. A brilliant scholar, she wrote extensively about gender and nationalism, ethnicity and political violence in relation to Northern Ireland and the Basque Country. Among her publications are *Shattering Silence: Women, Nationalism and Political Subjectivity in Northern Ireland* (Princeton: Princeton University Press, 1997) and *Los funerales en el nacionalismo radical vasco* (San Sebastián: Baroja 1987). At the time of her death to lung cancer she was writing a book about youth violence and the cultural imaginary of the state in the Basque Country.

William A. Douglass is a social anthropologist. In 1967 he was co-founder of the Basque Studies Program of the University of Nevada, Reno which he then directed for 33 years. He was the first editor of the Basque Series of Nevada University Press. He has authored many books and articles on Old World Basque society, the Basque diaspora, Italian emigration, identity, ethnonationalism, and political violence, including (with Jon Bilbao) *Amerikanuak: Basques in the New World* (Reno: University of Nevada Press, 1975), *Death In Murélaga: Funerary Ritual in a Spanish Basque Village* (Seattle: University of Washington Press, 1969) and *La Vasconia global. Ensayos sobre las diásporas vascas* (Vitoria-Gasteiz: Eusko Jaurlaritzaren Argitalpen Zerbitzu Nagusia; Servicio Central de Publicaciones del Gobierno Vasco, 2003). He is now professor emeritus with the Center for Basque Studies, University of Nevada, Reno.

Christopher H. Gray is a cyberculture expert and social activist. He edited (with the assistance of Heidi Figueroa-Sarriera and Steven Mentor) *The Cyborg Handbook* (New York and London: Routledge, 1995) and has authored two books: *Postmodern War: The New Politics of Conflict* (New York: Guilford Publications; London: Routledge, 1997) and *The Cyborg Citizen: Politics in The Posthuman Age* (New York: Routledge, 2001). He has worked for NASA, the Smithsonian Institutions, and the computer industry, and is currently Associate Professor of Cultural Studies of Science and Technology at the University of Great Falls in Montana.

Alfonso Pérez-Agote holds a chair of sociology at the Universidad Complutense in Madrid, Spain. He is the author of *La reproducción del nacionalismo. El caso vasco* (Madrid: Centro de Investigaciones Sociológicas; Siglo XXI de España, 1984) and *La sociedad y lo social. Ensayos de sociología* (Bilbao: Servicio Editorial de la Universidad del País Vasco, 1989). He is also the editor of *Sociología del nacionalismo* (Vitoria: Gobierno Vasco; Servicio Editorial de la Universidad del País Vasco, 1989) and *El nacionalismo vasco a la salida del franquismo* (Madrid: Centro de Investigaciones Sociológicas; Siglo Veintiuno de España Editores, 1987), and has coauthored several books. His specialty is the sociology of nationalism and in particular Basque nationalism.